T0224060

Communications
in Computer and Information Science   768

Commenced Publication in 2007
Founding and Former Series Editors:
Alfredo Cuzzocrea, Xiaoyong Du, Orhun Kara, Ting Liu, Dominik Ślęzak,
and Xiaokang Yang

More information about this series at http://www.springer.com/series/7899

Dingzhu Du · Lian Li
En Zhu · Kun He (Eds.)

Theoretical
Computer Science

35th National Conference, NCTCS 2017
Wuhan, China, October 14–15, 2017
Proceedings

 Springer

Editors
Dingzhu Du
The University of Texas at Dallas
Richardson, TX
USA

En Zhu
National University of Defense Technology
Changsha, Hunan
China

Lian Li
Hefei University of Technology
Hefei, Anhui Province
China

Kun He
Huazhong University of Science
  and Technology
Wuhan, Hubei
China

ISSN 1865-0929   ISSN 1865-0937 (electronic)
Communications in Computer and Information Science
ISBN 978-981-10-6892-8   ISBN 978-981-10-6893-5   (eBook)
https://doi.org/10.1007/978-981-10-6893-5

Library of Congress Control Number: 2017956724

This Springer imprint is published by Springer Nature
The registered company is Springer Nature Singapore Pte Ltd.
The registered company address is: 152 Beach Road, #21-01/04 Gateway East, Singapore 189721, Singapore

Preface

The National Conference of Theoretical Computer Science (NCTCS) is the main academic activity in the area of theoretical computer science in China. To date, NCTCS has been successfully held 34 times in over 20 cities. It provides a platform for researchers in theoretical computer science or related areas to exchange ideas and start cooperations.

This volume contains the papers presented at NCTCS 2017: the 35th National Conference of Theoretical Computer Science held during October 14–15, 2017, in Wuhan, China. Sponsored by the China Computer Forum (CCF), NCTCS 2017 was hosted by the CCF Theoretical Computer Science Committee and School of Computer Science Technology at Huazhong University of Science (HUST).

NCTCS 2017 received 84 English submissions (including seven published papers accepted only for communication at the conference) in the area of algorithms and complexity, software theory and methods, data science and machine learning theory, web science base theory, parallel and distributed computing and computational models, etc. Each of the 77 submissions was reviewed by at least three Program Committee members. The committee decided to accept 25 papers that are included in these proceedings published Springer's *Communications in Computer and Information Science* (CCIS) series.

NCTCS 2017 invited well-reputed researchers in the field of theoretical computer science to give keynote speeches, carry out a wide range of academic activities, and introduce recent advanced research results. We had seven invited plenary speakers at NCTCS 2017: Wei Chen (Microsoft Research Asia), Jin-Kao Hao (University of Angers, France), Jian Li (Tsinghua University, China), Qing Li (City University of Hong Kong), Pinyan Lu (Shanghai University of Finance and Economics), Liwei Wang (Peking University), and Jianping Yin (National University of Defense Technology). We express our sincere thanks to them for their contributions to the conference and the proceedings.

We would like to thank the Program Committee members and external reviewers for their hard work in reviewing and selecting papers. We are also very grateful to all the editors at Springer and the local organization chairs for their hard work in the preparation of the conference.

September 2017

Dingzhu Du
Lian Li
En Zhu
Kun He

Organization

General Chairs

Dingzhu Du   The University of Texas at Dallas, USA
Lian Li   Hefei University of Technology, China

Program Chairs

Dingzhu Du   The University of Texas at Dallas, USA
Lian Li   Hefei University of Technology, China

Program Co-chairs

En Zhu   National University of Defense Technology, China
Kun He   Huazhong University of Science and Technology, China

Organization Chair

Kun He   Huazhong University of Science and Technology, China

Program Committee

Saddek Bensalem   Joseph Fourier University, France
Longbing Cao   University of Technology Sydney, Australia
Jinkao Hao   University of Angers, France
Chumin Li   University of Picardie Jules Verne, France
Lingqiao Liu   University of Adelaide, Australia
Shaoying Liu   Hosei University, China
Stephan
   Reiff-Marganiec   University of Leicester, UK

Lei Wang   University of Wollongong, Australia
Jinsong Wu   University of Chile, Chile
Songyuan Yan   Univerity of Bedfordshire, UK
Mingsheng Ying   University of Technology Sydney, Australia
Changqing Zhang   University of North Carolina at Chapel Hill, USA
Jian Zhang   University of Technology Sydney, Australia
Kerong Ben   Naval University of Engineering, China
Yijia Chen   Fudan University, China
Jianer Chen   Central South University, China
Zhigang Chen   Central South University, China
Wei Chen   Microsoft Research Asia, China
Jieren Cheng   Hainan University, China

Yuxi Fu	Shanghai Jiaotong University, China
Qiangsheng Hua	Huazhong University of Science and Technology, China
Jian Li	Tsinghua University, China
Renren Liu	Xiangtan University, China
Tian Liu	Beijing University, China
Zhiming Liu	Southwest University, China
Pinyan Lu	Shanghai University of Finance and Economics, China
Rui Mao	Shenzhen University, China
Xiaoming Sun	Institute of Computing Technology, CAS, China
JIgang Wu	Guangdong University of Technology, China
Guoqing Wu	Wuhan University, China
Daoyun Xu	Guizhou University, China
Yun Xu	University of Science and Technology of China
Jingyun Xue	Jiangxi Normal University, China
Ke Yi	Hong Kong University of Science and Technology, SAR China
Jianping Yin	National University of Defense Technology, China
Zhao Zhang	Zhejiang Normal University, China

Abstracts for Invited Talks

Combinatorial Online Learning

Wei Chen

Theory Group, Microsoft Research Asia, Beijing, China
weic@microsoft.com

Abstract. Combinatorial optimization is one of the core areas in theoretical computer science and operations research, with many classical problems such as graph shortest paths, minimum spanning trees, maximum weighted matchings, and it also has numerous modern applications such as in networking, online advertising, crowd sourcing, and viral marketing. However, in many of these modern applications, the exact parameters needed as inputs, such as link latencies in wireless networking, click-through rates in online advertising, worker-task performance in crowd sourcing, and diffusion probabilities in viral marketing, are stochastic and unknown, and thus have to be learned over time. On the other hand, well-studied online learning and optimization frameworks, exemplified by the classical multi-armed bandit problem, cannot be applied directly to address these problems due to the exponential blowup in the solution space. Therefore, it demands a new framework that could incorporate combinatorial learning seamlessly into the existing combinatorial optimization framework, without re-engineering the optimization tasks from scratch. In this talk, I will introduce a series of works I and my collaborators have done in the recent years to systematically build such a framework. I will first introduce our work on the general combinatorial multi-armed bandit (CMAB) framework that incorporates optimization tasks with non-linear objective functions and approximation guarantees, and provide a modularized learning algorithm with tight regret analysis. I will then introduce our recent studies including CMAB with probabilistically triggered arms, CMAB with general reward functions, and combinatorial pure exploration, which cover different aspects of combinatorial online learning. Throughout my talk I will illustrate how the framework and the results can be applied to applications such as online advertising, crowd-sourcing, and viral marketing, and discuss many opportunities in further advancing this line of research.

Learning and Data Mining for Combinatorial Optimization: Some Case Studies

Jin-Kao Hao

University of Angers, Angers, France
jin-kao.hao@univ-angers.fr

Abstract. We present some case studies of using learning and data mining techniques for solving combinatorial optimization: multidimensional scaling and reinforcement learning for graph coloring, opposition-based learning for subset selection with maximum diversity, and frequent patterns for quadratic assignment. We show how learning and data mining techniques techniques can be advantageously combined with an optimization method to obtain high-quality results for difficult combinatorial optimization problems.

Stochastic Combinatorial and Geometric Optimization

Jian Li

Institute for Interdisciplinary Information Sciences, Tsinghua University,
Beijing, China
lapordge@gmail.com

Abstract. The world is full of uncertainty and very often decisions have to be made way before the uncertainty is resolved. Stochastic optimization studies optimization problems with uncertain inputs or parameters, in which the uncertainty is modeled using probability theory. The area was initiated by Danzig in 1950s and has been subject to extensive research in many disciplines including computer science, math, operation research, economics, management science and social science. In this talk, I will talk about some of my recent efforts on stochastic geometric and combinatorial optimization problems. In particular, I will talk about some new results on the stochastic models for several fundamental geometric and combinatorial problems, such as minimum spanning tree, closest pair, minimum enclosing ball, shortest path and knapsack.

Towards Truth: Mechanism Design vs. Data Mining

Qing Li, Minming Li

City University of Hong Kong, Hong Kong, China
qing.li@cityu.edu.hk

Abstract. Eliciting true information from the input is of critical importance for meaningful output. There are two ways to secure true information. One is mechanism design where agents reporting wrong information will not gain them any benefit. The other is data mining where true information is dug out from multi-sourced (and perhaps multi-modal) data upon which cross validation can be carried out.

About mechanism design, we use facility location games as an example to illustrate how the truthfulness can be guaranteed by sacrificing some efficiency. Various models are discussed for this setting of mechanism design without money. Especially for one of the variants, we consider how agents affect each other in their utilities. We assume that the coefficients are already known as input when the mechanism is applied. However, in reality, the way people (agents) affect each other needs to be learned from historical data. Therefore, we also analyze how to learn those coefficients in the underlying social networks. For data mining, we use social event discovery as an example, where multi-sourced social media data is collected, integrated, and fused, upon which clustering and classification algorithms are then applied to discover or detect significant/interested events. In dealing with incomplete or inconsistent data from multiple sources, a multi-dimensional model is devised to facilitate cross checking and validation, thereby achieving the objective of digging out true information.

Interdisciplinary Researches through the Lenses of Theoretical Computer Science

Pinyan Lu

School of Information Management and Engineering,
Shanghai University of Finance and Economics, Shanghai, China
Lu.pinyan@mail.shufe.edu.cn

Abstract. Researches in of Theoretical Computer Science (TCS) cover core problems in computer science such as algorithm and complexity. However, there are also many interdisciplinary researches through the Lenses of TCS such as mathematics, physics, economics and so on. The key concepts, ideas and computational thinking in TCS influence other disciplines deeply. In this talk, I will share a few case studies from my own research.

Towards Understanding Deep Learning: Two Theories of Stochastic Gradient Langevin Dynamics

Liwei Wang

Peking University, Beijing, China
wanglw@pku.edu.cn

Abstract. Deep learning has achieved great success in many applications. However, deep learning is a mystery from a learning theory point of view. In all typical deep learning tasks, the number of free parameters of the networks is at least an order of magnitude larger than the number of training data. This rules out the possibility of using any model complexity-based learning theory (VC dimension, Rademacher complexity etc.) to explain the good generalization ability of deep learning. Indeed, the best paper of ICLR 2017 "Understanding Deep Learning Requires Rethinking Generalization" conducted a series of carefully designed experiments and concluded that all previously well-known learning theories fail to explain the phenomenon of deep learning.

In this talk, I will give two theories characterizing the generalization ability of Stochastic Gradient Langevin Dynamics (SGLD), a variant of the commonly used Stochastic Gradient Decent (SGD) algorithm in deep learning. Building upon tools from stochastic differential equation and partial differential equation, I show that SGLD has strong generalization power. The theory also explains several phenomena observed in deep learning experiments.

The Past, the Present and the Future of Theoretical Computer Science in China

Jianpin Yin

School of Computer, National University of Defense Technology,
Changsha, Hunan, China
jpyin@nudt.edu.cn

Abstract. Taking theory of computation and theory of programs as the core, researchers of theoretical computer science in China have made many achievements in the past. Combined with mathematical research, they have also contributed quite a lot on the field of discrete mathematics and numerical computation. In recent years, computing systems characterized by parallel and distributed computing have developed rapidly. The development models of computer software have changed thoroughly. New types of computing represented by quantum computation have received widespread attention. Computing technologies have been widely used in all walks of life. Computer networks have linked the world closely together. Security problem of computing systems, network systems and information systems is getting attention from all sides. Artificial intelligence is leading the application trend of computing technology. Big data and its effective processing is changing the way we research. All these changes have been deeply affecting the researchers of theoretical computer science in China. Although some researchers are still sticking to the positions of theory, more researchers have been pushed to drift around by the tide of technology development and they are free between theory and application. Even if those in the theoretical positions sometimes lack deep understanding about the significance and value of their research, only rest on the state to research for publishing papers. To develop theoretical computer science of China in the long run, it is time to think the following questions calmly. What problems should be researched on theoretical computer science? How to make the research on theoretical computer science both to fit the requirements of technology development and to keep its theoretical characteristics, even to guide the development of technology. Taking history and other countries as a mirror, this report tries to give our experience and thinking about the above questions.

Contents

Data Science and Machine Learning Theory

Parallel and Distributed Computing

Computational Model

Algorithms and Complexity

Multi-resource Fair Allocation with Bounded Number of Tasks in Cloud Computing Systems

Weidong Li[1,2], Xi Liu[1], Xiaolu Zhang[1], and Xuejie Zhang[1(✉)]

[1] Yunnan University, Kunming 650091, People's Republic of China
{weidong,zxl,xjzhang}@ynu.edu.cn
[2] Dianchi College of Yunnan University, Kunming 650228, People's Republic of China

Abstract. Dominant resource fairness (DRF) is a popular mechanism for multi-resource allocation in cloud computing systems. In this paper, we consider the problem of multi-resource fair allocation with bounded number of tasks. We propose the lexicographically max-min normalized share (LMMNS) fair allocation mechanism, which is a natural generalization of DRF, and design a non-trivial optimal algorithm to find a LMMNS fair allocation, whose running time is linear in the number of users. Then, we prove that LMMNS satisfies envy-freeness and group strategy-proofness, and analyze the approximation ratios of LMMNS with some assumptions, by exploiting the properties of the optimal solution.

Keywords: Lexicographically max-min normalized share · Dominant resource fairness · Multi-resource fair allocation · Approximation ratio

1 Introduction

Multi-resource fair (or efficient) allocation is a fundamental problem in any shared computer system including cloud computing systems. As pointed by Ghodsi et al. [8], the traditional slot-based scheduler for state-of-the-art cloud computing frameworks (for example, Hapdoop) can lead to poor performance, unfairly punishing certain workloads. Ghodsi et al. [8] are the first to suggest a compelling alternative known as the *dominant resource fairness* (DRF) mechanism, which is to maximize the minimum dominant share of users, where the dominant share is the maximum share of any resource allocated to that user. DRF is generally applicable to multi-resource environments where users have heterogeneous demands, and is now implemented in the Hadoop Next Generation Fair Scheduler.

In recent years, DRF has attracted much attention and been generalized to many dimensions. Joe-Wong et al. [20] designed a unifying multi-resource allocation framework that captures the trade-offs between fairness and efficiency, which generalizes the DRF measure. Parkes et al. [15] extended DRF in several ways, including the presence of zero demands and the case of indivisible tasks. Bhattacharya et al. [2] adapted the definition of DRF to suport hierarchies.

© Springer Nature Singapore Pte Ltd. 2017
D. Du et al. (Eds.): NCTCS 2017, CCIS 768, pp. 3–17, 2017.
https://doi.org/10.1007/978-981-10-6893-5_1

Wang et al. [19] generalized the DRF measure into the cloud computing systems with heterogeneous servers. Friedman, Ghodsi, and Psomas [7] studied the multi-resource allocation of indivisible tasks on multiple machines. Recently, Zarchy et al. [22] considered the multi-resource allocation with multiple demands, and compared two proposed mechanisms.

For the online case, Zeldes and Feitelson [23] proposed an online algorithm based on bottlenecks and global priorities. Kash, Procaccia and Shah [10] developed a dynamic model of fair division and proposed some dynamic resource allocation mechanisms based on DRF. Li et al. [12] gave a linear-time optimal algorithm and the approximation ratios of the dynamic DRF mechanism [10]. Also, Li et al. [11] generalized the dynamic dominate resource fairness mechanism to the bounded case, where each user has finite number of tasks.

Notably, Dolev et al. [6] suggested another notion of fairness, called Bottleneck-Based Fairness (BBF), which guarantees that each user either receives all he wishes for, or else gets at least his entitlement on some bottleneck resource. Gutman and Nisan [9] situated DRF and BBF in a common economics framework, obtaining a general economic perspective. Bonald and Roberts [4] argued that proportional fairness is preferable to DRF, especially assuming that the population of jobs in progress is a stochastic process. They also [5] introduced the bottleneck max fairness for the case of router resources allocation, which is a variant of BBF. Zahedi and Lee [21] applied the concept of Competitive Equilibrium from Equal Outcomes (CEEI) in the case of Cobb-Douglas utilities to achieve properties similar to DRF. Tan et al. [17] considered multi-resource fair sharing for multiclass workflows. Liu and He [13] presented a cooperative resource management system for Infrastructure-as-a-Service cloud. We refer to [16] to find other related works.

As mentioned by Wang, Liang and Li [19], the users have a bounded number of tasks in a real-world cloud computing system. They studied the multi-resource allocation problem in heterogeneous cloud computing systems with bounded number of tasks, and proposed a generalized version of the well-known water-filling algorithm. However, the running time of the water-filling is pseudo-polynomial. It is desired to design an efficient polynomial-time algorithm. In fact, this is not the only paper studied multi-resource allocation problem with bounded number of tasks. In [6], a user u_i receiving all he wishes for is equivalent to that all the tasks (finite) of u_i are processed. Recently, Tang et al. [18] studied the multi-resource fair allocation in pay-as-you-go computing, where the number of tasks is bounded for each user at a given time, too. Note that DRF is a special case of generalized resource fairness (GRF) [9], which includes both DRF and asset fairness [8]. Therefore, it is desired to generalize GRF to the bounded case, where the users have a finite number of tasks.

In this paper, we consider the multi-resource allocation problem in a single server with bounded number of tasks, which is a special case of the model studied in [19]. We propose the lexicographically max-min normalized share (LMMNS) fair allocation mechanism, which is a natural generalization of DRF. Moreover, we design a non-trivial optimal algorithm to find a LMMNS fair allocation, whose running time is linear in the number of users. Also, we prove that LMMNS satisfies envy-freeness and group strategy-proofness. Most importantly, we present the approximation ratios of LMMNS, by exploiting the properties of the optimal solution. Our results imply that the approximation ratio of DRF is exactly n, which improves the result in [15].

The rest of the paper is organized as follows. Section 2 introduces the LMMNS mechanism. Section 3 presents a non-trivial polynomial-time optimal algorithm. Section 4 lists the allocation properties LMMNS satisfies, while Sect. 5 analyzes the approximation ratios of LMMNS. Finally, Sect. 6 concludes the paper and gives the future work.

2   LMMNS Mechanism

In a cloud computing system, assume that we are given a server with m resources and n users. As in [8,15], assume that each user u_i has a publicly known weight w_{ij} for resource j, which represents the amount of resource j contributed by user u_i to the resource pool. Without loss of generality, assume that $\sum_{i=1}^{n} w_{ij} = 1$, for every resource $j = 1, \ldots, m$. Each user u_i requires r_{ij}-fraction of resource j per task.

Let x_i be the number of tasks processed on the server for user u_i. The resource requirement constraints are

$$\sum_{i=1}^{n} r_{ij} x_i \leq 1, \quad j = 1, \ldots, m. \tag{1}$$

The *weighted share* of resource j per task for user u_i is defined as

$$ws_{ij} = \frac{r_{ij}}{w_{ij}}, \text{ for } j = 1, \ldots, m,$$

and the *dominant share* for user u_i is defined as

$$DS_i = x_i \max_j ws_{ij}.$$

As mentioned in [19], the number of tasks need to be processed on the server is bounded in the realistic multi-resource environment, i.e.,

$$x_i \leq B_i, \quad \text{for} \quad i = 1, \ldots, n. \tag{2}$$

As in [9], let $\| \cdot \|_p$ $(p \geq 1)$ be a norm on $\mathcal{R}^m$, where

$$\|\mathbf{ws}_i\|_p = (\sum_{j=1}^{m} ws_{ij}^p)^{1/p}, \tag{3}$$

called the normalized share, is the measure of "how much" per task of user i obtains-a scalar that quantifies the weighted-share vector $\mathbf{ws}_i = (ws_{i1}, \ldots, ws_{im})$. For convenience, let

$$NS_i = \|\mathbf{ws}_i\|_p \cdot x_i \tag{4}$$

be the (total) normalized share for user u_i. Therefore, for the multi-resource fair allocation problem with bounded number of tasks, it is to allocate the resources as fair (may not equal) as possible, and the objective is to maximize system utilization $(x_1, \ldots, x_n)$, as in [8]. The main problem we face is how to define "fair". The well-known lexicographically max-min fairness [14] is a good choice. Given a feasible allocation, we compute the normalized share for each user. For convenience, let $\mathbf{NS} = (NS_1, \ldots, NS_n)$ be the normalized share vector.

Definition 1. A normalized share vector $\mathbf{NS}$ is called *lexicographically max-min* (LMM)-optimal, if for every feasible normalized share vector $\mathbf{NS}' = (NS_1', \ldots, NS_n')$, $\mathbf{NS}_\tau$ is lexicographically greater than $\mathbf{NS}_\tau'$, where $\mathbf{NS}_\tau$ ($\mathbf{NS}_\tau'$) is the vector obtained by arranging the normalized shares in $\mathbf{NS}$ ($\mathbf{NS}'$) in order of increasing magnitude.

For example, given two feasible normalized share vectors $\mathbf{NS} = (0.8, 0.9, 0.4)$ and $\mathbf{NS}' = (0.6, 0.7, 0.5)$, $\mathbf{NS}$ is not LMM-optimal, as $\mathbf{NS}_\tau' = (0.5, 0.6, 0.7)$ is lexicographically greater than $\mathbf{NS}_\tau = (0.4, 0.8, 0.9)$.

In this paper, we propose the *lexicographically max-min normalized share* (LMMNS) mechanism for the multi-resource fair allocation problem with bounded number of tasks, which is to find the LMM-optimal share vector $\mathbf{NS}$, subject to the constraints (1) and (2). Clearly, when $p = \infty$ implying $\|\mathbf{ws}_i\|_\infty = \max_j ws_{ij}$ and $B_i = \infty$, LMMNS is exactly DRF in [8].

3   Scheduling Algorithm

Although a LMM-optimal solution can be computed approximately by using the water-filling algorithm [19], or by modifying the algorithms in [9,15], the running time is high. In this section, we use a somewhat different algorithm to find the LMM-optimal solution. Here, if $r_{ij} = 0$ for some i, j, we can allocate the resources in multiple rounds as in [9,15]. Thus, for purpose of exposition, we will generally restrict our attention to $r_{ij} > 0$ for all i, j throughout this paper. When we violate this convention, we will be explicit about it.

Since the number of tasks for each user u_i is bounded by B_i, in any feasible allocation, the maximum normalized share for user u_i is $NS_i^{max} = \|\mathbf{ws}_i\|_p \cdot B_i$. For a positive number $NS > 0$, let $\mathbf{A}(NS) = (NS_1, \ldots, NS_n)$ be the share vector such that $NS_i = \min\{NS_i^{max}, NS\}$ for each user u_i.

Lemma 2. There exists a positive number NS^* such that $\mathbf{A}(NS^*)$ is the LMM-optimal normalized share vector.

Proof. Let $(NS_1^*, \ldots, NS_n^*)$ be a LMM-optimal normalized share vector and $NS^* = \max_i NS_i^*$. If there is a user u_k satisfying $NS_k^* \neq \min\{NS_k^{max}, NS^*\}$, we have $NS_k^* < NS_k^{max}$ and $NS_k^* < NS^*$. Consider the user u_h satisfying $NS_h^* = NS^* > NS_k^*$. Let $x_i^* = NS_i^*/\|\mathbf{ws}_i\|_p$, for $i = 1, \ldots, n$. We construct a feasible normalized share vector $\mathbf{NS}' = (NS_1', \ldots, NS_n')$, where

$$NS_i' = \begin{cases} \|\mathbf{ws}_h\|_p \cdot (x_h^* - \epsilon_1), & i = h, \\ \|\mathbf{ws}_k\|_p \cdot (x_k^* + \epsilon_2), & i = k, \\ NS_i^*, & i \neq k, h. \end{cases} \quad (5)$$

Here, ϵ_1, ϵ_1 are small enough positive numbers such that $NS_h' > NS_k'$, and $\epsilon_2 \leq \epsilon_1 \min_j r_{hj}/r_{kj}$. Clearly, $\epsilon_2 r_{kj} \leq \epsilon_1 r_{hj}$ for every resource j, which implies that $\mathbf{NS'}$ is a feasible normalized share vector. Thus,

$$NS_k^* < NS_k' < NS_h' < NS_h^*, \text{and } NS_i' = NS_i^*, \text{ for } i \neq k, h.$$

This contradictions the fact $(NS_1^*, \ldots, NS_n^*)$ is a LMM-optimal normalized share vector. ∎

Theorem 3. The LMM-optimal solution can be found within time $O(n)$.

Proof. According to Lemma 2, a simple way is to use the binary method to find the maximum NS^* such that $\mathbf{A}(NS^*) = (NS_1^*, \ldots, NS_n^*)$ is a feasible share vector satisfying (1) and (2). However, this naive algorithm is not efficient enough. Our algorithm is described as follows. Using Blum et al.'s method [3] to find the median value NS in $\{NS_1^{\max}, \ldots, NS_n^{\max}\}$, let $NS_i = \min\{NS, NS_i^{\max}\}$ and $x_i = NS_i/\|\mathbf{ws}_i\|_p$ for every user u_i. Clearly, if $\sum_{i=1}^n r_{ij}x_i \leq 1$ for every $j = 1, \ldots, m$, we have $NS^* \geq NS$. Otherwise, we have $NS^* < NS$. We distinguish the following two cases:

Case 1. $NS^* \geq NS$. For each user u_i satisfying $NS_i = NS_i^{\max}$, which implies $NS_i^{\max} \leq NS \leq NS^*$, by Lemma 2, we have $NS_i^* = \min\{NS_i^{\max}, NS^*\} = NS_i^{\max}$. Delete user u_i and decrease the corresponding resources consumed by u_i from the instance.

Case 2. $NS^* < NS$. For each user u_i satisfying $NS_i = NS$, which implies $NS_i^{\max} \geq NS > NS^*$, by Lemma 2, we have $NS_i^* = \min\{NS_i^{\max}, NS^*\} = NS^*$. Thus, these users satisfying $NS_i = NS$ have the same normalized share NS^* in the LMM-optimal solution $(NS_1^*, \ldots, NS_n^*)$, and can be merged into a "dummy" user u_{dum}. Let U_{dum} be the set of users satisfying $NS_i = NS$. Given a possible normalized "share" NS_{dum} of the dummy user u_{dum}, for each user u_i in U_{dum}, it consumes $r_{ij}x_i$-fraction resource of type j, where $x_i = NS_{dum}/\|\mathbf{ws}_i\|_p$. Thus, the dummy user u_{dum} consumes $NS_{dum}\mu_j$-fraction resource of type j, where

$$\mu_j = \sum_{i:u_i \in U_{dum}} \frac{r_{ij}}{\|\mathbf{ws}_i\|_p}.$$

Note that the number of users is reduced by half. Again, use Blum et al.'s method [3] to find the median value NS in $\{NS_i^{\max}|u_i$ is the remaining user and is not the dummy user$\}$. Then, compare NS and NS^* similarly to the above discussion, and reduce the number of users by half correspondingly until that there is only one dummy user. Finally, we will find the user u_τ with maximum value $NS_\tau^{\max}$ such that $NS_\tau^{\max} \leq NS^*$. For each user u_i satisfying $NS_i^{\max} \leq NS_\tau^{\max} \leq NS^*$, set $NS_i^* = NS_i^{\max}$. For each user u_i in U_{dum} such that $NS_i^{\max} > NS_\tau^{\max}$, consider the following linear program (LP):

$$\max \quad NS$$
$$\sum_{i:u_i \in U_{dum}} NS \cdot \frac{r_{ij}}{\|\mathbf{ws}_i\|_p} \leq 1 - \sum_{i:NS_i^{\max} \leq NS_\tau^{\max}} r_{ij}B_i, \text{ for } j = 1, \ldots, m.$$

It is easy to verify that the optimal value of the above LP is

$$NS^* = \min_j \frac{1 - \sum_{i:NS_i^{\max} \leq NS_\tau^{\max}} r_{ij} B_i}{\sum_{i:u_i \in U_{dum}} \frac{r_{ij}}{\|\mathbf{ws}_i\|_p}}$$

$$= \min_j \frac{1 - \sum_{i:NS_i^{\max} \leq NS_\tau^{\max}} r_{ij} B_i}{\mu_j}.$$

is the optimal solution to the above LP. For each user $u_i \in U_{dum}$, set $NS_i^* = NS^*$, and then we obtain the LMM-optimal solution $\mathbf{A}(NS^*) = (NS_1^*, \ldots, NS_n^*)$.

The optimal algorithm for the LMMNS mechanism is described as follows.

Algorithm 1. LMMNS scheduling algorithm

Step 1. Initialization. $\mathbf{rc} = (1, \ldots, 1)$, $NS_i^* = 0$, for $i = 1, \ldots, n$
$$U = \{u_1, \ldots, u_n\}, \mathcal{NS} = \{NS_1^{max}, \ldots, NS_n^{max}\}$$
$$U_{dum} = \phi, NS_{dum} = 0, \mu_j = 0, j = 1, \ldots, m.$$
Step 2. Using the method in [3] to find the median NS in $\mathcal{NS}$, set $NS_{dum} = NS$ and $NS_i^* = \min\{NS, NS_i^{max}\}$ for $u_i \in U$.
    If $NS_{dum} \mu_j + \sum_{i:u_i \in U} r_{ij} B_i \leq \mathbf{rc}_j, \forall j$, set

$$\mathbf{rc}_j \leftarrow \mathbf{rc}_j - \sum_{\substack{i:u_i \in U, \\ NS_i^* = NS_i^{max}}} r_{ij} B_i, \text{ for } j = 1, \ldots, m;$$

$$U \leftarrow U \setminus \{u_i | NS_i^* = NS_i^{max}\}.$$

    else, set

$$\mu_j \leftarrow \mu_j + \sum_{\substack{i:u_i \in U, \\ NS_i^* < NS_i^{max}}} r_{ij} \cdot \frac{1}{\|\mathbf{ws}_i\|_p}, \text{ for every} j;$$

$$U_{dum} \leftarrow U_{dum} \cup \{u_i | NS_i^* < NS_i^{max}, u_i \in U\};$$

$$U \leftarrow U \setminus \{u_i | NS_i^* < NS_i^{max}\}.$$

Step 3. If $U \neq \phi$, goto **Step 2**;
    else, for each user $u_i \in U_{dum}$, set

$$NS_i^* \leftarrow \min_j \frac{1 - \sum_{i:NS_i^{max} \leq NS} r_{ij} B_i}{\mu_j}.$$

Step 4. Output NS_i^*, for $i = 1, \ldots, n$.

At each iteration k, since we have at most $n/2^{k-1} + 1$ users, deciding whether $NS \geq NS^*$ can be done within $O(mn/2^{k-1})$ time. Thus, the overall running time is $O(m(n + n/2 + n/2^2 + \ldots + 1)) = O(mn)$, which is linear in n when m is a bounded number. When we allow $r_{ij} = 0$, we can execute Algorithm 1 at most m rounds as in [9,15] to find the LMM-optimal solution. The running time is also linear in n, as m is a bounded number in reality.   ∎

4   Allocation Properties

Similarly to [8,15], the following are important and desirable properties of a fair multi-resource allocation with bounded number of tasks:

1. **Pareto efficiency** (PE). It should not be possible to increase the number of tasks processed on the server without decreasing the allocation of at least another user.
2. **Sharing incentive** (SI). For all users u_i: either $x_i = B_i$ or there exists a resource j such that $r_{ij}x_i \geq w_{ij}$.
3. **Envy-freeness** (EF). For all users u_i: either $x_i = B_i$ or for every user k, there exists a resource j such that

$$\frac{r_{ij}x_i}{w_{ij}} \geq \frac{r_{kj}x_k}{w_{kj}}.$$

4. **Group Strategy-proofness** (GSP). No user can schedule more tasks by forming a coalition with others to misreports their requirements r_{ij}.

PE is to maximize system utilization subject to satisfying the other properties. SI means that the number of tasks processed for each user u_i is no less than the case where a w_{ij}-fraction of each resource j is allocated to every user. EF requires that for every user u_i such that $x_i < B_i$, she do not envy user u_k when the allocation of u_k is scaled by w_{ij}/w_{kj}. GSP means no user can get a better allocation by lying about r_{ij}.

As before, for purpose of exposition, we restrict our attention to $r_{ij} > 0$ for all i, j. Consider the LMM-optimal normalized share vector $\mathbf{NS}^* = (NS_1^*, \ldots, NS_n^*)$ and the corresponding utility vector $(x_1^*, \ldots, x_n^*)$, where $x_i^* = NS_i^*/\|\mathbf{ws}_i\|_p \leq B_i$ for $i = 1, \ldots, n$.

Lemma 4. If $x_k^* < B_k$ for user u_k, we have $NS_k^* \geq NS_i^*$ for every $i = 1, \ldots, n$.

Proof. If there is a user u_h satisfying $NS_h^* = \|\mathbf{ws}_h\|_p \cdot x_h^* > \|\mathbf{ws}_k\|_p \cdot x_k^* = NS_k^*$, we construct a feasible normalized share vector $\mathbf{NS}' = (NS_1', \ldots, NS_n')$, as defined in (5), where $NS_h^* > NS_h' > NS_k' > NS_k^*$. It is easy to verify that $\mathbf{NS}_\tau'$ is lexicographically greater than $\mathbf{NS}_\tau^*$, which contradicts the fact that $\mathbf{NS}^*$ is the LMM-optimal normalized share vector.   ∎

It is straightforward to verify that LMMNS satisfy the PE property. We will prove that LMMNS satisfies the other properties.

Theorem 5. LMMNS satisfies the SI property, if and only if $p = \infty$.

Proof. If $x_i^* = B_i$ for every user i, all users are satisfied. If there is a user u_k such that $x_k^* < B_k$, there exists at least one saturated resource. If not, we can allocate $(x_k^* + \epsilon)(r_{k1}, \ldots, r_{km})$ to user u_k without changing the other x_is, where $\epsilon = \min_j(1 - \sum_{i=1}^n r_{ij}x_i^*)/r_{kj}$. Then, we obtain a new normalized share vector

$\mathbf{NS}' = (NS'_1, \ldots, NS'_n)$, where $NS'_k = (x^*_k + \epsilon)\|\mathbf{ws}_k\|_p$ and $NS'_i = NS^*_i$ for $i \neq k$. Clearly, $\mathbf{NS}'_r$ is feasible and lexicographically greater than $\mathbf{NS}^*$, which contradicts the fact that $\mathbf{NS}^*$ is the LMM-optimal normalized share vector.

When $p = \infty$, $\|\mathbf{ws}_i\|_p = \max_j r_{ij}/w_{ij}$, for every user i. For convenience, let $j_i = \mathrm{argmax}\ r_{ij}/w_{ij}$, which implies that $r_{ij_i}/w_{ij_i} = \max_j r_{ij}/w_{ij}$. For an arbitrary user u_k such that $x^*_k < B_k$, if there is a resource j satisfying $r_{kj}x^*_k \geq w_{kj}$, then u_k is satisfied. Otherwise, $NS^*_k = r_{ij_k}x^*_k/w_{ij_k} < 1$ and for an arbitrary saturated resource j', we have $r_{kj'}x^*_k < w_{kj'}$. As $\sum_{i=1}^n w_{ij} = 1$ and the resource j' is saturated, i.e., $\sum_{i=1}^n r_{ij'}x^*_{ij'} = 1$, there is a user u_h satisfying $r_{hj'}x^*_h > w_{hj'}$, implying that

$$NS^*_h = \|\mathbf{ws}_h\|_\infty \cdot x^*_h = \frac{r_{hj_h}}{w_{hj_h}} \cdot x^*_h \geq \frac{r_{hj'}}{w_{hj'}} \cdot x^*_h > 1 > NS^*_k.$$

But this contradicts Lemma 4. Thus, for every user u_i, either $x^*_i = B_i$ or there exists a resource j such that $r_{ij}x^*_i \geq w_{ij}$, i.e., LMMNS satisfies the SI property, if $p = \infty$.

For any fixed constant $p < \infty$, it is sufficient to show that LMMNS violates the SI property with an example. Consider a system with of 18CPUs, 18GB RAM, and two users. Assume that $B_1 = B_2 = 18$ and $w_{ij} = 1/2$ for all $i, j = 1, 2$. User u_1's task requires $(1, 1)$, and user u_2's task requires $(1, \epsilon)$, where ϵ is a small enough positive number. For convenience, let $\epsilon = 0$ to obtain an approximate result. Clearly, $x^*_1 = x^*_2/2^{1/p} = 1/(2^{1/p} + 1)$ is a LMMNS allocation. Thus, for $j = 1, 2$, we have

$$r_{1j}x^*_1 = x^*_1 = \frac{1}{2^{1/p} + 1} < \frac{1}{2} = w_{1j},$$

which implies that LMMNS violates the SI property, if $1 \leq p < \infty$. ∎

Theorem 6. LMMNS satisfies the EF property.

Proof. For an arbitrary user u_k, if $x^*_k = B_k$, u_k does not envy any user. If $x^*_k < B_k$, by Lemma 4, we have $NS^*_k \geq NS^*_i$ for every user u_i. If user u_k envies another user u_h, u_h must have a strictly higher weighted share of every resource than that of user u_k, i.e., $r_{kj}x^*_k/w_{kj} < r_{hj}x^*_h/w_{hj}$, for $j = 1, \ldots, m$, which implies that

$$NS^*_k = \|\mathbf{ws}_k\|_p \cdot x^*_k = \|(\frac{r_{k1}}{w_{k1}} \cdot x^*_k, \ldots, \frac{r_{km}}{w_{km}} \cdot x^*_k)\|_p$$
$$< \|(\frac{r_{h1}}{w_{h1}} \cdot x^*_h, \ldots, \frac{r_{hm}}{w_{hm}} \cdot x^*_h)\|_p = NS^*_h,$$

where the inequality follows from the monotonicity of $\|\cdot\|_p$. A contradiction. Thus, LMMNS satisfies the EF property. ∎

Theorem 7. LMMNS satisfies the GSP property.

Proof. Denote by $\bar{\mathbf{NS}} = (\bar{NS}_1, \ldots, \bar{NS}_n)$ the LMM-optimal normalized share vector when a coalition of users $\bar{U} \subseteq \{u_1, \ldots, u_n\}$ misreports requirement $\bar{r}_{ik}$ instead of r_{ik} for all $u_k \in \bar{U}$. For an arbitrary user u_k, if $x_k^* = B_k$, user u_k cannot increase its utility by altering the demand vector or B_k. Thus, we assume that $x_k^* < B_k$ for each user $u_k \in \bar{U}$. By Lemma 4, for an arbitrary user $u_k \in \bar{U}$, we have

$$NS_k^* \geq NS_i^*, \text{ for } i = 1, \ldots, n. \tag{6}$$

Let $\bar{\mathbf{NS}} = (\bar{NS}_1, \ldots, \bar{NS}_n)$ be the LMM-optimal solution for the modified system. Denote by $(\bar{x}_1, \ldots, \bar{x}_n)$ the corresponding numbers of tasks processed in the LMMNS solution of the modified system. Thus, for each user $u_k \in \bar{U}$, $\bar{NS}_k = \|\bar{\mathbf{ws}}_k\|_p \cdot \bar{x}_k$, where $\bar{ws}_{kj} = \bar{r}_{kj}/w_{kj}$, and for each user $u_i \notin \bar{U}$, $\bar{NS}_i = \|\mathbf{ws}_i\|_p \cdot \bar{x}_i$, where $ws_{ij} = r_{ij}/w_{ij}$. For an arbitrary user $u_k \in \bar{U}$, since the true utility of user u_k is increased in the modified system, we have

$$r_{kj}x_k^* < \bar{r}_{kj}\bar{x}_k, \text{ for } j = 1, \ldots, m, \text{ and } NS_k^* < \bar{NS}_k. \tag{7}$$

Consider an arbitrary saturated resource j in the original system (there must exist, as in the proof of Theorem 5). As $\sum_{i=1}^n r_{ij}x_i^* = 1$, $\sum_{i:u_i \in \bar{U}} \bar{r}_{ij}\bar{x}_i + \sum_{i:u_i \in U \setminus \bar{U}} r_{ij}\bar{x}_i \leq 1$, and $r_{kj}x_k^* < \bar{r}_{kj}\bar{x}_k$ for each user $u_k \in \bar{U}$, there is a user $u_h \in U \setminus \bar{U}$ such that $r_{hj}x_h^* > r_{hj}\bar{x}_h$, which implies that

$$\bar{x}_h < x_h^* \leq B_h,$$

and

$$\bar{NS}_h = \|\mathbf{ws}_h\|_p \cdot \bar{x}_h < \|\mathbf{ws}_h\|_p \cdot x_h^* = NS_h^*. \tag{8}$$

Thus, by the optimality of $\bar{\mathbf{NS}} = (\bar{NS}_1, \ldots, \bar{NS}_n)$ and Lemma 2, we have

$$\bar{NS}_h \geq \bar{NS}_k. \tag{9}$$

Combining (6)–(9), we have

$$\bar{NS}_h \geq \bar{NS}_k > NS_k^* \geq NS_h^* > \bar{NS}_h.$$

A contradiction. Therefore, every user $u_k \in \bar{U}$ cannot increase her utility by altering the requirement vector, which implies that LMMNS satisfies the GSP property. ∎

5 Approximation Ratios

In the last section, we have proved that LMMNS satisfies some highly desirable fairness properties. In this section, we examine the approximation ratios of LMMNS. Let $(x_1, \ldots, x_n)$ be the LMMNS solution throughout this section. Consider a setting with one resource and two users. Assume that $w_{11} = r_{11} = 1/K$, $w_{21} = r_{21} = 1 - 1/K$, and $B_1 = B_2 = K + 1$, where K is a large positive number. The LMMNS mechanism produces a fair allocation with $x_1 = x_2 = 1$ and $NS_1 = NS_2 = 2^{1/p}$. It is easy to verify that the social welfare of the optimal solution is K obtained by allocating all resources to user u_1. Thus, the approximation ratio is $K/2$, which approaches infinity when $K \to +\infty$. It also holds for the utilization maximization objective which will be defined in the next subsection. The main reason for the bad approximation ratio is that every user has a different weight w_{ij}. Thus, we only consider the case where each user contributes equal amount for every type of resource as in [8], i.e., $w_{ij} = 1/n$ for every i, j.

Since LMMNS satisfies the SI property only if $p = +\infty$ and the worst-case scenario occurs when $B_i = +\infty$ for every user u_i, we only consider the case where $p = +\infty$ and $B_i = +\infty$ for every user u_i. In fact, based on our assumptions $w_{ij} = 1/n$, $p = +\infty$ and $B_i = +\infty$, LMMNS is exactly DRF. In the section, we analyze the approximation ratios of DRF under two different objectives.

5.1 Welfare Maximization

As in [15], given an allocation, define its (utilitarian) social welfare as $\sum_i x_i$. The *approximation ratio* of a mechanism is the worst-case ratio between the social welfare of the optimal solution and the social welfare of the mechanism's solution, i.e.,

$$\text{approximation ration} = \sup_I \frac{\sum_{i=1}^n x_i^*}{\sum_{i=1}^n x_i},$$

where $(x_1, \ldots, x_n)$ is the solution produced by the mechanism, and $(x_1^*, \ldots, x_n^*)$ is the social welfare maximized solution obtained by solving the following program:

$$\begin{cases} \max \sum_{i=1}^n x_i \\ \sum_{i=1}^n r_{ij} x_i \leq 1, \text{ for } j = 1, \ldots, m. \end{cases}$$

Note that approximation ratio is equivalent to price of fairness defined in [1]. Parkes, Procaccia, and Shah [15] show that the approximation ratio of DRF is at least m. In this section, we obtain the following results.

Theorem 8. When the objective is welfare maximization, the approximation ratio of DRF is exactly n.

Proof. Let $(x_1^*, \ldots, x_n^*)$ be a social welfare maximized solution. As $(x_1, \ldots, x_n)$ satisfies the SI property, for each user u_i, there is a resource j such that u_i receives at least $1/n$-fraction of it. Thus, for each $i = 1, \ldots, n$, we have $x_i \leq nx_i^*$, implying that $\sum_{i=1}^n x_i \leq n \sum_{i=1}^n x_i^*$.

Consider a setting with one resource and n users. For $i = 1, \ldots, n - 1$, the requirement of user u_i is $r_{i1} = 1/n$, and the requirement of user u_n is $r_{n1} = 1/n^K$, where K is a large enough positive number. The optimal allocation will give all of resource to user u_n, for a social welfare n^K. In contrast, under DRF each user will receive a $1/n$-fraction of the resource, for a social welfare $n^{K-1} + n - 1$. When K grows larger, the approximation ratio of DRF approaches

$$\lim_{K \to \infty} \frac{n^K}{n^{K-1} + n - 1} = \lim_{K \to \infty} \frac{n}{1 + \frac{1}{n^{K-2}} - \frac{1}{n^{K-1}}} = n.$$

Thus, for every $\delta > 0$, DRF cannot have an approximation ratio better than $n - \delta$ for the social welfare, which implies that the approximation ratio of DRF is exactly n.   ∎

Since DRF satisfies some important highly desirable fairness properties including SI, it is more reasonable to compare DRF with the mechanisms satisfying the desirable fairness properties. For example, consider a setting with one resource and n users. Comparing with the mechanisms satisfying SI, the approximation ratio of DRF is 1. It is easy to verify that DRF is the unique mechanism satisfying PE, SI, EF, and GSP. A nature question is that whether DRF is the only possible mechanism satisfying PE, SI, EF and GSP, when the number of resources is at least two. Although we do not find another mechanism, we can compute the approximation ratio of DRF, comparing with the mechanisms satisfying certain properties.

Theorem 9. The approximation ratio of DRF lies in $[n-1, n]$, comparing with the welfare maximization mechanisms satisfying PE, SI and EF.

Proof. Following from Theorem 8, the approximation ratio of DRF is at most n. Let $(x_1^*, \ldots, x_n^*)$ be a social welfare maximized solution satisfying PE, SI and EF. Consider a setting with two resources (for example, CPUs and memory) and n users. For $i = 1, \ldots, n - 1$, the requirements of user u_i are $r_{i1} = 1/n$ and $r_{i2} = 1/n^K$, and the requirements of user u_n are $r_{n1} = 1/n^{2K}$ and $r_{n2} = 1/n^{K+1}$, where K is a large positive integer. Clearly, $x_i = 1/(1 - 1/n + 1/n^K)$ for $i = 1, \ldots, n-1$ and $x_n = n^K/(1 - 1/n + 1/n^K)$, for a social welfare $(n^K + n - 1)/(1 - 1/n + 1/n^K)$. In contrast, the social welfare of $(x_1^*, \ldots, x_n^*)$ is $n^{K+1} - n^2 + 2n - 1$, where $x_i^* = 1$ for $i = 1, \ldots, n-1$ and $x_n^* = n^{K+1} - n^2 + n$. It is easy to verify that $(x_1^*, x_2^*, \ldots, x_n^*)$ satisfies PE, SI and EF. When k grows larger, the approximation ratio of DRF approaches

$$\lim_{K \to \infty} \frac{n^{K+1} - n^2 + 2n - 1}{(n^K + n - 1)/(1 - 1/n + 1/n^K)}$$

$$= (1 - \frac{1}{n}) \lim_{K \to \infty} \frac{n - 1/n^{K-2} + 2/n^{K-1} - 1/n^K}{1 + 1/n^{K-1} - 1/n^K} = n - 1.$$

Thus, the theorem holds.   ∎

Although DRF does not perform well on PE, SI and EF in the worst-case scenario, we believe that DRF performs well on GSP. Let $(x_1^*, \ldots, x_n^*)$ be a solution produced by a social welfare maximized mechanism $\mathcal{M}^*$ satisfying PE, SI, EF and GSP. If there is a user u_k satisfying $x_k^* > x_k$, there must be a user

u_l satisfying $x_l^* < x_l$, following the PE property of DRF. Combining the SI property of $(x_1^*, \ldots, x_n^*)$, we have

$$\max_j r_{kj} x_k^* > \max_j r_{kj} x_k = \max_j r_{lj} x_l > \max_j r_{lj} x_l^* \geq \frac{1}{n}.$$

If user u_l claims that its requirement vector is $(r_{l1}/K, \ldots, r_{lm}/K)$, where K is a large positive number approaching infinity. By the optimality of $\mathcal{M}^*$, the mechanism $\mathcal{M}^*$ will possibly reallocate some resources of user u_k to user u_l to improve welfare, without violating the PE, SI and EF properties. However, this violates the GSP property of $\mathcal{M}^*$. Thus, $(x_1, \ldots, x_n)$ is possibly the optimal solution satisfying PE, SI, EF and GSP, when the objective is welfare maximization.

5.2   Utilization Maximization

In cloud computing systems, the resource managers care more about the utilization rate of the resources. For example, Ghodsi et al. [8] shows CPU and memory utilization for the small workload when using DRF compared to Hadoop's fair scheduler (slot). Given an allocation $(x_1, \ldots, x_n)$, let $c_j = \sum_{i=1}^n r_{ij} x_i$ be the utilization rate (or consumption) of resource j. Define *utilization* of $(x_1, \ldots, x_n)$ as $\min_j c_j$, which is the minimum utilization rate of m resources. Similarly to that in [15], define *approximation ratio* of a mechanism is the worst-case ratio between the utilization of the optimal solution and the utilization of the mechanism's solution.

As in the last subsection, when $m = 1$, DRF is an optimal mechanism, because all the resources are allocated, following from the PE property. When $m \geq 2$, DRF will not always be optimal. As in the last subsection, we obtain the following results.

Theorem 10. When the objective is utilization maximization, the approximation ratio of DRF is exactly n.

Proof. Let $(x_1^*, \ldots, x_n^*)$ be a utilization maximized solution with utilization c^*. Since DRF satisfies the SI property, for each user u_i, we have $r_{ij_i} x_i \geq 1/n$. Combining the constraint $r_{ij_i} x_i^* \leq \sum_{k=1}^n r_{kj_k} x_k^* \leq 1$, we have $x_i \geq x_i^*/n$, for $i = 1, \ldots, n$. Let j' be the resource such that $\sum_{i=1}^n r_{ij} x_i^*$ is the minimized, which implies that the utilization of $(x_1^*, \ldots, x_n^*)$ is $c^* = \sum_{i=1}^n r_{ij'} x_i^*$. Obviously, for every resource $j = 1, 2, \ldots, m$, we have

$$\sum_{i=1}^n r_{ij} x_i \geq \frac{1}{n} \sum_{i=1}^n r_{ij} x_i^* \geq \frac{1}{n} \sum_{i=1}^n r_{ij'} x_i^* \geq \frac{c^*}{n}. \tag{10}$$

It implies that the approximation ratio of DRF is at most n.

Consider a setting with two resources and n users. The requirements of user u_1 are $r_{11} = 1/n$ and $r_{12} = 1/n$. For $i = 2, \ldots, n$, the requirements of user u_i are $r_{i1} = 1/n$ and $r_{i2} = 1/n^K$, where K is a large positive integer. The optimal allocation will give all of resource to user u_1, for a utilization 1. In contrast, under DRF, each user will receive a $1/n$-fraction of the resource 1, for a utilization $1/n+(n-1)/n^K$. When K grows larger, the approximation ratio of DRF approaches

$$\lim_{K\to\infty} \frac{1}{1/n + (n-1)/n^K} = \lim_{K\to\infty} \frac{n^K}{n^{K-1} + (n-1)} = n.$$

Thus, the approximation ratio of DRF is at least n. Therefore, the theorem holds. ∎

As in the last subsection, we compare DRF with the mechanisms satisfying certain properties. Similarly, we obtain

Theorem 11. The approximation ratio of DRF lies in $[n - 1, n]$, comparing with the utilization maximization mechanisms satisfying the PE, SI, and EF properties.

Proof. Following from Theorem 10, the approximation ratio of DRF is at most n. Let $(x_1^*, \ldots, x_n^*)$ be a utilization maximized solution satisfying PE, SI, and EF. Consider a setting with three resources and n users. For $i = 1, \ldots, n-1$, the requirements of user u_i are $r_{i1} = 1/n$, $r_{i2} = 1/n^K$, and $r_{i3} = 1/n^{4K}$, and the requirements of user u_n are $r_{n1} = 1/n^{2K}$, $r_{n2} = 1/n^{K+1}$, and $r_{n3} = 1/n^{2K}$, where K is a large positive integer. Clearly, $x_i = 1/(1 - 1/n + 1/n^K)$ for $i = 1, \ldots, n-1$ and $x_n = n^K/(1 - 1/n + 1/n^K)$, for a utilization $\sum_{i=1}^{n} x_i = (n-1)/n^{4K}(1 - 1/n + 1/n^K) + 1/n^K(1 - 1/n + 1/n^K)$. In contrast, the utilization of $(x_1^*, \ldots, x_n^*)$ is $\sum_{i=1}^{n} x_i^* = (n-1)/n^{4K} + (n^{K+1} - n^2 + n)/n^{2K}$, where $x_i^* = 1$ for $i = 1, \ldots, n-1$ and $x_n^* = n^{K+1} - n^2 + n$. When $K \to +\infty$, the approximation ratio approaches

$$\lim_{K\to\infty} \frac{1}{1 - 1/n + 1/n^K} \frac{n - 1 + (n^{K+1} - n^2 + n)n^{2K}}{n - 1 + n^{3K}}$$

$$= (1 - \frac{1}{n}) \lim_{K\to\infty} \frac{n - 1 + n^{3K+1} - n^{2K+2} + n^{2K+1}}{n - 1 + n^{3K}}$$

$$= n - 1.$$

Thus, the theorem holds. ∎

6   Discussions and Future Work

We have presented a linear-time algorithm to find a solution for the LMMNS mechanism, which a natural generalization of the well-known DRF mechanism. One important direction is to generalize our algorithm to multiple heterogeneous servers [19]. In addition, we have presented the approximation ratios of DRF, where the approximation ratio is somewhat different from that defined in [15]. It is interesting to find an optimal welfare (or utilization) maximization mechanism satisfying PE, SI, EF and GSP.

As mentioned in [4], proportional fairness (PF) is preferable to DRF under the assumption that the population of jobs in progress is a stochastic process.

It is interesting to design an efficient algorithm to find a PF (approximate) solution for multi-resource allocation with bounded number of tasks, which can also be used in the dynamic environment.

Acknowledgment. The work is supported in part by the National Natural Science Foundation of China [Nos. 61662088, 11301466], the Natural Science Foundation of Yunnan Province of China [No. 2014FB114] and IRTSTYN.

References

1. Bertsimas, D., Farias, V.F., Trichakis, N.: The price of fairness. Oper. Res. **59**(1), 17–31 (2011)
2. Bhattacharya, A.A., Culler, D., Friedman, E., Ghodsi, A., Shenker, S., Stoica, I.: Hierarchical scheduling for diverse datacenter workloads. In: Proceedings of the 4th Annual Symposium on Cloud Computing, SOCC 2013 (2013). Article No. 4
3. Blum, M., Floyd, R.W., Pratt, V., Rivest, R.R., Tarjan, R.E.: Time bounds for selection. J. Comput. Syst. Sci. **7**(4), 448–461 (1973)
4. Bonald, T., Roberts, J.: Enhanced cluster computing performance through proportional fairness. Perform. Eval. **79**, 134–145 (2014)
5. Bonald, T., Roberts, J.: Multi-resource fairness: objectives, algorithms and performance. In: Proceedings of the 2015 ACM SIGMETRICS International Conference on Measurement and Modeling of Computer Systems, pp. 31–42 (2015)
6. Dolev, D., Feitelson, D.G., Halpern, J.Y., Kupferman, R., Linial, N.: No justified complaints: on fair sharing of multiple resources. In: Proceedings of the 3rd Innovations in Theoretical Computer Science Conference, ITCS 2012, pp. 68–75 (2012)
7. Friedman, E., Ghodsi, A., Psomas, C.-A.: Strategyproof allocation of discrete jobs on multiple machines. In: Proceedings of the Fifteenth ACM Conference on Economics and Computation, pp. 529–546 (2014)
8. Ghodsi, A., Zaharia, M., Hindman, B., Konwinski, A., Shenker, S., Stoica, I.: Dominant resource fairness: fair allocation of multiple resource types. In: Proceedings of the 8th USENIX Conference on Networked Systems Design and Implementation, NSDI 2011, pp. 24–24 (2011)
9. Gutman, A., Nisan, N.: Fair allocation without trade. In: Proceedings of the 11th International Conference on Autonomous Agents and Multiagent Systems, AAMAS 2012, pp. 719–728 (2012)
10. Kash, I., Procaccia, A., Shah, N.: No agent left behind: dynamic fair division of multiple resources. J. Artif. Intell. Res. **51**, 351–358 (2014)
11. Li, W., Liu, X., Zhang, X., Zhang, X.: Dynamic fair allocation of multiple resources with bounded number of tasks in cloud computing systems. Multiagent Grid Syst. Int. J. **11**, 245–257 (2015)
12. Li, W., Liu, X., Zhang, X., Zhang, X.: A further analysis of the dynamic dominant resource fairness mechanism. In: Xiao, M., Rosamond, F. (eds.) FAW 2017. LNCS, vol. 10336, pp. 163–174. Springer, Cham (2017). doi:10.1007/978-3-319-59605-1_15
13. Liu, H., He, B.: F2C: enabling fair and fine-grained resource sharing in multi-tenant IaaS clouds. IEEE Trans. Parallel Distrib. Syst. **27**(9), 2589–2602 (2016)
14. Megiddo, N.: Optimal flows in networks with multiple sources and sinks. Math. Program. **7**(3), 97–107 (1974)

15. Parkes, D.C., Procaccia, A.D., Shah, N.: Beyond dominant resource fairness: extensions, limitations, and indivisibilities. ACM Trans. Econ. Comput. **3**(1) (2015). Article No. 3
16. Procaccia, A.D.: Cake cutting: not just child's play. Commun. ACM **56**(7), 78–87 (2013)
17. Tan, J., Zhang, L., Li, M., Wang, Y.: Multi-resource fair sharing for multiclass workflows. ACM SIGMETRICS Perform. Eval. Rev. **42**(4), 31–37 (2015)
18. Tang, S., Niu, Z., Lee, B., He, B.: Multi-resource fair allocation in pay-as-you-go cloud computing. Manuscript (2014)
19. Wang, W., Liang, B., Li, B.: Multi-resource fair allocation in heterogeneous cloud computing systems. IEEE Trans. Parallel Distrib. Syst. **26**(10), 2822–2835 (2015)
20. Wong, C.J., Sen, S., Lan, T., Chiang, M.: Multi-resource allocation: fairness efficiency tradeoffs in a unifying framework. IEEE/ACM Trans. Netw. **21**(6), 1785–1798 (2013)
21. Zahedi, S.M., Lee, B.C.: REF: resource elasticity fairness with sharing incentives for multiprocessors. In: Proceedings of the 19th International Conference on Architectural Support for Programming Languages and Operating Systems (ASPLOS), pp. 145–160 (2014)
22. Zarchy, D., Hay, D., Schapira, M.: Capturing resource tradeoffs in fair multi-resource allocation. In: IEEE INFOCOM, pp. 1062–1070 (2015)
23. Zeldes, Y., Feitelson, D.G.: On-line fair allocations based on bottlenecks and global priorities. In: Proceedings of the 4th ACM/SPEC International Conference on Performance Engineering, ICPE 2013, pp. 229–240 (2013)

Learning Latent Topics from the Word Co-occurrence Network

Wu Wang[1,3], Houquan Zhou[1], Kun He[1,2(✉)], and John E. Hopcroft[2]

[1] Huazhong University of Science and Technology, Wuhan 430074, China
{U201110084,U201417183,brooklet60}@hust.edu.cn
[2] Computer Science Department, Cornell University, Ithaca, NY 14853, USA
jeh@cs.cornell.edu
[3] Shenzhen Research Institute of Huazhong University of Science and Technology,
Shenzhen 518057, China

Abstract. Topic modeling is widely used to uncover the latent thematic structure in corpora. Based on the separability assumption, the spectral method focuses on the word co-occurrence patterns at the document-level and it includes two steps: anchor selection and topic recovery. Biterm Topic Model (BTM) utilizes the word co-occurrence patterns in the whole corpus. Inspired by the word-pair pattern in BTM, we build a Word Co-occurrence Network (WCN) where nodes correspond to words and weights of edges stand for the empirical co-occurrence probability of word pairs. We exploit existing methods to deal with the word co-occurrence network for anchor selection. We find a K-clique in the unweighted complementary graph, or the maximum edge-weight clique in the weighted complementary graph for the anchor word selection. Experiments on real-world corpora evaluated on topic quality and interpretability demonstrate the effectiveness of the proposed approach.

Keywords: Topic model · Word co-occurrence network · Maximum edge-weight clique · K-clique

1 Introduction

Topic modeling is an important technique used for text mining. The main idea of topic modeling is that documents arise as a distribution on a small number of topic vectors, where each topic vector is a distribution on words. Topic modeling can uncover the thematic structure from a large collection of text documents without human supervision. Topic models are of high importance in many machine learning applications, such as document analysis, classification and clustering, and it plays a key role on some specific context tasks. Topic modeling over short texts has attracted a lot of interests as short texts are prevalent on web application [15,17,18,26–28,30]. For a time-stamped document collection, discovering the evolution of topics over time has drawn much attention as well [4,14,29]. In practice, Targeted Topic Modeling (TTM) for focused analysis can perform more detailed analysis on some specific aspects [25]. The Web

© Springer Nature Singapore Pte Ltd. 2017
D. Du et al. (Eds.): NCTCS 2017, CCIS 768, pp. 18–30, 2017.
https://doi.org/10.1007/978-981-10-6893-5_2

Search Stream Model (WSSM), a novel and highly practical probabilistic topic model, is delicately calibrated for handling two salient features of the web search data [13].

Existing topic modeling approaches can be divided into two main categories: probabilistic models [6,12] and spectral methods [2,3,21]. The first is based on some basic probabilistic models, such as Probabilistic Latent Semantic Indexing (PLSI) [12] and Latent Dirichlet Allocation (LDA) [6]. The LDA model is the most popular and frequently-used topic modeling method. As it is intractable to learn the parameters directly, the LDA model uses approximation inference techniques such as Markov Chain Monte Carlo (MCMC) [11] and variational inference [6] to learn the parameters. A number of variations of LDA have been studied. The Correlated Topic Model (CTM) [5] exhibits correlation of topics via the logistic normal distribution. Gibbs sampling [7,16] and parallel inference [8,19,28] have been widely studied to improve the performance and scalability.

The second category, spectral methods, suggests an algebraic recovery perspective and utilizes nonnegative matrix factorization (NMF) as a main technique. By making some reasonable assumption, these methods are able to provide provable polynomial-time algorithms. Instead of doing inference on document-word matrix, which is very sparse, they focus on the word co-occurrence matrix. Arora et al. [3] propose an approach to recover the topic distribution assuming that every topic contains at least one anchor word which occurs with non-zero probability only in that topic. They first select an anchor word for each topic by solving numerous linear programs; then, in the recovery step, reconstruct the topic distributions given these anchor words. Bittorf et al. [24] and Gillis et al. [9] reduce the number of linear programs. Gillis et al. [10] propose a linear projection instead of linear programming. Arora et al. [2] replace the linear programming with a combinatorial anchor selection algorithm that is efficient and scalable as compared with other approaches. Nguyen et al. [21] develop a new regularized algorithms to mathematically resemble the rich priors and improves the interpretability of topic models.

Inspired by the word-pair pattern of Biterm Topic Model (BTM) [26], we develop a word co-occurrence network (WCN) that utilizes the word co-occurrence information in the whole corpus. More specifically, rather than considering words as vectors in the high dimensional space, we regard each word as a node in the word co-occurrence network. Exploiting the word-pair patterns of BTM and the separability assumption, we conclude that the anchor words do not appear simultaneously in any single document. Based on this observation, we propose two new anchor word selection algorithms. The first, denoted as HARDCLIQUE, finds K-clique in the unweighted complementary graph to select the anchor words. The second, denoted as SOFTCLIQUE, finds a maximum edge-weight clique of size K in the weighted complementary graph as the alternative.

To the best of our knowledge, this is the first attempt to use graph theory for the anchor selection in topic modeling. It is a novel and interesting perspective by transforming the corpus into a word co-occurrence network and finding cliques in the network so as to find the anchor words in the original corpus. We perform our methods on two types of real-world corpora and compare with two classical methods, the LDA method [6] and the anchor word method [2]. Experiments show that our method is very promising when evaluated on topic quality as well as interpretability. Our work relates the anchor selection problem in the area of data mining to the classic area of combinatorial optimization. In this way, other advanced methods for related problems in this classic area, such as theory and method for maximal independent set, can be transferred smoothly into the comparatively new area of topic modeling. Moreover, our method can be further investigated for many applications. For example, we might be able to determine the number of topics automatically by finding maximal cliques in the generated network.

2   Related Work

We review two related works: the Anchor Word Algorithm (AWA) [2] and the word-pair pattern of Biterm Topic Model (BTM) [26]. AWA is a provable learning algorithm for topic model inference. The algorithm can be divided into two steps: anchor selection and recovery. A better anchor word selection plays a key role in this algorithm. BTM is a probabilistic generative model that learns topics by directly modeling the generation of the word-pair patterns in the whole corpus.

2.1   The Anchor Word Algorithm

Learning Topics. The Anchor Word Algorithm (AWA) is based on the reasonable separability assumption. It assumes that there exists at least a special word to identify each topic. For example, "winger", "field", "shot" are likely to appear in articles related to football, but only "winger" is suitable to be the anchor word as it is most unambiguous.

Compared with the probabilistic models that work directly on the documents and words, AWA mainly focuses on the probability of the word co-occurrence. Denote the vocabulary size by V and the number of topics by K. At the first step, AWA generates the word co-occurrence matrix $\mathbf{Q}$ by applying a simple calculation [2]. $\mathbf{Q}$ is a $V \times V$ matrix whose element $Q_{i,j}$ stands for the probability of word i and word j simultaneously appear in a single document. The $\overline{\mathbf{Q}}$ matrix is the row normalized version of $\mathbf{Q}$ and its element stands for the conditional probability that word j appears given that word i appears in the same document.

AWA finds a set of anchor words from the co-occurrence matrix. Denote the indices of the anchor words as $S = \{s_1, s_2, ..., s_K\}$, the rows of $\overline{\mathbf{Q}}$ can be reconstructed as a convex combination of the rows corresponding to the anchor words [2]. We denote the coefficient of the reconstruction as a matrix C, where $C_{i,k} = p(z = k|w = i)$. More specifically,

$$\overline{Q}_{i,j} = \sum_{k=1}^{K} p(z = k|w = i)\overline{Q}_{s_k,j} = \sum_{k=1}^{K} C_{i,k}\overline{Q}_{s_k,j} \qquad (1)$$

To find the topic distribution $p(w = i | z = k)$, the probability of word i given topic k, denoted as $A_{i,k}$, it is necessary to calculate $C_{i,k}$, the probability of topic k given word i. Once $C_{i,k}$ is learned, we can easily discover the topic distribution by the Bayes formula.

$$A_{i,k} \propto C_{i,k} p(w = i) = C_{i,k} \sum_j \overline{Q}_{i,j} \tag{2}$$

The reconstruction coefficients, $C_{i,k}$, can be uncovered with respect to two measures, RecoverKL and RecoverL2 [2]:

$$\text{RecoverKL: } C_{i,\cdot} = \underset{C_{i,\cdot}}{\operatorname{argmin}} D_{(KL)}(\overline{Q}_{i,\cdot} \| \sum_k C_{i,k} \overline{Q}_{s_k,\cdot}) \tag{3}$$

$$\text{RecoverL2: } C_{i,\cdot} = \underset{C_{i,\cdot}}{\operatorname{argmin}} D_{(L2)}(\overline{Q}_{i,\cdot} \| \sum_k C_{i,k} \overline{Q}_{s_k,\cdot}) \tag{4}$$

Finding Anchor Words. Figure 1 illustrates the conclusion drawn by Eq. (1) that normal words (in grey) lie in the convex hull of anchor words (in dark).

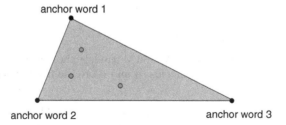

Fig. 1. Relations of anchor words and normal words. A anchor word is a vertex of the convex hull and the normal words lie in the convex hull.

Arora et al. propose a pure combinatorial algorithm, referred to as the FASTANCHORWORDS algorithm [2], to find the anchor words in the anchor selection phase that totally avoids using the linear programming method. Each row of the matrix $\mathbf{Q}$ is regarded as a point in a V-dimensional space, and we can get V points as the input of the FASTANCHORWORDS algorithm. FASTANCHORWORDS algorithm then iteratively finds the furthest point from the subspace spanned by the set of anchor words found so far. Meanwhile, when faced with many choices for the next anchor word, this algorithm adopts a greedy strategy to find a point that is furthest to the set of points found so far. Arora et al. also provide analysis to guarantee the feasibility of the algorithm.

2.2   The Biterm Topic Model

The Biterm Topic Model (BTM) [26] is a probabilistic generative model that models the generation of the biterms (word co-occurrence pattern) in the whole corpus rather than documents. Figure 2 shows the graphical representation of BTM. The main purpose of BTM is to tackle the sparsity problem in topic modeling over short texts. Notice that the method yields great results even in normal text data. In BTM, any two distinct words extracted from a document is a biterm. The probability that a biterm drawn from a specific topic is further captured by the probability that two words in the biterm are drawn from the topic.

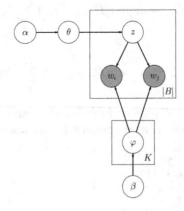

Fig. 2. Graphic representation of BTM. BTM models the generation procedure of biterms in a corpus rather than documents. α and β are the fixed hyperparameters.

For each biterm $b = (w_i, w_j)$, we should choose a topic first and draw the two words independently. Thus, the joint probability of a biterm can be written as [26]:

$$p(w_i, w_j) = \sum_z p(z)p(w_i|z)p(w_j|z) \tag{5}$$

where z is a topic.

Inspired by the word-pair pattern in BTM, we propose two novel anchor selection algorithms by regarding the corpus as a word co-occurrence network.

3   The Proposed Method

3.1   The Word Co-occurrence Network (WCN)

Generally speaking, a specific topic is represented as a group of semantically related words in topic models, while the correlation is revealed by word co-occurrence patterns in the documents. AWA and BTM both utilize the information of the word co-occurrence.

BTM assumes that the whole corpus is a mixture of topics, where each word-pair is independently drawn from a specific topic. The probability that a word-pair is drawn from a specific topic is further captured by the chance that two words in the word-pair are drawn from the same topic [26]. Inspired by the word-pair pattern, we build a word co-occurrence network by regarding words as nodes in the network and the word co-occurrence probability as the edge weights. The constructed word co-occurrence network can fully leverage the rich global word co-occurrence patterns to better reveal the latent topics. Meanwhile, from the probabilistic perspective, each entry of **Q** stands for the empirical word co-occurrence probability in the corpus. Figure 3 illustrates an example of the constructed word co-occurrence sub-network. The nodes in the network stand for words and the lighter color line indicates the lower-weight relationship. For example, edge between "layer" and "recognition" is of high weight while edge between "operate" and "redundancy" is of low weight.

Fig. 3. An example of word co-occurrence sub-network. The nodes in the network stand for words and the lighter color line indicates the lower-weight relationship.

Fig. 4. An example of the complementary graph G. Edge exists between two words if their joint probability is smaller than a threshold ε.

3.2   Finding Cliques of Anchor Words

The separability assumption claims that an anchor word only appears in a specific topic, and it strongly indicates the corresponding topic. Thus, based on the main idea of BTM that the whole corpus is a mixture of topics, where each word-pair is independently drawn from a specific topic, we can draw an interesting conclusion that anchor words belonging to different topics will not appear simultaneously in the same document.

$$p(w_{s_k}, w_{s_{k'}}) = \sum_z p(z)p(w_{s_k}|z)p(w_{s_{k'}}|z) = 0 \qquad (6)$$

Now consider the anchor selection phase and our goal is to find anchor words from the word co-occurrence network. Since we only have finitely many documents in the corpus, matrix **Q** is only an approximation to its expectation. Thus, each entry of $\mathbf{Q}$ stands for the empirical word co-occurrence probability in the corpus. The constraint in Eq. (6) may not be strictly satisfied. Strictly speaking, anchor words belonging to different topics will not appear simultaneously or they appear together with a very low probability.

$$p(w_{s_k}, w_{s_{k'}}) = \sum_z p(z)p(w_{s_k}|z)p(w_{s_{k'}}|z) \xrightarrow{threshold:\varepsilon} 0 \qquad (7)$$

Thus, the constraint in Eq. (6) need to be updated to Eq. (7). Accordingly, in the word co-occurrence network, the anchor word selection is to find a set of nodes which are connected with each other by very low-value edges. In practice, we propose two methods to find nodes corresponding to anchor words in the complementary graph. In this section, we describe the two proposed methods.

The HardClique Method. In the HARDCLIQUE method, we allow the probability between anchor words to be lower than a small value ε. In order to find anchor words in the word co-occurrence network, we transform the network into a variant of complementary graph $G = (V, E)$ where V is the same set of nodes and $E = \{(v_i, v_j)|w_{ij} < \varepsilon\}$. If the joint probability of two words is sufficiently small, then there exists an edge connecting them in the complementary graph G. Figure 4 shows an example.

Thus, based on the complementary graph and the conclusion drawn from Eq. (6) or (7), we could choose the set of K nodes contained in a K-clique as the anchor words. The details are in Algorithm 1.

Algorithm 1. The HARDCLIQUE method

Input: Corpus D, number of topics K, threshold ε
Output: Topic distribution matrix $\mathbf{A}$
 1: Calculate the word co-occurrence matrix $\mathbf{Q}$ from corpus D
 2: Transform the word co-occurrence network to graph G with respect to threshold ε
 3: $S \leftarrow$ FIND-K-CLIQUE(G)
 4: $\mathbf{A} \leftarrow$ RECOVERL2($S, \mathbf{Q}$)

In practice, it is possible to find multiple sets of K-cliques, as one topic contains more than one anchor word. For example, "winger" and "goalkeeper" both strongly imply the football topic so they can both play the role of the anchor word. How to select the threshold ε plays a key role in the HARDCLIQUE method. If the threshold is too small, we may not find any K-clique. On the contrary, if the threshold is too large, there could exist many candidates of anchor word cliques, and cause low topic quality. A trade-off between the quality and the feasibility should be carefully considered in practice. As nodes that stand for anchor words have at least $K - 1$ degrees in the graph, we can recursively remove nodes whose degree is less than $K - 1$ to reduce the size of graph and speed up the calculation.

The SoftClique Method. The other method we propose is with less restriction. As an alternative, we find K nodes whose sum of joint probability among each node pair is the smallest. We first replace the weight of edges w_{ij} by $1 - w_{ij}$ to get the complementary graph. The problem turns out to be the maximum edge-weighted clique problem (MEWCP), a well-known NP-hard problem [1,23].

Algorithm 2. GENETIC-MEWCP

Input: Graph G, number of topics K, number of iterations T, population size N
Output: Maximum edge-weighted clique $S = \{v_1, v_2, \cdots, v_K\}$
1: maxweight $\leftarrow 0$
2: population $\leftarrow$ A set of N k-cliques randomly chosen from G
3: do simple move to cliques in the population
4: **for** $i \leftarrow 1$ to T **do**
5:     exchange nodes between cliques in population
6:     do simple move to cliques in the population
7:     **for** $i \leftarrow 1$ to |population| **do**
8:         **if** weight(population[i]) > maxweight **then**
9:             $S \leftarrow$ population[i]
10:            maxweight $\leftarrow$ weight(population[i])
11:        **end if**
12:    **end for**
13: **end for**

Algorithm 3. The SOFTCLIQUE method

Input: Corpus D, number of topics K, number of iterations T, population size N
Output: Topic distribution matrix $\mathbf{A}$
1: Calculate word co-occurrence $\mathbf{Q}$ from corpus D
2: Replace weight of edges in word co-occurrence network G
3: $S \leftarrow$ GENETIC-MEWCP(G, K, T, N)
4: $A \leftarrow$ RECOVERL2$(S, \mathbf{Q})$

We could apply a simple local search method with the following genetic strategy. Find a clique by some greedy method, then define a simple move as swapping a node in the current clique that could increase the sum of the weights until a local maximum is achieved. To jump out of the local maximum, we exchange nodes between local maximum cliques and do a simple move again. This process is excuted iteratively to get a maximum edge-weight clique of size K. The GENETIC-MEWCP is given in Algorithm 2. The overall SOFTCLIQUE method is shown in Algorithm 3. Note that we could use any existing algorithm for the MEWCP.

Once the anchor words are found, the remaining of the procedure is the same as what was described in Sect. 2. We choose RecoverL2 measure in Eq. 4 to recover the topic distributions.

4   Experiments

In this section, we introduce the experiments conducted on real-world corpora to demonstrate the effectiveness of the proposed approaches. We take two typical methods as our baselines, namely LDA and AWA. All experiments are carried on a Linux server with Intel(R) Xeon(R) 2.00 GHz CPU and 56 GB memory.

4.1   Datasets

Two real-world corpora in different domains are used in the experiments, namely KOS and NIPS. The KOS corpus contains 3430 documents from the Daily Kos blog. The NIPS corpus contains 1500 papers from the NIPS conferences. All the corpora have been preprocessed into the bag of words format and stopwords are removed based on a stopword list.

We learn 10 or 20 topics on the corpora by four methods: LDA, AWA, and our HARDCLIQUE and SOFTCLIQUE methods. For LDA, we use an open-source python code implementation of LDA using Gibbs sampling[1]. The prior parameters are tuned via grid search: $\alpha = 0.1$ and $\beta = 0.01$. In our experiments, Gibbs sampling was run for 2000 iterations. For the HARDCLIQUE method, we use the clique-finding algorithm proposed in [22]. For the SOFTCLIQUE method, we use our own algorithm shown in Algorithm 3.

4.2   Evaluation Metrics

To compare the quality of topics found by different methods, we use a numeric metric called the coherence score [20]. Given a topic T and M words that appear most in topic $V^{(T)} = \{v_1, v_2, \cdots, v_M\}$, the coherence score is calculated as follows:

$$\text{Coherence}(T, V^{(T)}) = \sum_{i=2}^{M} \sum_{j=1}^{i-1} \log \frac{D(v_i, v_j) + 1}{D(v_j)} \tag{8}$$

$D(v_i, v_j)$ is the number of documents that v_i and v_j appear simultaneously and $D(v_i)$ is the number of documents v_i appears. 1 in the numerator of Eq. (8) is a smoothing constant to avoid zero value. As words strongly related to the same topic tend to co-occur in the same document, higher coherence score implies higher topic quality. It has been found that the coherence score is highly correlated with topic coherence.

To make a general evaluation, we compare the average of the coherence scores of K topics found by the four methods, namely $\frac{1}{K} \sum_k \text{Coherence}(T_k, V^{(T_k)})$. In the experiments, M is set to 10 and K is set to 10 or 20. As HARDCLIQUE may find several sets of anchor words, we calculate the average value over all sets.

---

[1] https://pypi.python.org/pypi/lda.

Besides the coherence score, we also compute the held-out likelihood, the logarithm probability of previous unseen data. Higher held-out likelihood value indicates stronger ability to fit unseen data. As held-out likelihoods can not be calculated directly by the anchor methods, we use variational inference [6] with the topic distribution learned by the anchor methods. The parameter α of variational inference is set to 0.1.

4.3 Results

Coherence. The result on coherence is averaged over three random runs, as shown in Fig. 5. In general, our two methods outperform the two baselines. For the NIPS corpus, HARDCLIQUE and SOFTCLIQUE show the best coherence when K is set to 10 and 20 respectively. For the KOS corpus, when K is set to 10, our two methods both outperform the two baselines. When K is set to 20, SOFT-CLIQUE method produces the best coherence. In general, our methods achieve considerable improvement for the topic quality.

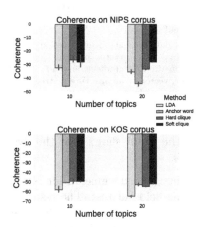

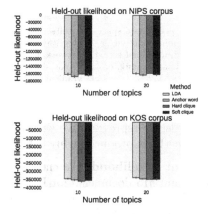

Fig. 5. Coherence score on two corpora. SOFTCLIQUE performs the best on the two corpora when K is set to 20, and HARDCLIQUE performs the best when K is set to 10.

Fig. 6. Held-out likelihood on two corpora. The four methods show very similar performance and LDA is slightly better.

Recall that HARDCLIQUE may find several sets of anchor words from the same corpus. For example, two cliques share 19 words and possess 1 exclusive word (in dark black) respectively. It indicates the exclusive words of two cliques are anchor words corresponding to the same topic. This gives reasonable interpretation for the result.

For more intuitive demonstration, we list top 10 words of some topics in Table 1. A more coherent topic is supposed to have more related top words, as

Table 1. The top 10 words given by 4 different methods on NIPS corpus for 5 topics. Top words of clique method are highly coherent.

Topic	LDA	Anchor word	HARDCLIQUE	SOFTCLIQUE
Topic 1	image, object images recognition features, feature pixel, view face, visual	network, set data, image system, neural images, training input, algorithm	data, image unit, input network, images output, hidden set, field	data, vector map, space point, feature set, input cluster, image
Topic 2	network, unit input, output weight, layer neural, hidden training, net	network, word training, input unit, set neural, system data, error	network, unit neural, weight hidden, input error, architecture output, algorithm	network, weight unit, input output, neural training, layer hidden, error
Topic 3	signal, filter information frequency noise, channel component system correlation auditory	speech, signal network, output recognition information layer, input speaker, acoustic	network, system pattern, neural output, training signal, recognition speech, input	word, signal speech, processing system, control training, subject recognition adaptation
Topic 4	image, object image recognition features, feature pixel, view face, visual	visual, signal object, image neuron, orientation map, spatial cortex, response	visual, processing direction, object motion, input activity, science spatial, field	system, image data, visual object, point images, direction recognition, feature
Topic 5	vector, data space, point function dimensional kernel, linear matrix, basis	architecture algorithm problem, network unit, weight vector, data set, gradient	algorithm, data set, distribution problem, method parameter, vector information, number	algorithm function vector, problem gradient, method architecture matrix error, space

top words are representative words for a topic. The result shows that the two clique methods produce highly coherent top words.

Held-out Likelihood. We choose 15% documents (165 documents for NIPS corpus and 515 documents for KOS corpus) for the held-out test. The result is averaged over three random runs and demonstrated in Fig. 6. We find that the HARDCLIQUE method and LDA provide the best held-out likelihood on NIPS and KOS corpus respectively. In general, the difference is within the range of variability between documents.

5   Conclusion and Future Work

How to do a better anchor word selection is an open problem. We build a word co-occurrence network that considers words as nodes and the co-occurrence probability as edge weights. We propose two new anchor selection methods, namely finding K-clique in the unweighted complementary graph and finding maximum edge-weight clique in the weighted complementary graph. Experimental results on real-world corpora suggest that our methods outperform AWA and Gibbs sampling for LDA for the topic quality, the four methods provide comparable results for the held-out likelihood.

We apply a simple local search method with genetic strategy to get a maximum edge-weight clique of size K. It provides promising space for potential improvement utilizing more sophisticated algorithms in graph theory. Also, our method probably does not require the anchor words to form a clique for the anchor selection. In future work, we will conduct other combinatorial algorithm on the word co-occurrence graph.

Acknowledgments. This research work is supported by National Natural Science Foundation of China (61772219, 61472147), US Army Research Office (W911NF-14-1-0477) and Shenzhen Science and Technology Planning Project (JCYJ2017030715474 9425). We also thank Junru Shao for valuable discussions.

References

1. Alidaee, B., Glover, F., Kochenberger, G., Wang, H.: Solving the maximum edge weight clique problem via unconstrained quadratic programming. European Journal of Operational Research **181**(2), 592–597 (2007)
2. Arora, S., Ge, R., Halpern, Y., Mimno, D., Moitra, A., Sontag, D., Wu, Y., Zhu, M.: A practical algorithm for topic modeling with provable guarantees. In: ICML, pp. 280–288 (2013)
3. Arora, S., Ge, R., Moitra, A.: Learning topic models-going beyond SVD. In: FOCS, pp. 1–10. IEEE, (2012)
4. Bhadury, A., Chen, J., Zhu, J., Liu, S.: Scaling up dynamic topic models. In: WWW, pp. 381–390 (2016)
5. Blei, D.M., Lafferty, J.D.: A correlated topic model of science. In: The Annals of Applied Statistics, pp. 17–35 (2007)
6. Blei, D.M., Ng, A.Y., Jordan, M.I.: Latent dirichlet allocation. J. Mach. Learn. Res. 3, 993–1022 (2003)
7. Chen, J., Zhu, J., Wang, Z., Zheng, X., Zhang, B.: Scalable inference for logistic-normal topic models. In: NIPS, pp. 2445–2453 (2013)
8. Foulds, J., Boyles, L., DuBois, C., Smyth, P., Welling, M.: Stochastic collapsed variational Bayesian inference for latent Dirichlet allocation. In: KDD, pp. 446–454. ACM, (2013)
9. Gillis, N.: Robustness analysis of Hottopixx, a linear programming model for factoring nonnegative matrices. SIAM Journal on Matrix Analysis and Applications **34**(3), 1189–1212 (2013)
10. Gillis, N., Vavasis, S.A.: Fast and robust recursive algorithmsfor separable nonnegative matrix factorization. IEEE transactions on pattern analysis and machine intelligence **36**(4), 698–714 (2014)
11. Griffiths, T.L., Steyvers, M.: Finding scientific topics. Proceedings of the National academy of Sciences **101**(Suppl. 1), 5228–5235 (2004)
12. Hofmann, T.: Probabilistic latent semantic indexing. In: Proceedings of the 22nd annual international conference on Research and development in information retrieval, pp. 50–57. ACM, (1999)
13. Jiang, D., Leung, K.W.T., Ng, W.: Fast topic discovery from web search streams. In: WWW, pp. 949–960. ACM, (2014)
14. Jo, Y., Hopcroft, J.E., Lagoze, C.The web of topics: discovering the topology of topic evolution in a corpus. InWWW, pp. 257–266. ACM, (2011)

15. Kataria, S., Agarwal, A.: Supervised Topic Models for Microblog Classification. In: ICDM, pp. 793–798. IEEE, (2015)
16. Li, A.Q., Ahmed, A., Ravi, S., Smola, A.J.: Reducing the sampling complexity of topic models. In: KDD, pp. 891–900. ACM, (2014)
17. Li, C., Wang, H., Zhang, Z., Sun, A., Ma, Z.: Topic modeling for short texts with auxiliary word embeddings. In: Proceedings of the 39th International conference on Research and Development in Information Retrieval, pp. 165–174. ACM, (2016)
18. Lin, T., Tian, W., Mei, Q., Cheng, H.: The dual-sparse topic model: mining focused topics and focused terms in short text. In: WWW, pp. 539–550. ACM, (2014)
19. Liu, X., Zeng, J., Yang, X., Yan, J., Yang, Q.: Scalable parallel EM algorithms for latent Dirichlet allocation in multi-core systems. In: WWW, pp. 669–679. (2015)
20. Mimno, D., Wallach, H.M., Talley, E., Leenders, M., McCallum, A.: Optimizing semantic coherence in topic models. In: EMNLP, pp. 262–272. ACL, (2011)
21. Nguyen, T., Hu, Y., Boyd-Graber, J.L.: Anchors Regularized: Adding Robustness and Extensibility to Scalable Topic-Modeling Algorithms. In: ACL, pp. 359–369 (2014)
22. Palla, G., Dernyi, I., Farkas, I., Vicsek, T.: Uncovering the overlapping community structure of complex networks in nature and society. (2005)
23. Pullan, W.: Approximating the maximum vertex/edge weighted clique using local search. Journal of Heuristics **14**(2), 117–134 (2008)
24. Recht, B., Re, C., Tropp, J., Bittorf, V.: Factoring nonnegative matrices with linear programs. In: NIPS, pp. 1214–1222 (2012)
25. Wang, S., Chen, Z., Fei, G., Liu, B., Emery, S.: Targeted Topic Modeling for Focused Analysis. In: KDD, pp. 1235–1244 (2016)
26. Yan, X., Guo, J., Lan, Y., Cheng, X.: A biterm topic model for short texts. In: WWW, pp. 1445–1456. ACM, (2013)
27. Yan, X., Guo, J., Liu, S., Cheng, X., Wang, Y.: Learning topics in short texts by non-negative matrix factorization on term correlation matrix. In: Proceedings of the 2013 International Conference on Data Mining, pp. 749–757. SIAM, (2013)
28. Yang, S.H., Kolcz, A., Schlaikjer, A., Gupta, P.: Large-scale high-precision topic modeling on twitter. In: KDD, pp. 1907–1916. ACM, (2014)
29. Zhang, H., Kim, G., Xing, E.P.: Dynamic topic modeling for monitoring market competition from online text and image data. In: KDD, pp. 1425–1434. ACM, (2015)
30. Zuo, Y., Wu, J., Zhang, H., Lin, H., Wang, F., Xu, K., Xiong, H.: Topic Modeling of Short Texts: A Pseudo-Document View. In: KDD, pp. 2105–2114. ACM, (2016)

Fusion of Global and Local Deep Representation for Effective Object Retrieval

Mao Wang[1](✉), Yuewei Ming[1], Qiang Liu[1], and Jianping Yin[2]

[1] College of Computer, National University of Defense Technology,
Changsha 410073, Hunan, China
{wangmao,ywming,qiangliu06}@nudt.edu.cn
[2] State Key Laboratory of High Performance Computing,
National University of Defense Technology, Changsha 410073, Hunan, China
jpyin@nudt.edu.cn

Abstract. Recently, Regional Max Aggregating Convolutional (R-MAC) feature built upon Convolutional Neural Networks (CNNs) has shown great feature representation power in object retrieval. Combing with re-ranking step by object localization and post-processing step by query expansion, R-MAC can achieve a good retrieval accuracy. However, we have found that performing retrieval with R-MAC feature from local query object will result in a lost of global information. In this paper, we propose to fuse global and local R-MAC feature to improve retrieval accuracy. Specifically, we use the global R-MAC deriving from entire image to issue the initial query, which can rank more positive results in the top. Then, the global and local R-MAC are concatenated to represent the entire image for re-ranking and query expansion, which can be a more comprehensive descriptor for object retrieval and avoid possible failure in object localization step. In addition, the concatenation is performed on the fly, needing no extra saving space. Experimental results on the public Oxford5k, Paris6k, Oxford105k and Paris106k dataset demonstrate that the proposed approach can improve retrieval accuracy with negligible computation and memory cost.

Keywords: Objec retrieval · Feature fusion · Deep feature · CNN

1 Introduction

Object retrieval refers to retrieving database images containing similar content to the query object image, which has attracted increasing attention in compute vision community. Current state-of-the-art approaches usually rely on Bag-of-visual-Word (BoW) model [1], involving extracting hand-craft local features such as SIFT [2] or SURF [3] from images and quantizing them into visual words and representing images as a histogram vector of visual words. Therefore, the similarity between query and database image is modeled as the cosine distance between normalized BoW representation. After initial retrieval, some additional re-ranking strategies are employed to refine the top-ranked list, such as spatial

© Springer Nature Singapore Pte Ltd. 2017
D. Du et al. (Eds.): NCTCS 2017, CCIS 768, pp. 31–45, 2017.
https://doi.org/10.1007/978-981-10-6893-5_3

verification [4,5] exploiting geometric information of local features, and query expansion [6,7] issuing new queries based on top-ranked results. But current approaches are heavily limited by the representative ability of hand-craft features. The accuracy of these approaches have reached a bottleneck and are hard to improve.

With the advance of deep learning in image classification, deep features deriving from Convolutional Neural Networks (CNNs) are becoming competitive descriptors to represent image, not only for classification but also for retrieval task. The deep representation deriving from the intermediate layers of CNNs pre-trained for image classification, such as the convolutional layer or fully connected layer, can be directly adopted for image retrieval. Depart from simply cropping intermediate activation, several works try to design better and compact image representation or fine-tune pre-trained networks to adapt to retrieval task. These carefully designed or fine-tuned deep features achieve competitive or even better retrieval accuracy compared to BoW-based approaches. In this paper, we concentrate on the Regional Max Aggregating Convolutional (R-MAC) feature, which extracts multiple regional features across image and can be employed for initial filtering and geometric-aware re-ranking simultaneously.

Typically, single feature is limit to represent the overall information of images. By merging different features, feature fusion is a popular method to improve the representative ability of features for accurate retrieval. In BoW-based approaches, color feature is commonly used as complementary information for local features such as SIFT and SURF which are extracted from gray-scale image and lost of color information. The color cue of local region or entire image are fused with local features to achieve a better performance in [8–10]. Recent works show that the hand-craft feature and deep feature can also be fused for a better representation [11]. The representation deriving from local feature is stable for illuminate and view point change, and the representation deriving from deep features is discriminative to distinguish similar but different visual structures. The combination of different features can benefit for representing the intrinsic property of image in multiple views. Based on the existing work of R-MAC, we propose to fuse R-MAC features to represent the overall image and Region of Interest (ROI) into a uniform representation, which can boost performance without extensive computation and extra saving cost.

Different from previous works that fuse multiple futures or merge the retrieval results returned by different features, we try to fuse the global and local ROI R-MAC into an effective representation. The proposed approach can be regard as a fusion of features from global and local spatial regions across an image. The R-MAC feature of overall image conveys the global information, and the R-MAC feature of ROI represents important information of query object. The combination of two R-MAC features can be complementary for each other and result in a better representation. In addition, the combination is performed on the fly and easy to implement. Summarily, we make the following contributions.

- Contrast to performing initial filtering by R-MAC feature of query ROIs, we leverage global R-MAC of entire query image to retrieval initial results, which can rank more positive results on the top list.
- After object localization, we combine global R-MAC and local R-MAC of ROI to form the new representation of images to perform re-ranking. The combination considers the global and regional information, avoiding ranking irrelevant images on the top caused by the failure of object location in previous work.

Experimental results on public object retrieval benchmarks demonstrate the proposed approach can boost retrieval accuracy compared with other approaches, even for some approaches based on fine-tuned CNNs.

The rest of the paper is organized as follows. Section 2 reviews related work of deep feature and feature fusion. Section 3 presents the R-MAC feature in details. Section 4 illustrates the detail of the proposed approach. Section 5 demonstrates the experimental results on public object retrieval benchmarks. At last, Sect. 6 draws conclusions.

2   Related Work

2.1   Deep Feature for Retrieval

CNNs based representations of image are widely employed in vision-related domains. The intermediate activations cropped from pre-trained CNNs for image classification can be served as global descriptors for image retrieval. For instance, the response of last fully connected layers with dimension reduction is widely used as the baseline feature to retrieval similar images in [12]. As fully connected layer is highly related to classification labels, its activation may less useful than the corresponding convolutional layers, which can convey information of local regions. Different from vector form of the activation of fully connected layers, the activation of convolutional layers forms a 3D tensor, consisting of multiple 2D feature maps. Sum-pooled convolutional features (SPoC) aggregates responses at the same spatial coordinate among the 3D tensor by sum pooling to form the final global descriptor with PCA compression in [13]. Maximum activation of convolutions (MAC) feature selects the maximum response of each 2D feature map and concatenates them into a compact global image descriptor in [14].

As the global representation will be influenced by image background and clutter, CNNs based regional features are developed to form regions of images to improve the representation power. In SPoC descriptor, the center region will receive a high weight as the important region is usually located in the center region, which can be viewed as a way to consider regional information. In [11], the response of fully connected layer is extracted by feeding multiple regions of an image into CNN, then aggregated by the Vector of Locally Aggregated Descriptors (VLAD) encoding [15]. Recently, R-MAC built upon Max Aggregating Convolutional (MAC) has shown to be an effective descriptor for image retrieval [14,16,17], which extracts MACs in different regions and scales across the 3D tensors. In [18], the ROI region of images are located for extracting R-MAC feature to alleviate image clutter.

Contrast to cropping activations from pre-trained CNN originally for classification, several works directly train CNN targeted at retrieval task. The fine-tuning of pre-trained CNN can transfer the deep feature from generic representation to fine-grained representation, avoiding influence of pre-trained classes in classification task. In [18], a landmark dataset is utilized to re-train CNN, allowing the intermediate representation suit for target landmark retrieval. In [17,18], based on MAC and R-MAC descriptor, carefully designed CNNs with extra annotated datasets from 3D reconstruction or classification are trained to directly generate fine-tuned MAC and R-MAC feature in an end-to-end way. Weakly geo-annotated street view dataset are utilized to trained a VLAD-like CNN to generate NetVLAD [19] descriptor, targeting at retrieving street view images in place recognition application. Fune-tuned CNNs for retrieval usually rely on triplet data with a contrast loss. Then re-training is performed on CNNs with large amount of annotated data. The fine-tuned CNNs can be served as a way for domain adaption, allowing the feature representation learning from CNNs is suitable for target task and dataset. Typically, fine-tuned CNNs will form a more effective descriptor than pre-trained CNN, both for global and regional representation.

2.2 Feature Fusion

In conventional retrieval system, the local descriptor will be fused with color and global information both in feature level and decision level. Multiple cues of different features can be complementary to represent different aspects of images benefiting for forming a more comprehensive representation of visual structure in images. Some irrelevant images can be very similar in local feature, but different in global feature. The fusion of different features can utilize multiple source of information to filter irrelevant images.

Feature fusion in feature level can be performed directly by representing image with independent descriptor or generate a uniform representation deriving from multiple features. In [9], local feature and color feature are fused in the inverted index file to filter false matched local region that is similar in SIFT space but different in color space. In [11], deep feature and hand-craft feature are merged to form the final descriptor of images, which can outperform single feature approach. Feature fusion can also be applied in same feature but for different spatial regions. In [11], the CNN-based feature are extracted from entire image and local regions returned by selective search or Edgebox [20,21], which can combine the global and local information to improve the accuracy.

After querying by different features, the result lists can also be fused for re-ranking to refine initial results. The fusion of decision level combines multiple information to return global optimized results compatible with different features. In conventional BoW-based approaches, color and global layout information such as HSV histogram and GIST descriptor [22], are used to fuse initial result lists. In [8], the result lists returned by local feature and global feature based approach are merged in the framework of graph ranking, leading to a performance boost in terms of accuracy. In [10], the rank scores of different feature are utilized to fuse different initial results for refinement.

Compared to previous works fusing different features in initial representation step or different rank lists in final re-rank step, we design a dynamic fusion of R-MAC deep feature inspired by the work in [11]. The simple and online feature fusion can lead to an effective representation of images without extensive computation and extra saving space.

3   Regional Maximum Activation of Convolutions

R-MAC feature is a popular global descriptor in object retrieval [16–18] since it was first proposed in [14], which is simply to extract and compact to represent large-scale images. The R-MAC is built upon MAC feature, but consists of local information across different regions of image. In addition, the R-MAC based approach can exploit the intermediate activation of CNNs for object localization, which is critical for refining initial results.

Considering the last convolutional layer after ReLU operation cropped from CNNs, we can obtain the activation represented by a 3D tensor of $W \times H \times K$ dimensions with non-negative elements, where W and H are the width and height of feature maps respectively, and K is the number of feature maps. For popular CNNs, such as AlexNet [23] or VGG-16 [24], K is 256 and 512 respectively. The size of feature map is determined by the structure of CNNs and the resolution of input images. Following the annotation in [14], the activation of 3D tensor $\mathcal{X}$ can be represented as a set of 2D feature maps $\mathcal{X} = \{\mathcal{X}_i\}, i = 1 \ldots K$, where $\mathcal{X}_i$ represents the ith feature map across the overall spatial location Ω, and $\mathcal{X}_i(p)$ represents the activation at the location $p \in \Omega$. The MAC feature is constructed by the vector consisting of maximum activation of each feature map, and is defined as

$$\mathbf{f}_\Omega = [\mathbf{f}_{\Omega,1} \ldots \mathbf{f}_{\Omega,i} \ldots \mathbf{f}_{\Omega,K}], \text{with } \mathbf{f}_{\Omega,i} = \max_{p\in\Omega} \mathcal{X}_i(p). \tag{1}$$

Then, the similarity of two images is computed as the dot product of their K dimension MAC features, which has a medium size (256 or 512-D) compared with previous popular hand-craft feature based descriptors such as VLAD and FV or the typically 4096-D deep feature cropped from fully connected layers.

The MAC feature only focuses on global information of images by considering the overall feature maps, neglecting the local region of feature maps. To encode local information of different image regions, the R-MAC is proposed based on the MAC. Contrast to perform max-pooling across the feature map, R-MAC merges MAC feature of sub-region of the overall feature map. For a region $\mathcal{R} \subseteq \Omega$, the MAC feature of $\mathcal{R}$ is given by

$$\mathbf{f}_\mathcal{R} = [\mathbf{f}_{\mathcal{R},1} \ldots \mathbf{f}_{\mathcal{R},i} \ldots \mathbf{f}_{\mathcal{R},K}], \text{with } \mathbf{f}_{\mathcal{R},i} = \max_{p\in\mathcal{R}} \mathcal{X}_i(p). \tag{2}$$

R-MAC feature selects different square regions in L different scales across the feature map. For the largest scale, the width and height of the region is $\min(W, H)$, and the corespondent at scale l is $2\min(W, H)/(l + 1)$. The square region will slide across the feature map with an overlapping of 40% in area. MAC features of these consecutive regions are extracted, then post-processed with ℓ_2 normalization, PCA-whitened and ℓ_2 normalization again. R-MAC feature is constructed by simply sum-pooling all regional MAC features and then ℓ_2 normalization. The final representation of R-MAC is the same K dimensions as MAC, but encodes information of multiple local regions. In [14], the initial retrieval is performed by computing similarities of R-MAC feature between query object and database images, which is better than retrieval by MAC feature.

Exploiting the region information not only can generate a better representation of images, but also can be used for object localization. Different visual structure of images result in different MAC or R-MAC features, and the feature map $\mathcal{X}$ can be mapped back to the original image $\mathcal{I}$. So, we can detect the location of query object in database images based on the MAC or R-MAC feature across different regions in $\mathcal{X}$. In [14], an approximate max-pooling localization (AML) is performed on feature maps to search the best region, whose MAC feature has a maximum similarity to the corresponding of query object. In this way, the matched region of query object in database images can be located. Then the initial similarity between query object and overall database image can be updated by calculating the similarity between query object and the located object region in database image.

In summary, previous R-MAC based object retrieval typically consists of three steps, the initial filtering, re-ranking by object localization and final query expansion [14,17,18]. R-MAC of database images are extracted from the global images, and R-MAC of queries are extracted from sub-region containing query objects. The initial filtering evaluates the similarity of R-MAC features to generate initial result lists. Then the re-ranking step searches the rough matched regions of query object among top-ranked database images, and the initial result list is re-ranked based on the refined similarities between query object and located region of database images. Finally, the query expansion merges the query and 5 top-ranked database R-MAC vectors to issue a new query and re-ranking again.

4   The Proposed Approach

R-MAC based approach gives a simple yet effective solution for object retrieval, which is the first time that deep feature based approach achieves a competitive performance compared to local feature based approach. But in practice, we have observed two problems that may challenge the effectiveness of R-MAC based approach. Firstly, in the filtering step, the similarity between object region of query image and overall database image is asymmetric, resulting in an under-estimated similarity. Secondly, in the re-ranking step, the matched object in database image may not accurately located due to background clutter or viewpoint variation. Then, the re-ranking will be failure as only the similarity between query and located object region is considered.

To tackle the above problems, we propose to use global R-MAC feature for initial filtering (Sect. 4.1) and merge global and local R-MAC feature for re-ranking and query expansion (Sect. 4.2).

4.1 Initial Filtering with Global Feature

In R-MAC based object retrieval, the initial filtering is critical for the following re-ranking steps. As the object localization is time consuming and only performed on top-ranked results, the initial filtering should rank positive database images in the top as many as possible. If there exist more positive database images in the top-ranked list, the re-ranking by object localization can detect more images containing matched objects and bring them to the top for refinement.

The initial similarity is simply calculated by dot product of R-MAC vectors between query object and database images, where the query object is usually a region of interest (ROI) of query image. However, we argue that this asymmetric similarity neglects the global information of query images and results in an under-estimated similarity. In many situations, the query object is just a part of the query image, and the remains can be helpful for retrieval. As we can see from Fig. 1, the first query object is only a sub-region of the overall image, and the database image typically contains many other visual structures. Therefore, directly comparison between the sub-region of query and the entire database image may result in a less accurate similarity. In addition, the visual content around the query object is discriminative and useful for retrieval, which is not fully exploited in previous initial filtering step.

To facilitate the object localization in re-ranking, we propose to use the global R-MAC of query image to perform initial filtering. In this way, we can avoid the asymmetric comparison and utilize the global information which not only contains query object but also other visual content. The proposed approach can be viewed as retrieval global similar database images at first, then the re-ranking is responsible for fine-grain detecting based on local similarity. In detail, the query R-MAC feature is constructed from the overall query image $\mathcal{I}$, no longer the cropped ROI $\mathcal{I}_{\text{Crop}}$. Compared to the previous initial filtering step, we only need to extract an extra R-MAC feature of the query image, which can be performed with negligible cost. For some public benchmark dataset, the query images are also among the database images, so the proposed approach can performed without extra computation overhead. In experiment (Sect. 5), we can see the simple replacement can result in an obvious boosting in terms of accuracy.

4.2   Re-ranking by Global and Local Feature

In previous work of R-MAC based object retrieval, the re-ranking step involves locating the query object in database images and updating similarities between query object region and the located database regions. In practice, we have found two limitation for the re-ranking only relying on local ROI information. At first, the comparison between local region neglects the global information that can also benefit for retrieving positive database images. Secondly, the object localization based on convolutional feature maps may fail in some situations. For example, some failed located examples are shown in Fig. 1, where the location of detected database objects are not perfectly overlapping with true location. In practice, there even exist some located regions out of the best location.

The reason can be from the low resolution of feature maps and the refinement process in AML. Owing to the max pooling operation in CNNs, the convolutional feature map is only an abstract of the original image. Typically, the raw image with resolution of 1024×768 will result in a feature map of 32×24. The localization performed on 3D feature maps can only determinate an approximate location of matched region. In addition, we have found the location refinement of AML will result in a worse localization as illustrate in Fig. 1. Even though the coarse search of AML can locate a large region containing the true object, the refining process will return a bad location.

To tackle the failure problem of object localization in re-ranking, we propose to merge the global and local R-MAC to replace the previous local R-MAC. The global R-MAC feature $\mathbf{f}_\mathcal{G}$ is constructed from the overall image $\mathcal{I}$ by Eq. (2),

Query   Database Images

Fig. 1. Illustration of query and corresponding database images (best viewed in color). The entire query images are given in the first column, where the query objects are located in blue rectangles. The rest is database image, where the green and red rectangle represent coarsely located and refined object region returned by AML approach in [14] respectively. As we can see, matched objects in database images are not accurately located, which can result in failures in re-ranking step. (Color figure online)

and the local R-MAC $\mathbf{f}_{\mathcal{L}}$ is constructed from $\mathcal{I}_{\text{Crop}}$, i.e. ROI of query image and located region of database image respectively. Then we combine the global and regional R-MAC feature simply by concatenating them into a uniform representation.

$$\mathbf{f}_{\mathcal{F}} = [\mathbf{f}_{\mathcal{G}}; \mathbf{f}_{\mathcal{L}}] \tag{3}$$

After merging, the newly representation $\mathbf{f}_{\mathcal{F}}$ is post-processed with ℓ_2 normalization. The combination is performed on the fly without extra computation of R-MAC feature. The dimension of $\mathbf{f}_{\mathcal{F}}$ are typically 1024 or 512 for VGG-16 and AlexNet respectively, which remains a medium size of representation. As the combination is performed only in re-ranking and query expansion step, there is no need to save the combined representation. The only change is a double memory footprint compared to the original approach. But the re-ranking is only performed on a short result list, typically top-1000 results in common setting. For R-MAC feature extracted from VGG-16 network, re-ranking top-1000 images will only need 2 MB memory if saving the 1000 1024-D features with single precision format, which is negligible for common desktop computer.

Compared to previous works fusing global and local features, the proposed approach utilizes existing features for fusion. A similar work in [11] extracts multiple local features of regions returned by selective search proposal [20], and then merges these local features in a VLAD-pooling manner, which needs to feed local regions into CNNs in multiple times and learn the PCA compression parameters. In the proposed approach, the only local feature is from the query or located ROIs, and there is no extra parameters to learn due to the simple post-processing of ℓ_2 normalization.

5   Experiments

5.1   Experimental Setup

We evaluate the proposed approach on four public datasets for object retrieval. The Oxford5k [4] dataset consists of 5063 high resolution images crawled from the image sharing site Flickr. There exist 55 queries depicting landmark building in Oxford University, and each has several or hundreds positive results. The Paris6k dataset [25] is similar to the Oxford5k and contains 6392 images. There also has 55 queries but depicting famous landmarks in Paris. For each query in Oxford5k and Paris6k, there exists a bounding box to locate the query object. To test the scalability, the Flickr100k dataset [25] containing 100,070 irrelevant images is merged with Oxford5k and Paris6k to form the Oxford105k and Paris106k dataset. We adopt the mean Average Precision (mAP) for evaluating the retrieval accuracy, which is the mean of average precision of all queries.

The R-MAC features for all evaluated datasets are provided by [26], avoiding extracting again. For object localization and query expansion, we used the public code and deep model released in [14] to extract feature maps. The code of the proposed approach is available at https://github.com/wangmaoCS/Fusion_RMAC.

5.2   Evaluation of Global Initial Filtering

Based on the public dataset provided in [26], we can evaluate the effectiveness of the proposed global initial filtering approach in Sect. 4.1. To compare with the query object based initial filtering, we use the original R-MAC based approach proposed in [14]. We test the proposed approach for R-MAC feature. As the result illustrated in Table 1, we can see that the global query can boost the mAP in all evaluated datasets.

The accuracy improve can be contributed to the symmetric comparison between the entire query image and database image, avoiding the global information absence in previous ROI based query. The simply replacement only need applied on query side with an extra computation of global deep feature of query image, which can also be benefit for the following re-ranking and query expansion step. For the Oxford5k and Oxford105k dataset, the mAP improvement is obvious as the query object is only part of the entire query image.

5.3   Evaluation of Fusion Re-ranking

To evaluate the proposed fusion of global and local deep feature, we keep the initial query with ROI of query and replace it with the fusion of global and local deep feature. The public code released in [14] is adopted to extract intermediate convolutional feature maps. After object localization performed on top-1000 results, we combine global and local deep feature by concatenating them into a uniform representation for calculating the updated similarity between query and top-ranked database images.

The experimental result is illustrated in Table 1. The original approach proposed in [14] is represented as R-MAC+R+QE, and the proposed approach is represented as R-MAC+F-R and R-MAC+F-(R+QE). We can see that the proposed approach can boost mAP both in re-ranking and query expansion step. Therefore, the proposed fusion of global and local deep feature can be a better representation of images. The only extra computation is from the post-process of concatenating global and local R-MAC feature, which is negligible.

Table 1. Retrieval results returned by different steps. For the initial filtering (R-MAC), re-ranking (R) and query expansion (QE) step, the proposed two steps (G-R-MAC in Sect. 4.1, F-R and F-(R+QE) in Sect. 4.2) are both better than the corresponding original steps.

Method	Oxford5k	Paris6k	Oxford105k	Paris106k
R-MAC	66.7	83.0	61.4	75.7
G-R-MAC	72.0	84.7	68.4	77.9
R-MAC+R	74.5	85.1	70.0	78.1
R-MAC+F-R	78.2	87.5	73.1	80.9
R-MAC+(R+QE)	77.3	86.4	73.2	79.8
R-MAC+F-(R+QE)	80.3	88.6	75.7	82.4

The reason for accuracy improvement is that the fused representation can be complementary of global and local ROI information. As the object localization is not stable, the located ROI region of database image can have a low Intersection over Union (IOU) with the true ROI. In this situation, the local deep feature extracted from false located region will not be similar to query object. However, the global deep feature can keep the global similarity and avoid re-ranking the initial top-ranked positive result to the bottom. Some examples can be viewed in Fig. 1. Moreover, for some false results with a located ROI similar to query object but with a dis-similar global layout, the fusion can allocate a lower similarity to them and avoid re-ranking them on the top only relying on ROI information. A typical example is illustrated in Fig. 2, where the right database image will be re-ranked on the top in [14] due to the high similarity of local rectangle regions. However, the proposed approach can down-weight their similarity as their global similarity is low. So, the fusion is an effective way to consider both global and local information for refinement.

Fig. 2. Illustration of a typical false result returned by re-ranking based on object localization. The left and right image are query and database image, where rectangles mean query and matched object respectively.

5.4 The Overall Approach

In this experiment, we evaluate the overall approach to illustrate the combination of global initial filtering and fusion of global and local R-MAC can boost the retrieval accuracy. The result is illustrated in Table 2. As we can see, the final accuracy is improved over these approaches only employing initial filtering or fusion re-ranking. The overall approach can utilize the global initial filtering to generate a better initial result list, which contains more positive images on the top. Then, the re-ranking and query expansion using fused features can discover positive images and re-rank them to the top.

Table 2. Full retrieval with different combinations of initial filtering, re-ranking and query expansion steps. Using the proposed steps (G-R-MAC and F-(R+QE)) can achieve the best retrieval accuracy.

Method	Oxford5k	Paris6k	Oxford105k	Paris106k
R-MAC+(R+QE) [14]	77.3	86.5	73.2	79.8
G-R-MAC+(R+QE)	77.9	86.8	74.2	80.9
R-MAC+**F-(R+QE)**	80.3	88.6	75.7	82.4
G-R-MAC+F-(R+QE)	**81.0**	**88.8**	**77.0**	**83.3**

Compared to the original approach [14], the extra computation overhead is calculating the R-MAC feature over the entire query feature. In the re-ranking step, we need to concatenate the global and local deep feature of top-ranked results, and the time and memory cost is negligible. So, the proposed approach can boost retrieval accuracy with a low computation overhead, which can be utilized as a replacement of the original approach.

5.5   Comparison with Other Approaches

We compare with other related approaches to demonstrate the effectiveness of the proposed approach. For fair comparison, We only present approaches employing query expansion. The results of the proposed approach and previous works are illustrated in Table 3. In summary, popular approaches can be divided into

Table 3. Comparison with other approaches. For deep feature based approaches, 'V' and 'fV' represent VGG-16 and fine-tuned VGG-16 CNN respectively. The proposed approach can outperform previous pre-trained CNNs based approach [14,27], and achieve a better retrieval accuracy than BoW-based approaches on the Paris6k and Paris106k dataset. The proposed approach can also outperform a fine-tuned CNN based approach [17] on the Paris6k and Paris106k dataset.

Method	Oxford5k	Paris6k	Oxford105k	Paris106k
BoW+QE [6]	82.7	80.5	76.7	71.0
Fine Vocabulary [28]	84.9	82.4	79.5	77.3
HEQ [29]	88.0	82.8	84.0	–
R-MAC+R+QE (V) [14]	77.3	86.5	73.2	79.8
CroW+QE (V) [27]	72.2	85.5	67.8	79.7
Faster RCNN+R+QE (fV) [30]	78.6	84.2	–	–
MAC+R+QE (fV) [17]	85.4	87.0	82.3	79.6
R-MAC+R+QE (fV) [17]	84.5	86.4	80.4	79.7
R-MAC+QE (fV) [18]	89.1	91.2	87.3	86.8
Our approach (V)	81.0	88.8	77.0	83.3

three categories, BoW-based approaches, pre-trained CNNs based approaches and fine-tuned CNNs based approaches. The proposed approach is better than pre-trained CNNs based approaches, and outperforms BoW-based approach and some fine-tuned CNNs based approaches.

Conventional BoW based approaches usually relies huge visual vocabulary and costly spatial verification, which challenges their scalability for large scale datasets. The fine-tuned approaches need vast amount of annotated images to re-train CNNs. Current state-of-the-art approach [18] involves re-training VGG-16 network by ranking task with annotated landmark data and located ROI region of images. However, the proposed approach can be useful if there is no available annotated data and computation resource to re-trained CNNs.

6 Conclusions and Discussion

In this paper, we present an approach fusing global and local deep feature for object retrieval. We propose to use global R-MAC feature of entire query image in initial filtering step, replacing the asymmetric comparison between ROI of query and entire image from database. Then, we combine the global and local deep feature to form the new representation of images for re-ranking and query expansion. Experimental results on four public object retrieval datasets demonstrate that the proposed approach can improve accuracy compared to the original R-MAC based approach.

The future work will focus on object localization, which is critical for the re-ranking and query expansion step. But current object localization based on convolutional feature maps is not accurate and stable in some situations. Locating the true ROI of database image can provide a better estimate of similarity between query object and ROI of database images, and then improve retrieval accuracy.

Acknowledgment. The authors would like to thank the financial support of National Natural Science Foundation of China (Project NO. 61672528, 61403405, 61232016, 61170287).

References

1. Sivic, J., Zisserman, A.: Video Google: efficient visual search of videos. In: Ponce, J., Hebert, M., Schmid, C., Zisserman, A. (eds.) Toward Category-Level Object Recognition. LNCS, vol. 4170, pp. 127–144. Springer, Heidelberg (2006). doi:10.1007/11957959_7

2. Lowe, D.: Distinctive image features from scale-invariant keypoints. Int. J. Comput. Vis. **60**, 91–110 (2004)

3. Bay, H., Ess, A., Tuytelaars, T., Van Gool, L.: Speeded-up robust features (SURF). Comput. Vis. Image Underst. **110**(3), 346–359 (2008)

4. Philbin, J., Chum, O., Isard, M., Sivic, J., Zisserman, A.: Object retrieval with large vocabularies and fast spatial matching. In: IEEE Conference on Computer Vision and Pattern Recognition (2007)

5. Zhou, Z., Wang, Y., Wu, Q.J., Yang, C.N., Sun, X.: Effective and efficient global context verification for image copy detection. IEEE Trans. Inf. Forensics Secur. **12**(1), 48–63 (2017). doi:10.1109/TIFS.2016.2601065. http://ieeexplore.ieee.org/document/7546839/
6. Chum, O., Mikulik, A., Perdoch, M., Matas, J.: Total recall II: query expansion revisited. In: Proceedings of the 2011 IEEE Computer Society Conference on Computer Vision and Pattern Recognition, CVPR 2011, pp. 889–896. IEEE Computer Society, Los Alamitos (2011). doi:10.1109/CVPR.2011.5995601. CD-ROM
7. Chum, O., Philbin, J., Sivic, J., Isard, M., Zisserman, A.: Total recall: automatic query expansion with a generative feature model for object retrieval. In: IEEE International Conference on Computer Vision (2007)
8. Zhang, S., Yang, M., Cour, T., Yu, K., Metaxas, D.: Query specific rank fusion for image retrieval. IEEE Trans. Pattern Anal. Mach. Intell. **37**(4), 803–815 (2015)
9. Zheng, L., Wang, S., Liu, Z., Tian, Q.: Packing and padding: coupled multi-index for accurate image retrieval. In: 2014 IEEE Conference on Computer Vision and Pattern Recognition (CVPR), pp. 1947–1954. IEEE (2014)
10. Zheng, L., Wang, S., Tian, L., He, F., Liu, Z., Tian, Q.: Query-adaptive late fusion for image search and person re-identification. In: IEEE Conference on Computer Vision and Pattern Recognition (CVPR) (2015)
11. Yan, K., Wang, Y., Liang, D., Huang, T., Tian, Y.: CNN vs. SIFT for image retrieval: alternative or complementary? In: Proceedings of the 2016 ACM on Multimedia Conference, MM 2016, pp. 407–411. ACM, New York (2016). doi:10.1145/2964284.2967252
12. Razavian, A.S., Azizpour, H., Sullivan, J., Carlsson, S.: CNN features off-the-shelf: an astounding baseline for recognition. In: 2014 IEEE Conference on Computer Vision and Pattern Recognition Workshops, pp. 512–519 (2014). doi:10.1109/CVPRW.2014.131
13. Babenko, A., Lempitsky, V.: Aggregating local deep features for image retrieval. In: The IEEE International Conference on Computer Vision (ICCV) (2015)
14. Tolias, G., Sicre, R., Jégou, H.: Particular object retrieval with integral max-pooling of CNN activations. arXiv preprint arXiv:1511.05879 (2015)
15. Jégou, H., Perronnin, F., Douze, M., Snchez, J., Prez, P., Schmid, C.: Aggregating local image descriptors into compact codes. IEEE Trans. Pattern Anal. Mach. Intell. **34**(9), 1704–1716 (2012). doi:10.1109/TPAMI.2011.235
16. Iscen, A., Tolias, G., Avrithis, Y.S., Furon, T., Chum, O.: Efficient diffusion on region manifolds: recovering small objects with compact CNN representations. CoRR abs/1611.05113 (2016). http://arxiv.org/abs/1611.05113
17. Radenović, F., Tolias, G., Chum, O.: CNN image retrieval learns from BoW: unsupervised fine-tuning with hard examples. In: Leibe, B., Matas, J., Sebe, N., Welling, M. (eds.) ECCV 2016. LNCS, vol. 9905, pp. 3–20. Springer, Cham (2016). doi:10.1007/978-3-319-46448-0_1
18. Gordo, A., Almazán, J., Revaud, J., Larlus, D.: Deep image retrieval: learning global representations for image search. In: Leibe, B., Matas, J., Sebe, N., Welling, M. (eds.) ECCV 2016. LNCS, vol. 9910, pp. 241–257. Springer, Cham (2016). doi:10.1007/978-3-319-46466-4_15
19. Arandjelović, R., Gronat, P., Torii, A., Pajdla, T., Sivic, J.: NetVLAD: CNN architecture for weakly supervised place recognition. In: IEEE Conference on Computer Vision and Pattern Recognition (2016)
20. van de Sande, K.E.A., Uijlings, J.R.R., Gevers, T., Smeulders, A.W.M.: Segmentation as selective search for object recognition. In: 2011 International Conference on Computer Vision, pp. 1879–1886 (2011). doi:10.1109/ICCV.2011.6126456

21. Zitnick, C.L., Dollár, P.: Edge boxes: locating object proposals from edges. In: Fleet, D., Pajdla, T., Schiele, B., Tuytelaars, T. (eds.) ECCV 2014. LNCS, vol. 8693, pp. 391–405. Springer, Cham (2014). doi:10.1007/978-3-319-10602-1_26

22. Oliva, A., Torralba, A.: Modeling the shape of the scene: a holistic representation f the spatial envelope. Int. J. Comput. Vis. **42**(3), 145–175 (2001). doi:10.1023/A:1011139631724

23. Krizhevsky, A., Sutskever, I., Hinton, G.E.: ImageNet classification with deep convolutional neural networks. In: Pereira, F., Burges, C.J.C., Bottou, L., Weinberger, K.Q. (eds.) Advances in Neural Information Processing Systems 25, pp. 1097–1105. Curran Associates, Inc. (2012). http://papers.nips.cc/paper/4824-imagenet-classification-with-deep-convolutional-neural-networks.pdf

24. Simonyan, K., Zisserman, A.: Very deep convolutional networks for large-scale image recognition. CoRR abs/1409.1556 (2014)

25. Philbin, J., Chum, O., Isard, M., Sivic, J., Zisserman, A.: Lost in quantization: improving particular object retrieval in large scale image databases. In: IEEE Conference on Computer Vision and Pattern Recognition (2008)

26. Iscen, A., Rabbat, M., Furon, T.: Efficient large-scale similarity search using matrix factorization. In: The IEEE Conference on Computer Vision and Pattern Recognition (CVPR) (2016)

27. Kalantidis, Y., Mellina, C., Osindero, S.: Cross-dimensional weighting for aggregated deep convolutional features. In: Hua, G., Jégou, H. (eds.) ECCV 2016. LNCS, vol. 9913, pp. 685–701. Springer, Cham (2016). doi:10.1007/978-3-319-46604-0_48

28. Mikulík, A., Perdoch, M., Chum, O., Matas, J.: Learning a fine vocabulary. In: Daniilidis, K., Maragos, P., Paragios, N. (eds.) ECCV 2010. LNCS, vol. 6313, pp. 1–14. Springer, Heidelberg (2010). doi:10.1007/978-3-642-15558-1_1

29. Tolias, G., Jégou, H.: Visual query expansion with or without geometry: refining local descriptors by feature aggregation. Pattern Recogn. **47**, 3466–3476 (2014). https://hal.inria.fr/hal-00971267

30. Salvador, A., Giro-i-Nieto, X., Marques, F., Satoh, S.: Faster R-CNN features for instance search. In: The IEEE Conference on Computer Vision and Pattern Recognition (CVPR) Workshops (2016)

ETSW: An Encounter History Tree Based Routing Protocol in Opportunistic Networks

Haoyan Liang, Zhigang Chen$^{(\boxtimes)}$, Jia Wu, and Peiyuan Guan

School of Software, Central South University, Changsha 410083, China
czg@csu.edu.cn

Abstract. The traditional flooding based routing protocols for the opportunistic networks like Epidemic or SnW (Spray and Wait) are blindfold on nodes selecting during the data packets forwarding, and besides, traditional probability based routing protocol like PRoPHET has the disadvantages of low transmission success rate and high transmission delay. So in this paper, we propose Encounter Tree Spray and Wait (ETSW) routing protocol combining with the respective advantages of them for routing in opportunistic networks, which exploits the encounter history of mobile nodes to reduce the blindness of data transmission between nodes. And the simulation results show that ETSW can improve the delivery rate, and reduce the transmission delay of data packets forwarding comparing with the traditional Spray and Wait routing protocols.

Keywords: Opportunistic networks · Routing protocol · Spray and wait routing · Nodes encounter tree

1 Introduction

Opportunistic networks (OppNets) [1] are emerging networks different from the traditional infrastructure-based communication, which has the significant feature that its communication between nodes does not require the existence of a complete path but is facilitated by means of nodes movement and forwarding messages to the next hop via "carry-store-forward". And therefore, the topology of opportunistic networks is constantly changing result in the fact that the traditional routing protocols are not applicable in this kind of network. Regarding the features of opportunistic networks, a lot of new routing protocols for it had been proposed, all of which have their own characteristics and are suitable for some specific scenes.

Owing to the fact that inherent characteristics of opportunistic networks can satisfy the requirements of some certain environments characterized by lack of end-to-end complete path and high delays, there are already some practical applications in the opportunistic networks. ZebraNet [2] is an opportunistic networks system explored by Princeton University to track steppe zebra in Kenya, which uses a tracking collar to study wild animals. DakNet [3], which is developed by MIT and deployed in remote areas of India to provide Internet services,

© Springer Nature Singapore Pte Ltd. 2017
D. Du et al. (Eds.): NCTCS 2017, CCIS 768, pp. 46–59, 2017.
https://doi.org/10.1007/978-981-10-6893-5_4

mainly provide solution for developing countries or remote areas which have incompleted network infrastructure and can not access the Internet. Besides, Pocket Switched Networks (PSNs) [4], Vehicular Ad-hoc Networks (VANETs) [5], Wireless Sensor Networks (WSN) [6] and Body Area Networks (BANs) [7] are also the typical applications in the opportunistic networks. Actually, no matter what kind of application it is, the mobile nodes in the actual scenes usually move in some certain regular way instead of totally random ones. Especially for human mobility [8], mobile nodes have some spatial, temporal, and connectivity characteristics.

However, the traditional flooding based routing protocols for OppNets do not take the regular movement of nodes into consideration. And thus, this paper proposes a routing protocol combined with the patterns of nodes' movement, which is relatively more suitable for some high genetically scenes.

2   Related Work

Since the traditional routing algorithm does not apply to the continuous changing characteristics of the network topology in opportunistic networks caused by the continuous movement of nodes, a number of researchers have proposed some new routing algorithms for the opportunistic networks, including the classical routing algorithms as follow:

First-Contact [9] and *Direct-Transmission* [10]. Both of these two are forwarding-based routing algorithm, which means that only a copy of the message is forwarding in the network during transmission process, and the message will not be copied during the forwarding between the nodes. In First-Contact, message generated from the source node will be forwarded to the first node it met, while in Direct-Transmission, the message of source will kept in its buffer until it meets the destination directly.

Epidemic-routing [11] and *Spray-and-Wait* [12]. Epidemic and Spray-and-Wait are Flooding-based routing algorithm. Epidemic proposes that the nodes will copy the message toward each other, while Spray-and-Wait will spread limited number of message copies generated from the source node over the network initially during the Spray phase, and the nodes which have the copy of the message will transmit them via "Direct-Transmission".

Prophet-routing [13]. Prophet-routing is a routing algorithm based on probability, which can estimate the probability of successful transmission and replicate the message selectively.

MaxProp-routing [14]. MaxProp-routing is a Scheduling-Strategy-based routing. The priorities of data packet are set before, and the data packets are copied to each other according to the priorities of the them as the nodes meet.

Some simulator experiments have shown that SnW has a relatively good overall performance among the routing protocols mentioned above. Compared with flooding based Epidemic, Spray and Wait (SnW) can reduce the amount of transmission, and thus can reduce the overhead of routing. While compared with Direct-Transmission, SnW can reduce the delay. Owing to the fact that the

SnW protocol can strike a balance between Epidemic and Direct-Transmission, this paper utilises the advantages of SnW and proposes an optimized protocol.

Spray and Wait, which is one of the well-known protocol in opportunistic networks, is a flooding-based routing algorithm. For every data packets generating from the source node, L copies of data packets are initially spread and forward to L nodes that the source node has encountered (which are called the "relays") during the Spray phase. And if the target node is not a part of the "relays", each of the "relays" just carries a data packets copy until they encounter with the target node and forward the data packets to it directly (which is called the Direct Delivery routing algorithm) during the Wait phase.

Binary Spray and Wait (BSW) [15], which is an optimal Spray and Wait routing algorithm, initially starts with L copies of data packets from the source node, and hands over half of the copies to the first node it encounters and keeps a half for itself. After that, every node which has the copies of data packets will deliver half of its copies of data packets toward the node that it met.

It has been proved that BSW is optimal, nonetheless, the source node ν_α forward $n/2$ data packets to the node ν_β as long as ν_α encountered ν_β, without considering that whether the node ν_β is "suitable" or not during the spray phase, which results in the blindness of data packets forwarding.

And therefore, we exploit the ETSW (Encounter Tree based Spray and Wait Routing protocol) in this paper for node selection during the Spray phase, which can evaluate the "message arriving destination capablity" of the next hop, and offer a better choice for message forwarding.

3   Encounter Tree Spray and Wait Routing Algorithm

3.1   Opportunistic Networks Architecture

Opportunistic networks is characterized by the fact that the message transmission between nodes do not necessarily have a complete path, that is, the whole network can be divided into multiple connected domains in a certain period of time, and only the nodes in the same domain can communicate with each other. Assuming that node S intends to deliver several data packets to node G, as shown in Fig. 1, during the period of time T, data of node S can only be transmitted to node A, C and M. Nodes B, D and G, which are in another area at this moment, are not able to receive the data.

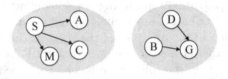

Fig. 1. Opportunistic networks topology.

For most of the realistic opportunistic networks scenes, mobile nodes all move in some certain regular way, instead of completely random moving. For example, the PSNs which takes advantage of the device mobility for data transmission. Generally speaking, when people go to work during the day, their moving scopes basically are industrial districts, commercial districts or financial districts, and mainly stay in residential districts while going home from work at night. In short, if a mobile node has been moving within a certain range for several times recently, we could generally consider that it will very likely visit this area again. And if a node encounter with another node frequently over a period of time, we are able to infer that the probability of the encounter between these two nodes next time will increase. In that case, routing can benefits considerably if one can make good use of the history of nodes encounter during the message forwarding period.

3.2 Calculation of Node's Probability of Encounter with Target Node

First of all, we shall establish a record $\eta \in H_N = \{\eta_A, \eta_B, \eta_C, ...\}$ for each node $\nu \in N = \{\nu_A, \nu_B, \nu_C, ...\}$ with its nodes encounter history and meeting time separately. Such as: $\eta_A = \{(\nu_B, \tau_{ab}), (\nu_H, \tau_{ah}), (\nu_I, \tau_{ai}), ...\}$, which means that node ν_A encounter with node ν_B at time τ_{ab}, node ν_H at time τ_{ah}, node ν_I at time τ_{ai} and so on.

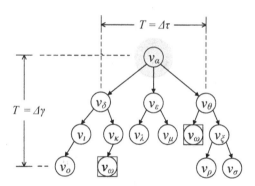

Fig. 2. Node encounter tree.

And then, we start to build the nodes encounter tree. As shown in Fig. 2, we take the node ν_α as an example to calculate the probability of its nodes encounter tree. Assuming that node ν_ω is the destination and node ν_α is a source node or a relay node. All the nodes (node ν_δ, ν_ϵ and ν_θ) that node ν_α has encountered in the past $T = \Delta\tau$ period (T is one of the control parameters that can be set by user, the longer the $\Delta\tau$, the more encounter nodes.) will be regarded as the children nodes of ν_α. And the encounter history of each child node of node ν_α is also regarded as the child node of it. Give an example, the node ν_ι and ν_κ which have met node ν_δ in the past $\Delta\tau$ period are regarded as the children nodes of ν_δ, and so on. Besides, the searching depth Γ ($\Gamma = \Delta\gamma$) of nodes-encounter tree is needed to be initialized by user too. So the parameters T and Γ can control the width and the depth of the node encounting tree respectively.

After that, we calculate the probability P_{ν_α} of node ν_α. We calculate the times of target node ν_ω's appearance and the depth of each appearance in nodes-encounter tree of node ν_α. Concretely speaking, we traverse the tree in depth-first search (or breadth-first search), recording the depth of each layer i, and calculating the probability of the target node's appearance among all the nodes $\nu \in N_i$ in each layer i ($1 \leq i \leq \Gamma$) with Eq. 1:

$$P(\nu_\omega|i,T,\nu) = \frac{n_\nu(\nu_\omega|i,T)}{n_\nu(N_i|i,T)} \quad (1 \leq i \leq \Gamma) \tag{1}$$

where $n_\nu(\nu_\omega|i,T)$ means that the number of target node's appearing in layer i, and $n_\nu(N_i|i,T)$ means that the total number of nodes in the i th layer.

And then, we need to calculate the weight of each layer i ($1 \leq i \leq \Gamma$) with Eq. 2:

$$W_i = \frac{\Gamma - i + 1}{\Gamma} \quad (1 \leq i \leq \Gamma) \tag{2}$$

At last, we calculate the probability that each $\nu \in N_S$ will encounter with the target node by combining the Eq. 1 with the Eq. 2 (i.e., Eq. 3):

$$
\begin{aligned}
P(\nu_\omega|\Gamma,T,\nu) &= \sum_{i=1}^{\Gamma} P(\nu_\omega|i,T,\nu)W_i \\
&= \sum_{i=1}^{\Gamma} \left(\frac{n_\nu(\nu_\omega|i,T)}{n_\nu(N_i|i,T)} \times \frac{\Gamma - i + 1}{\Gamma} \right)
\end{aligned}
\tag{3}
$$

where $\Gamma = \Delta\gamma$, $T = \Delta\tau$, and the calculation process can be described as shown in Algorithm 1.

3.3 Encounter Tree Spray and Wait Routing

So the process of optimized Spray and Wait routing ETSW can be described as follow:

(a) Spray phase

Since we state that BSW is blindfold in data packets forwarding, we are able to minimize the blindness of node selection at data packets forwarding as good as possible. When node ν_α encounters some new nodes, it evaluate their "capablity of data packets arriving destination", and distributes the copies of data packets the other nodes according to their capabilities.

Concretely speaking, assume that the node ν_α encounters node ν_β, node ν_χ, node ν_ψ at some point, the probabilities of them will be calculated according to the Eq. 3 (for convenience, we abbreviate $P(\nu_\omega|\Gamma,T,\nu)$ as P_ν). And assume that

---

Algorithm 1. Encounter Tree Probability Calculation

Intput: *host, dest, depth, time* //host for source node, dest for destination node, depth
    for depth of tree(Γ), time for past period(T)
Output: result
 1: //calculate the node's probability
 2: **function** PROCALC(*host, dest, depth, time*)
 3:    *result* $\leftarrow$ 0
 4:    *queue* $\leftarrow$ *null*
 5:    *children* $\leftarrow$ *null*
 6:    push(*queue, host*)
 7:    **for** $i = 1 \rightarrow depth$ **do**
 8:        *layerS* $\leftarrow$ 0 //total nodes of this layer
 9:        *layerD* $\leftarrow$ 0 //total destination nodes
10:        clear(*children*)
11:        **while** *queue* not empty **do**
12:            *layerS* + +
13:            *node* $\leftarrow$ pop(*queue*)
14:            **if** *node* $==$ *dest* **then**
15:                *layerD* + +
16:            **else**
17:                *children* $\leftarrow$ getChildren(*node, time*)
18:            **end if**
19:        **end while**
20:        *layerW* $\leftarrow$ (*depth* $- i + 1$)/*depth* //weight
21:        *result* $\leftarrow$ *result* + *layerD*/*layerS* $*$ *layerW*
22:        push(*queue, children*)
23:    **end for**
24:    **return** *result*
25: **end function**

---

the calculation result is that $P_\beta > P_\alpha = P_\chi > P_\psi$. Then we sort all the nodes order by their probabilities and add them to a queue in order of probabilities from large to small. As a result, we can get a nodes queue $Q = \{\nu_\beta, \nu_\chi, \nu_\psi\}$.

Similar to BSW, L copies of data packets D are generated form the source node ν_α initially (i.e. $D_\alpha = D_{init} = L$), and than the L copies of data packets are forwarded in the order of queue Q. But there's something different from BSW that the node ν_α is not going to hand over to the other node $D_\alpha/2$ and keep $D_\alpha/2$ for itself. We use the following formula (Eq. 4) to calculate the forwarding amount of data packets:

$$D_B = \begin{cases} \lceil \dfrac{P_B}{P_A + P_B} \times D_A \rceil & (P_A + P_B \neq 0) \\ 0.5 & (P_A + P_B = 0) \end{cases} \tag{4}$$

where A is the sender and B is the receiver. Firstly, we have L copies of data in node ν_α (i.e. $D_\alpha = L$). And then, we calculate the amount of data which is needed to be forwarded to node ν_β in the head of queue Q with $D_\beta = \lceil \frac{P_\beta}{P_\alpha + P_\beta} \times D_\alpha \rceil$

(i.e. D_β copies of data packets are needed to be forwarded from node ν_α to ν_β). So the remain amount of data in node ν_α is $D_\alpha = D_\alpha - D_\beta$. Repeat those operations for node ν_χ, node ν_ψ, and so on. While node ν_β enters another subnet, it acts as the source node and repeats the operations above. In other words, during the Spray phase, we spread the copies of data by calculating the probability of reaching destination of each nodes in the subnet with nodes encounter tree, and node ν_A will forward $P_B/(P_B + P_A)$ amount of data toward node ν_B from itself. Repeat the process above until the node in the network which is carrying the copy of data just have one copy of the data, then the data enter the Wait phase.

(b) Wait phase

During the Wait phase, the nodes which are carrying a copy of the data can also calculate the probability of all the nodes they are encountering with.

Algorithm 2. Encounter Tree Spray and Wait Process

Intput: $depth, time$ //depth for depth of tree(Γ), time for past period(T)
1: //Spray phase
2: **procedure** SPRAY($depth, time$)
3:    $list \leftarrow null$
4:    $queue \leftarrow null$
5:    **for** each node i in N **do**
6:        updateHistory(i)
7:        $p \leftarrow$ proCalc($i, dest, depth, time$)
8:        add($list, p$)
9:        **for** each encounter node j **do**
10:            $p \leftarrow$ proCalc($i, dest, depth, time$)
11:            add($list, p$)
12:            $queue \leftarrow$ sort($list$) //descending
13:        **end for**
14:        **if** $D_i == 1$ **then**
15:            **goto** WAIT($queue$)
16:            break
17:        **end if**
18:        **for** each node k in $queue$ **do**
19:            $D_k \leftarrow D_i * P_k/(P_i * P_k)$
20:            //distribute D_k
21:            $D_i \leftarrow D_i - D_k$
22:        **end for**
23:    **end for**
24: **end procedure**
25: //Wait phase
26: **procedure** WAIT($queue$)
27:    $k \leftarrow queue[0]$
28:    $D_k \leftarrow D_i$
29:    //distribute D_k
30:    $D_i \leftarrow 0$
31: **end procedure**

But unlike the Spray phase, all the nodes which are carrying one copy of data only forward their copy to the node in the head of the queue Q, which means the copy of data packets is not distributed but transferred toward the node with the highest probability in the neighbor nodes queue Q (i.e. the head of the queue, if the head of the queue Q is the node itself, it won't transfer the data packets) until it can be delivered to destination node directly.

The whole process above can be described with pseudocode as shown in Algorithm 2.

3.4   Specific Process of Node Traversal

So we come back to the subnet topology with node ν_S. Assume that while the user has set the parameters T and Γ (we set $T = t$, and $\Gamma = 4$), and the nodes-encounter trees of nodes ν_S, ν_A, ν_C, ν_M are as shown in Fig. 3.

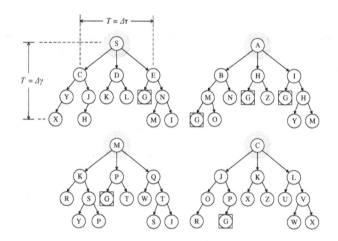

Fig. 3. Nodes encounter tree case.

Based on the Fig. 3, the specific process of ETSW algorithm can be described as follows:

(a) Spray phase

(1) Firstly, we can calculate the weight of each layer in each subtree of each node with Eq. 2 as follow (the depth of subtree of each nodes are the same, because Γ has been initialized): $W_1 = 1(i = 1)$, $W_2 = 3/4(i = 2)$, $W_3 = 1/2(i = 3)$, $W_4 = 1/4(i = 4)$.

(2) And then we need to calculate the probability of node ν_S. we first use the Eq. 1 to calculate the probability of target node's appearance in each layer of subtree ν_S: $P(\nu_G|1, t, \nu_S) = 0(i = 1)$, $P(\nu_G|2, t, \nu_S) = 0(i = 2)$,

$P(\nu_G|3,t,\nu_S) = 1/6(i = 3)$, $P(\nu_G|4,t,\nu_S) = 0(i = 4)$. After that we calculate the probability of node ν_S with Eq. 3: $P(\nu_G|\Delta\gamma, \Delta\tau, \nu_S) = 1/12$. At last we add P_S into a node probability list l.

(3) Similarly, we can calculate the probability of node ν_A: $P(\nu_G|\Delta\gamma, \Delta\tau, \nu_A) = 11/48$, ν_M: $P(\nu_G|\Delta\gamma, \Delta\tau, \nu_M) = 1/12$, ν_C: $P(\nu_G|\Delta\gamma, \Delta\tau, \nu_C) = 1/16$, and add them to l respectively.

(4) Then we sort the list l from big to small, and add them into a queue Q. So we can get the nodes queue $Q = \{\nu_A, \nu_S, \nu_M, \nu_C\}$. And node ν_S can start forwarding messages according to Q as shown in Fig. 4(a).

(5) We traverse the Q, and calculate the amount of data packets that node ν_S is going to forward to the node in the head of Q. Firstly, we calculate the amount of data packets that ν_S will transmit to ν_S with Eq. 4: $D_A = \lceil 11L/12 \rceil$. So D_S remain $L - \lceil 11L/12 \rceil$.

(6) Similarly, we can calculate that the amout of data packets: $D_M = \lceil (L - \lceil 11L/12 \rceil)/2 \rceil$, $D_C = \lceil 7[L - \lceil (L - \lceil 11L/12 \rceil)/2 \rceil]/48 \rceil$.

(7) And node ν_A, ν_M, ν_C that carry the copies of data serve as the relay nodes. While they enter another communication area, they become the "source node", and do as what ν_S does. Repeat the operations above till the node just carries one copy of the data packets, than the data in this node enter the Wait phase.

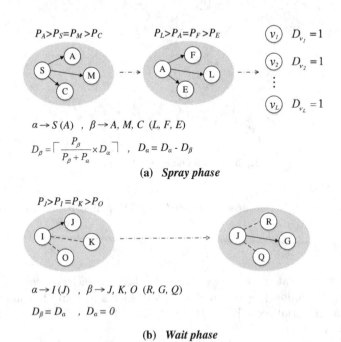

Fig. 4. Spray phase and Wait phase.

(b) Wait phase

(8) Assume that the node ν_I carries a copy of the data packets as shown in Fig. 4(b), and it encounters the node ν_J, ν_K and ν_O. The calculation result of nodes-encounter tree probabilities of each nodes is that $P(\nu_J) > P(\nu_I) = P(\nu_K) > P(\nu_O)$, and thus we could get the queue $Q = \{\nu_J, \nu_I, \nu_K, \nu_O\}$. And then node ν_I will transfer its copy of data toward the node in the head of Q (i.e. node ν_J) till the message can arrive the destination directly.

4 Simulation and Results

In order to obtain a more realistic network scenario, we apply the ONE 1.6 (Opportunistic Network Environment) simulator [16] to simulate real-life in the city of Helsinki (capital of Finland). The setting of simulation environment is shown in Table 1.

Table 1. Simulation setting in the ONE 1.6 simulator.

	Pedestrians	Cars	Trams
Number of nodes	100 (30–400)	40 (10–200)	10
Moving speed (m/s)	0.5–1.5	2.7–13.9	7–10
Transmission range (m)	10	10	100
Transmission speed (Kbps)	250	250	10000
Buffer size (Mbyte)	20	20	50
Message sizes (Kbyte)	500		
Message creation interval (s)	25–35		
Message TTL (h)	5		
Message copies L	6 (6–12)		
Encounter Tree period T (s)	120 (60–240)		
Encounter Tree depth Γ	2 (2–4)		
Simulation time (h)	12		
Simulation area (m^2)	4500 × 3400		

The ETSW is mainly compared with the classical algorithms BSW and SnW. As shown in Fig. 5, the number of nodes is used as an independent variable (we mainly alter the number of pedestrians) to analyze the changes of delivery rate.

From Fig. 5, we can see that the delivery rate grows as the number of nodes increases, and the delivery rate of ETSW is about 5% higher than SnW and BSW on average. That's because ETSW can distribute more copies of data packets toward the nodes which are more likely to encounter with the target node, while the nodes which have lower probabilities of reaching target node will get less

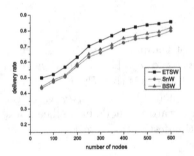
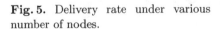
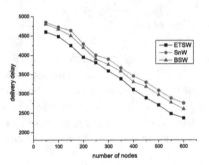

Fig. 5. Delivery rate under various number of nodes.

Fig. 6. Delivery delay under various number of nodes.

copies of data packets. Besides, as shown in Fig. 6, we can see that the delivery delay of ETSW are generally lower than that of BSW and SnW as the number of nodes grow. The reason is that ETSW will transfer the data packets to the node with a higher probability of arriving destination during the Wait phase.

And then, we analyze how parameters L (Message copies) affect the delivery rate and delay of transmission. As shown in Fig. 7, the delivery rate of ETSW will be risen as the copies L increases, and also a little bit higher than that of classic BSW or SnW. Besides ETSW has the lower overhead than BSW or SnW as shown in Fig. 8.

Besides, we also compare the overhead ratio of ETSW with that of SnW and BSW. As shown in Figs. 9 and 10, the overhead ratio of ETSW routing increases with the increasement in the number of nodes or the number of copies, and is basically consistent with SnW and BSW.

Copies L is the common parameter of ETSW, BSW and SnW, so we compare them with each other under various number of copies. But both T (Encounter Tree period) and Γ (Encounter Tree depth) are peculiar parameters of ETSW, and thus, we compare the delivery rates of different parameters T and Γ. As we

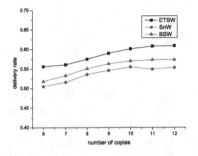
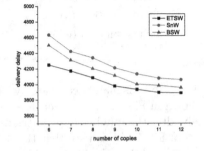

Fig. 7. Delivery rate under various number of copies.

Fig. 8. Delivery delay under various number of copies.

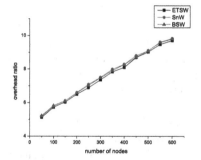

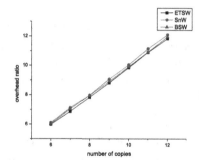

Fig. 9. Overhead ratio various number of nodes.

Fig. 10. Overhead ratio various number of copies.

could see in Fig. 11, for different Γ, with the increasement of T, the delivery rate is also growing at the beginning. However, when T grows to a certain number, the delivery rate grow slower. For $\Gamma > 1$, the delivery rate even drop. We could analyze that with the increasing depth of Encounter Tree, the complexity of probability calculation will also increase, which results in the overhead of the routing and thus reducing the delivery rate. And thus, L, T and Γ are the important parameters for ETSW protocol and needed to be adjusted according to different actual scenes.

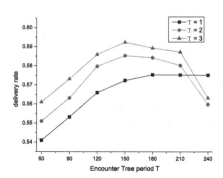

Fig. 11. Delivery rate under various period of time.

5   Conclusions

In this paper, we propose an optimized routing protocol (ETSW) based on the node encounter history in opportunistic networks. Both in the Spray phase and Wait phase, the probability of encountering with destination node of each node in the subnet will be calculated, and the next hop of that the message will forward to is selected by the calculating results. By comparing with the typical BSW or SnW routing protocol, the simulation results show that ETSW can improve the delivery rate, and reduce the transmission delay of data packets forwarding. And compared with other traditional routing protocols for OppNets, ETSW can also reduce the replicas of invalid data in the network, and thus reducing the overhead of messages transmission. Owing to the fact that the overhead of BSW routing is much lower than other classical algorithms like Epidemic or PRoPHET routing and ETSW is based on the BSW, and thus, ETSW also has the advantage of low routing overhead.

However, it is noteworthy that the width and depth of the nodes encounter history tree in the ETSW routing algorithm must to be controlled. Otherwise, the overhead of the routing will increase because of the probability calculating between nodes, which will affect the improvement of the delivery rate and reduction of the transmission delay. Only the depth of nodes encounter tree and the time period (i.e., the width of the tree) can be well controlled, the ETSW routing protocol can improve efficiency of data transmission. The experiment results show that the depth of the node tree is preferably 2–3 layers. When the number of layers increases, the computational complexity will also increase rapidly, and thus the transmission performance will be affected. While time period of nodes encounter tree can be set according to the actual situation. In contrast, the length of the time segment has less impact on the computational overhead than the depth. Besides, due to the characteristics of ETSW, it is more applicable to the more realistic scenes. That is, when the nodes movement model is more regular, its improvement of transmission rate of BSW is more obvious.

References

1. Trifunovic, S., Kouyoumdjieva, S.T., Distl, B., et al.: A decade of research in opportunistic networks: challenges, relevance, and future directions. IEEE Commun. Mag. **55**(1), 168–173 (2017)
2. Martonosi, M.: MOBILE SENSING: Retrospectives and Trends. GetMobile Mob. Comput. Commun. **20**(1), 14–19 (2016)
3. Tang, L., Wu, W.: Data forwarding with selectively partial flooding in opportunistic networks. In: Zeng, Q.-A. (ed.) Wireless Communications, Networking and Applications. LNEE, vol. 348, pp. 1233–1241. Springer, New Delhi (2016). doi:10.1007/978-81-322-2580-5_112
4. Wang, E., Yang, Y., Wu, J., et al.: Phone-to-phone communication utilizing WiFi hotspot in energy-constrained pocket switched networks. IEEE Trans. Veh. Technol. **65**(10), 8578–8590 (2016)
5. Eze, E.C., Zhang, S.J., Liu, E.J., et al.: Advances in vehicular ad-hoc networks (VANETs): challenges and road-map for future development. Int. J. Autom. Comput. **13**(1), 1–18 (2016)
6. Liu, D., Hou, M., Cao, Z., et al.: Duplicate detectable opportunistic forwarding in duty-cycled wireless sensor networks. IEEE/ACM Trans. Netw. (TON) **24**(2), 662–673 (2016)
7. He, D., Zeadally, S., Kumar, N., et al.: Anonymous authentication for wireless body area networks with provable security. IEEE Syst. J. **99**, 1–12 (2016)
8. Hess, A., Hummel, K.A., Gansterer, W.N., et al.: Data-driven human mobility modeling: a survey and engineering guidance for mobile networking. ACM Comput. Surv. (CSUR) **48**(3), 38 (2016)

9. Liu, X., João Nicolau, M., Costa, A., Macedo, J., Santos, A.: A geographic opportunistic forwarding strategy for vehicular named data networking. In: Novais, P., Camacho, D., Analide, C., El Fallah Seghrouchni, A., Badica, C. (eds.) Intelligent Distributed Computing IX. SCI, vol. 616, pp. 509–521. Springer, Cham (2016). doi:10.1007/978-3-319-25017-5_48

10. Ning, Z., Xia, F., Hu, X., et al.: Social-oriented adaptive transmission in opportunistic Internet of smartphones. IEEE Trans. Ind. Inform. **13**(2), 810–820 (2017)

11. Tian, D., Zhou, J., Wang, Y., et al.: An adaptive vehicular epidemic routing method based on attractor selection model. Ad Hoc Netw. **36**, 465–481 (2016)

12. Jain, S., Chawla, M., Soares, V.N.G.J., et al.: Enhanced fuzzy logic-based spray and wait routing protocol for delay tolerant networks. Int. J. Commun. Syst. **29**(12), 1820–1843 (2016)

13. Agarwal, N., Bhadouria, S.S.: Crime detection in rural areas using enhanced prophet routing algorithm in DTN. In: Symposium on Colossal Data Analysis and Networking (CDAN), pp. 1–5. IEEE (2016)

14. Das, M., Sarkar, S., Iqbal, S.M.A.: TTL based MaxProp routing protocol. In: 2016 19th International Conference on Computer and Information Technology (ICCIT), pp. 7–12. IEEE (2016)

15. Derakhshanfard, N., Sabaei, M., Rahmani, A.M.: Sharing spray and wait routing algorithm in opportunistic networks. Wirel. Netw. **22**(7), 2403–2414 (2016)

16. Keränen, A., Ott, J., Kärkkäinen, T.: The ONE simulator for DTN protocol evaluation. In: Proceedings of the 2nd International Conference on Simulation Tools and Techniques. Institute for Computer Sciences, Social-Informatics and Telecommunications Engineering (ICST), p. 55 (2009)

DFP: A Data Fragment Protection Scheme for mHealth in Wireless Network

Lin Zhang[1,2], Zhigang Chen[1,2(✉)], and Deyu Zhang[1,2]

[1] School of Software, Central South University, Changsha, China
`czg@mail.csu.edu.cn`
[2] Mobile Health Ministry of Education China Mobile Joint Laboratory,
Changsha, China

Abstract. The mHealth system gradually become widely promoted, the user data privacy issues by the community a strong concern in the complex wireless network environment. In this paper, we propose a data fragment protection scheme, named DFP. The proposed DFP scheme according to the characteristics of the medical environment to system preprocessing, let the wearable equipment or implantation equipment to collect the patient information classified as patient personal privacy data and general medical data, the two types of data on the degree of privacy of different treatment. And according to the data connectivity design reliable transmission scheme. Our framework can not only more reasonable protection of medical data privacy and security, but also to reduce communication consumption and reduce the average time delay. Extensive performance analysis and experimental results proves its effectiveness and reliability.

Keywords: Data fragment · Mobile health · Privacy protection · Security

1 Introduction

With the continuous development of science and technology, social medical level has been significantly improved, at the same time the problem is that the aging of the population has gradually emerged. Society has made great efforts to tackle the health problems [17] of the elderly. In recent years, a variety of health clinics and medical monitoring equipment continue to come out. In addition to the health needs of the elderly, these health clinics are also urgently needed by hospital patients to monitor the various parameters of the body indicators. (Such as blood pressure, blood sugar, heartbeat and so on). In addition, healthy people began to wear smart bracelet, download smart health APP or other wearable equipment to pay attention to their own health. Therefore, in the urgent needs of society, mobile health (mHealth) system [2] began to appear. Its core philosophy is to deal with and transmit medical information, combined with traditional medical services to improve the efficiency of medical services while meeting the

© Springer Nature Singapore Pte Ltd. 2017
D. Du et al. (Eds.): NCTCS 2017, CCIS 768, pp. 60–74, 2017.
https://doi.org/10.1007/978-981-10-6893-5_5

medical needs of different people. The widespread use of mobile medical electronic health systems has improved people's daily lives. Mobile medical systems use portable devices to facilitate the efficient collection of personal health data and provide better health care for different groups of people. For most mobile medical systems, patients use sensors, implantable medical devices (IMDS) [13] and mobile phones to collect personal health records (PHR) [11], Medical data is sent to the designated medical infrastructure via a wireless interface for medical diagnosis.

What is worth noting in this field is, as a result of mobile medical information such as electronic medical records [3], there is a variety of information closely related to patients with sensitive private personal information (such as identity card number, social insurance number, address, date of birth, illness history), once the information is stolen, it is easy for the attacker to pretend to be a real patient to steal data, tamper with the relevant information or attack system, and may even use these data to do some illegal acts. A number of medical records have been reported to be stolen, some attackers steal and publish patient health information to third parties or publish them on the Internet. According to a recent survey, the researchers estimated that the US medical identity theft [16] generated at least 41.3 billion in annual economic impact. Especially for mobile medical systems, the potential privacy [5] of mobile devices and the efficiency of mobile medical use is also another important concern for patients.

Over the past few years, mobile medical data privacy protection has been rapid development and achieved some achievements, these achievements have aroused close attention of academia and industry. At present the more popular mobile medical end to end transmission is, use personal implantable sensors or wearable sensing devices for personal medical data collection [1], The health data of each sensor is collected by a mobile device such as a mobile phone and transmitted to a medical center for medical treatment, and to provide daily health problems in patients with rationalization of the diagnosis and treatment recommendations. Because of the privacy of medical data and mobile devices themselves some of the irresistible insecurity factors leading to mobile medical system security issues become increasingly prominent. In this process, how to collect the information of each body sensor, the data itself how to carry out encryption protection have become a research hot spots, at the same time, the data in the transmission process how efficient and accurate transmission has become the academic community close attention problem. For example, Mobil-Health [9], UbiMon [6] and other projects to promote the implementation of mobile medical development.

To address the patient privacy issues lying in mHealth field, in this paper, we propose a Data Fragment Protection scheme for mHealth in wireless network called DFP. First of all, we pretreatment of the mobile medical system, according to the medical field characteristics of the implanted sensor and wearable equipment to collect the patient data is divided into personal sensitive data and general medical data. Second, we have different types of data to take the corresponding security program, Thirdly, taking into account the sensitivity of mobile medical data, our DFP framework considers the transmission security of medical data while reducing the communication consumption and average time delay. We will further illustrate the specific feasibility and superiority of the framework.

The rest of this article is arranged as follows. The description of related work in Sect. 2, and then formalize the problem in Sect. 3. The proposed DFP is presented in Sect. 4. Sections 5 and 6 presents the performance analysis and simulation. Finally, conclusions remarks are given in Sect. 7.

2   Related Work

In recent years, several research works on privacy protection of mHealth have been proposed, In particular, in order to achieve data privacy There have been many ways in the academic community, we will be divided into two types of existing methods to *protect the location of privacy* [7,14,19] and *protection of data privacy* [15,18,20]. In the literature [19], a scheme of broadcast source data is proposed, which solves the problem of data protection geographical limitation through the anonymity of the data to protect the data itself. However, its large forwarding leads to excessive resource waste and routing Consumption. In literature [7,14], there is a route that a route that uses pseudo-source, when the source wants to send data, it involves several pseudo-sources, and then the real and false sources send data at the same time. In addition, in a virtual single path route, after the source generates the data it will take a random path before reaching the destination. By taking the random path, the source data can prevent local eavesdropping. Literature [7,14,19] from different angles using the source of protection or the location of the way to bring the system security, but have to admit the fact that they are prevalent to increase the cost of routing, waste of network resources. In [15], It uses super-incremental sequences to construct multidimensional data and encrypt structured data through homomorphic paillier cryptography. Directly in the local gateway on the ciphertext data aggregation without decryption, the article also uses batch verification technology to reduce the cost of certification. Literature [18] present the mHealth sensing protocol, which provides powerful security and privacy link layer performance with low energy overhead. The protocol uses three new technologies: adaptive security, dynamic modification of transmission overhead; MAC fragmentation, even for small size message authentication code is also difficult to forge; Literature [20] for reduce the privacy of the participants by disconnecting data from the data source. This method allows the polymerizer to obtain an accurate distribution data aggregation, thus enabling the aggregator to efficiently calculate arbitrary complex aggregate functions. Literature [15,18,20] from the data itself, the use of different programs to achieve the purpose of ensuring data security, but there are such as increasing the burden of data transmission, affecting the efficiency of data transmission.

Different from the above works, the proposed DFP scheme not only from the protection of data to protect the security of medical data, but also to reduce the burden of data transmission, classification of different medical information.

3   Problem Formalization

In this section, we provide a concise problem formalization, including system model, security model and design goal.

3.1   System Model

In system model, we consider four parts of the medical health system: body sensor nodes, mobile devices, wireless networks [4] and physician center, Body sensor nodes may collect patients health information of their body, while the mobile devices can processing and transimission the information to physician, and the wireless network provides convenient network support for data communications, while physician center diagnosis and return the information as a recipient, so that the patient could get quick and accurate healthcare [8] form the physician. Here, we define the system model by dividing the eHealth system into three parts: mobile devices, wireless network and physician center as shown in Fig. 1.

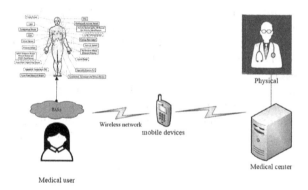

Fig. 1. Pervasive health monitoring in m-Healthcare system.

Mobile Devices. Body devices include body sensors [21] and mobile phone or other mobile devices that can be placed inside a human body or worn on a human body, The Body sensor could be accelerometer, blood pressure, oxygen saturation or temperature sensors, as well as collect the patient health information by the sensors nodes. The mobile devices is used to process and deliver medical information from body sensors. Simultaneously, mobile devices deliver the data to physician center by wireless network, then when doctor receive and return a diagnostic suggestion, we use the mobile device to receive it.

Wireless Network. In mHealth system, we adopt wireless network technology connection and transmission of sender and the receiver of the effective information to ensure continuity and transmission of node security. We will use elliptic curve discrete logarithm encryption technology to ensure the privacy of medical data.

mHealth Physician Center. mHealth [12] physician center as a receiver to receive medical information form the patient side and make timely professional diagnosis, and then send diagnostic information to the mobile devices of patient.

3.2 Security Model

Through the description of the system model, we know the specific composition of the eHealth system, however, there are many security problem during this process. At first, mobile devices collect the medical information form body sensors, we consider there are N body sensors $S = \{S_1, S_2, ..., S_N\}$ in the patient, these sensor carry I patient information, the total information (i) is carried $Info_{total} = \sum_{i=1}^{I} \sum_{s=1}^{N} i_s$ respectively. Due to the sensor come form different manufactures, and each sensor device is bound and collected a variety of user information, according to the particularity of eHealth environment [10], we consider a phenomenon, when medical data loss of patient-related information (such as gender and age of patient), the information is declared invalid in medicine, the reason is that many illnesses are related to the patients age and gender. Combine this phenomenon, we proposed a data fragmentation strategy that make the data collected form the body sensors are divided into two categories: personal privacy data and purely medical data. The two types of data are then transmitted separately to ensure data security. This is security than the previous data overall transmission, the reason is that if a third-party attacker breaks any communication channel, such as medical data, if the attacker can not tell the data and a patient information to connect, then the attack to obtain the data for the attacker does not make much sense. This is linkability, we proposed a DFP framework to protect the security of eHealth system. The model composition is shown in Fig. 2.

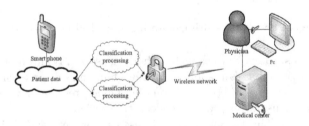

Fig. 2. Security model in m-Healthcare system.

3.3 Design Goal

Our design goal is to develop a Data Fragment Protection scheme for wireless network in mHealth. Specifically, with medical health system, it is necessary to protect the medical data privacy of patients. We consider the data collected form the sensor is divided into personal data and medical data, and allowed to be transmitted separately to the medical end. Even if the system encounters a third-party attack, an attack can be called a useless attack if the attacker can not accurately match the obtained medical data to the patient data. The design enhances the security of the medical system.

4 DFP Framework

In this section, we proposed a DFP (Data Fragment Protection) framework, which consists of three phases: elliptic curve discrete logarithm, system pre-processing and system initialization.

4.1 Elliptic Curve Discrete Logarithm

In this section we introduce elliptic curve discrete logarithm, which is the basic knowledge of the DFP framework. Let $K = \mathbb{F}_q(2^n)$ be a finite field containing q elements. P is the m order point of the elliptic curve $\mathbb{F}_q(2^n)$ in the domain K. From the equation.

$$f(x,y) = y^2 + (a_1 x + a_3)y - x^3 - a_2 x^2 - a_4 x - a_6 = 0 \tag{1}$$

The definition of non-singular algebraic curve E is called the finite field $\mathbb{F}_q(2^n)$ on the elliptic curve, where $x, y, a_1, a_2, a_3, a_4, a_6 \in \mathbb{F}_q, a_6 \neq 0$.

Definition 1. *A generator ϱen is a probabilistic algorithm that takes a security parameter n as input, and outputs a 5-tuple $(q, \mathbb{F}_q, E, P, n)$: $q \in \{p, 2^n\}$, p as a large prime number, finite field $\mathbb{F}_q$, the group of secure elliptic curves E, as well as a point for a large number of n points $P \in E(\mathbb{F}_q)$.*

Definition 2. *Select the random number $a(b) \in Z^*$, compute $Q_a = aP(Q_b = bP)$, and sends it to the other party.*

Definition 3. *Using the respective random numbers and the information obtained form the other party, can be calculated $S = a(Q_b) = b(Q_a)$. And s is the key common to users A and B.*

4.2 System Pre-processing

Now we need to do is according to the characteristics of medical data on the existing data fragment processing, according to the foregoing description, if there is no patient personal information such as gender, age, etc. as an auxiliary judge, the medical data itself is not of great use value or research value. At first, we abstract the body sensor nodes of a patient into a connected graph $G(V, E)$, where V is the set of sensor nodes, $|V| = N$ represents the number of sensors, edge E represents the communication link between the sensor and the mobile devices. In this stage, we consider to fragment the merged data, the classification rule is defined as procedures to determine the interception of patients with personal information, the above segmentation is performed for all data, we assume that Fig. 3 is the information collected form the patients body sensor, and the 0 state represents the personal privacy information, and the 1 state represents the professional medical information, and the 0 state and the 1 state data are separated by cutting.

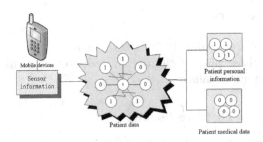

Fig. 3. Data segmentation.

We know that all data collected by a mobile device is represented as $Info_{total}$. We classify all medical information into two states (e), labeled as $e \in \{0, 1\}$. For ease of understanding and reading, we use $\vartheta(e)_{state}$ represents a classification function, which is:

$$\vartheta(e)_{state} = \begin{cases} 0, & \text{person privacy data} \\ 1, & \text{security medical data} \end{cases} \tag{2}$$

After the completion of the data will be placed in two containers, the state storage function is shown below, In addition, we consider to domains are assigned to users who have successfully registered through the trust authority TA, for example, TA assigns $1-10$ space to the patient *Alice*, after data fragmentation, a field of data is randomly selected as a flag. It means when the doctor-side to receive information, just decrypt the information, and the flag in the same region of the data to match, you can successfully obtain complete medical information. We domain flag is defined by the θ.

$$f(\vartheta(e)_{state}) = \begin{cases} \theta_{rand}||Info_{\vartheta(e)}, e=0 \\ \sum_{i=0}^{N}(\theta i_{rand}||Info(\vartheta(e)_{state})), e=1 \end{cases} \tag{3}$$

Obviously, we find that:

$$\theta_{rand}||Info_{\vartheta(e)} + \sum_{i=0}^{N}(\theta i_{rand}||Info(\vartheta(e)_{state}) = Info_{(\frac{1}{I})} \tag{4}$$

That is, the sum of the two items in Eq. (3) is one of the complete sensor information (I) in the patient information. After finishing, waiting for the next handler.

4.3   System Initialization

In this phase, we consider there is a trusted party (TA) to initializes the system parameter, assigns key materials for medical devices in the system. The workflow of TA is as follows:

Step 1. Generator ϱen given a secure random parameter n, the public key of sender $(q, \mathbb{F}_q, E, P, n)$ are first generated. Then, the TA select two random numbers $x_1, y_1 \in \mathbb{Z}_q^*$ as the master keys of sender, and computes the public keys $Q_{x_1} = x_1 P (Q_{y_1} = y_1 P)$. In addition, TA chooses two secure cryptographic hash functions H_0, H_1, where $H_0 : \{0,1\} \rightarrow \mathbb{F}$, and $H_1 : \{0,1\} \rightarrow \mathbb{Z}_q^*$. Finally, the TA sets the system public parameters $P_k = \{q, \mathbb{F}_q, E, P, n, Q_{x_1}, Q_{y_1}, H_0, H_1\}$. Each patient user completes the key exchange in this way.

Step 2. According to the system pre-processing results, First of all, we patients focus on personal privacy data. That is, remove the value of $f(\vartheta(0))_{state}$, Assume that there are pd patient users who have been legally registered with the medical system, and they completed the Step 1, and obtained the secret key is $S = x_1(Q_{y_1}) = y_1(Q_{x_1})$, Now, we consider to use S to encryption information pd like AES symmetric encryption algorithm. The process of exchanging the keys and encrypting the data by the patient user is illustrated in Algorithm 1.

Algorithm 1. Data encryption

    Data: $q, \mathbb{F}_q, E, P, n$,message $f(\vartheta(0))_{state}$.
    Result: secret key S, Encryption information $f(\vartheta(0))_{state}'$.
    `/* Key exchange process                                              */`
1 generator ϱen given a secure random parameter n $(n \rightarrow \varrho en)$
2 TA select two random numbers $x_1, y_1 \in \mathbb{Z}_q^*$, $Q_{x_1} = x_1 P (Q_{y_1} = y_1 P)$
3 let hash function as: $H_0 : \{0,1\} \rightarrow \mathbb{F}$ and
4 $H_1 : \{0,1\} \rightarrow \mathbb{Z}_q^*$
5 the system public parameters: $P_k = \{q, \mathbb{F}_q, E, P, n, Q_{x_1}, Q_{y_1}, H_0, H_1\}$
6 then, let $S = x_1(Q_{y_1}) = y_1(Q_{x_1})$
    `/* Symmetric encryption of patient data                              */`
7 use S to encryption information pd like AES symmetric encryption algorithm
8 Obtain the patient privacy data encrypted content

Step 3. For other medical data that part of the information collected form the body sensor data $f(\vartheta(1))_{state}$, we use two hash function H_0, H_1 and the key S obtained in the first step for message authentication by $HMAC$ technology. The general flow performance is as follows. $HMAC$ algorithm formula is expressed as:

$$HMAC(S, f(\vartheta(1))_{state}) = H_i(S \oplus opad \| H_i(S \oplus ipad \| f(\vartheta(1))_{state})) \quad (5)$$

Algorithm 2. Message authentication

Data: secret $Key S$,hash function H_1, H_2,message $f(\vartheta(1))_{state}$.
Result: authentication information $f(\vartheta(1))_{state}'$.
/* Message authentication process   */
1 Add 0 after the key S to create a string with a word length of K.
2 $Key(K) \oplus IPAD \rightarrow S$.
3 $H_1 \longleftarrow S \parallel f(\vartheta(1))_{state}$
4 $Key(K) \oplus OPAD \rightarrow S$.
5 $S \parallel H_2 \rightarrow f(\vartheta(1))_{state}$
6 Output the final result $f(\vartheta(1))_{state}'$.

The authentication algorithm is described Algorithm 2.

As described above, with the mobile devices of mhealth system and data security protection technology, the patient's personal data and medical data are effectively protected.

5 Security Analysis

we analyze the security of the proposed DFP framework to verify that the data fragment protection scheme for wireless network in mHealth is privacy-preserving against external and man-in-the-middle attack. Specifically, based on the hardness of ECCDH problem, we will prove this paper is semantic secure under the attack. We will analyze the security of the framework from a theoretical and technical, respectively.

In our framework, We pretreatment of the system according to the characteristics of the mobile medical environment, that is, the data collected by WBANs is fragmented. The fragmented data is used to divide the collected data into patient personal data and medical data. After the system preprocessing is complete, the two kinds of data were encrypted and message authentication processing, Finally, the data transmission, the receiver through the reverse compilation and combination of plaintext. In addition to the security of data transmission from the point of view of security, At the same time clever combination of mobile medical features, the data for effective fragmentation, and according to the different characteristics of different data processing, Such as the high personal data privacy, the effective elliptic curve key exchange and encryption processing, and isolated medical data relative to the reduction of privacy, we message authentication processing, which reduces the data transmission pressure, but also improve and to ensure the accuracy of data transmission and security. At the same time, by reducing the data encryption ratio, the communication consumption and the average transmission time delay are reduced.

Example 1. We simulated an experiment $Pr[AT_{A,\gamma}^{DFP}(\varphi)]$.

(1) Assume that Alice and Bob run the protocol γ to generate a bunch of shared secret keys and hold separate security parameters φ with each other. After

execution, a copy of all the information sent by both parties*copy* and the key S;

(2) Randomly select a $b \in \{0,1\}$. if $b = 0$, let $k = rand(0,1)^n$; if $b = 1$, let $k = S$;

(3) $\mathcal{A}$ get the message *copy* and the key k, output a b', if $b' = b$, the experimental output is true (1), else, the output is false (0).

Theorem 1. *For each probability polynomial of time attacker $\mathcal{A}$, there is a neglect function $negl(\varphi)$ that satisfies*

$$Pr[AT^{DFP}_{\mathcal{A},\gamma}(\varphi) = 1] \leq \frac{1}{2} + negl(\varphi) \tag{6}$$

The key exchange protocol is safe in the presence of an eavesdropper.

Proof. Due $Pr[b=0] = Pr[b=1] = \frac{1}{2}$, and

$$Pr[AT^{DFP}_{\mathcal{A},\gamma}(\varphi) = 1] = \frac{1}{2} * Pr[AT^{DFP}_{\mathcal{A},\gamma}(\varphi) = 1|b = 1]$$
$$+ \frac{1}{2} * Pr[AT^{DFP}_{\mathcal{A},\gamma}(\varphi) = 1|b = 0] \tag{7}$$

$\mathcal{A}$ get $(q, \mathbb{F}_q, n, Q_{x_1}, Q_{y_1}, k)$ through eavesdropping, the result is either the true secret key $S = x_1 y_1 P$ ($b = 1$) calculated by the data receiver, or a random group element k (if $b = 0$). That is derived from Eq. (7):

$$Pr[AT^{DFP}_{\mathcal{A},\gamma}(\varphi) = 1] = \frac{1}{2} * Pr[AT^{DFP}_{\mathcal{A},\gamma}(\varphi) = 1|b = 1]$$
$$+ \frac{1}{2} * Pr[AT^{DFP}_{\mathcal{A},\gamma}(\varphi) = 1|b = 0]$$
$$= \frac{1}{2} * Pr[\mathcal{A}(q, \mathbb{F}_q, n, Q_{x_1}, Q_{y_1}, S) = 1|b = 1]$$
$$+ \frac{1}{2} * Pr[\mathcal{A}(q, \mathbb{F}_q, n, Q_{x_1}, Q_{y_1}, k) = 0|b = 0]$$
$$= \frac{1}{2} * Pr[\mathcal{A}(q, \mathbb{F}_q, n, Q_{x_1}, Q_{y_1}, S) = 1|b = 1]$$
$$+ \frac{1}{2} * (1 - Pr[\mathcal{A}(q, \mathbb{F}_q, n, Q_{x_1}, Q_{y_1}, k) = 1|b = 0]$$
$$= \frac{1}{2} + \frac{1}{2}(Pr[\mathcal{A}(q, \mathbb{F}_q, n, Q_{x_1}, Q_{y_1}, S) = 1|b = 1]$$
$$- Pr[\mathcal{A}(q, \mathbb{F}_q, n, Q_{x_1}, Q_{y_1}, k) = 1|b = 0])$$
$$\leqslant \frac{1}{2} + \frac{1}{2} * Pr[\mathcal{A}(q, \mathbb{F}_q, n, Q_{x_1}, Q_{y_1}, S) = 1|b = 1]$$
$$- Pr[\mathcal{A}(q, \mathbb{F}_q, n, Q_{x_1}, Q_{y_1}, k) = 1|b = 0] \tag{8}$$

Because the assumption is relatively difficult, there is a negligible function $negl(\varphi)$ to satisfy:

$$Pr[\mathcal{A}(q, \mathbb{F}_q, n, Q_{x_1}, Q_{y_1}, S) = 1|b = 1]$$
$$- Pr[\mathcal{A}(q, \mathbb{F}_q, n, Q_{x_1}, Q_{y_1}, k) = 1|b = 0] \leqslant negl(\varphi) \tag{9}$$

Therefore:

$$Pr[AT_{\mathcal{A},\gamma}^{DFP}(\varphi) = 1] \leqq \frac{1}{2} + negl(\varphi) \qquad (10)$$

proof finished.

As a result, the DFP framework is semantic secure under chosen attack. The privacy-preserving of mHealth is achieved in the proposed DFP scheme.

6   Performance Evaluation

In the mobile medical system, communication overhead and time delay are two important performance evaluation indicators. So, in this section, we're focusing on these two points of PHI in order to evaluate the performance of DFP. We using a custom simulator built in Java (use JPBC and MIRACL libraries running on a 4G Hz processor 4G memory computing to research costs). The measured performance metric is the average data transmission time delay (TTD) and communication overhead (CO), where the TTD is defined as the average time of data transfer from the mobile device to the healthcare center.

6.1   Simulation Settings

As our main focus is through data fragmentation and classification to protect medical data privacy and security, reduce communication consumption and improve the efficiency of data transmission in the premise of improving security. For the comparison with DFP, we consider a method (SAGE) [19] where let each user generate the data ciphertext and then transfer it. In the simulation, we initially set the medical patient Mu in the group to carry n sensor nodes, Mu with velocities varying from $0.5\,\mathrm{m/s}$ to $1.2\,\mathrm{m/s}$ in an area of $1000 * 1000\,\mathrm{m}^2$. Assuming that these nodes were previously registered with the user, at time $T = 10\,\mathrm{min}$, we pre-experiment several times in the evaluation of different parameters under the conditions of medical care to receive data on the time. For each case, we run the simulation until the Pc receives the packet. The detailed parameter settings in the simulation are summarized in Table 1.

6.2   Simulation Results

In Fig. 4, the BANS node n from 1 to 5. With the increase of n, the TTD of SAGE and DFP increases accordingly, because the more BANS is, the greater the amount of data that the mobile device needs to collect and the relative delay. But we can see that in the case of $n = 1$ and $n = 5$, DFP's time delay is slightly lower than $SAGE$, the reason is that DFP has preprocessed the system by data fragmentation, and made the important two kinds of data encryption and secondary authentication processing, although the classification of data produced a certain delay, the overall time delay is better than SAGE the program. In particular, in Fig. 5(a), when $n = 1$, DFP average time delay (TTD)

Table 1. Simulation setting

Parameter	Setting
Simulation area	$1000 * 1000$ m
Simulation time	$T = 10$ min
Simulation duration	Till Pc receives the packet
Communication mode	WIFI or 4G
Number of sensors nodes	$n = 1, 5$
Velocity of user	0.5–1.2 m/s
Mobile devices collect medical data intervals	Every 10 s

is lower than SAGE, SAGE's time delay is 424.8 ms, DFP delay is 378.5 ms, the difference between the two 37.3 ms, when n = 5, SAGE time delay average of 438.2 ms, DFP delay of 382.4 ms, the difference between 55.8 ms. Obviously, increasing the sensor node will increase the data and transmission delay, while the use of DFP system than the SAGE system to produce a smaller time delay, improve data transmission efficiency.

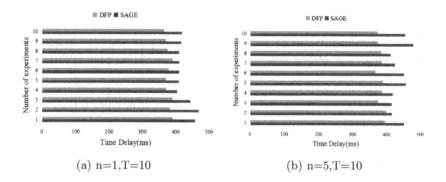

(a) n=1,T=10   (b) n=5,T=10

Fig. 4. Time delay

Similarly, we can see from Fig. 5(a) and (b), when the patient has only one sensor node, the communication gap between is relatively small, it is because the amount of data is relatively small, so the display is not very different, and two framework communication overhead in 9.9–10 MB, the gap is only 0.04 MB maximum. When the number of nodes is increased to 5, the amount of data that the mobile device needs to process increases, and the communication consumption of the DFP frame is more and more obvious than the SAGE. Obviously, the communication overhead of DFP is less than SAGE, and the gap is about 0.30 MB. The comparison of the parameters is shown in Table 2. Obviously, increasing the sensor node will increase the memory consumption of the device, while the use of DFP system than the SAGE system generated less communication overhead,

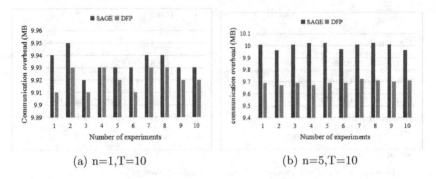

(a) n=1,T=10   (b) n=5,T=10

Fig. 5. Communication overhead

Table 2. DFP vs. SAGE performance comparison

Parameter	SAGE	DFP
Security design	Excellent	Excellent
CO (MB)	9.9/10.0	9.9/9.7
TTD (ms)	424.8/438.2	378.5/382.4

improve data communication efficiency. By the way, the ten experiments in the four graphs have resulted in different data fluctuations because the experimental equipment opens up other system processes that can cause some interference in the experiment, resulting in some error.

Through the above analysis, we can prove that our proposed DFP framework to ensure data security and reduce communication consumption, reduce the average transmission time delay of the superiority.

7   Conclusion

Data security is a matter of concern in the mobile medical field. In this paper, in order to study when mobile devices collect BANS data, how to handle these data security and efficiently, we proposed a data fragment protection (DFP) scheme for mHealth in wireless network. Formal security certification shows that DFP can achieve basic data security privacy protection and achieve data reduction. In addition, through extensive performance evaluation, DFP has proven to be advantageous in terms of average data transmission delays and communication consumption. Our future work will focus on researching more intelligent data segmentation algorithms and reducing data redundancy.

Acknowledgments. This work was supported in part by Major Program of National Natural Science Foundation of China (71633006); The National Natural Science Foundation of China (61672540, 61379057).

References

1. Huang, C.F., Lin, W.C.: Data collection for multiple mobile users in wireless sensor networks. J. Supercomput. **72**(7), 2651–2669 (2016)
2. Kotz, D., Gunter, C.A., Kumar, S., et al.: Privacy and security in mobile health: a research agenda. Computer **49**(6), 22 (2016)
3. Reuben, D.B., Hackbarth, A.S., Wenger, N.S., et al.: An automated approach to identifying patients with dementia using electronic medical records. J. Am. Geriatr. Soc. **65**(3), 658–659 (2017)
4. Zhang, D., Chen, Z., Zhou, H., et al.: Energy-balanced cooperative transmission based on relay selection and power control in energy harvesting wireless sensor network. Comput. Netw. **104**, 189–197 (2016)
5. Zhou, J., Cao, Z., Dong, X., et al.: PPDM: a privacy-preserving protocol for cloud-assisted e-healthcare systems. IEEE J. Sel. Top. Sig. Process. **9**(7), 1332–1344 (2015)
6. Ng, J.W.P., Lo, B.P.L., Wells, O., et al.: Ubiquitous monitoring environment for wearable and implantable sensors (UbiMon). In: International Workshop on Ubiquitous Computing (2004)
7. Schlamp, J., Holz, R., Jacquemart, Q., et al.: HEAP: reliable assessment of BGP hijacking attacks. IEEE J. Sel. Areas Commun. **34**(6), 1849–1861 (2016)
8. Wu, J., Chen, Z.: Data decision and transmission based on mobile data health records on sensor devices in wireless networks. Wirel. Pers. Commun. **90**(4), 2073–2087 (2016)
9. Konstantas, D., Van, H.A., Bults, R., et al.: Mobile patient monitoring: the Mobi-Health system. Conf. Proc. IEEE Eng. Med. Biol. Soc. **103**(5), 1238–1241 (2009)
10. Guo, L., Zhang, C., Sun, J., et al.: A privacy-preserving attribute-based authentication system for mobile health networks. IEEE Trans. Mob. Comput. **13**(9), 1927–1941 (2014)
11. Poulymenopoulou, M., Malamateniou, F., Vassilacopoulos, G.: A virtual PHR authorization system. In: IEEE-EMBS International Conference on Biomedical and Health Informatics, pp. 73–76. IEEE (2014)
12. Harvey, M.J., Harvey, M.G.: Privacy, security issues for mobile health platforms. J. Assoc. Inf. Sci. Technol. **65**, 1305–1318 (2014)
13. Ankarali, Z.E., Abbasi, Q.H., Demir, A.F., et al.: A comparative review on the wireless implantable medical devices privacy and security. In: EAI, International Conference on Wireless Mobile Communication and Healthcare, pp. 246–249. IEEE (2015)
14. Spachos, P., Toumpakaris, D., Hatzinakos, D.: Angle-based dynamic routing scheme for source location privacy in wireless sensor networks. In: Vehicular Technology Conference, pp. 1–5. IEEE (2014)
15. Lu, R., Liang, X., Li, X., et al.: EPPA: an efficient and privacy-preserving aggregation scheme for secure smart grid communications. IEEE Trans. Parallel Distrib. Syst. **23**(9), 1621–1631 (2012)
16. Sharma, A., Baweja, P.: Medical identity theft: a case report. Ann. Internal Med. **166**(5), 380 (2017)
17. Hambidge, S.J., Ross, C., Shoup, J.A., et al.: Integration of data from a safety net health care system into the vaccine safety datalink. Vaccine **35**(9), 1329–1334 (2017)
18. Mare, S., Sorber, J., Shin, M., et al.: Hide-n-Sense: preserving privacy efficiently in wireless mHealth. Mob. Netw. Appl. **19**(3), 331–344 (2014)

19. Lin, X., Lu, R., Shen, X., et al.: Sage: a strong privacy-preserving scheme against global eavesdropping for ehealth systems. IEEE J. Sel. Areas Commun. **27**(4), 365–378 (2009)
20. Zhang, Y., Chen, Q., Zhong, S.: Privacy-preserving data aggregation in mobile phone sensing. IEEE Trans. Inf. Forensics Secur. **11**(5), 980–992 (2016)
21. Zhang, Z., Wang, H., Lin, X., et al.: Effective epidemic control and source tracing through mobile social sensing over WBANs. In: 2013 Proceedings of IEEE INFOCOM, pp. 300–304. IEEE (2013)

A Greedy Heuristic Based on Corner Occupying Action for the 2D Circular Bin Packing Problem

Kun He[1,3] and Mohammed Dosh[1,2(✉)]

[1] School of Computer Science and Technology,
Huazhong University of Science and Technology, Wuhan 430074, China
i201522007@hust.edu.cn
[2] Faculty of Education for Girls, Kufa University, Najaf, Iraq
[3] Shenzhen Research Institute, Huazhong University of Science and Technology,
Shenzhen 518057, China

Abstract. The paper proposes a new two-dimensional circular bin packing problem (2D-CBPP) that is closely related to the well-known 2D rectangular bin packing problem and the single container circle packing problem. Inspired by Gold corner, silver side and strawy void for Chinese Go game, a greedy algorithm based on corner occupying action (GACOA) is proposed for solving the 2D-CBPP. We define the corner occupying action to pack the outside circles into a bin as compactly as possible, such that the number of used bins is minimized. As there are no existing benchmarks for this proposed problem, we generate two sets of benchmark instances with equal and unequal circles respectively. Experimental results show that the proposed algorithm performs quite well on these 2D-CBPP instances.

Keywords: Circular bin packing · Corner occupying · Heuristic · Greedy algorithm

1 Introduction

Given a set of n circular items with integer radii $r_1, r_2, \ldots, r_n$ and n identical rectangular bins with integer side lengths L and W. Without loss of generality, assume each single item can be packed into the bin. The two-dimensional circular bin packing problem (2D-CBPP) is to allocate all the circular items to a minimum number of bins without overlapping. The 2D-CBPP problem is a new variant of two-dimensional geometric bin packing problem, as in the classic 2D Bin Packing Problem the container and items are of rectangles. The 2D-CBPP can find wide applications in cutting stock, pallet packing, scheduling, logistics and resource allocation problems, etc. According to the typology proposed by Wscher, Hauner, and Schumann [1], the 2D-CBPP can be classified as a two-dimensional single-bin-size bin packing problem with the refinement that the items are circles.

The 2D-CBPP problem is closely related to an extensively studied problem in the family of bin packing, the 2D rectangular bin packing problem (2D-RBPP).

© Springer Nature Singapore Pte Ltd. 2017
D. Du et al. (Eds.): NCTCS 2017, CCIS 768, pp. 75–85, 2017.
https://doi.org/10.1007/978-981-10-6893-5_6

The 2D-RBPP aims to pack a set of rectangular items into a minimum number of identical rectangular bins, usually unit size squares [2,3]. A wide range of meta-heuristics are proposed for solving the 2D-RBPP, including a tabu search [4], a guided local search [5], a hybrid GRASP/VND approach [6], and various heuristics based on greedy heuristics [6–8]. Moreover, Christensen et al. [2] present ten major open problems, which are related to the multidimensional bin packing. On the other hand, the 2D-CBPP is an important extension of the 2D Circle Packing Problem (2D-CPP). The 2D-CPP is to pack all circular items into a single container of circular or square shape such that the size of the container is minimized [9–11]. The 2D-CPP is also well studied, and variants include packing circular items in different types of containers [12] and CPP with equilibrium constraints [13,14].

This paper introduces a 2D Circular Bin Packing problem. To the best of our knowledge, this is the first case to address this type of the geometric bin packing problem. We then propose a greedy algorithm based on the corner occupying action (GACOA) for solving the 2D-CBPP. The main idea is inspired by an old adage "Gold corner, silver side and strawy void" for playing Chinese Go game, which has been successfully applied for the rectangular packing problem [15–17]. The proposed GACOA always lets the circular item occupy a corner in order to pack the items as compactly as possible, such that the bins can be fully utilized and the number of used bins is minimized. Experiments are conducted on two sets of benchmark instances that include equal circular items and unequal circular items respectively, generated using the best-known results downloaded from the packomania website for single container circle packing problem (CPP) [18]. Computational results show that the proposed GACOA performs quite well for these instances.

The rest of this paper is organized as follows. Section 2 gives the problem definition of the 2D-CBPP. Section 3 describes the proposed GACOA algorithm, and Sect. 4 provides the computational results. Conclusion is presented in the end.

2   Problem Formulation

We introduce a formal definition for the two-dimensional circular bin packing problem (2D-CBPP). For most common case, here we consider identical square bins. However, note that the problem definition and the proposed approach can be easily extended for rectangular bins.

Assume we have n square bins with equal side length L. Let $\mathcal{C} = \{C_i \mid 1 \leq i \leq n\}$ be the set of n circular items with integer radii $r_1, r_2, \ldots, r_n (r_i \geq r_{i+1})$. Without loss of generality, assume the size of each item is no greater than the size of the bin, i.e., $L \geq 2max\{r_i \mid 1 \leq i \leq n\}$. We are asked to find a number of bins $K(K \leq n)$ and a K-partition $S_1 \cup S_2 \cup \cdots \cup S_K$ of the items such that all items in each set $S_k(1 \leq k \leq K)$ can be packed completely in bin B_k without overlapping.

Let X_{ik} be the indicator on whether item i is packed in bin B_k, and Y_k be the indicator on whether bin B_k is used. Let the centre of the kth bin be located at $(0, 0, k)$ in a three-dimensional Cartesian coordinate system, and (x_i, y_i, k)

be the centre coordinate of circle $C_i(1 \leq i \leq n)$ if $X_{ik} = 1$. A mathematical formulation of the 2D-CBPP is as follows:

$$\min K = \sum_{k=1}^{n} Y_k$$

s.t. (1) $\sum_{k=1}^{n} X_{ik} = 1, i \in \{1, \ldots, n\}$.

(2) $Y_k = \begin{cases} 1 \text{ if } \sum_{k=1}^{n} X_{ik} > 0 \\ 0 \text{ otherwise.} \end{cases} \quad k \in \{1, \ldots, n\}$

(3) $max(|x_i| + r_i, |y_i| + r_i) \leq 0.5L, i \in \{1, \ldots, n\}$.

(4) $D_{ij} = \sqrt{(x_i - x_j)^2 + (y_i - y_j)^2} \geq (r_i + r_j), for X_{ik} = X_{jk} = 1,$
$$i, j \in \{1, \ldots, n\}, i \neq j, k \in \{1, \ldots, n\}.$$

(5) $X_{ik} \in \{0, 1\}, i \in \{1, \ldots, n\}, k \in \{1, \ldots, n\}$.

Constraint (1) indicates that each circular item C_i should be packed into exactly one bin, and (2) assigns 1 to Y_k if there are some items packed in the kth bin. Constraint (3) imposes that any item should not extrude the bin's boundary, and (4) imposes no overlap between any pair-wise circles packed in the same bin. Figure 1 provides an illustration for constraints (3) and (4) inside a container.

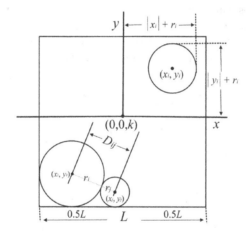

Fig. 1. The illustration of constraints (3) and (4).

3 A Greedy Algorithm Based on Corner Occupying Action

We first introduce some definitions before presenting the proposed algorithm. The most important definition is the corner occupying action, which is defined to pack the circular items from the margin of the bin to the center space and make the items as compactly as possible.

3.1 Definitions

Definition 1 (Packing Action). *It is an action that places an outside circular item into a bin so that it satisfies the constraints. The current circle being placed is called the action circle.*

Definition 2 (Corner Occupying Action). *A corner occupying action (COA) is a packing action that places a circle so that this circle is tangent to any two packed items (each side of the bin can be regarded as a special item).*

The concept of COA is borrowed from He et. al's work for rectangular packing [15,16]. Here a COA includes two aspects: which circle to be packed and which two packed circles to be tangent.

Definition 3 (Quality d_i of a COA). q_i *is the distance between the circle item to be packed and the borders of the bin, which is given by* $q_i = \{min(d_x, d_y), max(d_x, d_y)\}$. d_x *is a distance between the center point of the circle and the closer side of the bin in the horizontal direction, and d_y is a distance between the center point of the circle and the closer side of the bin in the vertical direction.*

The two distances can be compared in lexicographical order. The smaller the distance d_i is, the better a COA is. Since an action with the smaller distance packs the circle closer to the sides of the bins as well as to other packed circle items. Two COAs are shown in Fig. 2, and COA_1 is better than COA_2.

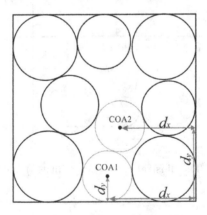

Fig. 2. The distances of two COAs.

3.2 The GACOA Algorithm

The proposed greedy algorithm based on COA is a constructive approach, which can rapidly generate a solution for the 2D-CBPP. It always selects a corner occupying action with the smallest distance at each iteration step. This packing step shows the evolution of the process, and at each step an outside circle is packed into one bin. Moreover, the packing process shows the circles are packed from the border of the bin to center of the bin.

The details of the GACOA algorithm are given in Algorithm 1. The GACOA packs the circular items into the bins one by one. For the current circle to be packed, we first find all the COAs of the first bin ($k = 1$) that do not violate the problem constraints (lines 3–6). If there is no available COA, we turn to the next bin ($k = k + 1$) to continue searching the COAs until at least one available COA is attained (lines 8–13). Then, we choose a best COA whose distance is the smallest and then execute the current COA. Hereby, one circle is packed into a bin (lines 14, 15). Repeat the above procedure until all circular items have been packed into the bins without overlapping and output the number of used bins as well as the occupying rate of each bin. One can easily observe that the GACOA intends to greedily pack the items to a bin as compactly as possible, such that the bins can be maximally utilized and the number of used bins is minimized.

Algorithm 1. GACOA algorithm.

---

input : The bin's side length L, n circles, a set of unpacked circles
$\{C_i \mid 1 \leq i \leq n\}$ with integer radii $r_1, r_2, \ldots, r_n (r_i \geq r_{i+1})$.
output: The total number K of used bins and the occupying rate of each bin.

1 $K = 1$;   ▷ /*The number of used bins */
2 **for** $i = 1$ to n ▷ /*The ith circle item to be packed */ **do**
3   **for** $k = 1$ to K **do**
4          $S = \phi$;   ▷ /*A set of COAs, initialized by ϕ */
5   **repeat**
6   Find a set S of all the feasible COAs in the kth bin;
7   ▷ /*Move to the next if there is no feasible COA in the current bin */
8   **if** $S = \phi$ **then**
9                  $k = k + 1$;
10   **if** $k > K$ **then**
11                     $K = k$;
12   **end**
13   **end**
14   **until** $(S \neq \phi)$;
15   A best COA from S is selected according to the distance d_i;
16   Execute this COA to pack the ith circle into the kth bin;
17   **end**
18 **end**
19 *Return K and the occupying rate of each bin.*

---

4   Computational results

To evaluate the performance of the proposed algorithm, we implemented the GACOA using Visual C++ and Matlab programming language. Experimental computation was employed on a personal computer with a 3.0 GHz CPU and 4.0 GB memory.

Since the 2D-CBPP problem is first addressed in the paper, there is no benchmark in the literature. As there are well-known benchmarks for the 2D-CPP which is to pack all circular items into a square container such that the container size is minimized [9], we first generate the 2D-CBPP instances using the 2D-CPP instances downloaded from the packomania website [18]. There are two sets of benchmark instances for the 2D-CPP, considering equal circular items and unequal circular items respectively. We select several instances for each set of 2D-CPP, use their current best results to fix the size of the square bin for each 2D-CBPP instance. Then for each item of the 2D-CPP instance, we get a random number, in {2, 3, 4, 5}, of copies for the items of the corresponding 2D-CBPP instance.

We generate three CBPP instances on each of the selected 2D-CPP instance and get 33×2 benchmark instances. As shown in Tables 1 and 2, n_0 is the number of items for 2D-CPP and n is the number of items for the generated 2D-CBPP instance. We run GACOA on each of the 2D-CBPP instances, and Tables 1 and 2 list the computational results for unequal and equal circles respectively. The third column presents the number of used bin K by GACOA. And columns 4–8 present the occupying rate of each used bin. Furthermore, in Fig. 3, we give a graphical display on two typical instances.

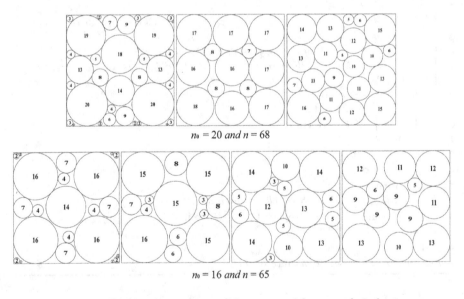

$n_0 = 20$ *and* $n = 68$

$n_0 = 16$ *and* $n = 65$

Fig. 3. Packing layouts on two instances with unequal circles.

Table 1. Computational results of GACOA on benchmarks with unequal circles.

n_0	n	K	Occupying rate of				
			bin1	bin2	bin3	bin4	bin5
10	35	3	0.819	0.780	0.760	——	——
	36	4	0.807	0.730	0.781	0.405	——
	49	5	0.845	0.783	0.780	0.734	0.721
11	41	3	0.824	0.797	0.720	——	——
	41	4	0.821	0.739	0.691	0.748	——
	53	5	0.824	0.767	0.731	0.723	0.767
12	43	3	0.834	0.791	0.782	——	——
	50	4	0.839	0.796	0.748	0.769	——
	59	5	0.839	0.769	0.774	0.716	0.748
13	43	3	0.823	0.791	0.782	——	——
	52	4	0.830	0.794	0.730	0.774	——
	64	5	0.830	0.820	0.791	0.758	0.732
14	51	3	0.851	0.805	0.771	——	——
	57	4	0.845	0.812	0.765	0.739	——
	67	5	0.858	0.799	0.781	0.710	0.736
15	57	3	0.836	0.812	0.758	——	——
	62	4	0.853	0.827	0.745	0.737	——
	73	5	0.854	0.816	0.800	0.619	0.721
16	55	3	0.856	0.818	0.795	——	——
	65	4	0.838	0.808	0.815	0.755	——
	77	5	0.840	0.819	0.800	0.719	0.773
17	55	3	0.829	0.811	0.760	——	——
	75	5	0.848	0.806	0.766	0.767	0.344
	78	5	0.848	0.819	0.817	0.757	0.736
18	62	3	0.851	0.803	0.790	——	——
	71	4	0.851	0.797	0.764	0.569	——
	76	4	0.856	0.789	0.772	0.697	——
19	61	3	0.892	0.828	0.808	——	——
	63	3	0.852	0.806	0.797	——	——
	91	5	0.898	0.832	0.810	0.798	0.766
20	68	3	0.871	0.820	0.788	——	——
	81	4	0.862	0.836	0.790	0.750	——
	97	5	0.856	0.813	0.773	0.766	0.742

Table 2. Computational results of GACOA on benchmarks with equal circles.

n_0	n	K	Occupying rate of				
			bin1	bin2	bin3	bin4	bin5
5	17	4	0.673	0.673	0.673	0.269	——
	19	4	0.673	0.673	0.673	0.539	——
	23	5	0.673	0.673	0.673	0.673	0.404
8	20	3	0.731	0.731	0.365	——	——
	23	3	0.731	0.731	0.639	——	——
	36	5	0.731	0.731	0.731	0.731	0.365
9	34	4	0.785	0.785	0.785	0.639	——
	36	4	0.785	0.785	0.785	0.785	——
	41	5	0.785	0.785	0.785	0.785	0.785
10	26	3	0.621	0.621	0.552	——	——
	35	4	0.621	0.621	0.621	0.552	——
	45	5	0.621	0.621	0.621	0.621	0.621
11	37	4	0.637	0.637	0.637	0.446	——
	40	4	0.637	0.637	0.637	0.637	——
	48	5	0.637	0.637	0.637	0.637	0.509
12	33	3	0.677	0.677	0.677	——	——
	40	4	0.677	0.677	0.677	0.431	——
	55	5	0.677	0.677	0.677	0.677	0.677
13	35	3	0.676	0.676	0.620	——	
	50	5	0.676	0.676	0.676	0.676	0.133
	58	5	0.676	0.676	0.676	0.676	0.564
14	39	3	0.683	0.683	0.683	——	——
	47	4	0.683	0.683	0.683	0.420	——
	51	4	0.683	0.683	0.683	0.630	——
15	44	3	0.762	0.762	0.711	——	——
	64	5	0.762	0.762	0.762	0.762	0.203
	73	5	0.762	0.762	0.762	0.762	0.660
16	47	3	0.785	0.785	0.736	——	——
	59	4	0.785	0.785	0.785	0.540	——
	77	5	0.785	0.785	0.785	0.785	0.638
17	58	4	0.690	0.690	0.690	0.431	——
	63	4	0.690	0.690	0.690	0.647	——
	76	5	0.690	0.690	0.690	0.690	0.518

To further compare the current best results on CPP and our results on CBPP in order to evaluate the proposed algorithm. We select three instances in the set of equal and unequal CPP respectively ($n = 8$, 9 and 10), and we still use the best results downloaded from the Packomania website [18] to set the bin size, but this time we generate one CBPP instance using each CPP instance by fixing the copy number to 5 for each item. Table 3 summarizes the current best results for 2D-CPP which are obtained by different researchers and the results of GACOA on 2D-CBPP. The first column is the number of circles in the original 2D-CPP, the second column is R_0 representing the occupying rate of Packomania website. Columns from 3–8 represent the occupying rate of each used bin of GACOA,

Table 3. Computational results for GACOA on benchmarks with 5 fixed copies of the circles (sampled on $n = 8$, 9, 10 and $m = 5$). R_0 denotes the best result of 2D-CPP on the Packomania website, listed as a reference. R_1 to R_6 correspond to the occupying rate of bin1 to bin6 for 2D-CBPP.

(a) Unequal circle instances						
n	R_0	R_1	R_2	R_3	R_4	R_5	R_6
8	0.756	0.834	0.741	0.712	0.760	0.734	——
9	0.785	0.785	0.717	0.752	0.750	0.717	0.207
10	0.812	0.835	0.783	0.795	0.747	0.719	0.181
(b) Equal circle instances						
n	R_0	R_1	R_2	R_3	R_4	R_5	R_6
8	0.730	0.730	0.730	0.730	0.730	0.730	——
9	0.785	0.785	0.785	0.785	0.785	0.785	——
10	0.690	0.621	0.621	0.621	0.621	0.621	0.345

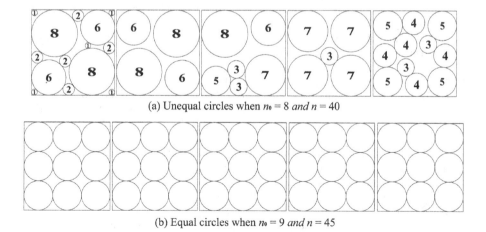

(a) Unequal circles when $n_0 = 8$ *and* $n = 40$

(b) Equal circles when $n_0 = 9$ *and* $n = 45$

Fig. 4. Packing layouts on two instances by fixing the copies of items to 5.

denoted by R_1 to R_6, respectively. As the number of items are copied 5 times for each item of the CPP instance, we know a current best solution for these instances should be of using 5 bins by copy the solution of the current best 2D-CPP algorithm 5 times. We see that GACOA is very competitive by yielding the current possible best solutions on three of the six instances.

With the new results of the instances, several of the new forms can seen in Fig. 4. Note that the layouts for the unequal circle items are different from the possible best results of simply copying the best solution of the corresponding 2D-CPP.

5   Conclusion

We addressed a new two-dimensional Circular Bin Packing problem (2D-CBPP) and proposed a greedy algorithm based on corner occupying action (GACOA). The proposed GACOA always employs the corner occupying action with the smallest distance and greedily packs the outside circles into the bins one by one in order to minimize the number of used bins. To evaluate the proposed algorithm, we provide four sets of benchmark instances with equal and unequal circles respectively. Experimental results on these instances showed that the proposed algorithm performs quite well. In future work, we would like to improve the current COA base approach considering sophisticated rules.

Acknowledgements. This work is supported by the National Natural Science Foundation of China (Grant No. 61472147, 61602196 and 61373016) and Shenzhen Science and Technology Planning Project (JCYJ20170307154749425).

References

1. Wscher, G., Hauner, H., Schumann, H.: An improved typology of cutting and packing problems. Eur. J. Oper. Res. **183**(3), 1109–30 (2007)
2. Christensen, H.I., Khan, A., Pokutta, S., Tetali, P.: Approximation and online algorithms for multidimensional bin packing: a survey. Comput. Sci. Rev. **24**, 63–79 (2017)
3. Wei, L., Oon, W.C., Zhu, W., Lim, A.: A skyline heuristic for the 2D rectangular packing and strip packing problems. Eur. J. Oper. Res. **215**(2), 337–46 (2011)
4. Lodi, A., Martello, S., Vigo, D.: Heuristic and metaheuristic approaches for a class of two-dimensional bin packing problems. INFORMS J. Comput. **11**(4), 345–357 (1999)
5. Faroe, O., Pisinger, D., Zachariasen, M.: Guided local search for the three-dimensional bin-packing problem. INFORMS J. Comput. **15**(3), 267–283 (2003)
6. Parreo, F., Alvarez-Valds, R., Oliveira, J.F., Tamarit, J.M.: A hybrid GRASP/VND algorithm for two-and three-dimensional bin packing. Annal. Oper. Res. **179**(1), 203–220 (2010)
7. Lodi, A., Martello, S., Monaci, M.: Two-dimensional packing problems: A survey. Eur. J. Oper. Res. **141**(2), 241–252 (2002)
8. Monaci, M., Toth, P.: A set-covering-based heuristic approach for bin-packing problems. INFORMS J. Comput. **18**(1), 71–85 (2006)

9. He, K., Huang, M., Yang, C.: An action-space-based global optimization algorithm for packing circles into a square container. Comput. Oper. Res. **30**(58), 67–74 (2015)
10. Lpez, C.O., Beasley, J.E.: Packing unequal circles using formulation space search. Comput. Oper. Res. **40**(5), 1276–1288 (2013)
11. Lpez, C.O., Beasley, J.E.: A formulation space search heuristic for packing unequal circles in a fixed size circular container. Eur. J. Oper. Res. **251**(1), 64–73 (2016)
12. Hifi, M., M'hallah, R.: A literature review on circle and sphere packing problems: models and methodologies. Adv. Oper. Res. **2009**, 22 (2009)
13. He, K., Mo, D., Ye, T., Huang, W.: A coarse-to-fine quasi-physical optimization method for solving the circle packing problem with equilibrium constraints. Comput. Indus. Eng. **66**(4), 1049–60 (2013)
14. Liu, J., Li, G., Chen, D., Liu, W., Wang, Y.: Two-dimensional equilibrium constraint layout using simulated annealing. Comput. Indus. Eng. **59**(4), 530–6 (2010)
15. Huang, W.Q., Li, Y., Jurkowiak, B., Li, C.M., Xu, R.C.: A two-level search strategy for packing unequal circles into a circle container. In: Rossi, F. (ed.) CP 2003. LNCS, vol. 2833, pp. 868–872. Springer, Heidelberg (2003). doi:10.1007/978-3-540-45193-8_69
16. He, K., Huang, W.: An efficient placement heuristic for three-dimensional rectangular packing. Comput. Oper. Res. **38**(1), 227–33 (2011)
17. He, K., Huang, W., Jin, Y.: An efficient deterministic heuristic for two-dimensional rectangular packing. Comput. Oper. Res. **39**(7), 1355–63 (2012)
18. Specht, E.: Packomania website 2017. www.packomania.com

Efficient Forwarding Strategy for Opportunistic Network Based on Node Similarity

Yucheng Lin, Zhigang Chen[(✉)], and Jia Wu

School of Software, Central South University, Changsha 410083, China
czg@csu.edu.cn

Abstract. In opportunistic network, it is a key problem to choose proper neighbors for forwarding messages. To avoid the low deliver ratio of transmission caused by node movement, dynamic change of network topology and other factors, a data forwarding algorithm——Efficient Forwarding Strategy for Opportunistic Network Based on Node Similarity(EFSNS) was proposed from the perspective of combining social network with opportunistic network. In the study, it is adopted the edit distance of data packets between nodes to calculate the social similarity, and then selects the appropriate neighbors according to the similarity to obtain one or more reliable communication paths. The experimental results show that the proposed algorithm outperforms typical routing algorithms in terms of the deliver ratio, delivery delay and routing overhead.

Keywords: Opportunistic network · Social network · Edit distance · Similarity · Routing algorithm

1 Introduction

Opportunistic network [1] is derived from delay tolerant network and mobile ad hoc network [2], which can be seen as a subclass of both. In opportunistic network, there is scarcely a end-to-end path between the source and destination [3], and the communication has to rely on the story-carry-forward paradigm [4]. Due to the limitations of application characteristics, environment, cost and other factors, the traditional wireless network [5] can not be established in many applications, and opportunistic network can meet especial requirements [6] owing to the fact that its inherent characteristics. The typical applications of opportunistic network are as follows: data collection for disconnected wireless sensor network [7], the network communication in remote areas [8], vehicular network [9], emergency evacuation and recovery [10], etc.

Figure 1 is a schematic diagram of opportunistic network, we assume that the source S is to send a message to the destination D. At time t_1, there is no connected path between node S and node D, hence the node S sends the message to the neighbor node 2. Since the node 2 does not have a appropriate next-hop for data transmission, it stores the message locally and waits for an opportunity

© Springer Nature Singapore Pte Ltd. 2017
D. Du et al. (Eds.): NCTCS 2017, CCIS 768, pp. 86–100, 2017.
https://doi.org/10.1007/978-981-10-6893-5_7

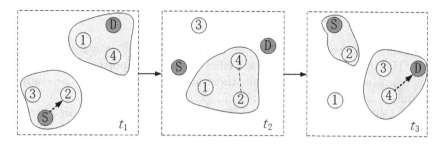

Fig. 1. Schematic diagram

to transmit. At time t_2, node 2 meets node 4 and forwards the message to node 4. Finally, node 4 meets the destination D and forwards the message to node D at time t_3.

The establishment of opportunistic network is flexible [11], but the routing algorithms of traditional wireless network can not adapt to the changes of network topology caused by node movement. Therefore, it is one of the key problems in the research of opportunistic network to select appropriate neighbor nodes and make the information can be delivered to the destination in a shorter delay. At present, a variety of solutions have been proposed for routing algorithm in opportunistic network, including prior knowledge, predictive routing based on mobile models and soon on. However, due to the intermittent connection of wireless network and the unreliability of the node itself, there are still many problems, such as the low deliver ratio and the lack of the purpose of transmission.

In the actual application scenario, the mobility of mobile users heavily depends on their social characteristics such as carriers' social relations and behaviors [12]. Compared with the frequent mobility of nodes and the continuous change of network topology, the social relationships of human beings are relatively stable [13], which is more suitable for the dynamic change of opportunistic network [14].

Through the analysis of the above problems, we propose a routing algorithm (Efficient Forwarding Strategy for Opportunistic Network Based on Node Similarity, EFSNS) based on the social similarity between nodes from the point of view of the combination of opportunistic network and social network, and the data packets carried by nodes are the key to measure the similarity. Firstly, we will compute the edit distance of the data packets between nodes, and then calculate the similarity based on the edit distance. When the similarity between two nodes is high, it shows that the two nodes have relatively close social relations in the network. By comparing the similarity between nodes to obtain one or more effective and reliable paths, it is more likely to forward the message to the communication area of destination to complete information transmission.

The rest of the paper is organized as follows. Section 2 explains the related work and Sect. 3 describes the proposed routing algorithm in detail. In Sect. 4, we present the simulation results. Finally, we conclude the paper in Sect. 5.

2　Related Work

In opportunistic network, the use of "storage-carry-forward" way for data transmission. How to transmit information efficiently is an important research field in opportunistic network. At present, there are some methods for the study of opportunistic network routing algorithm.

Direct Delivery algorithm [15] and First Content algorithm [16] are based on the forwarding strategy, the node does not copy the data packet in the forwarding process, there is only one copy of the data packet in the entire network. The difference is that the Direct Delivery algorithm is the source forwards the data packet to the destination only when the destination is encountered, and the First Content algorithm is that the source forwards the data packet when it encounters the first forwardable node. This kind of routing algorithm has the least network overhead, but the delivery delay is relatively large and the deliver ratio is extremely low.

Li et al. Proposed the Epidemic algorithm in the literature [17]. The core idea of the algorithm is that each node in the network maintains a message queue, and nodes exchange message queues with each other when they meet. Through the message queue to confirm the lack of datas in the other side of the cache, the two sides to exchange datas missing with each other. The advantage of this method is that it can maximize the deliver ratio and reduce the transmission delay. The main disadvantage is that there are a large number of copies of data packets in the network, which will consume a large amount of network resources.

Huang et al. In the literature [18] proposed Spary and Wait algorithm, the algorithm is divided into two stages, Spray stage and Wait stage. In the Spray phase, the source injects a certain number of copies of each data packet into the network, and then enters the Wait phase. If the destination does not receive the data packet during the Spray phase, then the node carrying the copy of the data packet transmits the data to the destination through the Direct Delivery algorithm. This strategy effectively controls the number of copies of data packets in the network and reduces the routing overhead.

Gibran proposed the PRoPHET algorithm based on probabilistic strategy in literature [19], which defines a value to describe the success of transmission between nodes. The nodes update their transmission prediction values when the two nodes meet, and then according to the value to decide whether to transmit the data. In the community model scenario, the PRoPHET algorithm performs better than the Epidemic algorithm [20].

Literature [21] proposed the SRBet routing algorithm. The algorithm uses the temporal evolution graph model to accurately capture the dynamic topology of the opportunistic network. Then, according to the historical contact records of the nodes, the social relations based on the intermediary centrality measure are proposed to ensure that the messages are forwarded through nodes with stronger social relations.

In this paper, we analyze the characteristics of node forwarding data from the angle of integrating opportunistic network and social network, and introduce a new routing algorithm different from all above studies. And we detail the design process of the algorithm in the next section.

3   Routing Algorithm Based on Similarity Between Nodes

3.1   Opportunistic Network Topology

According to the characteristics of opportunistic network, a subnet is selected randomly as the research object. In a certain period T, assuming that the subnet contains a set of nodes, $V = \{A, B, C, D, E, F, G, H, I, G, K, L\}$, a total of 12 nodes, and all nodes as relay nodes to carry and forward the message. The subnet topology shown in Fig. 2.

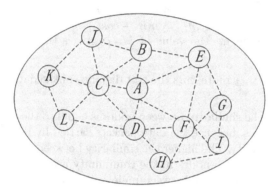

Fig. 2. Subnet topology

Assuming that node A needs to send information at the current time and the transfer speed of the information between the nodes is greater than the relative movement speed of nodes, that is, when the information is delivered in the subnet at the current time, the network topology of the subnet does not change in nature, there will be no nodes leave or come in. At this point, it is necessary to select the nodes with higher efficiency in the neighbor nodes to transmit information.

The nodes have a certain sociality in practical scenarios, compared with the frequently changing network topology, the social relations between nodes are relatively stable and reliable, and can be better adapt to the dynamic changes of the network. The EFSNS algorithm proposed in this paper selects the neighbor nodes in the subnet topology through the social similarity between nodes, and the similarity is calculated by the edit distance of the data packets.

3.2 Edit Distance Between Data Packets and Similarity Between Nodes

Edit distance(Dis). It is a way of quantifying how dissimilar two strings are to one another by counting the minimum number of operations required to transform one string into the other. Permitted editing operations include substituting a character with another character, inserting a character, and deleting a character. Assuming the string a of length m and the string b of length n, the edit distance of a and b is calculated as follows.

- Initialise: Create a matrix of $m + 1$ rows and $n + 1$ columns, M, where the first line is written with $0 - m$ and the first column is written with $0 - n$.
- Assignment: Assign a value to each element of the matrix, $M_{ij}(1 \leq i \leq m + 1, 1 \leq j \leq n + 1)$. If a_i is equal to b_j, then set the *cost* to 0 otherwise 1. Compare the value of the elements $M_{i,j-1}$, $M_{i-1,j}$, and $M_{i-1,j-1}$, and take the minimum(min) of the three. If the min is $M_{i,j-1}$ or $M_{i-1,j}$, set the $M_{i,j} = min + 1$, otherwise $M_{i,j} = min + cost$.
- Followed by assignment, the value of $M_{m+1,n+1}$ is the edit distance of the two strings.

In this paper, the $Dis_{a,b}$ represents the edit distance of the data packets of node a and node b.

Similarity(Sim). The similarity between nodes is equal to the similarity of data packets between nodes, because the data packets carried by nodes are the index to measure their sociality. The higher the similarity between nodes indicates that the relationships of the two nodes in the community are more closely. Sim_{ab} is used to represent the similarity between node a and node b, and the formula of similarity as shown in.

$$Sim_{ab} = 1 - Dis_{ab}/MaxLength(a,b) \tag{1}$$

$MaxLength(a, b)$ represents the maximum length of data packets of node a and node b.

Lower threshold(α). When the similarity between a node and its neighbor node is greater than the lower threshold α, the neighbor is considered as one of the candidates for the next-hop. If the similarity between a node and all its neighbors is less than the lower threshold α, the neighbor node with the highest similarity is selected to transmit the information. When the node traverses all neighbor nodes, it is probable to get multiple paths, which can effectively improve the deliver ratio.

Upper threshold(β). The upper threshold β is used to control the number of next-hop, to avoid excessive copies of the message in the network. If a node has multiple candidate nodes, it is necessary to calculate the similarity between the candidate nodes. If the similarity between two candidate nodes is greater than the upper threshold β, the candidate node with smaller similarity to the current node is discarded, and the larger one is reserved as the subnode of the current node. By defining the upper threshold β, the routing overhead can be effectively controlled while the deliver ratio is guaranteed.

3.3   The Traversal Process of Node

Each node in the network maintains a buffer to store the data packets that need to be forwarded by this node. Assuming that the data packets for each node in the set V are shown in Table 1.

Table 1. Data packets

Node	Data packet	Node	Data packet
A	a, b, c, d, e	G	h, g, n, o
B	e, f, c, h, i, k	H	c, f, y, j
C	a, c, d, e, g	I	j, k, m, e, y, n
D	a, d, e, g	J	m, i, d, f, h
E	m, p, q, d	K	g, k, c, n
F	k, i, c, d	L	h, y x, m, d, q

The node traversal process based on the subnet topology of Fig. 2 as follows.

(1) Initialize a tree T, insert node A that is currently sending the message into T as the root node. Create a set U_A to store the neighbor nodes of node A, $U_A = \{B, C, D, E, F\}$, and use the breadth-first search loop to traverse the neighbor nodes in U_A, as shown in the Fig. 3.

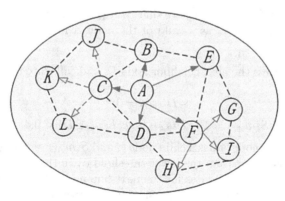

——▶ Node A loops through its neighbor nodes

---▷ Node C loops through its neighbor nodes

——▷ Node F loops through its neighbor nodes

Fig. 3. The traversal process

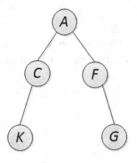

Fig. 4. The structure of the tree T   **Fig. 5.** Transmission paths

(2) Begin to access the neighbor node B of the current node A, and calculate
the edit distance and similarity between the data packets of node A and
node B.

$$Dis_{AB} = 5 \tag{2}$$

$$Sim_{AB} = 1 - Dis_{AB}/maxLen(A, B) = 0.17 \tag{3}$$

Since the current node A has no child nodes, the node B is inserted into the
tree T as a child of the node A.

(3) Continue to access the next neighbor C of node A, and calculate the edit
distance and similarity between of the data packets of node A and node C.

$$Dis_{AC} = 2 \tag{4}$$

$$Sim_{AC} = 1 - Dis_{AC}/maxLen(A, C) = 0.6 \tag{5}$$

Since $Sim_{AB} < Sim_{AC}$, postulate that Sim_{AB} is less than the lower threshold α, insert the node C as a child of the node A in the tree T and delete
the node B.

(4) Continue to access the next neighbor node D, and calculate the edit distance
and similarity.

$$Dis_{AD} = 3 \tag{6}$$

$$Sim_{AD} = 1 - Dis_{AD}/maxLen(A, D) = 0.4 \tag{7}$$

Since the current node A has a child node C and $Sim_{AC} > Sim_{AD}$, postulate
that Sim_{AD} is grater than the lower threshold α. In this case, the neighbor
nodes C and D are candidates for the next-hop node of the current node A,
and calculate the edit distance and similarity between node C and node D.

$$Dis_{CD} = 1 \tag{8}$$

$$Sim_{CD} = 1 - Dis_{CD}/maxLen(C, D) = 0.8 \tag{9}$$

Postulate that $Sim_{CD} > \beta$, according to $Sim_{AC} > Sim_{AD}$, therefore, node
D will be abandoned and the node C is reserved. At this point, the structure
of tree T remains unchanged and continues to access the next neighbor node.

(5) Access the neighbor node E, and calculate the edit distance and similarity.

$$Dis_{AE} = 4 \tag{10}$$

$$Sim_{AE} = 1 - Dis_{AE}/maxLen(A, E) = 0.2 \tag{11}$$

Since $Sim_{AE} < Sim_{AC}$, and postulate that $Sim_{AE} < \alpha$, then the node E is discarded and the structure of tree T remains unchanged.

(6) Continue to access the last neighbor F of the node A, and calculate the edit distance and similarity.

$$Dis_{AF} = 3 \tag{12}$$

$$Sim_{AF} = 1 - Dis_{AF}/maxLen(A, F) = 0.4 \tag{13}$$

Since the current node A has a child node C and $Sim_{AC} > Sim_{AF}$. Postulate that $Sim_{AF} > \alpha$, and then calculate the edit distance and similarity between node C and node F.

$$Dis_{CF} = 4 \tag{14}$$

$$Sim_{CF} = 1 - Dis_{CF}/maxLen(C, F) = 0.2 \tag{15}$$

Postulate that $Sim_{CF} < \beta$, then the node C is reserved and the node F is inserted into the tree T as another child node of the node A. At this point, the structure of the tree T is root node A and its two child nodes C and F.

(7) At present, all neighbor nodes of the current node A have traversed. According to the tree T obtained in step (6), a subnode C of the node A is selected as the current node. Create a set U_C to store the neighbor nodes of node C, $U_C = \{A, B, D, J, K, L\}$, and remove the intersection with the set U_A, $U_C = U_C - U_A$, get $U_C = \{J, K, L\}$. The neighbor nodes J, K, and L of the node C are sequentially accessed according to the above steps, as shown in the Fig. 3. When the all neighbor nodes of the node C in the set U_C are accessed, then get the next-hop node K of node C, and insert node K into the tree T as a child node of node C.

(8) Selects another subnode F of node A as the current node according to the tree T obtained in step (6), and repeats the operation of step (7). Finally, the next-hop node G of node F can be obtained, and insert node G into the tree T as the subnode of node the F. At this time, the structure of the tree T shown in Fig. 4.

(9) At present, the subnet topology shown in Fig. 2 has been accessed, and the final transmission paths are obtained according to the Fig. 4, the structure of the tree T, which is $A \rightarrow C \rightarrow K$ and $A \rightarrow F \rightarrow G$. The node A, which currently wants to send information, passes the message through the replication strategy on the two paths as shown in the Fig. 5.

3.4 Algorithm Design

According to the previous section of the traversal process of nodes in the sub-network topology, the implementation process of the EFSNS algorithm is deduced, as follows.

(1) Initialize a tree T, insert the node i that is currently sending information into the tree T as the root node.

(2) Create a set U_i to store the neighbor nodes of the current node i. If the node i has a parent node p in the tree T, then create a set U_p to store the neighbor nodes of node p, and make $U_i = U_i - U_p$.

(3) Access to the neighbor node j in the set U_i of the current node i by breadth-first search, and calculate the edit distance Dis_{ij} and the similarity Sim_{ij}.

(4) If the current node i does not have a subnode in the tree T, the neighbor j is inserted into the tree T as a subnode of node i.

(5) If the current node i has only one subnode k in the tree T, then determine the size of Sim_{ij} and Sim_{ik}.

If $min(Sim_{ij}, Sim_{ik}) \geq \alpha$, it is necessary to calculate the edit distance Dis_{jk} and the similarity Sim_{jk}. If $Sim_{jk} > \beta$, the node with smaller similarity to the current node i is discarded, and the larger one is reserved as the subnode of node i. Otherwise, the node j is inserted into the tree T as the other child of the current node i.

In the other case, such as $Sim_{ij} > \alpha > Sim_{ik}$, $Sim_{ik} > \alpha > Sim_{ij}$, $\alpha > Sim_{ij} > Sim_{ik}$, and soon on, the node with smaller similarity to the current node i is discarded, and the larger one is reserved as the subnode of node i.

(6) If there are two or more subnodes, $k_1, k_2, \cdots k_n$, in the current node i, then calculate the similarity between node j and subnode k_x, $k_x \in \{k_1, k_2, \cdots k_n\}$. If there are $Sim_{jk_x} \leq \beta$ for all the subnodes, the node j is inserted into the tree T as a subnode of the current node i.

If there is a subnode k_x and $Sim_{jk_x} > \beta$, the node with smaller similarity to the current node i is discarded, and the larger one is reserved as the subnode of node i.

(7) Continue to access other neighbor nodes of the current node i, repeat steps (3), (4), (5), (6) until all the neighbor nodes have finished accessing.

(8) Select all the subnodes of the current node i in turn as the current node, and repeat steps (2), (3), (4), (5), (6), (7) until all neighbor nodes of all nodes in tree T in the subnetwork topology are accessed.

(9) The tree T obtained according to the above steps is used to determine the path of the information transmission, and the date is forwarded on the path through the replication strategy.

The EFSNS algorithm as shown in Algorithm 1.

Algorithm 1. Efficient Forwarding Strategy for Opportunistic Network Based on Node Similarity

---

Input: A graph $G(V, E)$, a source node S, D_i/*the data packets of node i*/;
Output: One or more transmission paths;

1: Init:$InitTree(T)$;
2: Set: $CurrentNode(i, S)$, $T.setRootNode(i)$, U_i/*A set of neighbor nodes of node i */;
3: **while** (! $Empty(U_i)$) **do**
4:     **for** ($Neighbor\ j$: U_i) **do**
5:         Dis_{ij}; Sim_{ij};
6:         $Num = T.getChildNodeNum(i)$;/*get the number of child node of node i*/
7:         **if** ($Num == 0$) **then**
8:             $T.setChildNode(i, j)$;/*Set node j as the child node of node i*/
9:         **end if**
10:        **if** ($Num == 1$) **then**
11:           $ChildNode\ k = T.getChildNode(i)$;
12:           **if** (($min(Sim_{ij}, Sim_{ik}) \geq \alpha$)) **then**
13:              Dis_{ij}; Sim_{ij};
14:              **if** ($Sim_{kj} \geq \beta$) **then**
15:                 $T.setChildNode(i, max(Sim_{ij}, Sim_{ik}))$;
16:              **else** $T.setChildNode(i, j)$;
17:              **end if**
18:           **else**
19:              $T.setChildNode(i, max(Simij, Simik))$;
20:           **end if**
21:         **end if**
22:        **if** ($Num \geq 2$) **then**
23:           **for** ($Node\ k : T.getChildNode(i)$) **do**
24:              Dis_{ij}; Sim_{ij};
25:              **if** ($Simkj \geq \beta$) **then**
26:        $T.setChildNode(i, max(Sim_{ij}, Sim_{ik}))$, $break$;
27:              **else** $T.setChildNode(i, j)$;
28:              **end if**
29:           **end for**
30:         **end if**
31:     **end for**
32:     **for** ($ChildNode\ k : T.getChildNode(i)$) **do**
33:         $CurrentNode(i, k)$, $continue$;
34:     **end for**
35:     $Node\ p = T.getParentNode(i)$
36:     U_p /*the set of neighbors of node p*/
37:     $U_i = U_i - U_p$
38: **end while**
39: $getPath(T)$ /*get the transmission paths based on the tree T*/

---

4   Experimental Simulation and Result Analysis

4.1   Simulation Environment

We use the opportunistic network simulator ONE (Opportunistic Networking Environment) [22] for the simulation, and compare the performance of the EFSNS, Epidemic and PRoPHET algorithms. The three indexes of deliver ratio, delivery delay and routing overload are used to analyze and compare the algorithms. The Simulation environment as shown in Table 2.

Table 2. Simulation environment

Parameter	Value
Simulated time	12 h
Simulated area	4500 * 4000
Simulated city	Helsinki
Velocity of a node	1–9 (m/s)
Rate of node transmission	250 KB/s
Maximum transmission range	10 m
Communication mode	Bluetooth
Node cache	10 MB
Size of data packet	500 KB–1 MB
Lifetime of data packet	3 h

The algorithm parameters as shown in Table 3.

Table 3. Algorithm parameters

Parameter	Value
α	0.27
β	0.75

Experiments show that when $\alpha = 0.27$ and $\beta = 0.75$, the performance of the EFSNS algorithm is optimized.

4.2   Result Analysis

In the simulation, we compare the performances of the deliver ratio, delivery delay and overhead of EFSNS with those of the Epidemic and PRoPHET algorithms.

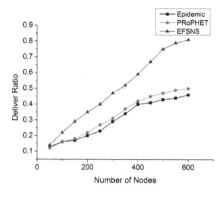

Fig. 6. Deliver ratio

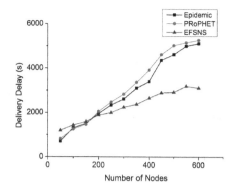

Fig. 7. Delivery delay

Figure 6 shows the experimental results of the deliver ratio of the three algorithms at different node densities.

As can be seen from Fig. 6, the node density has a greater impact on the deliver ratio of routing algorithms. When the node density is low, the deliver ratio of each routing algorithm is relatively low, and there is no significant difference between the algorithms. When the node density increases, the deliver ratio of the three algorithms is increased. The deliver ratio of the Epidemic and PRoPHET algorithms is relatively slow, when the number of nodes is greater than 400, the deliver ratio of Epidemic and PRoPHET algorithms is maintained at about 40%. And the increase of the deliver ratio of the EFSNS algorithm is more obvious, when the number of nodes reaches 600, the deliver ratio of the EFSNS algorithm is greater than 70%. The fundamental reason is that the EFSNS algorithm constructs the subnet topology, and selects one or more reliable and efficient transmission paths for information transmission by calculating the similarity between nodes.

The effect of the number of nodes on the propagation delay is shown in the Fig. 7. It can be seen from the Fig. 7 that with the increase of the number of nodes, the delivery delay of the Epidemic and PRoPHET algorithme is obviously increased. When the number of nodes reaches 400, the delivery delay of the two algorithms is kept at around 5000. The influence of the number of nodes on the delivery delay of EFSNS algorithm is relatively small. The delivery delay of EFSNS algorithm shows a slow increasing trend. When the number of nodes is less than 150, the delivery delay of the EFSNS algorithm is slightly higher than that of the two algorithms, because the complexity of EFSNS algorithm is higher than the two algorithms. With the increasing number of nodes, the number of transmission paths obtained by the EFSNS algorithm is increased and the reliability of the transmission path is improved, which reduces the influence of the algorithm complexity on the transmission delay to a certain extent. Finally, the delivery delay of the EFSNS algorithm is maintained at around 3000.

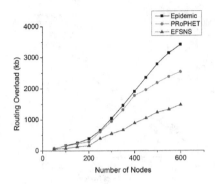

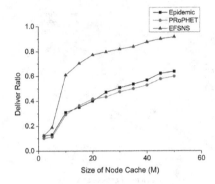

Fig. 8. Routing overhead   **Fig. 9.** Deliver ratio (node cache)

Figure 8 shows the effect of the number of nodes on the routing overhead of the three algorithms. In the case of fewer nodes, the routing overhead of the three algorithms is relatively low. With the increase of the number of nodes per unit area, the routing overhead of the Epidemic and PRoPHET algorithms is greatly increased, and the Epidemic algorithm is the largest. When the number of nodes reaches 600, the routing overhead of the Epidemic algorithm is about 4500, and the PRoPHET algorithm is about 3500, which means that the two algorithms have a large number of copies of data packets in the network with the increase of the number of nodes, it will be waste a lot of network resources. The routing overhead of the EFSNS algorithm is much lower than that of the two algorithms. With the increase of the number of nodes, the routing overhead of the EFSNS algorithm is growing slowly. When the number of nodes reaches 600, the routing overhead of the EFSNS algorithm is less than 2500, which is less than 3/5 of Epidemic algorithm, and it is less than the PRoPHET algorithm by about 1000. The experimental results show that the EFSNS algorithm can effectively reduce the routing overhead and save the network resources relative to the Epidemic and PRoPHET algorithms.

As shown in Fig. 9, the node cache has almost the same effect on the deliver ratio of the Epidemic and PRoPHET algorithms. With the increasing of the size of node cache, the deliver ratio of Epidemic algorithm and PRoPHET algorithm show the same growth trend. The effect of node cache on the deliver ratio of EFSNS algorithm is relatively significant. When the node cache is less than 20 M, the deliver ratio of EFSNS algorithm is more than two times that of the previous two algorithms. When the node buffer is greater than 20 M, the deliver ratio of EFSNS algorithm shows a slow growth trend, and finally remained at about 90%. It is about 30% higher than the Epidemic and PRoPHET algorithms, which greatly improves the deliver ratio of opportunistic network.

5   Conclusion and Future Work

Aiming at the characteristics of the information transmission between the nodes in the opportunistic network and the social relations among the nodes, a routing strategy based on the similarity between nodes is proposed from the perspective of the social network. The size of the social similarity between nodes is calculated by the edit distance of the data packets carried by nodes, and the number of next-hop nodes can be effectively controlled by the threshold α and β. Finally, we will get one or more relatively reliable transmission paths. Compared with Epidemic algorithm and PRoPHET algorithm, the simulation results show that EFSNS algorithm can effectively improve the deliver ratio and reduce the routing overhead and reduce the occupation of network resources. The high efficiency of EFSNS algorithm shows that the social attributes between nodes play a very important role in the transmission of information in opportunistic network.

In the actual scene, the human behavior model in the social network and the social relationship between people are extremely complex, and the spread of the message will be affected by many factors, such as the individual's interest, the degree of individual's willingness, the community in which the individual is located, and soon on. The future work is a comprehensive analysis of the various social relations between nodes, the behavior model of nodes and the group where the nodes are located in the opportunistic network. And further improve the deliver ratio on the basis of EFSNS algorithm and enhance the applicability of the algorithm in different realistic scenes.

Acknowledgements. This work is supported by the National Natural Science Foundation of China (Grant No. 71633006, Grant No. 61672540, Grant No. 61379057). This work is supported by the China Postdoctoral Science Foundation funded project (Grant No. 2017M612586). This work is supported by the Postdoctoral Science Foundation of Central South University (Grant No. 185684).

References

1. Boldrini, C., Lee, K., Önen, M., et al.: Opportunistic networks. Comput. Commun. **48**(14), 1–4 (2014)
2. Dong, L.: Opportunistic media access control and routing for delay-tolerant mobile ad hoc networks. Wireless Netw. **18**(8), 949–965 (2012)
3. Jang, K., Lee, J., Kim, S.K., et al.: An adaptive routing algorithm considering position and social similarities in an opportunistic network. Wireless Netw. **22**(5), 1537–1551 (2016)
4. Kerdsri, J., Wipusitwarakun, K.: Research article dynamic rendezvous based routing algorithm on sparse opportunistic network environment. Int. J. Distrib. Sens. Netw. **2015**, 12 (2015)
5. Chen, W., Chennikara-Varghese, J., Pang, M., et al.: Method to establish and organize an ad-hoc wireless peer to peer network: WO, US 7720026 B2[P] (2010)
6. Tamhane, S.A., Kumar, M., Passarella, A., et al.: Service composition in opportunistic networks. In: IEEE International Conference on Green Computing and Communications, pp. 285–292. IEEE (2012)

7. Tseng, Y.C., Wu, F.J., Lai, W.T.: Opportunistic data collection for disconnected wireless sensor networks by mobile mules. Ad Hoc Netw. **11**(3), 1150–1164 (2013)
8. Chakchouk, N.: A survey on opportunistic routing in wireless communication networks. IEEE Commun. Surv. Tutorials **17**(4), 1 (2015)
9. Zhu, L., Li, C., Li, B., et al.: Geographic routing in multilevel scenarios of vehicular ad hoc networks. IEEE Trans. Veh. Technol., 1 (2015)
10. Wang, X., Lin, Y., Zhang, S., et al.: A social activity and physical contact-based routing algorithm in mobile opportunistic networks for emergency response to sudden disasters. Enterprise Inf. Syst. **3**(2), 1–30 (2015)
11. Wu, J., Chen, Z.: Sensor communication area and node extend routing algorithm in opportunistic networks. Peer-to-Peer Network. Appl., 1–11 (2016)
12. Ying, Z., Zhang, C., Li, F., et al.: Geo-social: routing with location and social metrics in mobile opportunistic networks. In: IEEE International Conference on Communications, pp. 3405–3410. IEEE (2015)
13. Hui, P., Crowcroft, J., Yoneki, E.: BUBBLE rap: social-based forwarding in delay-tolerant networks. IEEE Trans. Mob. Comput. **10**(11), 1576–1589 (2010)
14. Yuan, P., Ma, H., Fu, H.: Hotspot-Entropy Based Data Forwarding in Opportunistic Social Networks. Elsevier Science Publishers B.V., Amsterdam (2015)
15. Risley, G.H.R., Elmore, A.C., Burken, J.G., et al.: Development of a waterjet system for direct delivery of granular iron and activated carbon to remediate contaminated aqueous sediments. Remediat. J. **21**(3), 103–119 (2011)
16. Rusli, M.E., Harris, R., Punchihewa, A.: Performance analysis of implicit acknowledgement coordination scheme for opportunistic routing in wireless sensor networks. In: International Symposium on Telecommunication Technologies, pp. 131–136. IEEE (2013)
17. Li, Y., Hui, P., Jin, D., et al.: Evaluating the impact of social selfishness on the epidemic routing in delay tolerant networks. IEEE Commun. Lett. **14**(11), 1026–1028 (2010)
18. Huang, W., Zhang, S., Zhou, W.: Spray and wait routing based on position prediction in opportunistic networks. In: International Conference on Computer Research and Development, pp. 232–236. IEEE (2011)
19. Gibran, K.: The PRoPHET: A New Annotated Edition. OneWorld Publications, London (2012)
20. Sok, P., Tan, S.C., Kim, K.: PRoPHET routing protocol based on neighbor node distance using a community mobility model in delay tolerant networks (2013)
21. Gao, Z., Shi, Y., Chen, S., et al.: Exploiting social relationship for opportunistic routing in mobile social networks. IEICE Trans. Commun. **E98.B**(10), 2040–2048 (2015)
22. Ker, N.A., Ott, J., et al.: The ONE simulator for DTN protocol evaluation. In: International Conference on Simulation TOOLS and Techniques. ICST (Institute for Computer Sciences, Social-Informatics and Telecommunications Engineering), p. 55 (2009)

Transmission Failure Tolerance and Node Punishment Mechanism in Opportunistic Network Based on Repeated-Game

Bin-an Yin[1,2], Zhigang Chen[1,2(✉)], and Jia Wu[1,2]

[1] School of Software, Central South University, Changsha 410075, China
ybastc@163.com, czg@csu.edu.cn, jiawu5110@163.com
[2] "Mobile Health" Ministry of Education, China Mobile Joint Laboratory,
Changsha 410083, China

Abstract. During the data forwarding in opportunistic network, the selfishness of rational nodes leads to a serious decline in network performance. To solve this problem, this paper proposes a mechanism referred as TFT-NP (transmission failure tolerance and node punishment). TFT-NP takes transmission failure into account, and judges whether the node is selfish or not. It introduces repeated-game theory and sets the penalty cycle of selfish node reasonably. It forces rational nodes to cooperate for a greater profit. Experimental results show that, in opportunistic network with selfish nodes, TFT-NP can improve message delivery rate and reduce message delay significantly.

Keywords: Opportunistic network · Repeated-game · Transmission failure

1 Introduction

Opportunistic network [1] requires no link between the source node and the target node. Data packets are transmitted hop-by-hop by using the communication opportunity formed by movement and encounter of nodes. Communications between nodes are implemented in Store Carry and Forward mode. Because opportunistic network can handle data transmission under the condition of network splitting, it has become a hot research in wireless network [2–4]. Nowadays, there are some specific applications based on opportunistic networks. In crowded places such as shopping malls, subways, supermarkets, message publisher sends popular video and discount information to pedestrians. These data are transferred between mobile intelligent terminals [5]. Wireless intelligent transmission equipments are installed along city roads, which can be used to inject real-time traffic information, news and entertainment information into vehicular ad hoc networks [6].

Opportunistic network consists of handheld devices or vehicular devices [7,8] which are used by people. Users are more concerned about the data they are

© Springer Nature Singapore Pte Ltd. 2017
D. Du et al. (Eds.): NCTCS 2017, CCIS 768, pp. 101–115, 2017.
https://doi.org/10.1007/978-981-10-6893-5_8

interested in. However, they are less concerned with the data to be forwarded to others. Energy of device is limited, and it is consumed quickly in data forwarding [9]. To save energy, selfish behavior that node refuses to forward data may occur. Especially in vehicular opportunistic network, node movement range is large, node movement speed is fast [10]. It is prone to cause transmission failure. Selfish nodes may use the phenomenon to show the false appearance that transmission failed. Selfish nodes do not take the initiative to attack network. However, as described in Reference [11], they make a serious decline in network performance.

This paper focuses on the opportunistic network contains publishers who inject information into it [12]. Nodes are interested in the information which they do not have. In this case, nodes will request for the information they do not have when encounter. When the node successfully receives the information, it will profit. Node may take selfish strategy that refusing to forward data for the sake of saving energy. To enforce cooperation between nodes, this paper introduces repeated-game theory in Economics [13], and reasonably isolates selfish node in a certain period by analysing its profit. The node which be punished cannot gain any profit in penalty cycle. It is forced to cooperate with other nodes.

Based on repeated-game, a mechanism of Transmission Failure Tolerance and Node Punishment (TFT-NP) is proposed in this paper to solve the problem of non-cooperation in data forwarding. Section 2 is related work. Section 3 is the illustration of TFT-NP in detail. Section 4 is simulation and analysis. And Sect. 5 is conclusion.

2   Related Work

At present, there are some methods to solve the problem of node selfishness, mainly in the following ways.

Marti et al. [14] propose Watchdog and Pathrater solution. The reliability of link is evaluated by detecting the historical cooperative behavior of nodes. The routing protocol for detecting the behavior of neighbor nodes is used to detect the behavior of selfish nodes. When the selfish node is detected, this method avoids selecting the communication link which the selfish node is located. However, this approach makes the selfish node no longer provide routing for other nodes. It indulges and rewards selfish nodes, and makes the network performance decline.

Buttyan et al. [15] propose a circulation model based on virtual currency Nuglet. Network services can only be used if users pay for it by virtual currency Nuglet. Node users can get some virtual currency by participating in data forwarding. So, node users are actively involved in data forwarding to earn more virtual currency. However, this method needs support of unmodifiable hardware or centralized management. So, it is not quite suitable in opportunistic network.

Srinivasan et al. [16] propose a model GTFT (Generous Tit-for-tat). By balancing the mutual contribution between nodes, the TFT model is improved. However, this method only considers the influence of historical profit on node decision, and it does not take future profit into account.

Zhang et al. [17] propose a model based on credit-cooperation and repeated games. Through setting the penalty cycle of selfish node, this method forces nodes to cooperate together. However, The setting of penalty cycle value is not explicitly given, and transmission failure is not taken into account.

To solve the above problems, transmission failure is taken into account based on opportunistic network characteristics. Historical credit of nodes and network transmission failure rate are used to judge whether the node is selfish or not. Based on repeated-game theory, the penalty cycle of selfish node is set reasonably. In this case, rational nodes will not take selfish strategy for a smaller profit when the short-term profit of selfishness is smaller than the long-term profit of cooperation.

3   TFT-NP

Because of nodes movement, the network connection between nodes is dynamically established. Large range movement and fast movement speed of nodes lead to an increase in end-to-end delay. Therefore, the transmission process is unstable and the link between nodes is easily broken off [18], and it can be used by selfish nodes. Meanwhile, transmission failure may occur in transmission process between normal nodes. For distinguishing selfish nodes and normal nodes, this paper sets the network transmission failure rate according to the statistical analysis of transmission failure in actual scene, and judges whether the node is selfish or not by comparing the history transmission failure rate of node and the network transmission failure rate.

3.1   Repeated-Game

For the convenience of analysis, following assumptions are given.

(1) There are N rational nodes in opportunistic network. Nodes make decisions by maximizing their profits.
(2) Network lifecycle T is unknown. A series of discrete time slots constitute T, $T = \sum_{i=1} t_i$.
(3) In slot t_i, each node interacts only once, the profit of the node which successfully receives data is r, and the loss of the node which forwards data is e, and $r > e$.
(4) In each interaction, the node always has the data which the other side does not have. Each node sends the same amount of data.

In slot t_i, There are 4 cases of interactions between node a and node b.

(1) If both of them are cooperative, then $U_{at} = U_{bt} = r - e$.
(2) If node a is cooperative, node b is uncooperative, then $U_{at} = -e$, $U_{bt} = r$.
(3) If node a is uncooperative, node b is cooperative, then $U_{at} = r$, $U_{bt} = -e$.
(4) If both of them are uncooperative, then $U_{at} = U_{bt} = 0$.

The profit function can be expressed as

$$U_{at}(S_{at}, S_{bt}) = S_{bt} \cdot r - S_{at} \cdot e \tag{1}$$

In Eq. (1), U_{at} represents the profit of node a in slot t_i, S_{at} and S_{bt} represent the strategy of node a and node b in slot t_i respectively. $S_{at}, S_{at} \in \{0, 1\}$, 0 represents it is uncooperative, and 1 represents it is cooperative. The payoff matrix is shown in Table 1.

Table 1. The payoff matrix of two nodes

a	b	
	Cooperate	Not cooperate
Cooperate	$(r-e, r-e)$	$(-e, r)$
Not cooperate	$(r, -e)$	$(0, 0)$

Table 1 shows that it is a prisoner's dilemma game. When the game between nodes is only once, selfish strategy will always be dominant strategy, regardless of whether the strategy of the other side is cooperative or not. The state that selfish strategy is taken by all nodes is Nash equilibrium state. At this point, the network delivery success rate is 0. To solve this dilemma, unknown lifecycle T is introduced. Nodes cannot predict the terminal time of the network. It is impossible that nodes use reverse derivation to select strategies in repeated games. Nodes can only treat T as infinity. When the profit of long-term cooperation is greater than that of selfishness, nodes driven by interests will choose cooperative strategy.

Considering time cost, nodes have a certain degree of patience to the repeated games. This paper uses discount factor [19] $\delta \in (0, 1)$ to convert future profit into current profit. The greater the δ is, the greater the degree of patience is. From t_i, after n times games, the profit of node a can be expressed as

$$E_a(n) = \sum_{j=t}^{t+n-1} \delta^{j-t} U_{aj}(S_{aj}, S_{bj}) \tag{2}$$

3.2   Punishment Mechanism

Supposing that node a plays n times games with other nodes from t_i, both of them take cooperative strategy. $\forall t$, $S_{at} = S_{bt} = 1$, substitute this into (2), then

$$E_a(n) = (r - e)\frac{1 - \delta^n}{1 - \delta} \tag{3}$$

If node a takes selfish strategy in the first game, as Fig. 1 shows, node b will broadcast the information of node a to the whole network.

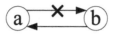

Fig. 1. Selfish behavior of node a

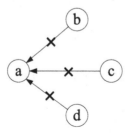

Fig. 2. Other nodes isolate node a

Node a will be isolated by other nodes in the next $n-1$ times games. Figure 2 shows this situation.

In this case, after n times games, the profit of node a is r. For eliminating uncooperative motivation of rational nodes, it is sure that $E_a > r$, then

$$n - 1 > \frac{\ln(r\delta - e) - \ln(r - e)}{\ln \delta} - 1 = F \tag{4}$$

In Eq. (4), $\delta > \frac{e}{r}$, $n-1$ is penalty cycle. Denote it as F_0, $F_0 \in (F, +\infty)$, F_0 is an integer. After F_0, the profit of node a is less than that of the node which cooperates all the time. In this case, rational nodes are forced to choose cooperative strategy.

Theorem 1. If $\delta < \frac{e}{r}$, the profit of the node with selfish strategy will be certainly greater than that of the node with cooperative strategy.

Proof: Because $\delta < \frac{e}{r}$, $\lim_{n \to +\infty} E_a(n) = \frac{r - e}{1 - \delta} < \frac{r - e}{1 - \frac{e}{r}} = r$.

It can be seen from Theorem 1, when $\delta > \frac{e}{r}$, increasing r and reducing e will promote cooperation. When $\delta = \frac{e}{r}$, permanently isolating the node will not affect whether it selects cooperative strategy. When $\delta < \frac{e}{r}$, the node will choose selfish strategy.

Supposing that in n times games, node a takes selfish strategy from 1 to $x - 1(1 < x < n)$, and initiatively forwards data for other nodes from x to n. It is defined as "repentance", as shown in Fig. 3.

Besides the first game, other nodes isolate node a, the profit of node a is

$$R_a(n, x) = r - e\frac{\delta^{x-1}(1 - \delta^{n-x+1})}{1 - \delta} \tag{5}$$

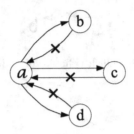

Fig. 3. Repentance of node a

Obviously, it is sure that $E_a > R_a$, which represents the profit of the node with cooperative strategy is greater than that of the node with repentance. Then

$$n - 1 > \frac{\ln(r\delta + e\delta^{x-1} - e) - \ln r}{\ln \delta} - 1 = M \tag{6}$$

In Eq. (6), the penalty cycle of repentance is denoted as M_0, $M_0 > M$, and M_0 is an integer. Repentant behavior helps to improve network performance. For stimulating selfish nodes to repent, the profit of the node with repentance in M_0 plus the profit of the node after penalty cycle in $F_0 - M_0$ should be greater than the profit of the node without repentance in F_0. So,

$$R_a(M_0 + 1, x) + (r - e)\frac{\delta^{M_0+1}(1 - \delta^{F_0-M_0})}{1 - \delta} > r \tag{7}$$

Then,

$$M_0 < \frac{\ln[(r - e)\delta^{F_0+1} + e\delta^{x-1}] - \ln r}{\ln \delta} - 1 = T \tag{8}$$

So, the penalty cycle of repentance should be set to M_0, $M_0 \in (M, T)$, and M_0 is an integer.

The differential of M is

$$\frac{dM}{dx} = \frac{\delta^{x-1}}{\delta^{x-1} + \frac{r\delta}{e} - 1} \tag{9}$$

Because $\delta > \frac{e}{r}$, $\frac{dM}{dx} > 0$, M is monotonically increasing on x. When $x = 2$, the minimum of M is

$$M_{min} = \frac{\ln(r\delta + e\delta - e) - \ln r}{\ln \delta} \tag{10}$$

So, when the node immediately repents after being punished, the penalty cycle should be set to M_{min}. It can stimulate selfish nodes to take the strategy of repentance immediately for shortening the penalty cycle.

By the above analysis, if selfish behavior occurs, the profit of selfish node will be less than that of normal node. In this case, nodes driven by interest are forced to choose cooperative strategy for a greater profit. According to the Nash equilibrium definition of mutual optimum response [13], the whole game situation is in the Nash equilibrium state.

3.3   Model Design and Algorithm Analysis

With the consideration of transmission failure in opportunistic network, this paper uses summary vector (SV) to exchange credit tables in the process of neighbor discovery. According to the statistical analysis of transmission failure in opportunistic network, the network transmission failure rate is set to α. By comparing the historical transmission failure rate of node and α, this paper tolerates selfish behavior of the node which historical transmission failure rate is less than α.

Table 2 describes a credit table header in each node. In this table, id is the node identifier, sn is the number of selfish behaviors, tn is the number of interactions, t is the latest updated time of this record. Credit table is used to record credit information of nodes besides the node itself. Credit information of the node is not saved on itself. It can increase the reliability of credit records.

Table 2. Credit table header

id	sn	tn	t

This paper uses formal method to describe the interaction of credit tables between two nodes.

(1) Node a and node b send credit table to each other via SV incidentally.
(2) If $r_b \notin T_a$, then $T_a = T_a \bigcup r_{b0}$, else, in record r_b of T_a, $tn = tn + 1$, update t to the current time. If $r_a \notin T_b$, then $T_b = T_b \bigcup r_{a0}$, else, in record r_a of T_b, $tn = tn + 1$, update t to the current time.
(3) $T_a' = T_a \bigcup_+ T_b \setminus r_a$, $T_b' = T_b \bigcup_+ T_a \setminus r_b$.

$\bigcup_+$ is based on the set operation $\bigcup$. The difference is that, it will only remain the record with the latest t if records have the same id. r_a represents the record which $id = a$. r_{a0} represents the record which $id = a$, $sn = 0$, $tn = 1$, and t is current time. T_a represents the record set of node a. T_a' represents the state of T_a after operation.

The specific steps of TFT-NP mechanism based on Epidemic routing algorithm is described as follows.

Undirected graph $G = (V, E)$ is used to represent the current network topology. The records in each node credit table are shown in Fig. 4.

Step 1. Each node performs neighbor discovery process. At time t_1, The nodes which discover each other are $<a, b>$, $<c, g>$ and $<d, h>$.

Step 2. For each node pair $<a, b>$, $<c, g>$ and $<d, h>$, nodes send credit tables to each other via SV incidentally. After that, $T_a' = \{b, c\}$, $T_b' = \{a, c\}$, $T_c' = \{d, g\}$, $T_g' = \{c, d\}$, $T_d' = \{a, b, c, h\}$, and $T_h' = \{a, b, c, d\}$, as shown in Fig. 5. Each node pair processes Step 3 to Step 6.

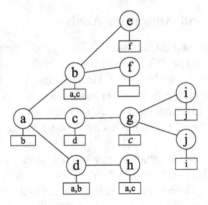

Fig. 4. Network topology with credit tables

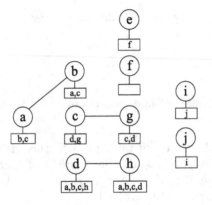

Fig. 5. Interactions between nodes at time t_1

Step 3. If node j is in penalty cycle, then node i does not send data packets to j. If penalty cycle of j is F_0, and j successfully sends data packets to i, then i broadcasts that the penalty cycle of j is changed to M_0; If penalty cycle of j is M_0, and j rejects or fails to send data packets to i, then i broadcasts that the penalty cycle of j is set to F_0.

Step 4. If i is in penalty cycle, then take the same operation to i as Step 3.

Step 5. If i and j are not in penalty cycle, then i and j send data packets to each other. If a failure occurs in the process of transmitting data packets to j by i, then j determines whether i is a selfish node based on the credit record of i, as Fig. 6 shows. If i is judged as a selfish node, then j broadcasts that the penalty cycle of i is set to F_0. If a failure occurs in the process of transmitting data packets to i by j, then taking the same operation to j.

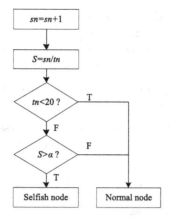

Fig. 6. Judgement of selfish node

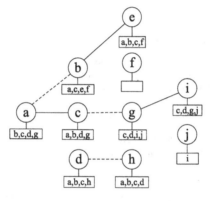

Fig. 7. Interactions between nodes at time t_2

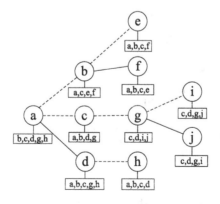

Fig. 8. Interactions between nodes at time t_3

It is worth noting that, if the node interacts too little, the statistical characteristics of network transmission failure cannot be reflected, it may cause misjudgment. When $tn < 20$, the node with selfish behavior will be judged as a normal node, but the selfish behavior will be recorded.

Step 6. If node i or node j is in penalty cycle, then add a unit of penalty time to it. If it reaches the penalty cycle, then remove its penalty cycle.

Step 7. Each node continues neighbor discovery process. At time t_2, The nodes which discover each other are $<a, c>$, $<b, e>$ and $<g, i>$.

Table 3. Pseudo-code of TFT-NP mechanism

Algorithm 1. TFT-NP mechanism algorithm

Input: node P[n], node neighbor, node credit table, packet, α, T, F_0, M_0.
Output: updated credit tables of nodes.
Start:

```
  while(t< T) {
    for each node i do
    while(node[i]->neighbor!=NULL) {
      if(!isVisit(node[i]->neighbor)) {
        Update(node[i].table,node[i]->neighbor.table);
          //update credit table of node i and its neighbor.
        Call TransmitProc(node[i],node[i]->neighbor);
          //invoke TransmitProc as below.
        Call TransmitProc(node[i]->neighbor,node[i]);
      }
      node[i]->neighbor=node[i].nextNeighbor;
        //go to the next neighbor of node i
    }
  }
```

End.

```
void TransmitProc(node i, node j) {
  if(timePenalty(j)==F0) { // penalty cycle of node j is F0.
    if(transmit(j,i,packet)==TRUE) // j successfully transmits a packet to i
      RevisePenalty(j,M0); //revise the penalty cycle of node j from F0 to M0
  }
  else if (timePenalty(j)==M0) {
    if(transmit(j,i,packet)==FALSE)
      RevisePenalty(j,F0);
  }
  else {      // j is not in penalty cycle
    if(transmit(i,j,packet)==FALSE)
      JudgeSelfish(i);
        /*judge whether node i is a selfish node,
        if it is a selfish node, then set its penalty cycle to F0. */
    if(transmit(j,i,packet)==FALSE)
      JudgeSelfish(j);
  }
  RemovePenalty(i,j);
    /*if i or j in the penalty cycle, then add a unit of penalty time
    i or j, if it reach to the penalty cycle, then remove it. */
}
```

Step 8. For each node pair $<a, c>$, $<b, e>$ and $<g, i>$, nodes send credit tables to each other via SV incidentally. After that, $T'_a = \{b, c, d, g\}$, $T'_c = \{a, b, d, g\}$, $T'_b = \{a, c, e, f\}$, $T'_e = \{a, b, c, f\}$, $T'_g = \{c, d, i, j\}$, and $T'_i = \{c, d, g, j\}$, as shown in Fig. 7. The dotted lines in the figure represent the links were discovered before. Each node pair processes Step 3 to Step 6.

Step 9. Each node continues neighbor discovery process. At time t_3, The nodes which discover each other are $<a, d>$, $<b, f>$ and $<g, j>$.

Step 10. For each node pair $<a, d>$, $<b, f>$ and $<g, j>$, nodes send credit tables to each other via SV incidentally. After that, $T'_a = \{b, c, d, g, h\}$, $T'_d = \{a, b, c, g, h\}$, $T'_b = \{a, c, e, f\}$, $T'_f = \{a, b, c, e\}$, $T'_g = \{c, d, i, j\}$, and $T'_j = \{c, d, g, j\}$, as shown in Fig. 8. Each node pair processes Step 3 to Step 6.

Step 11. All nodes are accessed at this time. Repeat the above steps in lifecycle T.

According to the above analysis and calculation, Table 3 shows the pseudo-code of TFT-NP mechanism based on Epidemic routing algorithm.

4   Simulation and Analysis

The simulation is based on ONE (opportunistic network environment simulator) v1.6.0 [20]. By introducing selfish nodes, this paper researches the profit between normal nodes and selfish nodes at first. After that, this paper applys TFT-NP mechanism based on Epidemic routing algorithm, and obtains its delivery success rate and average message delay, verifying the effectiveness of TFT-NP mechanism.

Let $F_0 = 5$, $M_0 = 1$ in the simulation. Figure 9 shows that, the selfish node without repentance gets a high short-term profit at time 1. After that, it is isolated by other nodes, and its profit remains the same. The profit of the normal node starts to exceed that of the selfish node at time 4. After the penalty cycle $[1, 6]$, the profit of the selfish node begins to increase.

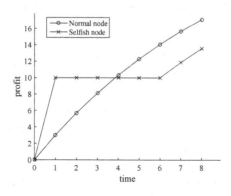

Fig. 9. The profit of selfish node without repentance

Figure 10 shows that, the node takes selfish strategy at the beginning. So, it gets a high short-term profit at time 1. After that, the node proactively forwards data for other nodes. So, its profit declines. Its penalty cycle is shortened to $[1, 2]$ because of its repentance. After time 2, the punishment is over and the node starts to profit. Its profit is less than that of the normal node, but greater than that of the selfish node without repentance.

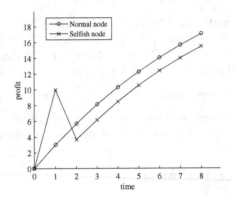

Fig. 10. The profit of selfish node with repentance

The road map of Finland's Capital, Helsinki is used to simulate the real scene. Nodes use the model of map route movement. According to 8 bus routes in real world, nodes do round-trip movement on their bus routes. When the node arrives at a waypoint, it will stop for a while. The Stopping time obeys the uniform distribution of $[10, 30]$ s. Then, the node moves to the next waypoint on its own bus route.

The simulation parameter settings are shown in Table 4.

Table 4. Simulation parameter settings

Parameter	Value	Parameter	Value
Simulation time	12 h	Storage capacity	30 M
Simulation area	9*9 km	Packets size	200 kB
The number of nodes	40	TTL	60 s
Speed of nodes	20–50 km/h	Data rate	250 kBps
Maximum transmission range	30 m	Message generation interval	5 h

Figure 11 shows the change of delivery success rate with selfish node ratio. When the selfish node ratio changes from 0 to 80%, the delivery success rate of Epidemic without TFT-NP mechanism will down from 96% to 36%.

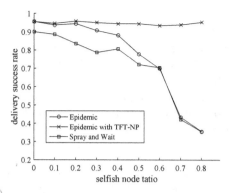

Fig. 11. Delivery success rate

However, with the increase of selfish node ratio, the delivery success rate of Epidemic with TFT-NP mechanism almost remains the same. Its average value is 95%. It is because TFT-NP mechanism forces selfish nodes to participate in data forwarding. Each selfish node becomes a normal node after the penalty cycle.

Figure 12 shows the change of average message delay with selfish node ratio. With the raise of selfish nodes, the average message delay of Spray and Wait is not ideal, and the average message delay of Epidemic without TFT-NP is increasing. It will basically remain the same when the selfish node ratio is greater than 30%. It is because the average message delay is very close to the TTL value. When TTL value increases, the average message delay will keep on increasing. The average message delay of Epidemic with TFT-NP mechanism slightly increases with the raise of selfish node ratio. It is caused by the penalty cycle of selfish nodes. After the penalty cycle, selfish nodes change to normal nodes. As a result, the average message delay does not become greater significantly.

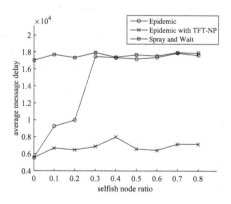

Fig. 12. Average message delay

5   Conclusion

In view of selfish behavior of nodes in opportunistic network, this paper introduces repeated-game based on the consideration of transmission failure. Through comparing the profit between selfish node and normal node, the penalty cycle of selfish node is set reasonably, so that rational nodes are forced to give up selfish strategy and choose to cooperate for a greater profit. In next step, we will study the statistical relationship between movement speed of nodes and network transmission failure, and get a reasonable transmission failure rate.

Acknowledgements. This work is supported by Major Program of National Natural Science Foundation of China (71633006); The National Natural Science Foundation of China (61672540, 61379057); China Postdoctoral Science Foundation funded project (2017M612586); The Postdoctoral Science Foundation of Central South University (185684).

References

1. Soelistijanto, B., Howarth, M.P.: Transfer reliability and congestion control strategies in opportunistic networks: a survey. IEEE Commun. Surv. Tutorials **16**(1), 538–555 (2014)
2. Liu, Q.L., Liu, M.S., Li, Y.: Novel game-based incentive strategy for opportunistic networks. Appl. Res. Comput. **25**(7), 65–71 (2015)
3. Pan, D.R., Zhang, H., Chen, W.J., et al.: Transmission of multimedia contents in opportunistic networks with social selfish nodes. Multimedia Syst. **21**(3), 277–288 (2015)
4. Wu, J., Chen, Z.G.: Sensor communication area and node extend routing algorithm in opportunistic networks. Peer-to-Peer Network. Appl. 1–12 (2016). https://doi.org/10.1007/s12083-016-0526-4
5. Kumar, M., Mishra, R.: An overview of MANET: history, challenges and applications. Indian J. Comput. Sci. Eng. **3**(1), 121–125 (2012)
6. Placzek, B.: Selective data collection in vehicular networks for traffic control applications. Transport. Res. Part C Emerg. Technol. **23**(7), 14–28 (2011)
7. Wang, D., Chen, Z.G., Wu, J.: Forwarding mechanism in opportunistic networks based on social relations. Appl. Res. Comput. **32**(5), 1461–1463 (2015)
8. Li, H., Chen, Z.G., Wu, J.: Opportunistic network routing algorithm based on community and sociality. Comput. Eng. **41**(12), 64–68+74 (2015)
9. Chen, Z.G., Wu, J.: Applying a sensor energy supply communication scheme to big data opportunistic networks. KSII Trans. Internet Inf. Syst. **10**(5), 2029–2046 (2016)
10. Pereira, P.R., Casaca, A., Rodrigues, J.J.P.C., et al.: From delay-tolerant networks to vehicular delay-tolerant networks. IEEE Commun. Surv. Tutorials **14**(4), 1166–1182 (2012)
11. Pelusi, L., Passarella, A., Conti, M.: Opportunistic networking: data forwarding in disconnected mobile ad hoc networks. IEEE Commun. Mag. **44**(11), 134–141 (2006)
12. Zhao, G.S., Chen, M.: Research of incentive-aware data dissemination in selfish opportunistic networks. J. Commun. **34**(2), 73–84 (2013)

13. Lu, Y., Shi, J., Xie, L.: Repeated-Game modeling of cooperation enforcement in wireless ad hoc network. J. Softw. **19**(3), 755–768 (2008)
14. Marti, S., Giuli, T., Lai, K.: Mitigating routing misbehavior in mobile ad hoc networks. In: Proceedings of the ACM MobiCom, vol. 6(11), pp. 255–265. ACM Press (2000)
15. Buttyan, L., Hubaux, J.P.: Stimulating cooperation in self-organizing mobile ad hoc networks. Mobile Netw. Appl. **8**(5), 579–592 (2003)
16. Srinivasan, V., Nuggehalli, P., Chiasserini, C.F., et al.: Cooperation in wireless ad hoc networks. Proc. IEEE INFOCOM **2**(7), 808–817 (2003)
17. Zhang, C., Liu, H.J., Chen, Z.Y., et al.: Credit-based repeated game model applied in transfer decision of opportunistic network. J. PLA Univ. Sci. Technol. **13**(2), 152–158 (2012)
18. Ye, H., Chen, Z.G., Zhao, M.: ON-CRP: cache replacement policy for opportunistic networks. J. Commun. **31**(5), 98–107 (2010)
19. Fudenberg, D., Maskin, E.: The folk theorem in repeated games with discounting or with incomplete information. Econometrica **54**(3), 533–554 (2015)
20. Wang, Z., Wang, X.H., Sui, J.Q.: Extending research for ONE simulator of opportunistic network. Appl. Res. Comput. **29**(1), 272–277 (2012)

Software Theory and Method

Formal Analysis and Verification for an Ultralightweight Authentication Protocol RAPP of RFID

Wei Li$^{(\boxtimes)}$ ⓘ, Meihua Xiao ⓘ, Yanan Li ⓘ, Yingtian Mei ⓘ,
Xiaomei Zhong ⓘ, and Jimin Tu ⓘ

School of Software, East China Jiaotong University, Nanchang 330013,
People's Republic of China
vic.me@foxmail.com, xiaomh@ecjtu.edu.cn,
yenalee@sina.com, myingtian@126.com,
zhongxm@ecjtu.ecjtu.edu.cn, tujimin@163.com

Abstract. Radio Frequency Identification (RFID) technique, as the core of Internet of Things, is facing security threats. It is critical to protect information security in RFID system. Ultralightweigh authentication protocols are an important class of RFID lightweight authentication protocols. RAPP is a recently proposed ultralightweight authentication protocol, which is different from any other existing protocols due to the use of permutation. Formal methods are vital for ensuring the security and reliability of software systems, especially safety-critical systems. A protocol abstract modeling method is presented to build abstract interaction model of RAPP which can be formalized by extracting interaction features. Due to the complexity of fundamental cryptograph operations in RAPP, the proposed method overcomes the limitation which is inconvenient to discuss security of RAPP directly with formal method. Using SPIN, authenticity and consistency of RAPP properties is verified. Analysis and verification result shows that RAPP is vulnerable against desynchronization attack. The proposed modeling method above has great significance in formal analysis of similar ultralightweight authentication protocols of RFID.

Keywords: RFID authentication protocol · RAPP · Model checking · Protocol abstract modeling · Desynchronization attack

1 Introduction

Radio frequency identification (RFID) is the key technique of Internet of things, and it has been widely used in public service, intelligent transportation, smart home and other fields [1]. Because of realizing the automatic identification of objects with radio frequency technology, the open wireless transmission channel is adopted between reader and tag, so it is more vulnerable to malicious attacks. It would even cause huge economic losses in the logistics, transportation and other critical areas [2]. Therefore, analyzing and verifying the security authentication protocol in RFID system with formal method takes an important place in finding the origin of vulnerability, and provides

© Springer Nature Singapore Pte Ltd. 2017
D. Du et al. (Eds.): NCTCS 2017, CCIS 768, pp. 119–132, 2017.
https://doi.org/10.1007/978-981-10-6893-5_9

strong power for building a secure and reliable RFID system. Formal analysis of RFID security protocols contributes to development of good appliance.

Authentication protocols can be divided into the lightweight authentication protocol and the non-lightweight authentication protocol on the basis of complexity. The non-lightweight authentication protocol uses symmetric encryption or public key encryption system based on high computational complexity of encryption. It can acquire a higher security, but return in much power consumption and more hardware resources. Hence, there is a certain application limitation of non-lightweight authentication protocol. However, the lightweight authentication protocol gains lower power consumption and higher efficiency in the use of basic bit operations and logic functions of encryption method, while meeting the demand of security. So the lightweight authentication protocol can be applied extensively [3].

Ultralightweight authentication protocols are an important class of the lightweight authentication protocol in which the operation used in tag side is restricted to simple bitwise operations (like XOR, AND, OR, rotation, modular addition, etc.) [4]. At present, RFID ultralightweight authentication protocols mainly include: Gossamer [5], SASI [6], LMAP++ [7] and etc.

RAPP [8] is a new ultralightweight RFID authentication protocol, whose operations are totally different from the other existing ultralightweight protocols. A new data dependent permutation operation is introduced into this protocol, and traditional unbalanced OR and AND operations are no longer used. Three operations in RAPP, which are bitwise XOR, left rotation, and permutation, cast down the computational complexity and the cost of tag effectively, while ensuring security properties.

Formal method is an important means to improve the security and reliability of software system, especially safety-critical system. Formal methods mainly includes two branches [9]: model checking and theorem proving. SPIN (Simple Promela Interpreter) [10] is a well-known model checker, which was recognized by the ACM with its most prestigious Software System Award. Maggi et al. [11] takes the Needham-Schroeder public key protocol as an example to propose a security protocol modeling method based on the Dolev-Yao attacker model [12], and then has found the NS public key protocol flaws using SPIN. In this paper, those method is improved, so it can be applied to verify RFID ultralightweight authentication protocols.

2   Related Work

In [13], the author proposed a Mutual Authentication Protocol for RFID System Based on EPC C1G2 Standard, and then applied BAN logic for analysis of the protocol. But not for flaws detection, they employed them for encryption. Security protocol validation tool named AVISPA was applied to validate the security properties of LMAP. AVISPA discovered attacks in LMAP and author gave patch scheme in [14]. Yuan [15] utilized model checker nuXmv for analysis of hash-lock protocol, and they presented a methodology for verifying RFID protocols. In the model check results, nuXmv gives some counterexamples.

So far Baghri et al. [16] proposed dissimilar attacks to check the properties of permutation based on the protocol. Wang et al. [17] performed the security analysis of RAPP, and evaluated performance in some specific environments. Ahmadian et al. [18] has done cryptanalysis of RAPP, and a desynchronization attack was found. As RFID ultralightweight authentication protocols do not use classic encryption (like symmetric encryption, public key system, etc.), the related research works of this class protocols are still insufficient with the use of formal method, especially in model checking. Most scholars [2, 13, 19] adopt modal logic (BAN logic, GNY logic, etc.) to verify protocol security properties, but it is difficult to achieve automation.

This paper explores formal analysis and verification of RAPP by applying model checking. A protocol abstract modeling method is presented through extracting inter-action features to build abstract interaction model of RAPP. Then protocol behaviour is described precisely with formal method, and eventually the protocol model is converted into Promela code. The SPIN's experiment result reveals that desynchronization flaw exists in RAPP.

Following is the organization of this paper. Section 3 introduces RAPP and the formal representation of abstract protocol model. In Sect. 4, we illustrate modeling approach of RAPP in details. In Sect. 5, SPIN is used to verify the RAPP protocol and analysis result is given. Section 6 concludes.

3   RAPP and Abstract Protocol Modeling Method

RAPP is a mutual ultralightweight authentication protocol. In RAPP, every tag and a reader share an unchanged and unique identifier (ID). When the authentication is done, it shares a pseudonym IDS and three secret keys: $K1, K2, K3$. In short, Tag stores $\{IDS, K1, K2, K3\}$; Reader stores two sets of data, one is the previous version of fundamental data $\{ID, IDS^{old}, K1^{old}, K2^{old}, K3^{old}\}$, the other is latest version $\{ID, IDS^{new}, K1^{new}, K2^{new}, K3^{new}\}$. The protocol works as follows:

$$1.\, Reader \rightarrow Tag : Hello$$
$$2.\, Tag \rightarrow Reader : IDS$$

The reader first sends *Hello* message to the tag, and the tag sends *IDS* to the reader after receiving *Hello* message. The reader uses the received IDS as a search index to extract the secret information linked to the tag, i.e. $\{ID, K1, K2, K3\}$. Then, the reader generates a random number $n1$ to compute messages A and B and send them to the tag. (Notice: $Per()$ is a permutation operation function, $Rot()$ is a left rotation function)

$$3.\, Reader \rightarrow Tag : A, B$$

$$A = Per(K2, K1) \oplus n1$$
$$B = Per(K1 \oplus K2, Rot(n1, n1)) \oplus Per(n1, K1)$$

Upon receiving A and B, the tag extracts $n1$ from A and then $n1$ is used to verify the correctness of B. If the verification succeeds, the reader is authenticated by the tag and then the tag sends C to the reader as a response.

$$4.\, Tag \rightarrow Reader : C$$

$$C = Per(n1 \oplus K1, n1 \oplus K3) \oplus ID$$

Upon receiving C, the reader first validates its correctness. If succeeds, the tag is authenticated by the reader and then reader generates n2 to compute secret information update seeds D and E as follows. It updates its pseudonym and secret keys at the same time.

$$5.\, Reader \rightarrow Tag : D, E$$

$$D = Per(K3, K2) \oplus n2$$
$$E = Per(K1 \oplus K2, Rot(n2, n2)) \oplus Per(n1, K3 \oplus K2)$$

Reader: Updating $\{IDS^{old},\ K1^{old},\ K2^{old},\ K3^{old}\}$ and $\{IDS^{new},\ K1^{new},\ K2^{new},\ K3^{new}\}$
            with $n1$, $n2$

Tag: Updating $\{IDS,\ K1,\ K2,\ K3\}$ with $n1$, $n2$

The tag extracts n2 from D and verifies E. If succeeds, the *IDS* and the shared key *K1*, *K2*, and *K3* are updated in the same way as the reader side to stay consistency in the database.

In order to apply formal method into analysing RAPP, we need to abstract this protocol to overcome the limitation which is inconvenient to discuss security for the protocol directly due to the complexity of fundamental cryptograph operations in RAPP. A protocol abstract modeling method is proposed on the basis of principles that as follows:

(1) Assume that the cryptographic system used for this protocol is perfect, that is, there is no flaws in the encryption operation. Thus, we can focus on researching flaws that protocol itself really exists, not leaks of cryptosystem. To do this, we can abstract all cryptographic operations in RAPP into an *ENC()* function, and that function is supposed to be perfect.

(2) For convenience, the shared keychain *K1*, *K2*, *K3* in RAPP is denoted as the key tuple *Key*, that is, *Key* = {*K1*, *K2*, *K3*}.

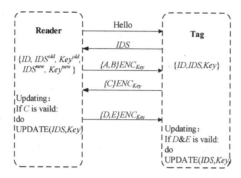

Fig. 1. The abstract protocol model of RAPP

(3) Define a key fundamental information updating function *UPDATE()* which proceeds update operation, and this function can be achieved both in reader and tag side.

Then, following three principles above, the abstract interactive model of RAPP can be built as shown in Fig. 1.

According to abstract protocol model above, the formal representation of reduced RAPP protocol is obtained as follows:

$$(1)\ Reader \rightarrow Tag{:}\{A,B\}ENC_{Key};$$
$$(2)\ Tag \rightarrow Reader{:}\{C\}ENC_{Key};$$
$$(3)\ Reader \rightarrow Tag{:}\{D,E\}ENC_{Key};$$
$$(4)\ Reader{:}UPDATE(IDS,Key);$$
$$(5)\ Tag{:}UPDATE(IDS,Key);$$

Here, *ID* is the unique identity of the tag, *IDS* is the pseudonym information of the tag, Key is the key tuple, *ENC()* is the encryption function, and *UPDATE()* is the update function.

4 Modeling RAPP with Promela

After formalizing the RAPP, we need to convert it into Promela model. The protocol model mainly include the protocol instance model and the intruder model. Intruder modeling method is guided by Dolve-Yao [12]. When building the protocol instance model and the intruder model with Promela, we assume that: ① Intruder can pretend to be any legal agents; ② The only way to decrypt an encrypted message is to know the corresponding key; ③ Intruder can always steal the *IDS* data of tag.

4.1 Modeling the Protocol Instance

RAPP consists two honest principals: Reader and Tag, so we need to define processes respectively for those two principals which are named as *proctype PReader()* and *proctype PTag()*. Messages exchanged in RAPP are divided into two categories based on the number of items in each message. As results, two different global channels are needed to transfer messages in RAPP. Thus, global channels are defined as follows:

$$\text{chan } ca = [0] \text{ of } \{\text{mtype}, \text{mtype}, \text{mtype}, \text{mtype}, \text{mtype}, \text{byte}\};$$
$$\text{chan } cb = [0] \text{ of } \{\text{mtype}, \text{mtype}, \text{mtype}, \text{byte}\};$$

Message (1) and (3) from the abstract model are transmitted by *ca* channel, whereas message (2) is transmitted by *cb* channel. Take *ca* as an example, if an agent wants to send messages via *ca* channel, the sending statement format should be *ca! x1, x2, x3, x4, x5*. In that pattern, *x1* represents message receiver, *x2* and *x3* is the data items, *x4* represents encryption key, *x5* represents session key version. The reception of a message by an agent is expressed similarly. The ultimate goal of protocol modeling is to transform the protocol into a concurrent system. However, state transitions between processes might be huge and could even cause state explosion problems [20]. To cut down the state transitions between processes, we can use *eval* function to judge which messages that can be received correctly. Like statement *ca? eval(x1), x2, x3, eval(x4), eval(x5)*, it acquires the receiver, key, and key version should be consistent with given parameters. If any of them does not meet the condition, receiver will drop the message.

As reader stores two sets of key information that is $\{Key^{old}, Key^{new}\}$, we use an array, which is expressed as *readerKeySet[2]*, to store previous key and latest key. In RAPP, the session key version needs to be negotiated before session begins. In other words, session key must be chosen from the previous key or the latest key when session tends to start. What's more, fundamental information update operation is required as long as protocol authentication is completed. To achieve that action, we define a *ChooseKey()* function to negotiate the session key version by matching the tag's key with *readerKeySet* array that stored in reader. More specifically, if the tag's key matches *readerKeySet[0]*, the session key version will be previous key; if the tag's key matches *readerKeySet[1]*, the session key version will be latest key. The next step is defining update operation function for RAPP. According to updating rules in RAPP, we define *Update(x,y,z)* function to reach that goal. In that function, *x* represents *IDS*, *y* represents *Key*, and *z* is Reader or Tag agent. *Update(x,y,z)* function is realized by proceeding these operations that as follows: ① Reader side. If the current session key version is an previous key, so the previous key remains unchanged, and the latest key's value performs update action as *readerKeySet[1]++*; If the current session key version is an latest key, the current session key is supposed to be assigned to the previous key, which is *readerKeySet[0] = readerKeySet[1]*, then the latest key version does *readerKeySet[1]++*. ② Tag side. Performing the operation as *tagKey_ver++*.

After *ChooseKey()* and *Update()* functions having been defined, we take *proctype PReader()* as an example, and code is shown below in details:

```
proctype PReader (mtype self;mtype party;mtype msg1;mtype msg2){
       mtype g1;
        atomic{
        ChooseKey();//Choose session key
        IniRunning(self,party);
        ca !party, msg1, msg2,Key,readerKey_use;
        }
        atomic{
        ChooseKey();
        cb ? eval(self),g1 eval(Key),eval(readerKey_use);
        Update(IDS,Key,Reader);//Perform update operations
        IniCommit(self,party);
        ca ! party, D, E,Key,readerKey_use;
        }
   }
```

Parameter *self* represents the identity of the host where the initiator process is running, whereas *party* is the identity of the host with which *self* host wants to run a protocol session. *g1* is a generic data item which is used to receive unknown data items. *atomic* is used to define a statement sequence executions which cannot be interruptible, so it can compress states. *IniRunning* and *IniCommit* are two macros used to update the values of variables recording the atomic predicates which are used to express the authentication properties. For example, *IniRunning(Reader,Tag)* expresses that Reader initiates a protocol session with Tag. *IniCommit(Reader,Tag)* expresses that Tag takes part in a protocol run with agent Reader. In the protocol configuration of RAPP we want to analyse, we need global boolean variables to describe them, so there are defined as follows:

```
bit ConsistencyRT=1;bit IniRunningRT = 0;bit IniCommitRT = 0;
bit ResRunningRT = 0;bit ResCommitRT = 0;
```

As for *ConsistencyRT*, it represents the consistency of key version between Reader and Tag. *ConsistencyRT* is true iff the key version stored in Reader always corresponds to Tag side. To do this, we define a *CheckConsistency()* method in the system to check consistency all the time between Rader and Tag.

In this paper, we dedicate to verifying authenticity and consistency properties of RAPP. Authentication of Tag to Reader in RAPP can be expressed that *ResRunningRT* must be true before *IniCommitRT*, whereas the converse authentication property corresponds to saying that *IniRunningRT* becomes true before *ResCommitRT*. Similarly, authentication of Reader to Tag can be defined following the same rules. Also, the key version of the two agents Reader and Tag always needs to be consistent. Thus, we have defined authenticity and consistency properties, and those properties in LTL formalism [21] can be expressed as:

- [] ((([]!IniCommitRT)||(!IniCommitRT∪ResRunningRT))
- [] ((([]!ResCommitRT)||(!ResCommitRT∪IniRunningRT))
- [] ([]ConsistencyRT)

With the same rules, we can define the processes of the other principals. The initial process is shown below:

```
init{
    atomic{
            run PReader(Reader,Tag,A,B);
            run PTag(Tag,Reader,C);
            run PI();
    }
}
```

PI() is intruder process which can intercept any messages from the message channel.

4.2   Modeling the Intruder

In Dolve-Yao attacker model, intruder has a powerful ability to intercept, recombine, and forward any messages in the channel. However, this capability is limited without knowing the session key. If intruder knows a few knowledge, it can learn new knowledge items through intercepting and eavesdropping messages. Therefore, it is important to build intruder's knowledge repository. The intruder's knowledge repository is divided into two parts that are the basic knowledge set and the learnt knowledge set. The basic knowledge set is the initial knowledge of intruder. The learnt knowledge set is the knowledge that intruder decrypts from intercepted messages, or the whole messages which cannot be decrypted.

In order to further reduce state transitions, it is necessary to simplify the knowledge item representation of intruder. So, the intersection of message elements which the intruder can eventually acquire and potentially needed are messages that needed to denote by the intruder. As is shown in Fig. 2.

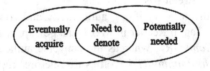

Fig. 2. The actual knowledge set which needs to be denoted.

The knowledge elements which can be learnt by attacker finally will be obtained through analyzing the sending statements of legal principals. In RAPP protocol, since the key is pre-shared between Reader and Tag, intruder can only store the intercepted messages completely which are shown as Table 1.

Table 1. Knowledge elements that the intruder can acquire

Received messages	Learnt item
$\{A,B\}ENC_{Key}$	$\{A,B\}ENC_{Key}$
$\{D,E\}ENC_{Key}$	$\{D,E\}ENC_{Key}$
$\{C\}ENC_{Key}$	$\{C\}ENC_{Key}$

The next step is to analyze the knowledge items which will be used to construct and send to the legal principals potentially by intruder. Therefore, the knowledge elements which intruder need to learn will be acquired while analyzing the received messages of legal principals. Following rules above, the knowledge elements results are as shown as Table 2.

Table 2. Knowledge elements that the intruder potentially needs

Messages	Needed knowledge
$\{A,A\}ENC_{Key}, \{A,B\}ENC_{Key},$ $\{A,C\}ENC_{Key} \{A,D\}ENC_{Key},$ $\{A,E\}ENC_{Key,}, \{A,gD\}ENC_{Key,}$ $\{B,A\}ENC_{Key}, \{B,B\}ENC_{Key},$ $\{B,C\}ENC_{Keyy} \{B,D\}ENC_{Key},$ $\{B,E\}ENC_{Key,}, \{B,gD\}ENC_{Key,}$ $\{C,A\}ENC_{Key}, \{C,B\}ENC_{Key},$ $\{C,C\}ENC_{Key} \{C,D\}ENC_{Key},$ $\{C,E\}ENC_{Key,}, \{C,gD\}ENC_{Key}$ $\{D,A\}ENC_{Key}, \{D,B\}ENC_{Key},$ $\{D,C\}ENC_{Key} \{D,D\}ENC_{Keyy},$ $\{D,E\}ENC_{Key,}, \{D,gD\}ENC_{Key}$ $\{E,A\}ENC_{Key}, \{E,B\}ENC_{Key},$ $\{E,C\}ENC_{Key} \{E,D\}ENC_{Key},$ $\{E,E\}ENC_{Key,}, \{E,gD\}ENC_{Key,}$ $\{gD,A\}ENC_{Key}, \{gD,B\}ENC_{Key},$ $\{gD,C\}ENC_{Key} \{gD,D\}ENC_{Key},$ $\{gD,E\}ENC_{Key,},\{gD,gD\}ENC_{Key}$	A, B, C, D, E, Key or $\{A,A\}ENC_{Key}, \{A,B\}ENC_{Key},$ $\{A,C\}ENC_{Key} \{A,D\}ENC_{Key},$ $\{A,E\}ENC_{Key,}.$ $\{A,gD\}ENC_{Key,}$ $\{B,A\}ENC_{Key}, \{B,B\}ENC_{Key},$ $\{B,C\}ENC_{Keyy} \{B,D\}ENC_{Key},$ $\{B,E\}ENC_{Key,}.$ $\{B,gD\}ENC_{Key,}$ $\{C,A\}ENC_{Key}, \{C,B\}ENC_{Key},$ $\{C,C\}ENC_{Key} \{C,D\}ENC_{Key},$ $\{C,E\}ENC_{Key,}, \{C,gD\}ENC_{Key}$ $\{D,A\}ENC_{Key}, \{D,B\}ENC_{Key},$ $\{D,C\}ENC_{Key} \{D,D\}ENC_{Keyy},$ $\{D,E\}ENC_{Key,}.$ $\{D,gD\}ENC_{Key}$ $\{E,A\}ENC_{Key}, \{E,B\}ENC_{Key},$ $\{E,C\}ENC_{Key} \{E,D\}ENC_{Key},$ $\{E,E\}ENC_{Key,}.$ $\{E,gD\}ENC_{Key,}$ $\{gD,A\}ENC_{Key}, \{gD,B\}ENC_{Key},$ $\{gD,C\}ENC_{Key} \{gD,D\}ENC_{Key},$ $\{gD,E\}ENC_{Key,},\{gD,gD\}ENC_{Key,}$
$\{A\}ENC_{Key}, \{B\}ENC_{Keyy},$ $\{C\}ENC_{Keyy} \{D\}ENC_{Keyy},$ $\{E\}ENC_{Key,}, \{gD\}ENC_{Key}$	A, B, C, D, E, Key或 $\{A\}ENC_{Key}, \{B\}ENC_{Keyy},$ $\{C\}ENC_{Keyy} \{D\}ENC_{Keyy},$ $\{E\}ENC_{Key,}, \{gD\}ENC_{Key}$

The knowledge items which the attacker needs to denote are the intersection of the right column of Tables 1 and 2, and results are shown as follows:

$$\{A, B\}ENC_{Key}; \quad \{D, E\}ENC_{Key}; \quad \{C\}ENC_{Key}$$

Based on analysis results mentioned above, the intruder's behaviors can be described in Promela. The coding framework of intruder is shown as follows:

```
proctype PI() {
        mtype x1=0;mtype x2=0;mtype x3=0;mtype x4=0;byte x5=0;
        bit k_A_B__Key = 0;/* knowledge items that need to denote*/
        bit k_C__Key = 0;
        bit k_D_E__Key =0;
        bit kA = 0;bit kB = 0;bit kC = 0;bit kD = 0;
        bit kE = 0;bit k_Key=0;
        do
        :: ca! (((kA && kB && k_Key) || k_A_B__Key) -> Tag:R), A, B, Key,0
        :: ca! ((kA && kC && k_Key) -> Tag:R), A, C, Key,0
        :: cb! ((kB && k_Key) -> Reader:R), B, Key,0
        :: cb! (((kC && k_Key) || k_C__Key) -> Reader:R), C, Key,0
        :: d_step{ca? x1,x2,x3,x4,x5; ···}/*intercepting messages from
        channel ca*/
        :: d_step{cb? x1,x2,x3,x5; ···}/*intercepting messages from  channel
        cb*/
        od
    }
```

Performing the verification in SPIN 5.2.0 with the environment of Window7 64bit system and Cygwin2.510.2.2, we discover the desynchronization attack.

5   Analysis of Verification Results

The error trail showing the desynchronization attack is reported in Fig. 3. Intruder aims at making invalidate state either in Reader or Tag. Hence, the attack basically breaks the synchronization among Tag and Reader. As soon as the attack sequence comes out, we perform analysis of verification results. The following is the attack process.

PIni:1
10
1!Tag,R,B,Key,0
PRes:3
11
16
2!Reader,C,Key,0
PI:2
17
25
2!Reader,C,Key,0
26
29
1!Tag,D,E,Key,0
30
34
1!Tag,R,B,Key,0
35
39
1!Tag,D,E,Key,0
40
44
2!Reader,C,Key,0
45
48
1!Tag,D,E,Key,0
49

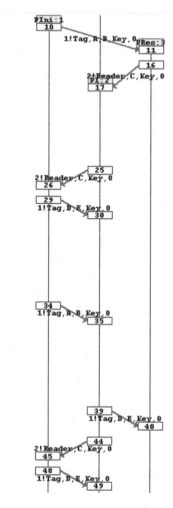

Fig. 3. Attack sequence diagram

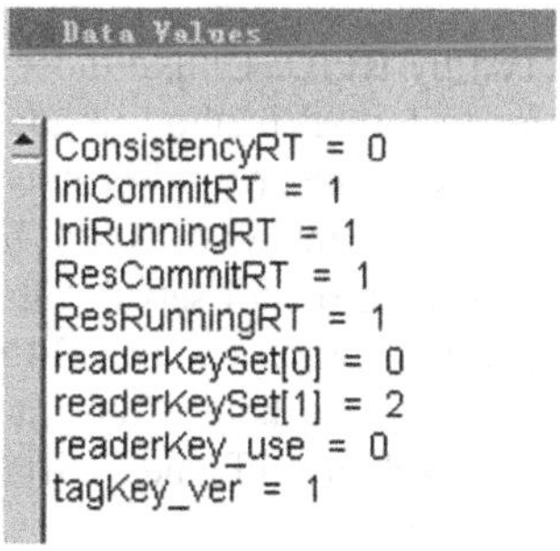

Data Values
ConsistencyRT = 0
IniCommitRT = 1
IniRunningRT = 1
ResCommitRT = 1
ResRunningRT = 1
readerKeySet[0] = 0
readerKeySet[1] = 2
readerKey_use = 0
tagKey_ver = 1

Fig. 4. Data values in the protocol

```
Stage1:
Key_version                      session_Key_version
Reader{0,0};Tag{0}                      [0]
Session flow:
Reader→Tag:{A,B}ENC_Key                              (1.1)
Tag→Intruder:{C} ENC_Key                             (1.2)
Intruder→Reader: {C} ENC_Key                         (1.3)
Reader→Intruder: {D,E} ENC_Key                       (1.4)


Stage2:
Key_version                      session_Key_version
Reader{0,1};Tag{0}                      [0]
Session flow:
Reader→Intruder:{A,B}ENC_Key                         (2.1)
Intruder→Tag:{D,E} ENC_Key                           (2.2)
Intruder→Reader: {C} ENC_Key                         (2.3)
Reader→Intruder: {D,E} ENC_Key                       (2.4)
```

Although intruder does not know the session key, they still has ability to steal messages $\{A,B\}ENC_{Key}$ and $\{C\}ENC_{Key}$. In stage1, with the intruder blocking message $\{D,E\} ENC_{Key}$. Tag cannot perform update operations while Reader has already updated its *Key*. In stage2, intruder uses intercepted messages of stage1 to disguise as a legal Tag to communicate with the reader. Since the intercepted messages of stage1 are used, Reader uses the previous key for the session. When intruder starts communicating with Reader, they also pretends as an another Reader to replay message $\{D,E\}$ ENC_{Key} of stage1 to Tag. After the end of whole session, Reader performs update operations twice, while Tag only has once. After the attack is complete, the previous key version in Reader is 0, the latest key version is 2, the key version in Tag is 1, and the key version used for the last session is 0. Data Values in RAPP protocol is shown in Fig. 4. In other words, the attack makes inconsistency of keys between Reader and Tag, which it is called desynchronization attack. Eventually, the legal tag cannot communicate with the reader any more.

6 Conclusion and Future Work

Security is the critical issue faced by RFID. Unlike those protocols that adopt public key cryptosystem, we cannot apply formal method to analyze ultralightweight protocols directly. Thus, in order to research security of protocol itself, this paper explores methods of building an abstract protocol model of RAPP by utilizing protocol abstract modeling method. It is found that the protocol satisfies the authenticity, but does not satisfy the consistency. From the verification results, SPIN has found desynchronization attack successfully in RAPP with the help of abstract modeling method. In the future, we will dedicate to improving the RAPP and verifying the security of improved protocol.

Acknowledgements. This work is supported by National Natural Science Foundation of China (NSFC) under grant of No. 61163005 and 61562026, the Natural Science Foundation of Jiangxi Province of China under grant of No. 20161BAB202063, and the Foreign Science Technology Cooperation Project of Jiangxi Province (No. 20151BDH80005).

References

1. Bruce, N., Kim, H., Kang, Y., Lee, Y., Lee, H.: On modeling protocol-based clustering tag in RFID systems with formal security analysis. In: 2015 IEEE 29th International Conference on Advanced Information Networking and Applications (AINA), pp. 498–505 (2015). doi:10.1109/AINA.2015.227

2. Qian, Q., Jia, Y.L., Zhang, R.: A lightweight RFID security protocol based on elliptic curve crytography. Int. J. Netw. Secur. **18**(2), 354–361 (2016)

3. López, P.P., Castro, D.D.J.C.H., Garnacho, D.D.A.R.: Lightweight cryptography in radio frequency identification (RFID) systems. Computer Science Department, Carlos III University of Madrid (2008)

4. Chien, H.Y., Huang, C.W.: Security of ultra-lightweight RFID authentication protocols and its improvements. ACM SIGOPS Oper. Syst. Rev. **41**(4), 83–86 (2007). doi:10.1145/1278901.1278916

5. Peris-Lopez, P., Hernandez-Castro, J.C., Tapiador, J.M.E., Ribagorda, A.: Advances in ultralightweight cryptography for low-cost RFID tags: Gossamer protocol. In: Chung, K., Sohn, K., Yung, M. (eds.) WISA 2008. LNCS, vol. 5379, pp. 56–68. Springer, Heidelberg (2009). doi:10.1007/978-3-642-00306-6_5

6. Chien, H.Y.: SASI: a new ultralightweight RFID authentication protocol providing strong authentication and strong integrity. IEEE Trans. Dependable Secure Comput. **4**(4), 337–340 (2007). doi:10.1109/tdsc.2007.70226

7. Gurubani, J.B., Thakkar, H., Patel, D.R.: Improvements over extended LMAP+: RFID authentication protocol. In: Dimitrakos, T., Moona, R., Patel, D., McKnight, D.H. (eds.) IFIPTM 2012. IAICT, vol. 374, pp. 225–231. Springer, Heidelberg (2012). doi:10.1007/978-3-642-29852-3_17

8. Tian, Y., Chen, G., Li, J.: A new ultralightweight RFID authentication protocol with permutation. IEEE Commun. Lett. **16**(5), 702–705 (2012). doi:10.1109/lcomm.2012.031212.120237

9. Xiao, M., Ma, C., Deng, C., Zhu, K.: A novel approach to automatic security protocol analysis based on authentication event logic. Chin. J. Electron. **24**(1), 187–192 (2015). doi:10.1049/cje.2015.01.031

10. Holzmann, G.J.: The model checker SPIN. IEEE Trans. Software Eng. **23**(5), 279–295 (1997)

11. Maggi, P., Sisto, R.: Using SPIN to verify security properties of cryptographic protocols. In: Bošnački, D., Leue, S. (eds.) SPIN 2002. LNCS, vol. 2318, pp. 187–204. Springer, Heidelberg (2002). doi:10.1007/3-540-46017-9_14

12. Dolev, D., Yao, A.: On the security of public key protocols. IEEE Trans. Inf. Theory **29**(2), 198–208 (1983)

13. Qingling, C., Yiju, Z., Yonghua, W.: A minimalist mutual authentication protocol for RFID system & BAN logic analysis. In: ISECS International Colloquium on Computing, Communication, Control, and Management, CCCM 2008, vol. 2, pp. 449–453. IEEE (2008). doi:10.1109/CCCM.2008.305

14. Islam, S.: Security analysis of LMAP using AVISPA. Int. J. Secure. Netw. **9**(1), 30–39 (2014). doi:10.1504/ijsn.2014.059325
15. Yuan, G., Long, S.: Formal verification of RFID protocols using nuXmv. In: 2016 10th IEEE International Conference on Anti-counterfeiting, Security, and Identification (ASID), pp. 58–62. IEEE (2016). doi:10.1109/ICASID.2016.7873917
16. Bagheri, N., Safkhani, M., Peris-Lopez, P., Tapiador, J.E.: Cryptanalysis of RAPP, an RFID authentication protocol. IACR Cryptology ePrint Archive, p. 702 (2012)
17. Shao-hui, W., Zhijie, H., Sujuan, L., Dan-wei, C.: Security analysis of RAPP an RFID authentication protocol based on permutation. College of computer, Nanjing University of Posts and Telecommunications, Nanjing, 210046 (2012)
18. Ahmadian, Z., Salmasizadeh, M., Aref, M.R.: Desynchronization attack on RAPP ultralightweight authentication protocol. Inf. Process. Lett. **113**(7), 205–209 (2013). doi:10.1016/j.ipl.2013.01.003
19. Bruce, N., Kim, H., Kang, Y., Lee, Y., Lee, H.: On modeling protocol-based clustering tag in RFID systems with formal security analysis. In: 2015 IEEE 29th International Conference on Advanced Information Networking and Applications (AINA), pp. 498–505. IEEE (2015). doi:10.1109/aina.2015.227
20. Hou, G., Zhou, K., Yong, J.: Survey of state explosion problem in model checking. Comput. Sci. **40**(06A), 77–86 (2013). doi:10.3969/j.issn.1002-137X.2013.z1.018
21. Xiao, M., Xue, J.: Formal description of properties of concurrency system by temporal logic. J. Naval Univ. Eng. **05**, 10–13 (2004). doi:10.3969/j.issn.1009-3486.2004.05.003

Double-Spending Detection for Fast Bitcoin Payment Based on Artificial Immune

Zhengjun Liu[1], Hui Zhao[2(✉)], Wen Chen[2], Xiaochun Cao[3], Haipeng Peng[4], Jin Yang[2], Tao Yang[1], and Ping Lin[1]

[1] College of Computer Science, Sichuan University, Chengdu 610065, China
[2] College of Cybersecurity, Sichuan University, Chengdu 610065, China
zhaohui@scu.edu.cn
[3] Institute of Information Engineering, Chinese Academy of Sciences,
Beijing 100093, China
[4] College of Cybersecurity, Beijing University of Posts and Telecommunications,
Beijing 100876, China

Abstract. With the rapid development of Bitcoin, it is frequently used in the scene of fast payment. But the strategy which Bitcoin takes to prevent the double-spending attack is waiting for six confirmations (about one hour), this is not suitable for the fast payment scenarios where service time is about tens of seconds. The default strategy in fast payment is that do not offer the service until a payment transaction is added to the wallet of vendor, which is useless for the detection of double-spending attack. In this paper, an immune-based model is proposed to detect the double-spending attack in the fast Bitcoin payment. This model is composed of many immune-based Bitcoin nodes which include a detection modula and a traditional node. Antigen character is first extracted from a transaction by the detection modula, and initial detectors (mature detectors) are generated based on these antigens. Then, memory detectors and mature detectors are used to detect the double-spending attack, and a mature detector which matches an attack will evolve into a memory detector and be delivered to other immune-based nodes in the Bitcoin network, in order to rapidly detect the double-spending attack. Experimental result shows that this model can efficiently detect double-spending attacks in fast Bitcoin payment.

Keywords: Artificial immune · Fast payment · Bitcoin · Double-spending

1 Introduction

Bitcoin, introduced in 2009 by Satoshi Nakamoto [1], is nowadays a very current currency and develops rapidly. The annual trade volume of Bitcoin in 2016 was five trillion and the market cap at April 2017 was 19.7 billion [2]. With the development of Bitcoin, many researchers focus on its security problems, where double-spending attack is one of the most serious problems [3]. The double-spending attack is in fact a successful attempt to first convince a merchant

© Springer Nature Singapore Pte Ltd. 2017
D. Du et al. (Eds.): NCTCS 2017, CCIS 768, pp. 133–143, 2017.
https://doi.org/10.1007/978-981-10-6893-5_10

that a transaction has been confirmed, and then convince the entire network to accept another transaction; the merchant would be left with neither product nor coins, while the attacker will get to keep both. In [1], Nakamoto used a consensus mechanism named Proof-of-Work and a public block chain to record all confirmed transactions, in order to prevent double-spending attacks. Rosenfeld [4] further derived the probability for a successful double-spending, and argued that the cost of a double-spending attack grew exponentially if vendors waited for six confirmations. Sompolinsky [5] investigated Bitcoin's security against double-spending attacks, and the results showed that at high throughput, substantially weaker attackers were able to reverse payments they had made, even well after they were considered accepted by recipients. Sompolinsky [6] further proposed a security model to improve the understanding of Bitcoin's security guarantees and to provide correct bounds for those wishing to safely accept transactions.

Nowadays, Bitcoin is increasingly utilized in many "fast payment" scenarios, where the trade time between the currency and goods is short, and the payment is followed by fast delivery of goods (such as tens of seconds). Examples include vending machine payments and fast-food payments (featured in media reports on Bitcoin [7]). However, the defence mechanisms mentioned above are just suitable for the detection of double-spending attacks in "slow payment" whose exchange time is tens of minutes. Therefore, they are inappropriate for "fast payments". Since users of Bitcoin are encouraged to hold many accounts, there is only limited value in verifying the payment after the user obtains the goods or services. Karame et al. [8,9] and Bambert et al. [10] have both considered double-spending in "fast payment" and argues that measures recommended by Bitcoin developers for the use of Bitcoin in fast transactions are not always effective in resisting double-spending.

In this work, we analyze the double-spending in fast Bitcoin payment, and propose a detection model based on artificial immune. In this model, a immune detection modula is added in each Bitcoin node. The main purposes of the detection modula are extracting antigens characters from Bitcoin transactions, generating detector with antigens, detecting double-spending attacks and spreading it on the Bitcoin network, in order to prevent the double-spending attack. Our contributions in this paper can be summarized as follows:

- We analyze the double-spending attack and three necessary conditions for performing successful double-spending attacks against fast payments in Bitcoin.
- We propose an immune-based detection model for the Bitcoin network, and give the basic definitions of Ag, $Self$, $nonself$ and $detector$ respectively.
- We define the dynamic evolution of $Self$, immature detector, mature detector and memory detector respectively, and analyze the way to detect double-spending attacks based on this model.

2   Double-Spending in Fast Bitcoin Payment

In the scenarios of fast Bitcoin payment, we can not wait one hour to confirm the payment, so the double-spending attack is feasible. As shown in Fig. 1, to perform

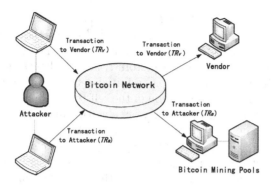

Fig. 1. Sketch of a double-spending attack against fast payment in Bitcoin. Attackers first dispatch a transaction (TR_v) to the vendor, then dispatch another transaction (TR_a) to a colluding address using the same BTCs. The double-spending attack is deemed successful if TR_a is included in the upcoming Bitcoin block.

a successful double-spending attack in fast Bitcoin payment, three necessary conditions should be satisfied:

(a) TR_v is added to the wallet of vendor. That is to say, TR_v should arrive to the vendor first, otherwise, it will be rejected (TR_a and TR_v use the same BTCs) and the vendor will ask the attacker to re-issue a new payment. TR_a will be rejected by the node(the vendor or its neighbor node) which has accepted TR_v, and the vendor never know TR_a exists.

(b) TR_a is confirmed in the Bitcoin block chain. If TR_v is confirmed first in the block chain, TR_a can never appear in subsequent blocks, so the attacker can not retrieve the spent BTCs.

(c) Service time of this vendor is shorter than the time to detect the misbehavior. Since Bitcoin users are anonymous and users hold many accounts, it is difficult to identify the attack after he obtains the vendor's service.

3   Proposed Theoretical Detection Models

Let $\Omega = \bigcup_{i=1}^{\infty}\{0,1\}^i$ be a set of binary strings. Given $\Upsilon \subset \Omega$, where Υ is the set of transaction packets transferred in the Bitcoin network. Given that $\Psi = \bigcup_{i=1}^{n}\Psi_i, \Psi_i = \{x = <x_1, \cdots, x_j, \cdots, x_d>|x_j \in \Upsilon\}$, where n is the number of Ψ, d is the dimension of x. x is similar to the characteristic code related to the corresponding Bitcoin transaction packet. Let $\Re = \{<a,b>|a \in \Psi, b \in \Upsilon\}$, Given antigen set $Ag \in \Re$, where $\forall x \in Ag$, $x.b$ is the original Bitcoin transaction packet and $x.a$ denotes the character of $x.b$, which is composed of timestamp, the hash of transaction, the source of BTCs, signature script, version, the count of BTCs, etc. Ag contains two subsets, $Self$ and $Nonself$, such that $Self \bigcup Nonself = Ag, Self \bigcap Nonself = \emptyset$. In this detection model, $Nonself$ represent the abnormal transactions from double-spending attacks, while $Self$ are normal transactions in the Bitcoin network. Detector set $Dts = \{\bigcup_{i=1}^{n} dt_i | dt_i = <a, age, count> | a \in \Psi, count \in N, age \in N\}$, where n is the number of Dts, a is the antibody of dt, age is the age of dt and $count$ is the number of antigens matched by dt. Dts contains three kinds of detectors: immature detectors I, mature detectors T and memory detectors M. An immature detector is an initial detector and a mature detector is an initial detector which passes through the self-tolerance but not activated by antigens. A memory detector is evolved from a mature one matching enough antigens in its lifecycle. Thus, $I = \{x | x \in Dts, x.age < \lambda \wedge x.count = 0\}$, $T = \{x | x \in Dts, \forall y \in Self, f_{match}(x.a, y) = 0 \wedge \lambda \leq x.age \leq max\_age \wedge x.count < \beta\}$, $M = \{x | x \in Dts, \forall y \in Self, f_{match}(x.a, y) = 0 \wedge x.age \geq max\_age \wedge x.count \geq \beta\}$, where λ is the period of self-tolerance, β is the activation threshold and f_{match} is a matching function based on the affinity between a detector and an antigen: if the affinity is greater than a specified threshold, then 1 is returned, otherwise, 0 is returned. The matching function can be r-contiguous-bits matching rule, Hamming distance, Euler distance, etc. [11].

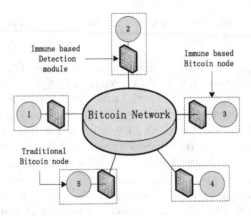

Fig. 2. Sketch of immune-based detection model. An immune-based detection module is added into each Bitcoin node. The purpose of this module is detecting double-spending attacks and delivering the corresponding vaccines to Bitcoin network.

In this paper, a new detection model based immune, named IMDM, is proposed to detect double-spending attacks in fast Bitcoin payment. As shown in Fig. 2, IMDM is composed of many immune-based Bitcoin nodes which include a traditional node and a detection module. The purpose of detection module is to detect attacks and to share information with other nodes. Figure 3 illustrates the framework of a detection module. There are three main stages in this module: (1) The dynamic evolution of $Self$. The antigen elements extracted from Bitcoin transactions are detected by memory detectors and mature detectors respectively. Meanwhile the survived elements are taken as self-antigens and used in the process of self-tolerance model; (2) The dynamic evolution of $Detector$. New immature detectors have to experience a self-tolerance period,

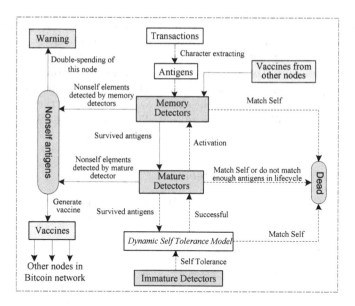

Fig. 3. The framework of Detection module. The solid arrows indicate *Self* evolution, the long dashed arrows indicate *Detector* evolution while the short dashed arrows indicate attack-detection and vaccine-generation.

and detectors which match any self-antigen will be eliminated (negative selection [12]). The survived immature detectors will evolve into mature detectors, having a fixed lifecycle. A mature detector that do not match enough antigens or matches self-antigen in its lifecycle will be eliminated, otherwise, it will evolve into a memory detector. The memory detector has an infinite lifecycle, and will be eliminated as soon as it matches a self-antigen. (3) The detection of attacks and the generation of vaccine. Antigens are extracted from Bitcoin transactions. When a nonself-antigen (double-spending) is detected by mature detector, a corresponding vaccine is generated and delivered to other immune-based nodes in Bitcoin network. If the double-spending is an attack for this node, a warning will be sent to node's owner.

3.1   Dynamic Evolution of Self

$$
Self(t) = \begin{cases} \{x_1, x_2, \cdots, x_n\}, & t = 0 \\ Self(t-1), & t \bmod \lambda \neq 0 \\ Self(t-1) \bigcup Self_{new}(t) - Self_{dead}(t), & else \end{cases} \tag{1}
$$

$$
Self_{dead}(t) \begin{cases} \emptyset, & Self(t-1) + Self_{new}(t) < max\_s \\ \{eariest\ Self_{new}(t)\ elements\ in\ Self(t-1)\}, & else \end{cases} \tag{2}
$$

Equation 1 simulates the dynamic evolution of self-antigens, where $Self(t) \subseteq Self$ is the self set at time t, $x_i \in Ag(0 < i < n)$ is an initial self element. $Self_{new}(t)$ is the new self-antigens which are not detected by detectors. $\lambda(>0)$ is called the evolution period of $Self$. $Self$ keeps stable in the period of λ, but will be supplemented at the end of evolution period λ. However, the earliest self elements ($Self_{dead}$) will be eliminated when the size of $Self$ exceeds the threshold max_s, thus, the size of $Self$ will not increase unlimitedly, therefore, the self-tolerance for immature detector can be carried out in a high efficient way.

3.2   Dynamic Evolution of Detector

In this section, the evolution of three kinds detectors (named immature detector I, mature detector T and memory detector M respectively) are discussed.

$$I(t) = \begin{cases} \{x_1, x_2, \cdots, x_k\}, & t = 0 \\ (f_{inc\_age}(I(t-1)) - I_{dead}(t) - I_{mature}(t)) \bigcup I_{new}(t), & t > 0 \end{cases} \tag{3}$$

$$I_{dead}(t) = \{x | x \in f_{inc\_age}(I(t-1)) \bigwedge \exists y \\ \in Self(t-1) \bigwedge (f_{match}(x.a, y) = 1)\} \tag{4}$$

$$I_{mature}(t) = \{x | x \in (f_{inc\_age}(I(t-1)) - I_{dead}(t)) \bigwedge x.age \geq \lambda\} \tag{5}$$

Equation 3 simulates the self-tolerance process of immature detector, where $x_i = \{<a, 0, 0> | a \in \Psi, 1 < i < k\}$ is an initial immature detector, λ is the period of self-tolerance. $f_{inc\_age}(X)$ is a function which increases the age of all elements in X by 1. $I_{new}(t)$ is the new randomly generated immature detectors at time t. I_{mature} is the survived immature detector which passed through the self-tolerance, and I_{dead} is the eliminated detectors in the process of self-tolerance.

$$T(t) = \begin{cases} \emptyset, & t = 0 \\ T'(t)) - T_{dead}(t) - T_{memory}(t) \bigcup I_{mature}(t), & t > 0 \end{cases} \tag{6}$$

$$T'(t) = f_{inc\_age}(f_{inc\_count}(T(t-1))) \tag{7}$$

$$T_{dead}(t) = \{x | x \in T'(t) \bigwedge x.age = max\_age \bigwedge x.count < \beta\} \tag{8}$$

$$T_{memory}(t) = \{x | x \in T'(t) \bigwedge x.age \leq max\_age \bigwedge x.count \geq \beta\} \tag{9}$$

Equation 6 depicts the lifecycle of mature detectors. All mature detectors have a fixed lifecycle (max_age). If a mature detector matches enough antigens ($\geq \beta$) in its lifecycle, it will evolve into a memory detector, otherwise, it will be killed and new mature detectors are supplemented. If a nonself-antigen is detected by a mature detector x, function $f_{inc\_count}(x)$ will increase the count of x by 1. T_{dead} is the eliminated detectors while T_{memory} is the detectors which evolve into memory detectors.

$$M(t) = \begin{cases} \emptyset, & t = 0 \\ M'(t)) - M_{dead}(t) \bigcup T_{memory}(t) \bigcup M_{vaccine}(t), & t > 0 \end{cases} \quad (10)$$

$$M'(t) = f_{inc\_age}(f_{inc\_count}(M(t-1))) \quad (11)$$

$$M_{dead}(t) = \{x | x \in M'(t) \bigwedge \exists y \in Self(t) \bigwedge (f_{match}(x.a, y) = 1)\} \quad (12)$$

Equation 10 depicts the dynamic evolution of immune memory. $M_{dead}(t)$ is the detectors which match a known self-antigen at time t. $M_{vaccine}(t)$ is the vaccines received from other immune-base nodes in Bitcoin network, and the generation of a vaccine will be discussed in next section. With these vaccines, a second attack will be found rapidly if it was detected on other immune-based node.

3.3 Detection of Double-Spending and Generation of Vaccine

The Bitcoin transactions are accepted by the immune-based module in the new model. Then some identity characters of each transaction are extracted to construct an element $b(b \in Ag)$. The identity characters include timestamp, the hash of transaction, the sources of BTCs, signature script, version, the count of BTCs, etc. If b is matched by mature detector, it indicates b is a new double-spending that never occurs. Therefore, this immune-based module will generate a vaccine (according to Eq. 13) and send it to Bitcoin network. If a double-spending aims at this node (the destination address of BTCs is this node), the immune-based module will show a "warning" to inform the node owner (maybe a vender or a merchant who accepts a fast Bitcoin payment) that he is attacked by a double-spending. This measure breaks the first necessary condition of the double-spending in fast Bitcoin payment, so this kind of attack can be rapidly detected in this immune-based Bitcoin network.

$$Vaccine(t) = M_{vaccine}(t) = \{x | x \in Dts, y \in T(t) \bigwedge (f_{match}(y.a, b) = 1) \\ \bigwedge x.a = y.a \bigwedge x.age = max\_age \bigwedge x.count = y.count + 1\} \quad (13)$$

4   Simulations and Experiment Results

According to the immune-based model, an antigen is defined as a fixed length binary string composed of timestamp, hash, the source of BTCs, signature script, the count of BTCs, etc. Table 1 shows the structure of an antigen extracted from a transaction in Bitcoin network. In order to test the performance of this model, we carried the simulation experiments on a real-world Bitcoin data set which is collected from a Bitcoin portal [13]. There are $1,000$ normal transactions ($Self$) and 500 double-spending attacks ($Nonself$) in this data set. Half of $Self$ and $Nonself$ is randomly selected as the train set, while the rest of them are test set.

Table 1. The antigen structure of Bitcoin transaction

Num	Field name	Size (bytes)
1	Timestamp	4
2	Hash	64
3	Version	4
4	Count of BTCs	8
5	Source of BTCs	32
6	Destination of BTCs	32
7	Length	8
8	Signature script	64

The selective rule of the model parameters is according to the situation in the real network environment. Due to the dynamic definition of $self$, the tolerance period λ decides the generation speed of mature detector, while the lifecycle max_age decides the death speed of mature detector and max_age should be greater than λ. The activation threshold β decides the generation speed of memory detector. A small β means that we can generate memory detector quickly. The size of $self$ (max_s) is based on the computer capability, i.e., max_s should be a great value if it is sure that the system efficiency do not decrease. Thus, in these experiments, refering to [14], we have $\lambda = 2$, $max\_age = 7$, $max\_s = 500$, $\beta = 4$ respectively. Two evaluation criterions, named Detection Rate (DR), False Alarm Rate (FAR), are adopted in these experiments, and they are defined as follows:

$$DR = \frac{nonself\ correctly\ classified}{total\ nonself} = \frac{TP}{TP + FN} \tag{14}$$

$$FAR = \frac{self\ incorrectly\ classified}{total\ self} = \frac{FP}{FP + TN} \tag{15}$$

where TP, TN, FP, FN are the number of true positive nonself-element, true negative self-element, false positive self-element and false negative nonself-element respectively.

Figure 4 illustrates the mature detector generating efficiency with different size of self set for both $IMDM$ and $IMDM\_0$, where the number of generated mature detectors is fixed, e.g., 100, $|Self|$ is the number of $Self$. $IMDM\_0$ is the $IMDM$ model without $Self$ dynamic evolution. In $IMDM$, due to the dynamic evolution of $Self$, the number of self elements used in the immune tolerance process is a small and constant number. Thus the time used to generate a fixed number of mature detector is stable. It does not increase too much when the size of self set increases.

As the mature detector will evolve into a memory detector when it is activated, so the number of memory detector ($|M|$) indicates the recognition ability of both mature and memory detector. Figure 5 shows the performance of $IMDM$

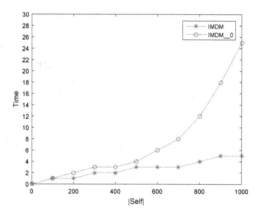

Fig. 4. The efficiency of mature detector generation.

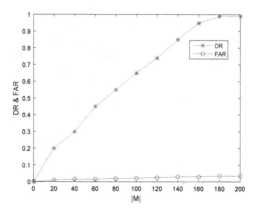

Fig. 5. The performance of IMDM.

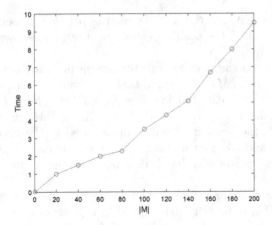

Fig. 6. The time expense of IMDM.

with different $|M|$. The FAR of this model is nearly 0%, which indicates that $IMDM$ has a better recognition for $Self$. With the increasing of $|M|$, the recognition ability (DR) is improved rapidly. When $|M|$ is greater than 90, $IMDM$ can recognize almost all attacks. This indicates that the proposed model has a strong ability of self learning. It also indicates that the detection ability will be improved while increasing the size of memory detector set. Figure 6 shows the time expense of $IMDM$ with different $|M|$. When $|M|$ equals to 200, the time expense is the biggest, but also less than 10 s, which indicates this model can rapidly detect double-spending attacks. So it is suitable for the fast Bitcoin payment.

5   Conclusion

The ability of Bitcoin to support and process fast payments in which the time to acquire a service is few seconds is of paramount importance to its growth and popularity among users. However, given its design, Bitcoin can only ensure the security of payments when a payment verification time of few tens of minutes can be tolerated. To solve this problem, an immune-based detection model is proposed. The basic definition of this model and the dynamic evolutions of $Self$ and $Detector$ are discussed in this paper. Experiments shows that $IMDM$ can rapidly detect the double-spending and it is suitable for the scenarios of fast Bitcoin payment.

Acknowledgment. This research is supported by National key research and development program of China (Grant No. 2016YFB0800604 and Grant No. 2016YFB0800605) and Natural Science Foundation of China (Grant No. 61402308 and No. 61572334).

References

1. Nakamoto, S.: Bitcoin: a peer-to-peer electronic cash system. Consulted (2009)
2. Currency transactions monitoring report of bitcoin, 18 April 2017. http://if.cert. org.cn/jsp/activitiesDetail2.jsp?id=49
3. Tschorsch, F., Scheuermann, B.: Bitcoin and beyond: a technical survey on decentralized digital currencies. IEEE Commun. Surv. Tutorials, 1 (2016)
4. Rosenfeld, M.: Analysis of hashrate-based double spending. Eprint Arxiv (2014)
5. Sompolinsky, Y., Zohar, A.: Secure High-rate transaction processing in bitcoin. In: Böhme, R., Okamoto, T. (eds.) FC 2015. LNCS, vol. 8975, pp. 507–527. Springer, Heidelberg (2015). doi:10.1007/978-3-662-47854-7_32
6. Sompolinsky, Y., Zohar, A.: Bitcoins security model revisited, May 2016. https:// arxiv.org/abs/1605.09193
7. Cnn: Bitcoin's uncertain future as currency, 4 April 2011. http://www.youtube. com/watch?v=75VaRGdzMM0
8. Karame, G.O., Androulaki, E., Capkun, S.: Two bitcoins at the price of one? double-spending attacks on fast payments in bitcoin. In: Conference on Computer & Communication Security (2012)
9. Karame, G.O., Androulaki, E., Roeschlin, M., Gervais, A., Apkun, S.: Misbehavior in bitcoin: a study of double-spending and accountability. ACM Trans. Inf. Syst. Secur. 18(1), 1–32 (2015)
10. Bamert, T., Decker, C., Elsen, L., Wattenhofer, R.: Have a snack, pay with bitcoins. In: IEEE Thirteenth International Conference on Peer-To-Peer Computing, pp. 1–5 (2013)
11. Forrest, S., Hofmeyr, S.A., Somayaji, A.: Computer immunology. Immunol. Rev. 216(1), 176–197 (2007)
12. Forrest, S., Perelson, A.S., Allen, L., Cherukuri, R.: Self-nonself discrimination in a computer. In: Proceedings of the 1994 IEEE Computer Society Symposium on Research in Security and Privacy, pp. 202–212 (1994)
13. A portal of bitcoin, luxembourg s.a., April 2017. https://blockchain.info/
14. Glickman, M., Balthrop, J., Forrest, S.: A machine learning evaluation of an artificial immune system. Evol. Comput. 13(2), 179–212 (2005)

Research on Information Organizations and Intelligent Retrievals for Digital Library Based on Ontology and Semantic Web

Guangjun Guo[1,2], Zhigang Chen[1(✉)], Dong Xie[3], and Mei Li[2]

[1] Central South University, Changsha, China
gjguo@163.com, czg@csu.edu.cn
[2] Loudi Vocational and Technical College, Loudi, China
lgxzy@163.com
[3] Hunan University of Humanities, Science and Technology, Loudi, China
ldzylm@163.com

Abstract. The semantic web provides a semantic interoperation model, and effectively realizes discoveries, sharing and application integrations of network resources. This paper expounds the key technologies such as semantic web, semantic intelligent retrieval, ontology construction, and metadata standards of digital literature resources, analyzes the relationship between ontology and metadata, and presents ontology construction based on bibliographic metadata and the organization method for digital literature resources. Moreover, we design an intelligent retrieval system model for semantic of digital literature resources based on ontology. The system consists of digital document repository, semantic annotators, ontology manager, retrieving the preprocessor, retrieving the reflector, and searching engine. The experiment shows that our method can improve the recall and precision of digital literature resources retrieval.

Keywords: Digital literature resources · Information organization · Intelligent retrieval · Ontology · Semantic web

1 Introduction

Digital library is an important part of the national information infrastructure as an important carrier of knowledge economy, so it has become an important symbol of a national information base level and the competition focus of national culture, science and technology. To heterogeneous, dynamic, distributed information, we need quick information and resource sharing to achieve integrated information retrieval by the most convenient and user-friendly, the most intelligent and the most effective way, and this has become the focus area of construction and development of the digital library in the library and information science.

Traditional information retrieval methods based on keyword matching do not support semantic organization, understanding, and treatment of information to identify real search intent, so retrieval results literally meet user requirements. This causes missing and false checks because of the low efficiency of information retrieval. As a

© Springer Nature Singapore Pte Ltd. 2017
D. Du et al. (Eds.): NCTCS 2017, CCIS 768, pp. 144–154, 2017.
https://doi.org/10.1007/978-981-10-6893-5_11

result, people need a breakthrough information retrieval technology to support more powerful information retrieval capabilities, which can understand, automatically expand and associate the semantic for supporting personal services to users. Ontologies and Semantic Web technology provide semantic interoperability models to effectively achieve organization, sharing, discovery, and integration of information resources, and provide new technology ways for improving automatic and intelligent information organization and retrieval in the digital library.

2   Key Technologies

2.1   Semantic Web

Semantic Web extend current Web, and it uses the ontology technology to describe Internet information and gives well define for understanding and identifying by computers. This can intelligently access to Web resources and retrieval. In 2006, Tim Berners-Lee gave the new model for the Semantic Web [1], as shown in Fig. 1.

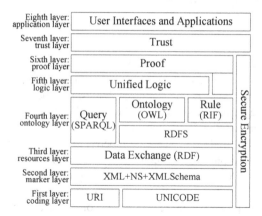

Fig. 1. The hierarchical model of the semantic web

The 1st layer, coding layer (UNICODE and URI): UNICODE use international uniform character to encodings of resources for achieve uniform coding of information on the Web; URI (Uniform Resource Identifier) supports identifications of objects and resources on Semantic Web.

The second layer, marker layer (XML+NS+XMLS): it will separate the structure, content, and forms of data resources on the Web to support seamless integrations with other XML-based standards.

The third layer, resources layer (RDF+RDFS): RDF is the basic data model for Semantic Web for describing Web resources. RDFS provides levels of modeling primitives by organizing Web objects, including classes, properties, subclasses, sub-properties relations, definition domain and value range constraints.

The fourth layer, ontology layer (Ontology+OWL): it uses OWL to represent ontology for describing complexities among resources and rich semantic information. It separates structures and contents of information, and makes fully formal description for information in order to Semantic Web information is readable for computers.

The fifth layer, logic layer: it is used to provide axioms and inference rules, and provides a basis for intelligent reasoning.

The sixth layer, proof layer: it implement rules of the logic layer, and judges whether we can trust given proofs Trusted application layer mechanisms according to application mechanisms of the trust layer.

The seventh layer, trust layer: it provides trust mechanisms, it guarantees to provide personalized services for user Agents on the Web and safe interactions each other.

The eighth layer, application layer: it provides user interfaces and specific business applications.

The second, third, and fourth layers (XML, RDF and Ontology) are used to describe semantic information of resources as the core of the whole system for the Semantic Web. Digital signatures are widely used in logic, proof and trust layers to determine whether documents are tampered, and this can ensure authenticities and reliabilities of data in the Semantic Web.

2.2   Ontology

Studer et al. [2] define that ontology is an explicit formal specifications of shared conceptual models. Some fields of the real world can be abstracted as a set of concepts and relationships among concepts by using ontologies, and they can provide universal, shared knowledge representations in the field achieving understanding and communication in heterogeneous distributed systems.

Ontology consists of [3] Concept, Property, Axiom, Value and Nominal. (1) Property is the description of the concept or the nature. Concept consists of the "original concept" and "definition concept" according to relationships between properties with concepts. "Original concept" may not contain the properties, and "definition concept" must contain properties in. (2) Axiom is constraint defined on "concept" and "properties" for further clarifying concept features. (3) Value generally refers to assigning values to attributes of concepts (specific characteristics of things). (4) Nominal usually includes two situations: some concepts in the ontology does not contain any instances; a concept is defined in the ontology by using a specific instance.

Ontology includes the top layer, field, tasks and application accordance to the field dependence [4]. Top-level ontology is the most common concepts and concept relationships such as space, time, event, action. Other types of ontologies are special cases of the ontology. Domain ontology (Digital literature) describes the relationship among concepts in specific domain. Task ontology describes concepts in specific tasks or actions and relationships of concepts. Application ontology describes concepts in specific tasks or fields and relationships of concepts.

3   Intelligent Semantic Retrieval

Bibliographic data with MARC format use the one-dimensional linear way. They are high structure degree and readable machine speed. Since they are lack of semantic information and object hierarchies, they are unable to adapt to requirements on information sharing and semantic knowledge discovery [5] and semantic retrieval under the Internet environment. On one hand, the intelligent semantic retrieval method uses the semantic technology to improve traditional information retrievals; on the other hand, the intelligent semantic retrieval method uses traditional information retrievals to help semantic queries. Traditional information retrievals can find reusable ontology in the semantic retrieval, and this can increase adaptabilities for semantic queries and improve performances of question-answering systems. Moreover, we may use inverted indexes of information retrievals to index semantic information and answer semantic queries.

4   Metadata of Digital Document Resources

Structured metadata provide information resources or data. They are structured descriptions of information resources for describing data characteristic and attributes of information resource and ruling organizations of digital information, so their functions are location, discovery, evidence, evaluation and selection, and so on.

Metadata determine the architecture of information resources in the digital library, and they are the basis of semantic interoperability across resources. Metadata mainly address definitions of the information architecture of digital objects and resources' organizational structures of digital objects. Digital objects are the basic logic unit of storing information in digital library, which determine the organization structure of information organization, utilization method, and resource library and provide unified interoperability. The metadata method is an important part of digital library construction shown in all aspects of the digital library development such as storage, retrieval, publishing and management. Metadata consist of several types such as management, descriptive, structural, access control, preservation, technical, usability, evaluation, and so on.

4.1   Metadata Standards

According to application fields of metadata, there several types: (1) the metadata standard for traditional books and journals includes MARC etc. (2) the metadata standard for network resources includes Dublin Core, IAFA/WHOIS++ Templates, LDIF (LDAP Data Interchange Format), SOIF (Summary Object Interchange Format), and URCs (Uniform Resource Characteristics/Citations) etc. (3) the metadata standard for government information includes GILS (Government Information Locator Service) and DC-Gov (DC-Government Application Profile) etc. (4) the metadata standard for science and technologies includes ibTEX, EELS (The Engineering Electronic Library), EEVL (The Edinburgh Engineering Virtual Library), and RFC1807 etc. (5) the metadata standard for resources of humanities and social sciences includes TEI Header and ICPSR SGML Codebook Initiative etc. (6) the metadata standard for educational resources includes IEEE LOM (Learn Object Model), GEM (GEM Element List), and DC-Ed (DC-Education) etc. (7) the metadata standard for museum collections or special collection includes CDWA (Categories for the Description of Works of Art), CIMI (Computer Interchange of Museum Information), VRA Core (Visual Resources Association Core), and REACH element sets etc. (8) the metadata standard for preservation scheme includes CEDARS, NLA, and NEDLIB etc. (9) the metadata standard for geospatial resources includes FGDC/CSDGM etc. (10) the metadata standard for preservation manuscripts and documents includes EAD etc. (11) the metadata standard for network multimedia and copyright managements includes INDECS etc.

Based on OAIS [6] (Open Archival Information System), the preservation Chinese metadata scheme of the reference model shown as Table 1.

Table 1. The Chinese metadata scheme

No.	Chinese names of metadata	English names of metadata
1	Chinese Title	Title
2	Chinese Subject	Subject
3	Chinese Edition	Edition
4	Chinese Abstract	Abstract
5	Chinese Content Type	ContentType
6	Languages	Language
7	Chinese Content Coverage	Coverage
8	Chinese Content Creator	Creator
9	Chinese Other Contributor	Contributor
10	Date of Chinese Content Creation	DateofCreation
11	Chinese Publisher	Publisher
12	Chinese Copyright Holder	CopyrightHolder
13	Chinese Resource Identifier	Identifier
14	Chinese Related Objects	RelatedObjects
15	Chinese Digital Publisher Name	DigitalPublisherName
16	Chinese Digital Publisher Date	DigitalPublisherDate
17	Chinese Digital Publisher Place	DigitalPublisherPlace
18	Chinese Rights Warning	RightsWarning
19	Chinese Open Actors	Actors
20	Chinese Actions	Actions
21	Chinese Original Technical Environments	OriginalTechnicalEnvironments
22	Chinese Ingest Process History	IngestProcessHistory
23	Chinese Administration History	AdministrationHistory
24	Chinese Authentication Indicator	AuthenticationIndicator
25	Chinese UAF-Description	UAF-Description

4.2 Bibliographic Metadata Standards

(1) DCMI [7] (Dublin Core Metadata Initiative) standard includes fifteen core elements. Where, (1) content property includes Title, Subject, Description, Source, Language, Relation, Coverage; (2) intellectual property includes Creator, Publisher, Contributor, Rights; (3) formality property includes Date, Type, Format, Identifier.

(2) FRBR [8] (Functional Requirements of Bibliographic Records) standard. The first group of entities includes names of bibliographic records or products described by knowledge or artistic creation: work, expression, manifestation and item. The second group of entities is responsible for knowledge or artistic content, material production, dissemination and managing products: person, corporation; the third group of entities include a serial of additional entities as subject of knowledge or artistic creations: concept, object, event, and place.

(3) RDA [9] (Resource Description & Access) standard inherits entities used in the FRBR whose core elements are from properties and relations with high matching values of users' tasks defined by FRBR and FRAD (Functional Requirements for Authority Data). Entities of FRBR are equivalent to Class of RDF (Resource Description Framework) model. However, RDA glossary downgrades second and three groups of entities to Subclass, and borrow from agent and subject of FRBROO (FRBR orient object) as their upper classes for two sets of entities.

5 Information Organization and Ontology Construction for Digital Literature Resources

5.1 Constructing Methods for Ontologies

Currently, constructing ontologies [10] is no a uniform standard. In 1995, Gruber proposed five principles for constructing ontologies: (1) clarity and objectivity: ontology should use natural language to provide clear and objective semantics definitions for terms. (2) completeness: proposed definitions are complete and fully able to express described meanings of terms. (3) consistency: inferences from terms are compatible with meanings of terms itself. (4) maximum monotonous scalability: existing content need not to be modified while ontologies are added into general or special terms. (5) Minimal ontological commitment: modeling object is given a minimum of constraints. Current important methods for constructing ontologies are shown as following: TOVE (Toronto Virtual Enterprise) [11], Skeletal [12], Methodology [13], KACTUS [14], SENSUS [15], IDEF5 [16], and seven steps [17].

5.2 Relationships Between Ontologies and Metadata

Ontologies and metadata are new methods with network information processing developments, and they are important for organizations and managements of knowledge and information retrieval. There are similarities and differences between them. Metadata is understandable information about Web resources and a number of other entities for machines [18]. Metadata and ontology have some same features shown as the followings: they use standard coding languages for formal processing; they can provide the semantic foundation for resources; they can organize and discover resources. The differences express that metadata cannot satisfy to describe different knowledge systems and different granularities of resources. Ontology can provide a mutual mapping mechanism for among different metadata, and can achieve interoperability among heterogeneous systems [19]. Ontology can make up lacks of metadata: (1) Ontology can solve the heterogeneity problem of semantic information systems including heterogeneous of microstructures of resources as well as complex relationships among resources objects. (2) Ontology use the framework for semantic Web services to provide an automatic mapping mechanism among metadata for addressing Universal adaptability issues of metadata. (3) Evolving Ontology. It can apply new metadata programmers by automatic and semi-automatic means. (4) Ontology describes different knowledge systems and different granularities of resources for

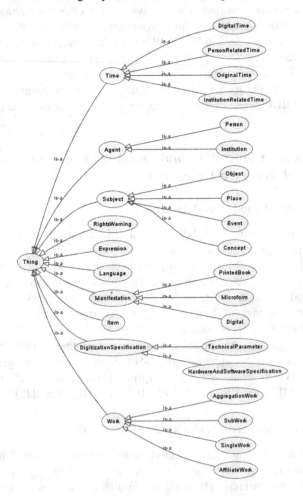

Fig. 2. The bibliographic ontology classes

achieving semantic relationships between heterogeneous resources and systems. (5) Ontology can describe the whole life cycle of digital resources.

5.3 Ontology Construction Based on Bibliographic Metadata

In order to construct ontologies based on the bibliographical metadata, we need to fully consider elements in the process of bibliographic data, set related classes, and give detailed properties and instances. As results, isolated descriptive information are related to convenient realize semantic smart retrieval by mappings and linkages. Here, references to conceptual models and standards such as DCMI, FRBR and RDA and so on, we extract and identify bibliographic metadata including title, creator, subject, description, publisher, contributor, date original, date digital, type, format, digitization specification, resource identifier, source, language, relation, coverage, rights management, contributing institution.

We divide the bibliographic ontology into top-level categories and their subcategories. Where, top-level categories include Work, Expression, Manifestation, Item, Time, Agent, Subject, Digitization Specification, Language, and Rights Warning. Where, 21 second-level classes, 33 third-level classes, 7 fourth-level classes, and 6 fifth-level classes. Totally, there are 75 classes and subclasses, as shown in Fig. 2.

6 The Intelligent Retrieval System of Digital Document Resources Based on Ontology

In order to achieve semantic retrievals for digital document resources, we firstly collect and store digital document resources, and annotate and index semantic based on semantic template. We normalize them after users submit query requests extended by query expansion mechanisms for semantics. Moreover, we retrieve according to extended query requests, and retrieval results are returned to users according to specific sort logic.

The intelligent retrieval system framework of digital document resource based on ontology shown in Fig. 3, which include five major parts such as digital document repository, semantic annotation, ontology manager, retrieval preprocessor, retrieval reconstruction, and retrieval engine.

6.1 Digital Document Repository

The subsystem of digital document repository pre-processes digital documents, so can classify, store them, modify, delete, and manage resources.

6.2 Semantic Annotation

According to task ontologies of digital document resources, the semantic annotation constructs corresponding semantic templates for different type of digital document resources.

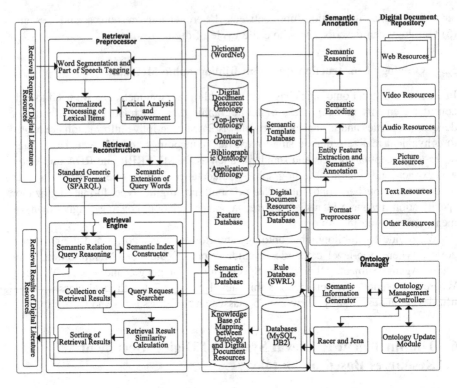

Fig. 3. The intelligent retrieval system framework for digital literature resources based on ontology

The model automatically extracts metadata of digital document resources to represent top semantics for digital document resources according to semantic templates. Subsequently, the library store featured files including metadata and top level semantic identifications of digital document resources.

6.3 Ontology Manager

The ontology manager responses for the MySQL database stores and accesses ontologies with the OWL format. It uses a reasoning engine to infer and store results into the ontology information database for achieving updating for existing ontologies and the ontology information database.

6.4 Retrieval Preprocessor

According to each retrieval word whether is an ontology vocabulary are determined in user query requests by the ontology library of digital document resources and the general dictionary, the retrieval preprocessor firstly separate words and labels their attributes. The retrieval preprocessor normalizes the query requests with Chinese form according to the specific statics of weight assignments for query words. These query words are assigned corresponding semantic layers and weights to finally form query vectors to retrieval reconstruction.

6.5 Retrieval Reconstruction

The retrieval reconstruction accesses the ontologies repository of digital documents, obtains semantic extension results, related concepts, and their semantic distances of each word in query vectors. Standard general SPARQL queries reconstructed by semantic extensions are submitted to the search engine.

6.6 Retrieval Engine

The search engine infers semantics relations for SPARQL queries, and creates semantic indexing files to respond to query requests according to the featured file library for achieving semantic classification of query words. Finally, search results are sorted to users according to weights of query words and their own sorting logic.

7 Experimental Results

Test environment: (1) hardware: CPU Quad-core Intel(R) Core(TM) i5-3230 M CPU@ 2.60 GHz, memory 4 GB; (2) Development environment: Microsoft Windows 8 64-bits operating system. System architecture: Struts 2; development platform: JDK-7u71-Windows-x64; Ontology editing and management tool: Protégé 4.3; Word segmentation toolkit: ICTCLAS 5.0; DBMS: MySQL 5.6.21 (For windows7/8_64bits); Semantic development toolkit: Jena 2.8.8 (Jena is HP's a semantic web toolkit opened by source codes based on Java developed, and it provides a programming environment and a rule-based inference engine for parsing RDF, RDFS and OWL ontologies.

Experimental results show that the intelligent retrieval prototype system of digital document resources is available based on ontology, and its advantages show as the followings: (1) it can effectively realize discoveries of digital document resources, sharing, and application integrations; (2) it can improve recalls and precisions of digital document resource retrievals to satisfy with users.

8 Conclusion

This paper describes semantic web, semantic retrieval, ontology construction, and metadata standard, and analyzes the relationships between ontologies and metadata. Moreover, this paper presents the construction methods of ontologies of digital document resources based on metadata, and designs the intelligent retrieval system for digital document resources based on ontology. Experimental results show that the semantic search based on ontology can improve recalls and precisions of digital document resource retrievals.

Acknowledgments. This work is supported in part by the Hunan Philosophy and Social Science Foundation of China (12YBA267).

References

1. Berners-Lee, T., Weitzner, D.J., Hall, W., O'Hara, K., Shadbolt, N., Hendler, J.A.: A framework for web science. Found. Trends® Web Sci. **1**(1), 1–130 (2006). Now Publishers Inc.
2. Studer, R., Benjamins, V.R., Fensel, D.: Knowledge engineering, principles and methods. Data Knowl. Eng. **25**(1-2), 161–197 (1998)
3. Gómez-Pérez, A., Benjamins, R.: Overview of knowledge sharing and reuse components: ontologies and problem-solving methods. In: IJCAI and the Scandinavian AI Societies. CEUR Workshop Proceedings (1999)
4. Durbha, S., King, R.L.: Interoperability in costal zone monitoring systems: resolving semantic heterogeneities. In: Proceedings of IEEE International Geoscience and Remote Sensing Symposium, IGARSS 2005, pp. 4236–4239 (2005)
5. Wei, Y., Junpeng, C.H.: Linking and mapping of library catalogue data based on MapReduce. New Technol. Libr. Inf. Serv. **9**, 15–22 (2013)
6. CCSDS.ORG. http://en.wikipedia.org/wiki/Open_Archival_Information_System#The_reference_model
7. DCMI-Terms. http://www.niso.org/apps/group_public/download.php/10256/Z39-85-2012_dublin_core.pdf
8. IFLA Bibliographic Control and International MARC Project Team: Functional requirements for bibliographic records: final report. http://www.bengu.cn/homepage/paper/FRBR_Chinese.pdf
9. Joint Steering Committee for Development of RDA: RDA: resource description and access prospectus. http://www.rda-jsc.org/rdaprospectus.html
10. Huazhu, S., Luo, Z., Hui, W., Ruitao, L.: Ontology and metadata for online learning resource repository management based on semantic web. J. Southeast Univ. (Engl. Ed.) **22**(3), 399–403 (2006)
11. Grüninger, M., Atefi, K., Fox, M.S.: Ontologies to support process integration in enterprise engineering. Comput. Math. Organ. Theor. **6**, 381–394 (2000)
12. Uschold, M., King, M.: Towards a methodology for building ontologies. In: Workshop on Basic Ontological Issues in Knowledge Sharing, Held in Conjunction with IJCAI 1995, Montreal, Canada (1995)
13. López, M.F.: Overview of methodologies for building ontologies. In: Proceedings of IJCAI 1999's Workshop on Ontologies and Problem Solving Methods, Stockholm, Sweden (1999)
14. Esprit Project 8145: The KACTUS booklet version 1.0. http://hcs.science.uva.nl/projects/NewKACTUS/home.html
15. ISI Natural Language Processing Research Group: Ontology creation and use SENSUS. http://www.isi.edu/natural-language/projects/SENSUS-demo.html
16. Knowledge Based Systems, Inc.: IDEF5 ontology description capture. http://www.idef.com/IDEF5.htm
17. Noy, N.F., McGuinness, D.L.: Ontology development 101: a guide to creating your first ontology. Stanford Knowledge Systems Laboratory Technical Report (2001)
18. Berners-Lee, T.: Metadata architecture. http://www.w3.org/DesignIssues/Metadata.html
19. Jinding, L.: Exploring the relationship between thesaurus, metadata and ontology. Res. Libr. Sci. **8**, 61–64 (2007)

Data Science and Machine Learning
Theory

Deep Compression on Convolutional Neural Network for Artistic Style Transfer

Jian Hu[1,3], Kun He[1,3(✉)], John E. Hopcroft[2], and Yaren Zhang[1]

[1] School of Computer Science and Technology,
Huazhong University of Science and Technology, Wuhan 430074, China
{lelouch,brooklet60,hhxjzyr}@hust.edu.cn
[2] Department of Computer Science, Cornell University, Ithaca 14850, NY, USA
jeh@cs.cornell.edu
[3] Shenzhen Research Institute of Huazhong University of Science and Technology,
Shenzhen 518057, Guangdong, China

Abstract. Deep artistic style transfer is popular yet costly as it is computationally expensive to generate artistic images using deep neural networks. We first ignore the network and only try an optimization method to generate artistic pictures, but the variation is limited. Then we speed up the style transfer by deep compression on the CNN layers of VGG. We simply remove inner ReLU functions within each convolutional block, such that each block containing two to three convolutional operation layers with ReLU in between collapses to a fully connected layer followed by a ReLU and a pooling layer. We use activation vectors in the modified network to morph the generated image. Experiments show that using the same loss function of Gatys et al. for style transfer the compressed neural network is competitive to the original VGG but is 2 to 3 times faster. The deep compression on convolutional neural networks shows alternative ways of generating artistic pictures.

Keywords: Convolutional neural network · Deep compression · Artistic style · Back-propagation · Computer vision

1 Introduction

In recent year, Deep neural networks (DNNs) have shown high performance in various image or speech recognition tasks. Specifically in the domain of computer vision, convolutional neural networks (CNNs) have demonstrated state-of-art performance on image classification and object detection [3–5]. Deep neural networks can extract features from data through the process of training [8,11], and for CNNs the convolutional kernels gradually capture different levels of the hierarchical architecture.

Gatys et al. first use the features extracted from CNNs to synthesize textures [2], and expand their work to artistic style transfer [1]. As an iterative optimization procedure, their generative algorithm relies on back-propagation

© Springer Nature Singapore Pte Ltd. 2017
D. Du et al. (Eds.): NCTCS 2017, CCIS 768, pp. 157–166, 2017.
https://doi.org/10.1007/978-981-10-6893-5_12

to morph images such that they match the desired image statistics. Here back-propagation means doing gradient descent to the loss function with respect to the input rather than the weights. However, such process is slow and memory inefficient [13].

Ulyanov et al. [7] train a feed-forward texture network that can generate artistic images by a feed-forward process. They move the computational burden to the learning stage so the pre-training task is very costly. Moreover, the style of the generated images is confined to a single form. Johnson et al. [9] further apply the perceptual loss and tailor the feed-forward network for real time video style transfer.

We do deep compression to speed up the image generation. We first try to optimize the loss function directly without using any neural network. Then, we build a simplified network by using the corresponding convolutional blocks of VGG. For each convolutional block, containing two or three convolutional layers and ReLU in between, followed by a pooling layer, we remove all internal ReLU layers such that the several convolutional layers collapse to a single fully connected layer, followed by one ReLU and a pooling layer. Then we do style transfer using the back-propagation algorithm to retain the flexibility in style transfer. Experiments show that we speed up the computation while generating similar quality artistic images.

2   Related Work

The key idea of artistic style transfer lies in the back-propagation process to morph the pixel values of the generated image driven by the loss function. So the most critical issue consists in **setting up the loss function properly**.

Early papers show evidence that CNNs automatically learn to capture local features of an image during the training process [8]. Layer by layer the learned features become more abstract and the activation vectors reflect the extracted prior information of the whole image [10]. So we can leverage a pre-trained neural network for image classification task (such as VGG [3]), and use the activation vectors generated through the feed-forward process to build the loss function.

2.1   Content Loss

Given a picture containing the semantic content, the goal is to generate an image resembling the content of the picture. The content loss is constructed by measuring the squared Euclidean loss of two representations. Let $\mathbf{p}$ and $\mathbf{x}$ denote the original picture and the generated image respectively, and matrices $P^{(l)}$ and $F^{(l)}$ denote the activation matrices of $\mathbf{p}$ and $\mathbf{x}$ in a forward pass through the VGG network in layer l. The content loss in layer l is:

$$L_{content}(\mathbf{x}, \mathbf{p}, l) = \frac{1}{2} \sum_{i,j} (F_{i,j}^{(l)} - P_{i,j}^{(l)})^2. \tag{1}$$

Accordingly the overall content loss is the weighted sum of the content loss in each layer:

$$L_{content}(\mathbf{x}, \mathbf{p}) = \sum_{l=1}^{L} \omega_l L_{content}(\mathbf{x}, \mathbf{p}, l). \tag{2}$$

The content loss directly measures the similarity of the two images by measuring the Euclidean distance between their activation vectors. Note that $\mathbf{x}$ is a variable but $\mathbf{p}$ is fixed. Apparently $L_{content}^{(l)}(\mathbf{x}, \mathbf{p}) \to 0$ as $\mathbf{x} \to \mathbf{p}$. If the generated image is similar to the picture in content, then the content loss is very small.

2.2   Style Loss

The most fascinating work of Gatys et al. is that they construct the style features by means of a delicate manually defined feature, the Gram matrix of the activation matrix. The Gram matrix reflects the texture of images [2]. Let $\mathbf{x}$ and $\mathbf{a}$ be the generated image and the art work respectively. Let G and A be the Gram matrix of the two activation matrices, namely $G = F^T F$, where F is the feature map. Then the style loss in each layer is:

$$L_{style}(\mathbf{x}, \mathbf{a}, l) = \frac{1}{4N_l^2 M_l^2} \sum_{i,j} (G_{i,j}^l - A_{i,j}^l)^2. \tag{3}$$

The overall style loss is:

$$L_{style}(\mathbf{x}, \mathbf{a}) = \sum_{l=0}^{L} \lambda_l L_{style}(\mathbf{x}, \mathbf{p}, l). \tag{4}$$

This style loss measures the spatial similarity of textures as every element of a Gram matrix is an inner product of two column vectors, which accordingly reflects the texture information.

Note that it is typical that only activation vectors from the convolutional layers are used, and activation vectors from fully-connected layers are not used in practice.

2.3   Gradient Descent

This generative method does gradient descent on the image pixel values to generate the desired image driven by specific loss function. It outputs a local optimal solution after convergence.

$$\mathbf{x}_{t+1} = \mathbf{x}_t - \gamma \left(\frac{\partial L}{\partial \mathbf{x}} \right) \Big|_{\mathbf{x} = \mathbf{x}_t} \tag{5}$$

Note that the initial image $\mathbf{x}_0$ can start from white noise. Practically we set its initial pixel values to those of the original picture so that the content loss is 0, leading to a faster convergence in practice.

If we set the loss L to the content loss, and solve the deep representation inversion problem [10], then:

$$\mathbf{x}^* = \arg\min_{\mathbf{x}} L_{content}(\mathbf{x}, \mathbf{p}). \tag{6}$$

If we set L to style loss, and solve the texture synthesis problem [2], then:

$$\mathbf{x}^* = \arg\min_{\mathbf{x}} L_{style}(\mathbf{x}, \mathbf{a}). \tag{7}$$

If we combine the two losses into a mixed optimization problem, and solve the artistic style transfer problem [1].

$$L_{total}(\mathbf{x}, \mathbf{a}, \mathbf{p}) = \alpha L_{content}(\mathbf{x}, \mathbf{p}) + \beta L_{style}(\mathbf{x}, \mathbf{a}). \tag{8}$$

Then we get

$$\mathbf{x}^* = \arg\min_{\mathbf{x}} L_{total}(\mathbf{x}, \mathbf{a}, \mathbf{p}). \tag{9}$$

The mixed loss guides the generated image to converge to a point in the corresponding high dimensional search space where both the content loss and the style loss reach small values, as illustrated in Fig. 1.

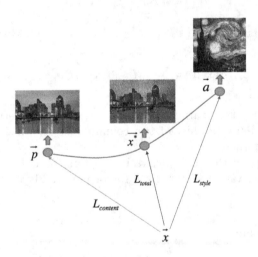

Fig. 1. Illustration of the style transfer process. Intuitively the picture and the art work lie on one manifold (denoted by the top curve). The style transfer process aims to morph the generated image by gradient descent. By the mixed loss (denote by the middle arrow) the generated image converges to a point between the picture and the art work, so that the generated image can resemble the picture in content and the art work in style.

3   Methods

3.1   Convergence Acceleration

There exists some weakness in the above generative algorithm. First, it entails a pre-trained neural network to extract spatial features of the images. The training is costly and it is not flexible to change the network architecture. Second, it relies on a back-propagation which takes a comparatively long time to generate a single image.

For the first weakness, He et al. [6] have shown that CNN with random weights can also extract features for style transfer, and generate competitive artistic images. For the second weakness, we explore a deep compression method to speed up the generation.

Optimizing the Loss without Deep Network. Inspired by the power of random weight CNN in style transfer, it is likely neither the values of weights nor the depth of the network impacts the style transfer. So we first try raw features of the images, i.e. we apply the content loss and the style loss on the raw pixel values without any neural network.

For the original artistic style transfer task, let f be the neural network and $\|\cdot\|$ be the Euclidean norm, then Eqs. (8) and (9) can be rewritten as:

$$\mathbf{x}^* = \arg\min_{\mathbf{x}}\{\alpha\,\|f(\mathbf{x}) - f(\mathbf{p})\|^2 + \beta\,\|Gram(f(\mathbf{x})) - Gram(f(\mathbf{a}))\|^2\} \qquad (10)$$

If we replace f with a less complicated function g where $g \approx f$, then the computation of gradients will be sped up. For the no-network case, g is just an identity mapping, namely:

$$\mathbf{x}^* = \arg\min_{\mathbf{x}}\{\alpha\,\|\mathbf{x} - \mathbf{p}\|^2 + \beta\,\|Gram(\mathbf{x}) - Gram(\mathbf{a})\|^2\} \qquad (11)$$

In practice only limited variation is achieved.

Compressing the Convolutional Layers into Dense Layers. As the computational complexity of back-propagation is aligned with the depth of neural networks, we do deep compression to speed up the computation. In such a scenario, g is a compressed network of f.

The key steps are as follows:

– Find the matrix representations of convolutional kernels, then use matrix multiplication to compress multiple convolutional layers into a single fully-connected layer.
– Supplant the nonlinear activation functions with linear functions with appropriate factors. This enables the matrices before and after the activation functions to multiply into a single matrix.

By carefully applying the above techniques we can greatly reduce the depth of the neural networks. E.g. the first block of VGG has conv1_1, conv1_2 and a pooling layer; the content loss and style loss are measured at the ReLU activation of conv1_2 layer. Let $K_1(x)$ and $K_2(x)$ be the kernel of conv1_1 and conv1_2 respectively, as shown in Fig. 2. Let the measured activation for loss function be y, then:

$$y = f(x) = ReLU(K_2(ReLU(K_1(x)))) = ReLU \circ K_2 \circ ReLU \circ K_1(x). \quad (12)$$

$$vec\left(\begin{pmatrix} a_{11} & a_{12} & a_{13} \\ a_{21} & a_{22} & a_{23} \\ a_{31} & a_{32} & a_{33} \end{pmatrix} * \begin{pmatrix} k_{11} & k_{12} \\ k_{21} & k_{22} \end{pmatrix}\right) = vec\left(\begin{matrix} k_{11}a_{11}+k_{12}a_{12}+k_{21}a_{21}+k_{22}a_{22} & k_{11}a_{12}+k_{12}a_{13}+k_{21}a_{22}+k_{22}a_{23} \\ k_{11}a_{21}+k_{12}a_{22}+k_{21}a_{31}+k_{22}a_{32} & k_{11}a_{22}+k_{12}a_{23}+k_{21}a_{32}+k_{22}a_{33} \end{matrix}\right)$$

$$= \begin{pmatrix} k_{11}a_{11}+k_{12}a_{12}+k_{21}a_{21}+k_{22}a_{22} \\ k_{11}a_{21}+k_{12}a_{22}+k_{21}a_{31}+k_{22}a_{32} \\ k_{11}a_{12}+k_{12}a_{13}+k_{21}a_{22}+k_{22}a_{23} \\ k_{11}a_{22}+k_{12}a_{23}+k_{21}a_{32}+k_{22}a_{33} \end{pmatrix}$$

$$= \begin{pmatrix} k_{11} & k_{21} & 0 & k_{12} & k_{22} & 0 & 0 & 0 & 0 \\ 0 & k_{11} & k_{21} & 0 & k_{12} & k_{22} & 0 & 0 & 0 \\ 0 & 0 & 0 & k_{11} & k_{21} & 0 & k_{12} & k_{22} & 0 \\ 0 & 0 & 0 & 0 & k_{11} & k_{21} & 0 & k_{12} & k_{22} \end{pmatrix} \begin{pmatrix} a_{11} \\ a_{21} \\ a_{31} \\ a_{12} \\ a_{22} \\ a_{32} \\ a_{13} \\ a_{23} \\ a_{33} \end{pmatrix} = Ka$$

Fig. 2. Converting convolutional kernels into matrices. It shows an example of how to convert a 3×3 feature map convoluted with a 2×2 kernel into the multiplication of a 4×9 matrix with a vector in 9-dimension.

The gradient computation is:

$$\frac{\partial f}{\partial x}(x) = \frac{\partial ReLU}{\partial K_2}\frac{\partial K_2}{\partial ReLU}\frac{\partial ReLU}{\partial K_1}\frac{\partial K_2}{\partial x}(x). \quad (13)$$

Then we can replace the ReLU activation at conv1_1 with identity functions and multiply the matrices of conv1_1 and conv1_2 into a single dense matrix. In this way we actually compress two convolutional layers into a single fully-connected layer, as shown in Fig. 3. Let M_1 and M_2 be the matrix representation of conv1_1 and conv1_2 respectively, and $M_3 = M_2M_1$ be the dense matrix of the corresponding fully-connected layer, then:

$$y = g(x) = ReLU(M_2(M_1(x))) = ReLU \circ M_3(x). \quad (14)$$

The reduced gradient flow is:

$$\frac{\partial g}{\partial x}(x) = \frac{\partial ReLU}{\partial M_3}\frac{\partial M_3}{\partial x}(x). \quad (15)$$

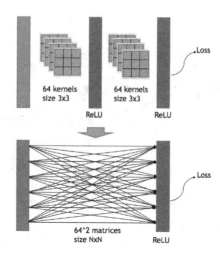

Fig. 3. Compressing conv1_1 and conv1_2 into a fully connected layer. It illustrates how to do deep compression for one convolutional block. By removing non-linear activation functions between conv1_1 and conv1_2, two sparse matrices that represent the convolutional kernels collapse into one dense matrix.

In this example the gradient flow is shortened so the computation of gradient descent per iteration is reduced.

Typically we substitute $y = \tanh x$ or $y = ReLU(x)$ activation with $y = x$, and we substitute sigmoid activation $y = \frac{1}{1+\exp(-x)}$ with $y = \frac{1}{4}x + \frac{1}{2}$ as they are the tangent lines to the activation functions at the point $x = 0$. However, we retain the nonlinear activation at the layer where loss is applied so as to maintain as much accurate information as possible in the activation vectors.

4   Experiments

4.1   Optimization with No Network

We first apply the content loss function directly to the pixel values of the images, and calculate the Gram matrix by directly do multiplications on the image matrices and the transposes. Experiments show that the quality of the generated images is limited for the style transfer problem. When directly optimizing the loss directly without a network, the loss function converges very fast. The generated images resemble the original pictures but they are far from the desired stylish image. Only some local parts are dyed in accordance with the art work, but the straight lines are barely changed into curves which typically occurs with the original algorithm. See Fig. 4 for comparison.

4.2   Deep Compression on VGG Network

We compress the first three blocks with a total of 13 layers of the VGG network into a 3-layer fully-connected network. At first we remove the loss measured

Fig. 4. Comparisons on style transfer. The first row are the original picture and the art work. The second row are images generated respectively by the first 13 convolutional layers of VGG-16 and the purely optimization method with no network.

at layers of conv4_3 and conv5_3, so the loss functions are measured at layers conv1_2, conv2_2 and conv3_3. We remove all internal rectified linear activations apart from the layers mentioned above, which techniquely compresses conv1_1 and 1_2 to a fully-connected layer fc1, and layers conv2_1 and conv2_2 to a layer fc2, and compress conv3_1, conv3_2 and conv3_3 to a layer fc3. Note that we retain all the pooling layers in order to retain as much original information as possible.

Figure 5 shows the comparison. The gradient descent process on a compressed network is 2 to 3 times faster than that on the original network, but the quality of the generated image is almost the same as that of the original method. This means we successfully speed up the computation by gaining similar artistic images. If we want the generated images to have higher quality, then we can slow down the training process. If we want to generate the image as soon as possible, we could just compress the shallow layers of the network and apply the same algorithm.

We apply a second experiment and compare the convergence between the original network and the compressed network. Gatys et al. use layers of conv1_2, conv2_2, conv3_3, conv4_3 and conv5_3, and we use the same corresponding layers. We set the same loss threshold such that they could generate reasonably good images. To reach the same quality, in the original network it takes at least 100 iterations, while in the compressed network it converges faster and only takes 60 iterations. Figure 6 shows the generated images by the two networks. All the experiments maintain the hyper-parameters $\frac{\beta}{\alpha} = 200$.

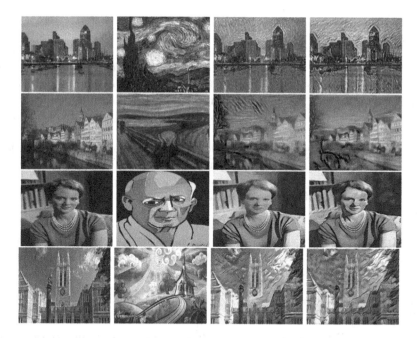

Fig. 5. Comparison on the compressed network and the original network. The first column corresponds to the original pictures, and the second column corresponds to the art work. The third column and the fourth column correspond to results from 13-layer VGG and compressed 3-layer VGG respectively, each of which takes 5000 iterations. The compressed VGG has almost the same quality as the deep network has, but for the latter it takes 2 to 3 times more time to update parameters per iteration. The algorithm converges faster on the compressed network because shallower depth leads to a simpler loss function.

Fig. 6. Comparison on deep VGG network and our compressed network with same layers. The style image is the second one at the second row in Fig. 5. The left image is generated using Gatys et al.'s original network and the right image is generated using our network. To reach the same quality, our network converges after 60 iterations while theirs needs 100 iterations. Each iteration of ours is 2–3 times faster than that of the original network.

5   Discussion

Experiments show that there is a trade off between the quality of the generated image and the time cost for computation. It is an application based on need. When we need to do style transfer on a large amount of images, we can do more deep compression on the network to speed up computation, and when on fewer images, we do less deep compression to maintain high quality of generated images.

Most computation lies in the calculation of the Gram matrix for the style loss. However the Gram matrix is defined manually to capture the texture feature. If this texture feature can be represented by a simpler model, then the computation could be reduced significantly. An ideal case is to use shallow layered neural networks to learn style features.

Acknowledgements. This research work was supported by National Science Foundation of China (61472147, 61772219) and Shenzhen Science and Technology Planning Project (JCYJ20170307154749425).

References

1. Gatys, L.A., Ecker, A.S., Bethge, M.: Image style transfer using convolutional neural networks. arXiv:1508.06576v2 [cs.CV], 2 September 2015
2. Gatys, L.A., Ecker, A.S., Bethge, M.: Texture synthesis and the controlled generation of natural stimuli using convolutional neural networks. arXiv:1505.07376
3. Simonyan, K., Zisserman, A.: Very deep convolutional networks for large-scale image recognition. arXiv:1409.1556 [cs.CV]
4. Russakovsky, O., Deng, J., Hao, S., et al.: ImageNet large scale visual recognition challenge. Int. J. Comput. Vis. (IJCV) **115**(3), 211–252 (2015)
5. He, K., Zhang, X., Ren, S., Sun, J.: Deep residual learning for image recognition. arXiv:1512.03385 [cs.CV]
6. He, K., Wang, Y., Hopcroft, J.: A powerful generative model using random weights for the deep image representation. arXiv:1606.04801 [cs.CV]
7. Ulyanov, D., Lebedev, V., Vedaldi, A., Lempitsky, V.S.: Texture networks: feed-forward synthesis of textures and stylized images. arXiv:1603.03417 [cs.CV]
8. Bengio, Y., Courville, A., Vincent, P.: Representation learning: a review and new perspectives. arXiv:1206.5538 [cs.LG]
9. Johnson, J., Alahi, A., Fei-Fei, L.: Perceptual losses for real-time style transfer and super-resolution. In: Leibe, B., Matas, J., Sebe, N., Welling, M. (eds.) ECCV 2016. LNCS, vol. 9906, pp. 694–711. Springer, Cham (2016). doi:10.1007/978-3-319-46475-6_43
10. Mahendran, A., Vedaldi, A.: Understanding deep image representations by inverting them. In: CVPR, pp. 5188–5196 (2015)
11. Jia, Y., Shelhamer, E., Donahue, J., et al.: Caffe: convolutional architecture for fast feature embedding. In: Proceedings of the ACM International Conference on Multimedia, pp. 675–678. ACM (2014)
12. Abadi, M., et al.: TensorFlow: large-scale machine learning on heterogeneous distributed systems (2015). http://tensorflow.org/
13. Nikulin, Y., Novak, R.: Exploring the neural algorithm of artistic style. arXiv preprint arXiv:1602.07188

Degree Correlations in Two Layer Growth Model with Nonlinear Preferential Attachment Rule

Youjun Lu[1], Daoyun Xu[1(✉)], and Jincheng Zhou[2]

[1] School of Computer Science and Technology, Guizhou University, Guiyang, China
yjlu111@126.com, dyxu@gzu.edu.cn
[2] School of Mathematics and Statistics, Qiannan Normal University for Nationalities, Duyun, China

Abstract. Most real-world complex systems have multiple subsystems and layers of connectivity. All such systems can be described and represented in terms of multiplex network model, where the edges at each layer stand for the interactions of a different type between the same set of vertices. To better characterize and simulate such multiplex systems, we propose a new two layers network growth model based on nonlinear preferential attachment rule. Moreover, we obtain the joint degree distribution expression of the model via the rate equation approach at the steady state, and discuss the joint degree distribution and conditional average degree for the models of two different vertex weighted function, respectively. It was found that some existing multiplex network model is one of special cases of the model, and the corresponding joint degree distribution and the conditional average degree can also be obtained by the joint degree distribution expression of the model. Also, we observe that the conditional average degree expression is identical for the models of two different vertex weighted function. To verify our theoretical results, we perform Monte Carlo simulations for the models of two different vertex weighted function. Experiments indicate that our theoretical results are in accordance with the Monte Carlo simulation results well.

Keywords: Multiplex network model · Nonlinear preferential attachment rule · Joint degree distribution · Conditional average degree

1 Introduction

It has been observed that a great quantity of real-world complex systems such as the Internet [1], world wide web [2,3], scientific collaboration networks [4,5] and others are well described by complex networks, in which vertices stand for basic units in these systems, while the edges represent interactions between them. In the last decades, a large number of scholars have been working to construct a set of models to characterize the basic properties and characteristics of the real-world systems such as the vertex degree distribution [6], the degree correlations

© Springer Nature Singapore Pte Ltd. 2017
D. Du et al. (Eds.): NCTCS 2017, CCIS 768, pp. 167–181, 2017.
https://doi.org/10.1007/978-981-10-6893-5_13

[7], the diameter [2], the clustering coefficient [8], the small-world effect [9], the scale-free property [10] and the community structure [11] and etc.

The traditional model assumes that the connections between vertices are equivalent. However, many complex systems comprises a set of basic constituents connected by relationships of different kinds. Hence, the traditional network model assumption might discard some important information with respect to the structure and function of the original system. In fact, these systems can be better characterized by multiplex networks, i.e. networks where vertices are members of distinct network layers, and all edges of a given type are described by each layer. Recently, a large amount of multiplex network models for describing and modeling the structure and function of these systems have been proposed in [12–16]. In Ref. [12], Nicosia et al. developed a generic growth multiplex model based on preferential attachment, in which the probability for a newly added vertex to establish connections to existing vertices in each layer is a function of the degree of other vertices at all layers. In Ref. [13], Kim et al. proposed a modeling framework according to coevolution of network layers, in which the probability that an existing vertex would obtain an edge from the new added is also a function of the degree of other vertices at all layers. In Ref. [14], Nicosia et al. introduced a general growth multiplex networks model based on a non-linear preferential attachment mechanism. In Refs. [15,16], Fotouhi and Momeni considered the homogeneous and heterogeneous growth multiplex networks with arbitrary number of layers, respectively. In order to characterize and quantify the function and properties of multiplex networks, a large number of theoretical measures have been introduced in the context of real-world multiplex networks, including the centrality and ranking of vertices [17,18], the clustering coefficient [19] and the degree correlations [20,21] and others [22,23]. Moreover, some researchers has been also devoted on investigating various kinds of dynamic process on multiplex topologies, including diffusion processes [24], epidemic spreading [25–28], cooperation [29], synchronization [30], percolation [31,32] and random walks [33,34] on multiplex networks.

The article is organized in the following way. In Sect. 2, we propose a new two layer network growth model based on nonlinear preferential attachment probability, in which the attachment probability at each layer is a function of the degree of vertices in the same layer. In Sect. 3, we focus on the analysis of the joint degree distribution of the model at the steady state. Moreover, we consider the general characteristics of vertex weighted function in the model, and investigate the joint degree distribution and the conditional degree distribution of the model corresponding to two different vertex weighted function, and obtain closed form solutions for the joint degree distribution and the conditional degree distribution. In Sect. 4, we perform the Monte Carlo simulations to verify the theoretical results are given in Sect. 3. The conclusions are given in Sect. 5.

2   Two Layers Growth Network Model

In order to obtain the two layers growth network model which adds vertices and edges, the vertex weighted function f was defined in Ref. [35], i.e. if $1 \leq m \leq$

$k \leq M \leq \infty$, then $f(k) > 0$, otherwise $f(k) = 0$. The nonlinear preferential attachment rule is called to be the probability $\Pi_i^{[1]}$ and $\Pi_i^{[2]}$ that a vertex i with replica vertex obtains an edge in layer 1 and in layer 2 is proportional to an nonnegative function $f(k_i)$ and $f(l_i)$, respectively. i.e.,

$$\Pi_i^{[1]} = \frac{f(k_i)}{\Sigma_j f(k_j)}, \quad \Pi_i^{[2]} = \frac{f(l_i)}{\Sigma_j f(l_j)}. \tag{1}$$

where k_i and l_i is the degree of vertex i in layer 1 and in layer 2, respectively.

The two layers growth network model $\mathcal{G}_2 = \{G(p, f, m_l, G_t^l) : l = 1, 2; \ t \geq 0\}$ is described by the following algorithm. At time $t = 0$, we start from a duplex network G_0^1 and G_0^2 with n_0 vertices connected by $0 < m_0 \leq \binom{n_0}{2}$ edges in each layer. At each time step $t \geq 1$, the networks $G_{t+1}^l, l = 1, 2$ is formed by modifying $G_t^l, l = 1, 2$ in that one of the following two steps is performed.

(1) With probability p we add a new vertex with a replica vertex in each of the two layers to the duplex network. Each newly added vertex with replica vertex has m_l, $l = 1, 2$ new edges that with probability $\Pi_i^{[l]}, l = 1, 2$ are attached to different old vertices i of the same layer.

(2) With probability $1 - p$ we add m_l, $l = 1, 2$ new edges to each layer of the duplex network, respectively. The new edges that with probability $\Pi_i^{[l]}, l = 1, 2$ are connected to vertex i of the corresponding layer.

In this model $\mathcal{G}_2 = \{G(p, f, m_l, G_t^l) : l = 1, 2; \ t \geq 0\}$, each layer consists of an undirected and unweighted network model $G(p, f, m, G_0)$ and all layers have the same vertices. In the case, the vertex degree distribution in each layer is given by the vertex degree distribution of the model $G(p, f, m, G_0)$ proposed by Ref. [36]. Moreover, the model does not allow multiple edges and self-loop.

3   Degree Correlations in Two Layer Model

The degree correlations is an important feature in multiplex networks, and the degrees of the same vertex in different layers may be positively or negatively correlated. Namely, the hub vertices of one layer are or are not the hub vertices of another layer. In the following, we first investigate the degree correlations of the model $\mathcal{G}_2 = \{G(p, f, m_l, G_t^l) : l = 1, 2; \ t \geq 0\}$, including the general joint degree distribution. Taking into account the general characteristics of vertex weighted function f, we also study the joint degree distribution and the conditional average degree of the model $\mathcal{G}_2 = \{G(p, f, m_l, G_t^l) : l = 1, 2; \ t \geq 0\}$ corresponding to the vertex weighted function $f(k) = k$ and $f(k) = c > 0$ using the general joint degree distribution expression.

The degree of a vertex i in the two layer network is represented by the vector $k_i = (k_i^{[1]}, k_i^{[2]})$, where $k_i^{[1]}$ and $k_i^{[2]}$ is the degree of vertex i in layer 1 and layer 2, respectively. For convenience, we assume $k_i^{[1]} = k$ and $k_i^{[2]} = l$. Let N be the total number of vertices of the networks, and $N(k, l)$ is the number of vertices that have degree k in layer 1 and degree l in layer 2, and $P(k,l)$ is the fraction of vertices with degree k in layer 1 and degree l in layer 2, respectively. Then the joint degree distribution $P(k,l)$ of the two layer network model is given by

$$P(k,l) = \frac{N(k,l)}{N}. \tag{2}$$

and the conditional average degree $\bar{l}(k)$, i.e. the average degree of vertex in layer 2 conditioned to the degree of the same vertex in layer 1, is characterized by

$$\bar{l}(k) = \sum_l l P(l|k). \tag{3}$$

where $P(l|k)$ is the condition probability that a vertex with degree k is attached to a vertex with degree l. If this function $\bar{l}(k)$ does not depend on k, the degrees in the two layers are uncorrelated. If this function $\bar{l}(k)$ is increasing and decreasing in k, the degrees of vertices in the two layers are positively and negatively correlated, respectively.

Theorem 1. *In this model $\mathcal{G}_2 = \{G(p, f, m_l, G_t^l) : l = 1, 2; t \geq 0\}$, let $f_k > 0, 1 \leq m \leq k \leq M \leq \infty$ and $f_{M+1} = 0$ be the vertex weighted function. The average weight of graph vertices is denoted by $\overline{f_1}, \overline{f_2}$ in layer 1 and layer 2, respectively. Supposed that $\overline{f_1}, \overline{f_2} \neq 0$, then the joint degree distribution $P(k,l)$ is given by*

$$P(k,l) = \frac{\overline{f_2} m_1 f_{k-1} \cdot P(k-1,l) + \overline{f_1} m_2 f_{l-1} \cdot P(k, l-1) + \frac{p}{2-p} \cdot \overline{f_1} \cdot \overline{f_2} \delta_{k,m_1} \delta_{l,m_2}}{\frac{p}{2-p} \cdot \overline{f_1} \cdot \overline{f_2} + \overline{f_2} m_1 f_k + \overline{f_1} m_2 f_l}.$$

where $\delta_{k,m_1} = 1$ if $k = m_1$, otherwise, $\delta_{k,m_1} = 0$. Similarly, $\delta_{l,m_2} = 1$ if $l = m_2$, otherwise, $\delta_{l,m_2} = 0$.

Proof. In Ref. [36], it has been shown that the total number of vertices $n_t \approx n_0 + p \cdot t \approx p \cdot t$ for $t \to \infty$. Thus, Eq. (1) can be equivalently rewritten as follows:

$$\Pi_i^{[1]} = \frac{f(k_i)}{\sum_j f(k_j)} = \frac{f(k_i)/n_t}{\Sigma_{r \geq m} f(r) n_r^t / n_t} \approx \frac{f_k/(p \cdot t)}{\Sigma_{r \geq m} f_r Q_r} = \frac{f_k}{p \cdot t \cdot \overline{f_1}} = P_k. \tag{4}$$

$$\Pi_i^{[2]} = \frac{f(l_i)}{\sum_j f(l_j)} = \frac{f(l_i)/n_t}{\Sigma_{h \geq m} f(h) n_h^t / n_t} \approx \frac{f_l/(p \cdot t)}{\Sigma_{h \geq m} f_h Q_h} = \frac{f_l}{p \cdot t \cdot \overline{f_2}} = P_l. \tag{5}$$

where the vertex weighted function $f(k)$ and $f(l)$ is written as f_k and f_l, $k_i = k_i^{[1]}$ and $l_i = l_i^{[2]}$ is the degree of the vertex i in the layer 1 and layer 2, $\overline{f_1} = \Sigma_{r \geq m} f_r Q_r$ and $\overline{f_2} = \Sigma_{h \geq m} f_h Q_h$ is the average weight of graph vertices in the layer 1 and layer 2, n_r^t and n_h^t denotes the number of vertices having the connectivity degree r and h at time t, Q_r and Q_h is the probability that a randomly selected vertex has degree r and h, respectively.

In this model $\mathcal{G}_2 = \{G(p, f, m_l, G_t^l) : l = 1, 2; t \geq 0\}$, the probability that vertex i obtains an edge in layer 1 and layer 2 is proportional to the function of k_i

and l_i, respectively. At time $t > 0$, when with probability p we add a new vertex with a replica vertex and the edges incident to new vertex, or with probability $1 - p$ we add new edges to each layer of the duplex network, respectively. The values of $N_t(k, l)$ can consequently change, i.e. if a vertex with degree $k - 1$ in layer 1 and degree l in layer 2 gets an edge in layer 1, its degree in layer 1 increases and becomes k, and the values $N_t(k, l)$ increases. Similarly, if a vertex with degree k in layer 1 and degree $l - 1$ in layer 2 obtains an edge in layer 2, its degree in layer 2 increases and the values of $N_t(k, l)$ also increases. Moreover, if a vertex with degree k in layer 1 and degree l in layer 2 receives an edge in either of the layers, the values of $N_t(k, l)$ decreases consequently. Finally, each new vertex with a replica vertex has degree m_1 in layer 1 and degree m_2 in layer 2 upon birth, so the values of $N_t(m_1, m_2)$ increases by one. The master equation captures the evolution of the expected value of $N_t(k, l)$ is given by

$$
\begin{aligned}
N_{t+1}(k, l) =\ & p \cdot m_1 \frac{f_{k-1} \cdot N_t(k-1, l) - f_k \cdot N_t(k, l)}{p \cdot t \cdot \overline{f_1}} + N_t(k, l) \\
& + p \cdot m_2 \frac{f_{l-1} \cdot N_t(k, l-1) - f_l \cdot N_t(k, l)}{p \cdot t \cdot \overline{f_2}} + p\delta_{k, m_1} \delta_{l, m_2} \\
& + 2(1-p) \cdot m_1 \frac{f_{k-1} \cdot N_t(k-1, l) - f_k \cdot N_t(k, l)}{p \cdot t \cdot \overline{f_1}} \\
& + 2(1-p) \cdot m_2 \frac{f_{l-1} \cdot N_t(k, l-1) - f_l \cdot N_t(k, l)}{p \cdot t \cdot \overline{f_2}}
\end{aligned}
\tag{6}
$$

Assuming that $N_t(k, l) \to n_t \cdot P(k, l) \approx p \cdot t \cdot P(k, l)$ is valid for $t \to \infty$, and combining this with Eq. (6), we can get the following expression for $P(k, l)$,

$$
\begin{aligned}
P(k, l) =\ & \frac{(2-p)m_1}{p} \frac{f_{k-1} \cdot P(k-1, l) - f_k \cdot P(k, l)}{\overline{f_1}} + \delta_{k, m_1} \delta_{l, m_2} \\
& + \frac{(2-p)m_2}{p} \frac{f_{l-1} \cdot P(k, l-1) - f_l \cdot P(k, l)}{\overline{f_2}}.
\end{aligned}
\tag{7}
$$

Solving Eq. (7), we obtain

$$
P(k, l) = \frac{\overline{f_2} m_1 f_{k-1} \cdot P(k-1, l) + \overline{f_1} m_2 f_{l-1} \cdot P(k, l-1) + \frac{p}{2-p} \cdot \overline{f_1} \cdot \overline{f_2} \delta_{k, m_1} \delta_{l, m_2}}{\frac{p}{2-p} \cdot \overline{f_1} \cdot \overline{f_2} + \overline{f_2} m_1 f_k + \overline{f_1} m_2 f_l}.
$$

The proof of the Theorem 1 is complete.

Specially, when $k = m_1$ and $l = m_2$, we have

$$
P(m_1, m_2) = \frac{p \cdot \overline{f_1} \cdot \overline{f_2}}{p \cdot \overline{f_1} \cdot \overline{f_2} + (2-p)\left(\overline{f_2} m_1 f_{m_1} + \overline{f_1} m_2 f_{m_2}\right)}.
\tag{8}
$$

Otherwise, we have

$$
P(k, l) = \frac{(2-p)\left(\overline{f_2} m_1 f_{k-1} \cdot P(k-1, l) + \overline{f_1} m_2 f_{l-1} \cdot P(k, l-1)\right)}{p \cdot \overline{f_1} \cdot \overline{f_2} + (2-p)\left(\overline{f_2} m_1 f_k + \overline{f_1} m_2 f_l\right)}.
\tag{9}
$$

Here we investigate the joint degree distribution $P(k, l)$ of the model corresponding to the vertex weighted function $f(k) = k$ and $f(k) = c > 0$, respectively. Notes that when the vertex weighted function $f(k) = k$ and $f(k) = c > 0$, the nonlinear preferential attachment probability reduces to the linear preferential attachment probability was given in Ref. [2] and the uniform random attachment probability, respectively.

Theorem 2. *In this model* $\mathcal{G}_2 = \{G(p, f, m_l, G_t^l) : l = 1, 2; \ t \geq 0\}$, *if the vertex weighted function* $f_k = k$, *then the joint degree distribution* $P(k, l)$ *is given by*

$$P(k, l) = \frac{2\Gamma\left(m_1 + m_2 + \frac{2}{2-p}\right)\Gamma(k)\Gamma(l)\Gamma(k + l - m_1 - m_2 + 1)}{(2-p)\Gamma(m_1)\Gamma(m_2)\Gamma\left(k + l + \frac{2}{2-p} + 1\right)\Gamma(k - m_1 + 1)\Gamma(l - m_2 + 1)}.$$

where $\Gamma(x)$ *is Gamma function for* $x > 0$.

Proof. In this model $\mathcal{G}_2 = \{G(p, f, m_l, G_t^l) : l = 1, 2; \ t \geq 0\}$, if the vertex weighted function $f = f_k = k$, then by Theorem 1, we have

$$P(k, l) = \frac{(k-1) \cdot P(k-1, l)}{k + l + \frac{2}{2-p}} + \frac{(l-1) \cdot P(k, l-1)}{k + l + \frac{2}{2-p}} + \frac{2\delta_{k, m_1}\delta_{l, m_2}}{2 + (2-p)(m_1 + m_2)} \quad (10)$$

In order to solve Eq. (10), we define the following new sequence

$$P(k, l) = \frac{\Gamma(k)\Gamma(l)}{\Gamma\left(k + l + \frac{2}{2-p} + 1\right)} m_{k, l}. \quad (11)$$

where $\Gamma(x) = \int_0^{+\infty} t^{x-1}e^{-t}dt$ is Gamma function for $x > 0$.

By Eq. (11), we observe that the following holds

$$\frac{k-1}{k + l + \frac{2}{2-p}} \cdot P(k-1, l) = \frac{\Gamma(k)\Gamma(l)}{\Gamma\left(k + l + \frac{2}{2-p} + 1\right)} m_{k-1, l}, \quad (12)$$

$$\frac{l-1}{k + l + \frac{2}{2-p}} \cdot P(k, l-1) = \frac{\Gamma(k)\Gamma(l)}{\Gamma\left(k + l + \frac{2}{2-p} + 1\right)} m_{k, l-1}. \quad (13)$$

Substituting Eqs. (11)–(13) into Eq. (10), we can rewrite it as

$$m_{k, l} = m_{k-1, l} + m_{k, l-1} + \frac{2\Gamma\left(m_1 + m_2 + \frac{2}{2-p}\right)}{(2-p)\Gamma(m_1)\Gamma(m_2)}\delta_{k, m_1}\delta_{l, m_2}. \quad (14)$$

Now, we define the Z-transform of sequence $m_{k, l}$ as follows:

$$\varphi(x, y) = \sum_k \sum_l m_{k, l} x^{-k} y^{-l}. \quad (15)$$

then the inverse transform is given by

$$m_{k,l} = \frac{1}{(2\pi i)^2} \oint \oint \varphi(x,y) x^{k-1} y^{l-1} dx dy. \tag{16}$$

Taking the Z-transform of every term in Eq. (14), we have

$$\varphi(x,y) = x^{-1}\varphi(x,y) + y^{-1}\varphi(x,y) + \frac{2\Gamma\left(m_1+m_2+\frac{2}{2-p}\right)}{(2-p)\Gamma(m_1)\Gamma(m_2)} x^{-m_1} y^{-m_2}. \tag{17}$$

and solving Eq. (17), we obtain

$$\varphi(x,y) = \frac{2\Gamma\left(m_1+m_2+\frac{2}{2-p}\right)}{(2-p)\Gamma(m_1)\Gamma(m_2)} \frac{x^{-m_1} y^{-m_2}}{1 - x^{-1} - y^{-1}}. \tag{18}$$

Combing Eq. (16) with Eq. (18), we can obtain the following expression for $m_{k,l}$,

$$
\begin{aligned}
m_{k,l} &= \frac{2\Gamma\left(m_1+m_2+\frac{2}{2-p}\right)}{(2-p)\Gamma(m_1)\Gamma(m_2)} \frac{1}{(2\pi i)^2} \oint \oint \frac{x^{k-m_1} y^{l-m_2}}{(y-1)\left(x-\frac{y}{y-1}\right)} dx dy \\
&= \frac{2\Gamma\left(m_1+m_2+\frac{2}{2-p}\right)}{(2-p)\Gamma(m_1)\Gamma(m_2)} \frac{1}{2\pi i} \oint \frac{y^{k+l-m_1-m_2}}{(y-1)^{k-m_1+1}} dy \\
&= \frac{2\Gamma\left(m_1+m_2+\frac{2}{2-p}\right)}{(2-p)\Gamma(m_1)\Gamma(m_2)} \binom{k+l-m_1-m_2}{k-m_1}.
\end{aligned}
\tag{19}
$$

Inserting Eq. (19) into Eq. (11), then the joint degree distribution $P(k,l)$ is given by

$$P(k,l) = \frac{2\Gamma\left(m_1+m_2+\frac{2}{2-p}\right)\Gamma(k)\Gamma(l)\Gamma(k+l-m_1-m_2+1)}{(2-p)\Gamma(m_1)\Gamma(m_2)\Gamma\left(k+l+\frac{2}{2-p}+1\right)\Gamma(k-m_1+1)\Gamma(l-m_2+1)}.$$

The proof of the Theorem 2 is complete.

Theorem 3. In this model $\mathcal{G}_2 = \{G(p, f, m_l, G_t^l) : l = 1, 2; \ t \geq 0\}$, if the vertex weighted function $f_k = c > 0$, then the joint degree distribution $P(k,l)$ is given by

$$P(k,l) = \frac{p m_1^{k-m_1} m_2^{l-m_2}}{(2-p)\left(m_1+m_2+\frac{p}{2-p}\right)^{k-m_1+l-m_2+1}} \binom{k+l-m_1-m_2}{k-m_1}.$$

Proof. In this model $\mathcal{G}_2 = \{G(p, f, m_l, G_t^l) : l = 1, 2; \; t \geq 0\}$, if the vertex weighted function $f = f_k = c > 0$, then by Theorem 1, we can get

$$
\begin{aligned}
P(k, l) &= \frac{m_1 \cdot P(k-1, l)}{m_1 + m_2 + \frac{2}{2-p}} + \frac{m_2 \cdot P(k, l-1)}{m_1 + m_2 + \frac{2}{2-p}} + \frac{p\delta_{k, m_1}\delta_{l, m_2}}{p + (2-p)(m_1 + m_2)} \\
&= q_1 \cdot P(k-1, l) + q_2 \cdot P(k, l-1) + \frac{p\delta_{k, m_1}\delta_{l, m_2}}{p + (2-p)(m_1 + m_2)}.
\end{aligned}
\tag{20}
$$

where

$$
q_1 = \frac{m_1}{m_1 + m_2 + \frac{2}{2-p}}, \quad q_2 = \frac{m_2}{m_1 + m_2 + \frac{2}{2-p}}.
\tag{21}
$$

Here, we define the Z-transform of sequence $P(k, l)$ as follows:

$$
\Phi(x, y) = \sum_k \sum_l P(k, l) x^{-k} y^{-l}.
\tag{22}
$$

then the inverse transform is given by

$$
P(k, l) = \frac{1}{(2\pi i)^2} \oint \oint \Phi(x, y) x^{k-1} y^{l-1} dx dy.
\tag{23}
$$

Taking the Z-transform of every term in Eq. (20), we have

$$
\Phi(x, y) = q_1 x^{-1} \Phi(x, y) + q_2 y^{-1} \Phi(x, y) + \frac{p x^{-m_1} y^{-m_2}}{p + (2-p)(m_1 + m_2)}.
\tag{24}
$$

Solving Eq. (24), we obtain

$$
\Phi(x, y) = \frac{p}{p + (2-p)(m_1 + m_2)} \frac{x^{-m_1} y^{-m_2}}{1 - q_1 x^{-1} - q_2 y^{-1}}.
\tag{25}
$$

Plugging Eq. (25) into Eq. (23), we can get

$$
\begin{aligned}
P(k, l) &= \frac{p}{p + (2-p)(m_1 + m_2)} \frac{1}{(2\pi i)^2} \oint \oint \frac{x^{k-m_1} y^{l-m_2}}{(y - q_2)\left(x - \frac{yq_1}{y - q_2}\right)} dx dy \\
&= \frac{p q_1^{k-m_1}}{p + (2-p)(m_1 + m_2)} \frac{1}{2\pi i} \oint \frac{y^{k+l-m_1-m_2}}{(y - q_2)^{k-m_1+1}} dy \\
&= \frac{p q_1^{k-m_1} q_2^{l-m_2}}{p + (2-p)(m_1 + m_2)} \binom{k+l-m_1-m_2}{k-m_1}.
\end{aligned}
\tag{26}
$$

Substituting Eq. (21) into Eq. (26), we finally obtain for $P(k, l)$

$$
P(k, l) = \frac{p m_1^{k-m_1} m_2^{l-m_2}}{(2-p)\left(m_1 + m_2 + \frac{p}{2-p}\right)^{k-m_1+l-m_2+1}} \binom{k+l-m_1-m_2}{k-m_1}.
$$

The proof of the Theorem 3 is complete.

Specially, when the probability $p = 1$, the results is given by Theorems 2 and 3 agrees with the finding in [15, 16]. Moreover, when the probability $p = 1$ and $m_1 = m_2$, the results is given by Theorems 2 and 3 agrees with the finding in [12, 14].

The another methods to evaluate the degree correlations between a layer 1 and a layer 2 is the conditional average degree $\bar{l}(k)$, i.e. the average degree of a vertex in layer 2 conditioned to the degree the same vertex in layer 1. In the following, we investigate the conditional average degree of the model $\mathcal{G}_2 = \{G(p, f, m_l, G_t^l) : l = 1, 2; \ t \geq 0\}$ corresponding to the vertex weighted function $f(k) = k$ and $f(k) = c > 0$ according to the results are given in Theorems 2 and 3, respectively.

Theorem 4. *In this model $\mathcal{G}_2 = \{G(p, f, m_l, G_t^l) : l = 1, 2; \ t \geq 0\}$, if the vertex weighted function $f_k = k$, then the average degree $\bar{l}(k)$ in layer 2 conditioned on the degree of the vertex in layer 1 is given by*

$$\bar{l}(k) = \frac{m_2 \cdot \left(k + \frac{2}{2-p}\right)}{m_1 + \frac{2}{2-p} - 1}.$$

Proof. In Ref. [36], it has been shown that the vertex degree distribution of the model $G(p, f, m, G_0)$ corresponding to the vertex weighted function $f_k = k$ is given by

$$Q_k = \frac{2}{2 - p} \frac{\Gamma(k)\Gamma(m + \frac{2}{2-p})}{\Gamma(m)\Gamma(k + \frac{2}{2-p} + 1)}. \tag{27}$$

According to the definition of the average degree $\bar{l}(k)$ in layer 2 conditioned on the degree of the vertex in layer 1, and combing the Theorem 2 with Eq. (27), we have

$$\bar{l}(k) = A \sum_l \frac{\Gamma(k + \frac{2}{2-p} + 1)\Gamma(l+1)}{\Gamma\left(k + l + \frac{2}{2-p} + 1\right)} \frac{\Gamma(k + l - m_1 - m_2 + 1)}{\Gamma(k - m_1 + 1)\Gamma(l - m_2 + 1)}. \tag{28}$$

where

$$A = \frac{\Gamma\left(m_1 + m_2 + \frac{2}{2-p}\right)}{\Gamma(m_2)\Gamma\left(m_1 + \frac{2}{2-p}\right)}. \tag{29}$$

According to the definition of the Beta function and the relation between the Gamma function and the Beta function $B(m, n) = \frac{\Gamma(m)\Gamma(n)}{\Gamma(m+n)}$ for $m, n > 0$, we obtain the following identity:

$$\frac{\Gamma(k + \frac{2}{2-p} + 1)\Gamma(l+1)}{\Gamma\left(k + l + \frac{2}{2-p} + 1\right)} = \left(k + l + \frac{2}{2-p} + 1\right)\int_0^1 t^l(1 - t)^{k + \frac{2}{2-p}} dt. \tag{30}$$

Substituting Eq. (30) into Eq. (28), we have

$$\bar{l}(k) = A \int_0^1 t^{-k-\frac{2}{2-p}} (1-t)^{k+\frac{2}{2-p}} \frac{d}{dt} \left[\sum_l \frac{\Gamma(k+l-m_1-m_2+1)}{\Gamma(k-m_1+1)\Gamma(l-m_2+1)} t^{k+l+\frac{2}{2-p}+1} \right] dt.$$

(31)

Because

$$\sum_l \frac{\Gamma(k+l-m_1-m_2+1)}{\Gamma(k-m_1+1)\Gamma(l-m_2+1)} t^{k+l-m_1-m_2} = \frac{t^{k-m_1}}{(1-t)^{k-m_1+1}}.$$

(32)

By Eq. (32), we get the following relation

$$\frac{d}{dt} \left[\sum_l \frac{\Gamma(k+l-m_1-m_2+1)}{\Gamma(k-m_1+1)\Gamma(l-m_2+1)} t^{k+l+\frac{2}{2-p}+1} \right]$$

$$= \frac{d}{dt} \left[t^{m_1+m_2+\frac{2}{2-p}+1} \sum_l \frac{\Gamma(k+l-m_1-m_2+1)}{\Gamma(k-m_1+1)\Gamma(l-m_2+1)} t^{k+l-m_1-m_2} \right]$$

$$= \frac{d}{dt} \left[\frac{t^{k+m_2+\frac{2}{2-p}+1}}{(1-t)^{k-m_1+1}} \right].$$

(33)

Taking into account Eq. (33) and the relation $B(m,n) = \frac{\Gamma(m)\Gamma(n)}{\Gamma(m+n)}$ for $m, n > 0$, we have

$$\int_0^1 t^{-k-\frac{2}{2-p}} (1-t)^{k+\frac{2}{2-p}} \frac{d}{dt} \left[\frac{t^{k+m_2+\frac{2}{2-p}+1}}{(1-t)^{k-m_1+1}} \right] dt$$

$$= \int_0^1 t^{m_2} (1-t)^{m_1+\frac{2}{2-p}-2} \left[(k+m_2+\tfrac{2}{2-p}+1) - (m_2+\tfrac{2}{2-p}+m_1)t \right] dt$$

$$= B(m_2+1, m_1+\tfrac{2}{2-p}-1) \cdot \left(k + \tfrac{2}{2-p} \right)$$

$$= \frac{\Gamma(m_2+1)\Gamma(m_1+\tfrac{2}{2-p}-1)}{\Gamma(m_1+m_2+\tfrac{2}{2-p})} \cdot \left(k + \tfrac{2}{2-p} \right).$$

(34)

Plugging Eqs. (29) and (34) into Eq. (28), we obtain

$$\bar{l}(k) = \frac{m_2 \cdot \left(k + \frac{2}{2-p} \right)}{m_1 + \frac{2}{2-p} - 1}.$$

(35)

The proof of the Theorem 4 is complete.

Theorem 5. *In this model $G_2 = \{G(p, f, m_l, G_t^l) : l = 1, 2; t \geq 0\}$, if the vertex weighted function $f_k = c > 0$, then the average degree $\bar{l}(k)$ in layer 1 conditioned on the degree of the vertex in layer 2 is given by*

$$\bar{l}(k) = \frac{m_2 \cdot \left(k + \frac{2}{2-p} \right)}{m_1 + \frac{2}{2-p} - 1}.$$

Proof. In Ref. [36], it has been shown that the vertex degree distribution of the model $G(p, f, m, G_0)$ corresponding to the vertex weighted function $f = f_k = c > 0$ is given by

$$Q_k = \frac{p}{(2-p) \cdot m + p} \left(\frac{(2-p) \cdot m}{(2-p) \cdot m + p} \right)^{k-m}. \tag{36}$$

According to the definition of the average degree $\bar{l}(k)$, and combing the Theorem 3 with Eq. (36), we have

$$\bar{l}(k) = B \sum_l l \cdot \frac{m_2^{l-m_2}}{\left(m_1 + m_2 + \frac{p}{2-p} \right)^{l-m_2}} \binom{k+l-m_1-m_2}{k-m_1}$$

$$= B \sum_{l'} (l' + m_2) \cdot \left(\frac{m_2}{m_1 + m_2 + \frac{p}{2-p}} \right)^{l'} \binom{k'+l'}{k'}. \tag{37}$$

where

$$B = \left(\frac{m_1 + \frac{p}{2-p}}{m_1 + m_2 + \frac{p}{2-p}} \right)^{k-m_1+1}, \quad k' = k - m_1, \ l' = l - m_2. \tag{38}$$

In Refs. [15,16], we see that $\sum_m x^m \binom{m}{n} = \frac{x^n}{(1-x)^{n+1}}$. Thus, we have

$$\sum_{l'} (l' + m_2) \cdot \left(\frac{m_2}{m_1 + m_2 + \frac{p}{2-p}} \right)^{l'} \binom{k'+l'}{k'}$$

$$= \left(\frac{m_1 + m_2 + \frac{p}{2-p}}{m_1 + \frac{p}{2-p}} \right)^{k'+2} \left(m_2 + \frac{m_2}{m_1 + m_2 + \frac{p}{2-p}} \cdot (k' - m_2 + 1) \right)$$

$$= \left(\frac{m_1 + m_2 + \frac{p}{2-p}}{m_1 + \frac{p}{2-p}} \right)^{k-m_1+2} \frac{m_2 \cdot (k + \frac{p}{2-p} + 1)}{m_1 + m_2 + \frac{p}{2-p}}. \tag{39}$$

Substituting Eqs. (39) and (38) into Eq. (37), we get

$$\bar{l}(k) = \frac{m_2 \cdot \left(k + \frac{2}{2-p} \right)}{m_1 + \frac{2}{2-p} - 1}. \tag{40}$$

The proof of the Theorem 5 is complete.

Specially, when the probability $p = 1$, the results is given by Theorems 4 and 5 agrees with the finding in [15,16]. Moreover, when the probability $p = 1$ and $m_1 = m_2$, the results is given by Theorems 4 and 5 agrees with the finding in [12,14]. Also, we observe that the conditional average degree expression $\bar{l}(k)$ is identical for the model $\mathcal{G}_2 = \{G(p, f, m_l, G_t^l) : l = 1, 2; t \geq 0\}$ with respect to two different vertex weighted function $f(k) = k$ and $f(k) = c > 0$, respectively. It was found that the conditional average degree $\bar{l}(k)$ is increasing in k, the degrees of vertices in the two layers are positively correlated.

4   Simulation Results

In this section, we perform the Monte Carlo simulations to verify our theoretical results. In the following simulations, we consider $m_1 = 3$ and $m_2 = 4$, and the initial seed networks are complete graphs with $n_0 = 10$ vertices in both layers, and time $t = 5000$. The results are averaged over 100 Monte Carlo simulations.

Figures 1 and 2 shows the variation trends of the simulation joint degree distribution and the theoretical joint degree distribution over time t for the model $\mathcal{G}_2 = \{G(p, f, m_l, G_t^l) : l = 1, 2; \ t \geq 0\}$ corresponding to the vertex weighted function $f(k) = k$ and $f(k) = 10$, respectively. In Figs. 1 and 2, the horizontal dashed stands for the theoretical joint degree distribution which accord with the Theorems 2 and 3, and the solid line represents the simulation results, respectively. We observe from Figs. 1 and 2 that the Monte Carlo simulation results visibly converge to theoretical results given by Theorems 2 and 3 with the increasing of time t.

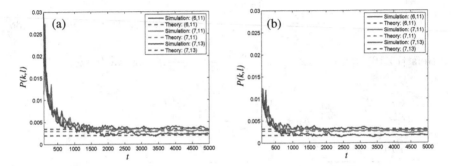

Fig. 1. Comparison between the steady state joint degree distribution and the theoretical joint degree distribution of Theorem 2 for the vertex weighted function $f(k) = k$ with parameters $m_1 = 3$, $m_2 = 4$. (a) $p = 0.4$, (b) $p = 0.8$.

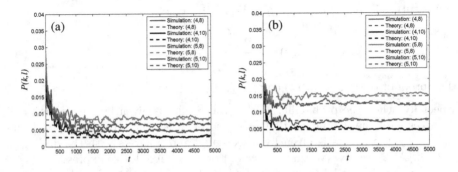

Fig. 2. Comparison between the steady state joint degree distribution and the theoretical results of Theorem 3 for the vertex weighted function $f(k) = 10$ with parameters $m_1 = 3$, $m_2 = 4$. (a) $p = 0.4$, (b) $p = 0.8$.

Figure 3 shows the variation trends of the simulations conditional average degree distribution and the theoretical conditional average degree distribution over time t for the model $\mathcal{G}_2 = \{G(p, f, m_l, G_t^l) : l = 1, 2; \ t \geq 0\}$ corresponding to the vertex weighted function $f(k) = k$ and $f(k) = 10$, respectively. We can see from Fig. 3 that the Monte Carlo simulation results are accord with the theoretical results given by the Theorems 4 and 5, respectively. Moreover, we also observe that the conditional average degree is identical for the model $\mathcal{G}_2 = \{G(p, f, m_l, G_t^l) : l = 1, 2; \ t \geq 0\}$ of two different vertex weighted function $f(k) = k$ and $f(k) = 10$.

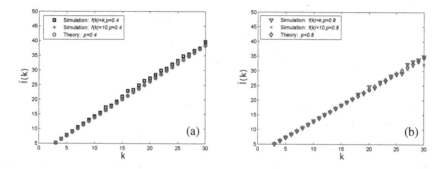

Fig. 3. Comparison between the steady state conditional average degree distribution and the theoretical analyses of Theorems 4 and 5 for the vertex weighted function $f(k) = k$ and $f(k) = 10$ with parameters $m_1 = 3$, $m_2 = 4$, respectively. (a) $p = 0.4$, (b) $p = 0.8$.

5   Conclusions

In this paper, we proposed a new two layer network growth model according to nonlinear preferential attachment rule. Moreover, we calculated the steady state joint degree distribution expression via the rate equation approach, and discussed the joint degree distribution $P(k, l)$ and conditional average degree $\bar{l}(k)$ for the model of two different vertex weighted function $f(k) = k$ and $f(k) = c > 0$, respectively. It was found that the conditional average degree $\bar{l}(k)$ is identical and increasing in k, the degrees of vertices in the two layers are positively correlated. To verify our theoretical results, we perform Monte Carlo simulations for the model of two different vertex weighted function. Experiments indicate that our theoretical results are coincide with the simulation results well.

Acknowledgment. This work was supported by the National Natural Science Foundation of China (Grant Nos. 61262006, 61462001, 61540050, 61762019), the Major Applied Basic Research Program of Guizhou Province (Grant No. JZ20142001), and the Graduate Student Innovation Foundation of Guizhou University (Grant No. 2016047).

References

1. Faioutsos, M., Faioutsos, P., Faioutsos, C.: On powerlaw relationships of the internet topology. ACM SIGCOMM Comput. Commun. Rev. **29**, 251–262 (1999)
2. Albert, R.: Diameter of the world wide web. Nat. Int. J. Sci. **401**, 130–131 (1999)
3. Dorogovtsev, S.N., Mendes, J.F.F., Oliveira, J.G.: Frequency of occurrence of numbers in the world wide web. Phys. A Stat. Mech. Appl. **360**, 548–556 (2005)
4. Newman, M.E.J.: From the cover: the structure of scientific collaboration networks. Proc. Nat. Acad. Sci. **98**, 404–409 (2001)
5. Savić, M., Ivanović, M., Radovanović, M., et al.: The structure and evolution of scientific collaboration in serbian mathematical journals. Scientometrics **101**, 1805–1830 (2014)
6. Boccaletti, S., Latora, V., Moreno, Y., et al.: Complex networks: structure and dynamics. Phys. Rep. **424**, 175–308 (2006)
7. Vazquez, A.: Degree correlations and clustering hierarchy in networks: measures, origin and consequences. Brain Res. **2**, 393–396 (2002)
8. Newman, M.E.J.: The structure and function of complex networks. SIAM Rev. **45**, 167–256 (2003)
9. Watts, D.J., Strogatz, S.H.: Collective dynamics of small-world networks. Nature **393**, 440–442 (1998)
10. Barabasi, A.L., Albert, R.: Emergence of scaling in random networks. Science **286**, 509–512 (1999)
11. Girvan, M., Newman, M.E.J.: Community structure in social and biological networks. Proc. Nat. Acad. Sci. U.S.A. **99**, 7821 (2002)
12. Nicosia, V., Bianconi, G., Latora, V., et al.: Growing multiplex networks. Phys. Rev. Lett. **111**, 058701 (2013)
13. Kim, J.Y., Goh, K.I.: Coevolution and correlated multiplexity in multiplex networks. Phys. Rev. Lett. **111**, 058702 (2013)
14. Nicosia, V., Bianconi, G., Latora, V., et al.: Nonlinear growth and condensation in multiplex networks. Phys. Rev. E Stat. Nonlin. Soft Matter Phys. **90**, 042807 (2013)
15. Fotouhi, B., Momeni, N.: Growing multiplex networks with arbitrary number of layers. Phys. Rev. E Stat. Nonlin. Soft Matter Phys. **92**, 062812 (2015)
16. Fotouhi, B., Momeni, N.: Inter-layer degree correlations in heterogeneously growing multiplex networks. In: Mangioni, G., Simini, F., Uzzo, S., Wang, D. (eds.) Complex Networks VI. Studies in Computational Intelligence, vol. 597, pp. 159–170. Springer International Publishing, Cham (2015). doi:10.1007/978-3-319-16112-9_16
17. Battiston, F., Nicosia, V., Latora, V.: Structural measures for multiplex networks. Phys. Rev. E Stat. Nonlin. Soft Matter Phys. **89**, 032804 (2014)
18. Solá, L., Romance, M., Criado, R., et al.: Eigenvector centrality of nodes in multiplex networks. Chaos **23**, 033131 (2013)
19. Criado, R., Flores, J., Amo, A.G.D.: A mathematical model for networks with structures in the mesoscale. Int. J. Comput. Math. **89**, 291–309 (2010)
20. Min, B., Yi, S.D., Lee, K.M., et al.: Network robustness of multiplex networks with interlayer degree correlations. Phys. Rev. E. **89**, 042811 (2014)
21. Nicosia, V., Latora, V.: Measuring and modeling correlations in multiplex networks. Phys. Rev. E. **92**, 032805 (2014)
22. Domenico, M.D., Solèribalta, A., Cozzo, E., et al.: Mathematical formulation of multi-layer networks. Phys. Rev. E. **3**, 4192–4195 (2013)

23. Kivelä, M., Arenas, A., Barthelemy, M., et al.: Multilayer networks. SSRN Electron. J. **2**, 261–268 (2013)
24. Gómezgardeñes, J.: Diffusion dynamics on multiplex networks. Phys. Rev. Lett. **110**, 028701 (2013)
25. Cozzo, E., Baños, R.A., Meloni, S., et al.: Contact-based social contagion in multiplex networks. Phys. Rev. E Stat. Nonlin. Soft Matter Phys. **88**, 050801 (2013)
26. Granell, C., Gómez, S., Arenas, A.: Dynamical interplay between awareness and epidemic spreading in multiplex networks. Phys. Rev. Lett. **111**, 128701 (2013)
27. Zhao, D., Li, L., Peng, H., et al.: Multiple routes transmitted epidemics on multiplex networks. Phys. Lett. A. **378**, 770–776 (2014)
28. Buono, C., Alvarezzuzek, L.G., Macri, P.A., et al.: Epidemics in partially overlapped multiplex networks. Plos One **9**, 92200 (2014)
29. Gómezgardeñes, J., Reinares, I., Arenas, A., et al.: Evolution of cooperation in multiplex networks. Sci. Rep. **2**, 620 (2012)
30. Nicosia, V., Valencia, M., Chavez, M., et al.: Remote synchronization reveals network symmetries and functional modules. Phys. Rev. Lett. **110**, 174102 (2012)
31. Zhou, J.: Percolation in multiplex networks with overlap. Phys. Rev. E Stat. Nonlin. Soft Matter Phys. **88**, 052811 (2013)
32. Bianconi, G., Dorogovtsev, S.N.: Multiple percolation transitions in a configuration model of a network of networks. Phys. Rev. E Stat. Nonlin. Soft Matter Phys. **89**, 062814 (2014)
33. Battiston, F., Nicosia, V., Latora, V.: Biased random walks on multiplex networks. Comput. Sci. **18**, 043035 (2015)
34. Guo, Q., Cozzo, E., Zheng, Z., et al.: Lévy random walks on multiplex networks. Sci. Rep. **6**, 37641 (2016)
35. Zadorozhnyi, V.N., Yudin, E.B.: Growing network: models following nonlinear preferential attachment rule. Phys. A Stat. Mech. Appl. **428**, 111–132 (2015)
36. Lu, Y.J., Xu, D.Y., Zhou, J.C.: Vertex degree distribution in growth models with nonlinear preferential attachment rule. J. Beijing Univ. Posts Telecommun. **39**, 116–123 (2016)

Improving Accuracy of Sybil Account Detection in OSNs by Leveraging Victim Prediction

Qingqing Zhou, Zhigang Chen$^{(\boxtimes)}$, and Rui Huang

School of Software, Central South University, Changsha, Hu'nan Province,
People's Republic of China
{qqzhou,czg}@csu.edu.cn, 958870977@qq.com

Abstract. The rapid development of social networks, led to a variety of abnormal accounts of the increasingly rampant, and one of the most representative is Sybil. They will create a variety of malicious activities, which seriously endanger the social network and user security. For Sybil account detection this problem, we propose a very efficient Sybil account detection model, which leverages victim prediction to improve the detection accuracy. First, given the exacted features, we design a classifier for victim prediction. Then, prediction results are applied to the social network graph model to modify the weight of the edge. Next, a modified random walk algorithm is used for trust propagation. Finally we rank all nodes according their trust value. And our detection model guarantees that most normal accounts rank higher than Sybil accounts so that operators of online social networks can take actions against low-ranking Sybil accounts.

Keywords: Sybil account detection · Social networks · Victim prediction

1 Introduction

In recent years, online social networks (OSNs) have developed rapidly, such as Facebook and Twitter abroad, domestic Microblogging and RenRen etc. OSNs provide people with the best platform for communication and sharing, and so attract a large number of users. However, due to the interests of the drive, OSNs also attract a lot of attackers [1–4], they create a variety of malicious activities on social networking sites, such as publishing malicious information, which include advertising, pornography and fishing etc. [5,6], sending spam [7], collecting personal privacy information [8] and so on. And social networks are particularly vulnerable to attack from Sybil accounts, Sybil was originally used to describe fake identities in distributed networks such as P2P [9], and was later cited as a fake account in the development of social networks. Sybil account by sending a large number of friends request, in an attempt to establish friendship with a large number of normal users, so as to create the condition for the subsequent launch of malicious activities. The credibility evaluation system and the user's

© Springer Nature Singapore Pte Ltd. 2017
D. Du et al. (Eds.): NCTCS 2017, CCIS 768, pp. 182–197, 2017.
https://doi.org/10.1007/978-981-10-6893-5_14

trust relationship of the social network all have been a serious threat to the Sybil attack. Therefore, the Sybil account for accurate detection is extremely important. In order to solve the problem, many detection schemes have been proposed by academia and industry. These schemes are generally based on graph model, and need to be based on some assumptions to achieve better results. Moreover, many studies have shown that the accuracy of these schemes is very low in practice, and it is easy for attackers to avoid detection of these schemes [8,10,11].

In this paper, we propose a scheme to detect Sybil account efficiently. We use the two-way social relationship between accounts for the establishment of social network model. And we use victim prediction to improve detection accuracy. The victim is the normal account that accepts the Sybil account buddy request, so there is a connection edge between the victim and the Sybil account in the graph model, which is the attack side. Thus, it is possible to reach the Sybil node through the victim node. We use victim forecast to improve sorting quality, thereby improving detection efficiency. First of all, we got the classifier through feature modeling to predict the victim. Then, we applied the forecasting result to the graph model of social network, and use the modified random walk algorithm to propagate trust. Finally, according to the trust value of the node to rank. Eventually, Sybil will be separated from the normal account based on the ranking result. Our detection model can ensure that most of normal nodes rank higher than Sybil nodes. The experimental result shows that Sybil accounts almost all at the bottom of the sequence.

The next section discusses related work. Section 3 provides the design goal and graph model. Section 4 elaborates on system model in depth. The effectiveness of our system model is shown experimentally in Sect. 5. Finally, Sect. 6 draws conclusions.

2   Related Work

At present, most of Sybil account detection mechanisms are graph-based. Depending on whether they utilize machine learning or graph analysis techniques in order to identify Sybil. Next, we discuss every approache in detail. As described in Table 1, including the core algorithm and whether based on the assumption that the number of attack edges is limited.

Cao et al. proposed the application of Markov random field to Sybil detection [12], which is to calculate the posterior probability of each node by the Markov random field, that is, the probability of the node is normal node, so as to judge whether the node is Sybil node. SybilRank adds the ranking process based on random walk [13]. First, random walks are power-iterated. The trust value of normal nodes is distributed to other nodes and normalized. Finally, the result is sorted according to the standardized result. Wei et al. improved the random walk, performed random walk several times [14], recorded the number of times each node was visited, and then judged whether the node is a normal node by calculating the average and standard deviation of the number of visits. Tran et al. combined random walk and breadth-first search to propose Gatekeeper [15].

Table 1. Each schemes described by the core algorithm and whether based on the assumption that the number of attack edges is limited. And Y means this scheme is based on the assumption. Adaptive max flow means adaptive maximum flow. Multi random walk means multiple random walk.

Schemes	Core algorithm	Assumption
SybilBelief [12]	Markov random field	Y
SybilRank [13]	Random walk	Y
SybilDefender [14]	Random walk	Y
GateKeeper [15]	Random walk	Y
SumUp [16]	Adaptive Max Flow	Y
SybilInfer [17]	Bayesian reasoning	Y
SybilLimit [18]	Multi random walk	Y
SybilGurad [19]	Random walk	Y

First, the root node is selected using random walk. Then, the graph is traversed by breadth-first search, whether the number of nodes searched is greater than Threshold Determines whether the node is a normal node.

SumUp proposed to use the voting mechanism to detect Sybil [16], the use of maximum flow theory for each node to allocate different votes, and to collect votes of normal nodes voting, but do not to collect the vote of Sybil nodes, the node with multiple violations is Sybil node. Danezis et al. Proposed SybilInfer, a detection scheme based on random walk and Bayesian reasoning [17]. SybilLimit is to determine whether the node is a normal node by whether the last edge of the node path is the same as normal node's [18]. Yu et al. proposed a modified random walk algorithm for each node to calculate the transfer path [19]. If the node's path intersects the path of the normal node, it is a normal node. Otherwise, it is a Sybil node. But this detection scheme has a high FPR (False Positive Rate).

The above detection scheme is based on the assumption that the number of attack edges is limited, that is, the connection edge between victim accounts and Sybil accounts is limited. However, due to the complexity of the reality of social networks, this assumption is not necessarily established [10,20]. Koll et al. [21] demonstrated that the proposed detection scheme was not satisfactory when the hypothesis was not valid [22]. The detection scheme proposed in this paper does not need to be based on this assumption, so the detection efficiency is greatly improved.

3   Design Goals and Graph Model

3.1   Design Goals

We aim to help OSN operators in detecting Sybil account using a precise scheme. In particular, we have the design goal of high-quality victim prediction. The system model should have an efficient classifier, which used to predict the victim. It should deliver a score of victim in only few minutes, this score is the probability that the user becomes a victim. Simultaneously, the system model should be able to extract low-cost and useful features, in order to ensure the high-quality victim prediction.

3.2 Graph Model

As illustrated in Fig. 1, Firstly, we model an OSN as an undirected graph $G = (A, E)$, each node $a_i \in A$ represents a user, and each edge $\{a_i, a_j\} \in E$ represents a bilateral social relationship among a_i and a_j. In the graph G, we define the number of nodes as n, which is $n = |A|$, and the number of edges as m, which is $m = |E|$. Each node $a_i \in A$ has a degree $deg(a_i)$, which is equal to the sum of weights on edges incident to a_i. And each edge $\{a_i, a_j\} \in E$ has a weight $w(a_i, a_j) \in (0, 1]$, which is initially set to $w(a_i, a_j) = 1$.

We divide the node set A into two disjoint sets, A_n and A_s, representing normal and Sybil accounts, respectively. And the sub-graph structured by A_n as the normal region G_n, which includes all normal accounts and the social relationship between them. Likewise, the another sub-graph structured by A_s as the Sybil region G_s, which includes all Sybil accounts and the social relationship between them. The set of attack edges E_a between victim and Sybil account connecting two regions. We assume social network operators already know a small set of trusted accounts A_t, which are verified to be normal accounts that are not victims.

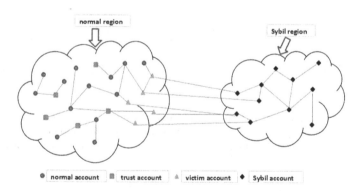

Fig. 1. We divide the social network graph into two disjoint region, normal region and Sybil region. There are normal accounts, trust accounts, victim accounts and their friendship in normal region. The Sybil region includes Sybil accounts and their friendship.

4 System Model Design

We propose to improve the accuracy of Sybil account detection by using victim prediction, the rationale for finding the Sybil account through the victim has been explained in the previous section. In fact, some users of social networks is more likely to become a victim. Therefore, we summarized the characteristics of the victim through experiments.

4.1 Overview

First of all, we have established the corresponding graph model for a social network, and then select characteristics of a account to model, which can obtain a classifier, we use the classifier to predict the victim. Next, prediction results are applied to the social network graph model, according to prediction results, we give different weights to edges in the graph. Finally, we use the modified random walk to walk in the social network graph, so as to sort account nodes in the graph. Eventually, Sybil accounts should be at the bottom of the sequence, and Sybil account separated from the normal account. In addition, the proposed detection model can ensure that most of normal account nodes rank higher than Sybil account nodes. The experimental result showed that Sybil accounts almost all at the bottom of the sequence. The detection process of the model shown in Fig. 2.

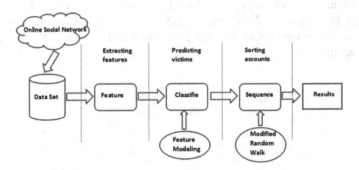

Fig. 2. We extracted features from the dataset, and then got a classifier by modeling feature, which used to predict victim. Next, integrating victim predictions and ranking accounts, we use modified random walk in this process. Finally, we sorted accounts.

4.2 Feature Selection

Victims in social networks have some common features. We summarized victim characteristics in three dimensions by several experiments, these dimensions are account personal information, account behavior and content of message, respectively. As described in Table 2, We calculated the contribution of each attribute to the normal account as a victim, which can obtain the relative importance of each feature. And then we extracted six victim characteristics based on relative importance, these features are, respectively, the number of friends and account age in the victim personal information, frequency of update and frequency of access of victim behavior, URL ratio and number of comments of the message

Table 2. Features extracted from dataset. A k-categorical feature means this feature can have one value out of k categories. The importance is the relative importance of the feature.

Feature	Type	Importance (%)
Friends	Numeric	100.0
Photos	Numeric	75.1
Messages	Numeric	53.3
Number of comments	Numeric	85.9
Frequency of update	Numeric	90.77
Age	Numeric	84.2
Frequency of access	Numeric	80.4
Gender	2-Categorical	13.8
URL ratio	Numeric	82.3

sent by the victim. The multidimensional feature ensures the high accuracy of the victim's prediction. Generally speaking, in order to improve the detection efficiency, we should select the feature of low-cost and easy access, that is, the time taken for feature extraction should be as small as possible. These six features are available for only $O(1)$ time.

Our approach models the following six features when building a user profile.

- The number of friends: This model captures the number of friends. Because attackers like to choose a user that have a lot of friends as the object of attack, send a large number of friend requests to them. these users' scope of influence is relatively large, attackers can spread malicious messages or links to more users through these users.
- Account age: In general, the longer the user registration, the more vulnerable to attack by the attacker. The long-term users have a greater impact on the surrounding users than those with shorter years, which can help the attacker to create malicious activities.
- Frequency of update: The frequency of update is the number of times the user has updated status for a period of time, The update frequency indicates that the user is active. Active users are more likely to spread messages and links than inactive users, so it's easier for these users to be the target of attacking.
- Frequency of access: The frequency of access is the number of times a user has been accessed over a period of time, The frequency of being visited is actually the user's influence.
- URL ratio: Often, messages posted on social network sites contain URL to additional resources, such as pictures, news articles, or videos. URL ratio is the percentage of a message that contains the URL over a period of time. A lot of advertising, porn sites, fishing, etc. are transmitted through the URL, so attackers are more willing to choose these users as an attack object.

- The number of comments: Users update a state, there will be a lot of friends in the comments below. The more comments, indicating that the more people care about the user, and such users tend to be an object of attack.

4.3   Victim Prediction

We propose to improve the accuracy of Sybil detection by using victim prediction. First, we extract six features from the user's profile, which are the number of friends, account age, the frequency of access, the frequency of update, the URL rate, and the number of comments. Then, the classifier is obtained by modeling features, and the classifier is used for the victim prediction. We compared our classifier with random forest classifier, Naive Bayes classifier and decision tree classifier through experiments, Experimental results show that our classifier is the most accurate predictor of the victim, and detailed experimental results are presented in the following sections. We determined whether the account is a victim by the size of victim score $s(a_i)$ and the operating threshold α. We say a_i is a potential victim if $s(a_i) \geq \alpha$, and if $s(a_i) < \alpha$, we think that a_i is a normal account. The forecasting process is shown in Fig. 3.

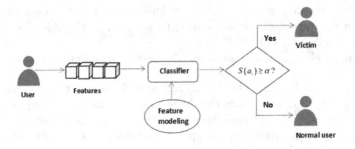

Fig. 3. We extracted six features from the user's profile, in order to obtain a classifier by modeling feature. We determined whether the account is a victim by the size of $s(a_i)$ and α. We say a_i is a potential victim if $s(a_i) \geq \alpha$, and if $s(a_i) < \alpha$, we think that a_i is a normal account.

Feature Modeling. We extracted characteristics from the user's profile, in order to establish a feature model for each account, we use the set F to represent the feature model of each account, and elements contained in F are two-tuple $\langle f_a, v \rangle$, f_a represents a feature, v represents the number or value of f_a. The total number of accounts contained in the data set is denoted by N. We calculate the score for each feature by comparing v and $\overline{F}$, $\overline{F}$ is calculated as follows:

$$\overline{F} = \frac{\sum_{i=1}^{\|F\|} v_i}{N},\tag{1}$$

If $v \geq \overline{F}$, which means that the feature may be abnormal, we need to calculate the frequency of the feature, which is $p = \frac{v_{f_a}}{N}$, and the score of the feature is

$g(f_a) = 1 - p$. If $v < \overline{F}$, which indicates that the feature is normal, the score for the feature is $g(f_a) = 0$. Finally, the average of scores for all features in each feature model is calculated, which as the victim score $s(a_i)$ of the account. In other words, $s(a_i)$ is equal to the average.

Predicting. For each account a_i, we compute a victim score $s(a_i) \in (0,1)$ that represent the probability of a_i to be a victim. At the same time, we set an operating threshold $\alpha \in (0,1)$ with a default value of $\alpha = 0.5$, we say a_i is a potential victim if $s(a_i) \geq \alpha$, and if $s(a_i) < \alpha$, we think that a_i is a normal account. As long as characteristics of the account a_i are extracted, and the value of α is determined, we can use the classifier to calculate the victim score of a_i, which can predict whether a_i is the victim. The feature model we design takes $O(n \log n)$ time to extract n feature set.

4.4   Ranking Users

We use the classifier to predict the victim, so that the victim and the normal account for separation. Next, we sort the account nodes. A known trust account node is randomly selected as the starting point of the modified random walk. We take the probability of a random walk landing a node as the trust value of the node, modeling the probability distribution of the walk at each step, which as a trust propagation process between account nodes. In this process, a weight $w(a_i, a_j)$ represents the rate at which trust may propagate from either side of the edge $\{a_i, a_j\} \in E$. We use the power iteration method to efficiently calculate the trust value of each node, and compute the trust distribution of all nodes in each iteration as the random walk proceeds by one step. We let $T_n(a_i)$ denote the trust value obtained by each node $a_i \in A$ after n iterations. The sum of trust values is denoted by $T \geq 1$. Initially, T is evenly distributed to all trust nodes $a_i \in A_t$. This process is shown in Eq. 2 [23].

$$T_0(a_i) = \{ \begin{matrix} \frac{T}{|A_t|} & if\, a_i \in A_t \\ 0 & otherwise \end{matrix}, \tag{2}$$

After the trust value of the node is initialized, we need to compute the trust value $T_n(a_i)$ of node a_i after n iterations. Where in iteration n, each node a_i collects its trust $T_n(a_i)$ from each neighbor a_j. The process then as follows:

$$T_n(a_i) = \sum_{\{a_i, a_j\} \in E} T_{n-1}(a_j) \cdot \frac{w(a_i, a_j)}{deg(a_j)}, \tag{3}$$

According to the law of conservation, the sum of propagated trust values of all nodes in each iteration is equal. Throughout this process, T is preserved such that for each iteration $n \geq 1$ we have:

$$\sum_{a_i \in A} T_n(a_i) = \sum_{a_i \in A} T_{n-1}(a_i) = T, \tag{4}$$

To ensure that the trust value of the normal account is greater than the Sybil account, we seek to limit the portion of T that escapes the normal region G_n and enters the Sybil region G_s. In order to achieve this goal, the trust propagation rate between the nodes is adjusted, so that edges of potential victim nodes are assigned a smaller weight than other nodes. If a_i and a_j are not potential victims, then the weight of edge $\{a_i, a_j\} \in E$ is the default value $w(a_i, a_j) = 1$. Otherwise, we modify the weight as follows:

$$w(a_i, a_j) = \min\{1, \mu \cdot (1 - \max\{s(a_i), s(a_j)\})\}, \tag{5}$$

Where μ is a scaling parameter with a default value of $\mu = 2$. Generally speaking, the trust propagation is influenced by individual node degrees. And as n grows large, the trust propagation begins to tend to high degree nodes. This implies that high-degree Sybil accounts may collect more trust than low-degree normal accounts. Therefore, in order to eliminate this trend, we normalize the trust by its degree after $k = O(\log n)$ iterations as the rank value $T'_k(a_i)$ of the node. And the rank value is equal to its degree-normalized trust:

$$T'_k(a_i) = \frac{T_k(a_i)}{deg(a_i)}, \tag{6}$$

Finally, we sort nodes by their rank values in a descending order. The experimental result shows that Sybil accounts are ranked at the bottom of the sequence, and normal accounts are listed in the middle and upper part of the sequence, so that Sybil accounts are separated from normal accounts.

4.5   Runtime Analysis

For an OSN with n accounts and m social relationship, our system model takes $O(n \log n)$ time to complete its computation. Predicting potential victims takes $O(n \log n)$ time, where it takes $O(n \log n)$ time to train a classifier and $O(n)$ time to compute victim scores. Also, the trust propagation of our system model takes $O(n \log n)$ time, the propagation process iterates for $O(\log n)$ times and each iteration takes $O(m)$ time. Finally, sorting accounts by their degree-normalized trust takes $O(n \log n)$ time. So the running time of our system model is $O(n \log n)$.

5   System Model Evaluation

We use real data sets collected from Facebook to analyze and evaluate our system model. Furthermore, our detection model was compared with Íntegro and SybilRank. We chose SybilRank and Íntegro for two main reasons. First, the victim prediction method we use is similar to the method used by Íntegro. Second, SybilRank utilizes a similar power iteration method to rank accounts albeit on a unweighted version of the graph. This similarity shows the impact of leveraging victim prediction on Sybil account detection. In addition, Íntegro and Sybil-Rank are state of the art in Sybil detection scheme. Compared to Íntegro and SybilRank, our system model requires the same $O(n \log n)$ time.

5.1   Datasets

The dataset we use was collected from Facebook from May to October 2015. Also, we validated the user of the dataset to verify whether these users are still active on Facebook. In October 2016, these users were visited and found that 8.1% of users were banned by Facebook or the user's own cancellation, after the exclusion of these accounts, and ultimately get 8,457 accounts. The dataset contains various types of Facebook users, accounting for 54.1% of male users and 45.9% of females, which are distributed in 2,001 cities in 131 countries around the world.

In addition, the dataset includes three graph samples of Facebook, which were collected by the breadth-first search algorithm [24]. Each graph consists of two parts, the normal region and Sybil region. The first graph consists of 3,015 normal accounts with 9,425 friendships (the normal region), 60 Sybil with 2,013 friendships (the Sybil region), and 804 attack edges. The second graph consists of 3,020 normal accounts with 8,042 friendships (the normal region), 62 Sybil with 1,987 friendships (the Sybil region), and 642 attack edges. The third graph consists of 2,400 normal accounts with 7,134 friendships, which represents the normal region.

5.2   Classifier Comparison

We use the method of feature modeling to get the classifier for victim prediction. The experimental result shows that the accuracy of our classifier is higher than other classifiers. We use random forest classifier, naive Bayesian classifier, decision tree classifier, and our classifier to predict victims of the same dataset. We randomly select 200 accounts from the data set to form the training set. Respectively, training random forest classifier, Naive Bayes classifier and decision tree classifier and our classifier. We use the manual verification method to verify 200

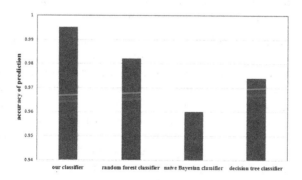

Fig. 4. We compared these four classifiers, the accuracy of random forest classifier is 0.982, And the accuracy of the Naive Bayes classifier and the decision tree classifier are 0.96 and 0.974, respectively. The accuracy of our classifier is as high as 0.995. We can see that our classifier predict the victim is the most accurate.

accounts to confirm whether a account is the victim. The result shows that 18 out of 200 accounts are victims. The experimental result shows in Fig. 4, We compared four classifiers, the accuracy of random forest classifier is 0.982, And the accuracy of the Naive Bayes classifier and the decision tree classifier are 0.96 and 0.974, respectively. The accuracy of our classifier is as high as 0.995. From the result we can see that our classifier performs best. Moreover, the accuracy of other classifiers is also very high, indicating that the extracted features are very efficient. Improving the accuracy of predicting victim, which can help to improve the quality of sorting.

5.3   Detection Efficiency

We compared our system model against Íntegro and SybilRank in terms of their detection efficiency under various attack scenarios, where ideally normal accounts should be ranked higher than Sybil accounts. We mainly consider the detection efficiency comparison under the two victim attack scenarios. In the first attack scenario, we consider attackers who establish attack edges with targeting accounts, attackers and targeting accounts have mutual Sybil friends. And we refer to this scenario as the targeted-victim attack. In the second attack scenario, we consider attackers who establish attack edges with targeting accounts at random. Regardless of whether the attacker and target victim have common Sybil friends. We refer to this scenario as the random-victim attack.

Performance Metric. We use the ROC (receiver operating characteristics) curve to analysis the final detection efficiency. And we performed ROC analysis by moving a pivot point along the list of accounts, starting from the bottom of the list. And if an account is behind the pivot, we marked it as Sybil; otherwise, we marked it as normal. And we also measured the true-positive rate (TPR) and the false-positive rate (FPR) across the whole list. Finally, we refer to the area under its ROC curve (AUC) [25] to measure the performance of the detection scheme. We utilize the AUC to quantify the probability that a random normal account is ranked higher than a random Sybil account.

Evaluation Program. In the two victim attack scenarios, we run our detection model, SybilRank and Íntegro, respectively. At the beginning, we only set one attack edge, and then add another attack edge, repeating the experiment until the number of attack edges to the maximum that the condition allows. At the end of each run, we measure the AUC of each model or system. Finally, the average AUC is compared to evaluate the performance of three detection schemes.

We pick 200 trust accounts that are non-victim or non-Sybil, which can make the chance of guessing seeds very small. We performed $\lceil \log_2(n) \rceil$ iterations for our model, SybilRank and Íntegro, n is the number of nodes in the given graph.

Experimental Results. The experimental result shows that our proposed Sybil account detection model is superior to both SybilRank and Íntegro in both victim attack scenarios. Especially as the number of attack edges increased. AUC of SybilRank is significantly decreased. AUC of Íntegro is showing a downward trend, but which is always greater than 0.93. While our detection model with the increased number of attack edges also shows a downward trend, but the AUC has been no less than 0.98.

In each attack scenario, if Sybil accounts are sparsely connect to normal accounts, and then regions were easily separated. In other words, each detection scheme performed well when the number of attack edges was very small. When the number of attack edges is relatively large, AUC of SybilRank is significantly degraded, Íntegro's AUC is also decreased, but performed better than Sybil-Rank's, however, our detection model maintains its performance, with at most 0.05 decrease in AUC.

In the first attack scenario, as the number of attack edges increases, the AUC of SybilRank decreases to about 0.71, and the AUC of Íntegro is finally kept at about 0.96, and the AUC of our proposed detection model finally decreases to 0.985. As shown in Fig. 5, we can see that under the first attack scenario, the detection efficiency of our proposed detection model is higher than the other two detection systems.

In the second attack scenario, the result is shown in Fig. 6, the quality of our detection model is still higher than the other two detection systems. Moreover, with the increase of the number of attack edges, SybilRank's AUC decreased significantly close to 0.72, and Íntegro's AUC decreased significantly close to 0.93, while our system model sustained its high performance with AUC greater than 0.98. The detection models we designed can maintain high detection efficiency under the two victim attack scenarios.

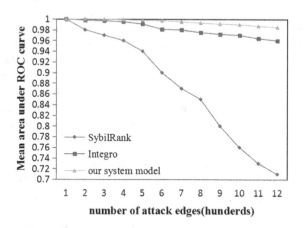

Fig. 5. The detection efficiency of each detection scheme in terms of its AUC under each victim attack scenario. In the first scenario, as the number of attack edges increased, SybilRank's AUC decreased significantly close to 0.71, and Íntegro's AUC decreased significantly close to 0.96, while our system model sustained its high performance with AUC greater than 0.985.

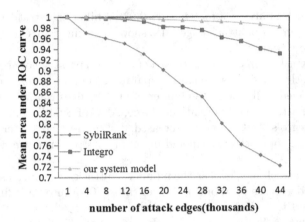

Fig. 6. In the second scenario, as the number of attack edges increased, SybilRank's AUC decreased significantly close to 0.72, and Íntegro's AUC decreased significantly close to 0.93, while our system model sustained its high performance with AUC greater than 0.98.

5.4   Sensitivity Evaluation

Attackers that have rich Experience might got a full or partial knowledge of which accounts are trusted by the OSN operator. And attackers can improve the ranking of Sybil by establishing attack edges directly with these trust accounts. We refer to this attack as the seed-targeting attack.

We consider two main attack scenarios. In the first attack scenario, the length of the shortest path from any Sybil account to any trusted account is exactly $k + 1$, representing the distance between the seed and the Sybil region. For example, each trusted account is a victim and located at a distance of 1 while $k = 0$. We refer to this scenario as the distant-seed attack.

In the second attack scenario, attackers target k trusted accounts picked at random, they have only a partial knowledge of which accounts are trusted by the OSN operator. We refer to this attack scenario as the random-seed attack.

Evaluation Program. We used the first Facebook graph to simulate each attack scenario, which can evaluate the sensitivity of each detection model or system to a seed-targeting attack. We achieve it by replacing the endpoint of each attack edge in the normal region with a normal account, and the normal account is picked at random from a set of candidates. And a candidate account is one that is k nodes away from all trusted accounts in the first attack scenario. A candidate account is any trusted account in the second scenario. We run each detection scheme under different values of k, at the same time, we measure the corresponding AUC at the end of each run.

Experimental Results. In Fig. 7, we can see that each detection model or system has a poor detection efficiency when the distance is small in the first attack

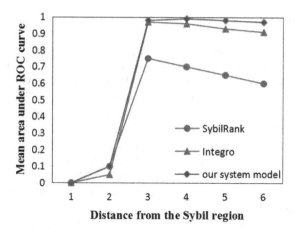

Fig. 7. An attacker befriends accounts that are at a particular distance from all trusted accounts in distant-seed attack. We can see that each detection model or system is sensitive to distant-seed attack

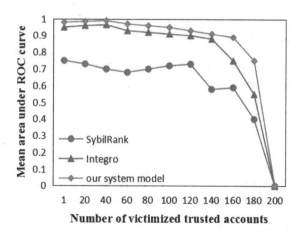

Fig. 8. The attacker directly befriends a subset of the trusted accounts in the random-seed attack. In general, each detection model or system is sensitive to random-seed attack.

scenario. However, our detection model outperforms SybilRank and Íntegro when the distance is larger. In the second attack scenario, with the increased number of victimized trusted accounts, the detection efficiency of each detection model or system degraded. But, in Fig. 8, we can see that our detection model consistently outperforms SybilRank and Íntegro.

6   Conclusion

Today, Sybil accounts on social networks are becoming increasingly rampant, seriously endangering the user's security and experience. And the crafty Sybil operator will mask itself by mimicking the behavior of normal users, which makes the detection of Sybil becomes very challenging. Aiming at the Sybil account detection problem, this paper designs an efficient Sybil detection model, which use victim forecasts to improve sorting quality, thereby improving detection efficiency. First of all, modeling the user characteristics to get a classifier, using the classifier to predict the victim account, and then the forecast result is applied to account sorting, and finally, according to sorting results from the normal account of Sybil separated. The detection model can help social network operators to accurately detect Sybil accounts.

Our detection model is compared with SybilRank and Íntegro, the result shows that the accuracy of our detection model is higher than other two detection systems in the two attack models. Moreover, SybilRank and Íntegro are the most efficient detection systems available today. Therefore, our Sybil detection model can effectively detect the Sybil account, and reduce the harm to users and social networking.

Acknowledgement. This work is supported by the National Natural Science Foundation of China (Grant No. 71633006, Grant No. 61672540), and China Postdoctoral Science Foundation funded project (Grant No. 2017M612586), and Central South University students innovation and entrepreneurship project (Grant No. 201710533511).

References

1. Gao, H., Hu, J., Huang, T., Wang, J.: Security issues in online social networks. IEEE Internet Comput. **15**, 56–63 (2011)
2. Fire, M., Goldschmidt, R., Elovici, Y.: Online social networks: threats and solutions. IEEE Commun. Surv. Tutor. **16**, 2019–2036 (2013)
3. Caviglione, L., Coccoli, M., Merlo, A.: A taxonomy-based model of security and privacy in online social networks. Int. J. Comput. Sci. Eng. **9**, 325–338 (2014)
4. Zhang, D., Chen, Z., Chen, L., Shen, X.: Energy-balanced cooperative transmission based on relay selection and power control in energy harvesting wireless sensor network. Comput. Netw. **104**, 189–197 (2016)
5. Thomas, K., Mccoy, D., Grier, C., Kolcz, A., Paxson, V.: Trafficking fraudulent accounts: the role of the underground market in Twitter spam and sbuse. In: USENIX Conference on Security, Washington, USA, pp. 195–210 (2014)
6. Huang, T.K., Rahman, M.S., Madhyastha, H.V., Faloutsos, M., Ribeiro, B.: An analysis of socware cascades in online social networks. In: WWW, pp. 619–630 (2013)
7. Thomas, K., Grier, C., Song, D., Paxson, V.: Suspended accounts in retrospect: an analysis of twitter spam. In: Proceedings of IMC, pp. 243–258 (2011)
8. Boshmaf, Y., Muslukhov, I., Beznosov, K., Ripeanu, M.: The socialbot network: when bots socialize for fame and money. In: Twenty-Seventh Computer Security Applications Conference, ACSAC 2011, Orlando, FL, USA, pp. 93–102 (2011)

9. Douceur, J.R.: The sybil attack. In: Druschel, P., Kaashoek, F., Rowstron, A. (eds.) IPTPS 2002. LNCS, vol. 2429, pp. 251–260. Springer, Heidelberg (2002). doi:10. 1007/3-540-45748-8_24

10. Bilge, L., Strufe, T., Balzarotti, D., Kirda, E.: All your contacts are belong to us: automated identity theft attacks on social networks. In: International Conference on World Wide Web, WWW 2009, Madrid, Spain, pp. 551–560 (2009)

11. Zhang, D., Chen, Z.: Energy-efficiency of cooperative communication with guaranteed E2E reliability in WSNs. Int. J. Distrib. Sensor Netw. **2013**, 94–100 (2013)

12. Gong, N.Z., Frank, M., Mittal, P.: SybilBelief: a semi-supervised learning approach for structure-based sybil detection. IEEE Trans. Inf. Forensics Secur. **9**, 976–987 (2013)

13. Cao, Q., Sirivianos, M., Yang, X., Pregueiro, T.: Aiding the detection of fake accounts in large scale social online services. In: USENIX Conference on Networked Systems Design and Implementation, p. 15 (2012)

14. Wei, W., Xu, F., Tan, C.C., Li, Q.: SybilDefender: defend against Sybil attacks in large social networks. In: Proceedings - IEEE INFOCOM, vol. 131, pp. 1951–1959 (2012)

15. Tran, N., Li, J., Subramanian, L.: Optimal Sybil-resilient node admission control. In: IEEE International Conference on Computer Communications, Joint Conference of the IEEE Computer and Communications Societies, INFOCOM 2011, Shanghai, China, pp. 3218–3226 (2011)

16. Tran, N., Min, B., Li, J.: Sybil-resilient online content voting. In: USENIX Symposium on Networked Systems Design and Implementation, NSDI 2009, Boston, MA, USA, pp. 15–28 (2009)

17. Danezis, G., Mittal, P.: SybilInfer: detecting Sybil nodes using social networks. In: Network and Distributed System Security Symposium, NDSS 2009, San Diego, California, USA (2009)

18. Yu, H., Gibbons, P.B., Kaminsky, M.: SybilLimit: a near-optimal social network defense against Sybil attacks. In: IEEE Symposium on Security and Privacy, SP 2008, NDSS 2008, pp. 3–17. IEEE (2008)

19. Yu, H., Kaminsky, M., Gibbons, P.B., Flaxman, A.D.: SybilGuard: defending against Sybil attacks via social networks. IEEE/ACM Trans. Netw. **16**, 576–589 (2008)

20. Mohaisen, A., Yun, A., Kim, Y.: Measuring the mixing time of social graphs. In: Proceedings of the 10th ACM SIGCOMM Conference on Internet Measurement, Melbourne, Australia, pp. 383–389 (2010)

21. Koll, D., Li, J., Stein, J., Fu, X.: On the effectiveness of sybil defenses based on online social networks. In: IEEE International Conference on Network Protocols, pp. 1–2 (2013)

22. Zhang, Y., Lv, S., Fan, D.: Anomaly detection in online social networks. Chin. J. Comput. **38**, 2011–2027 (2015)

23. Boshmaf, Y., Logothetis, D., Siganos, G., Leria, J., Lorenzo, J.: Íntegro: leveraging victim prediction for robust fake account detection in OSNs. In: Proceedings of the 22nd Annual Network and Distributed System Security Symposium, San Diego, USA (2015)

24. Leskovec, J., Faloutsos, C.: Sampling from large graphs. In: Proceedings of the ACM SIGKDD Conference, pp. 631–636 (2006)

25. Hastie, T., Tibshirani, R., Friedman, J.: The elements of statistical learning: data mining, inference, and prediction. Math. Intell. **27**, 83–85 (2009)

Landmark-Based Spectral Clustering with Local Similarity Representation

Wanpeng Yin[1(✉)], En Zhu[1], Xinzhong Zhu[2], and Jianping Yin[3]

[1] College of Computer, National University of Defense Technology,
Changsha 410073, Hunan, China
{wpyin,enzhu}@nudt.edu.cn
[2] Zhejiang Normal University, Jinhua 321004, Zhejiang, China
zxz@zjnu.cn
[3] State Key Laboratory of High Performance Computing,
National University of Defense Technology, Changsha 410073, Hunan, China
jpyin@nudt.edu.cn

Abstract. Clustering analysis is one of the most important tasks in statistics, machine learning, and image processing. Compared to those clustering methods based on Euclidean geometry, spectral clustering has no limitations on the shape of data and can detect linearly non-separable pattern. Due to the high computation complexity of spectral clustering, it is difficult to handle large-scale data sets. Recently, several methods have been proposed to accelerate spectral clustering. Among these methods, landmark-based spectral clustering is one of the most direct methods without losing much information embedded in the data sets. Unfortunately, the existing landmark-based spectral clustering methods do not utilize the prior knowledge embedded in a given similarity function. To address the aforementioned challenges, a landmark-based spectral clustering method with local similarity representation is proposed. The proposed method firstly encodes the original data points with their most 'similar' landmarks by using a given similarity function. Then the proposed method performs singular value decomposition on the encoded data points to get the spectral embedded data points. Finally run k-means on the embedded data points to get the clustering results. Extensive experiments show the effectiveness and efficiency of the proposed method.

Keywords: Landmark representation · Spectral clustering · Clustering analysis

1 Introduction

Spectral clustering is a class of clustering methods based on the eigen decomposition on Laplacian matrix with applications ranging from statistics [1], machine learning [2,3] and image processing [4,5]. Compared to those clustering methods based on Euclidean geometry [6], spectral clustering has no limitations on the

D. Du et al. (Eds.): NCTCS 2017, CCIS 768, pp. 198–207, 2017.
https://doi.org/10.1007/978-981-10-6893-5_15

shape of data and can detect linearly non-separable pattern. Despite these advantages, spectral clustering has less applicability to large-scale data set because of its high computation complexity. In general, spectral clustering needs to construct an affinity matrix to model the similarities between all pairs of data points. Then compute the first k eigenvectors of the corresponding Laplacian matrix, which is also called spectral embedding. Finally, run k-means on each row of the first k eigenvectors. Considering a data set consists of n data points, the time complexity of spectral clustering is $O(n^3)$, which makes it prohibitive for large-scale data application.

Recently, many methods are proposed to reduce the computational complexity of spectral clustering. Nyström method [7] is one of the most popular methods. It approximates the eigenvectors of entire affinity matrix by sampling its columns. Fast approximate spectral clustering(FASP) [8] samples a small subset of the original data to represent the whole data set, then performs spectral clustering on this small subset. Landmark-based spectral clustering methods [9] assume that all the data points can be represented by some selected landmarks. Inner product is used to model the similarities between all pairs of data points. The runtime of spectral embedding can be largely reduced by performing singular vector decomposition on a tall and thin matrix. However, the existing landmark-based spectral clustering methods do not take prior knowledge of the original data sets into consideration. In other words, the existing landmark-based representation do not use the information of a given similarity function.

In this paper, a landmark-based spectral clustering method is proposed not only to use the prior knowledge embedded in a given similarity function but also to reduce the computation complexity of spectral clustering. It can be summarized as the following steps. Firstly, all the data points are encoded with their most similar landmarks by using a given similarity function. Then, inner product between all pairs of the encoded data points is used as the affinity matrix. By using Singular Value Decomposition(SVD), the eigen decomposition of a large affinity matrix can be reduced as the eigen decomposition of a thin and tall matrix, which can largely reduce the time complexity of spectral embedding. Finally, treat each row of eigenvectors as an embedded data point and run k-means on these embedded data points to get the clustering results.

Our main contribution can be summarized as follow:

– A landmark-based spectral clustering with local similarity representation is proposed to accelerate spectral embedding. Compared to the existing landmark-based spectral clustering methods, the information embedded in a given similarity function is used for clustering.
– Compared to existing spectral clustering methods, the proposed method needs fewer parameters - the number of selected landmarks and nearest neighbors of a data point in selected landmarks.

The rest of paper is organized as follow: Sect. 1 covers related work on various kinds of spectral clustering. Section 2 presents the proposed method detailed. Section 3 provides the experimental results. Section 4 presents the concluding remarks of the proposed method.

2   Methodology

In this section, considering that the existing landmark-based spectral clustering methods do not use the prior knowledge embedded in the similarity function, a local similarity representation is proposed. By constructing a proper affinity matrix, the spectral embedding can be largely accelerated.

2.1   Limitations of Existing Landmark-Based Spectral Clustering

Existing landmark-based spectral clustering methods assume that all the data points can be represented with some selected landmarks. Given some selected landmarks $U = [u_1, u_2, ..., u_p]$ and original data set $X = [x_1, x_2, ..., x_n]$, these methods try to solve the following equation.

$$\min_Z \sum_{i=1}^{N} \|x_i - U_i z_i\|^2$$

$$\text{s.t.} \quad \mathbf{1}^T z_i = 1$$

where $Z = [z_1, z_2, ..., z_n]$ is the landmark representation of the original data set.

From the view of linear space, the above equation tries to "compress" all the data points by finding a set of basis vectors and the representation with respect to the basis for each data point. To explain it detailedly, U is regarded as the new basis of the original data points X and Z is regarded as the new coordinates of X under the new basis U. Compared to the original data points $X \in \mathbb{R}^{n \times d}$, such landmark representation $Z \in \mathbb{R}^{n \times p}$ largely decreases its dimensions and sometimes can be more sparse.

Considering the runtime of k-means is quite sensitive to the shape of the original data points, random selection is used to get the landmarks. The basis vectors U have the same dimensionality with the original data points. We can treat the basis vectors as the landmark points of the data set.

By using some proper methods such as N-W estimator [9], locality-constrained linear coding [10] or anchor graph embedding [11], the landmark representation of all the original data points is computed. Obviously, such representation does not use the information of a given similarity function $S(x_i, x_j)$.

2.2   Local Similarity Representation

To project each data point into its local-coordinate system using prior knowledge embedded in the similarity function $S(x_i, x_j)$, every original data point x_i is encoded by $z_i = [z_i^{(1)}, z_i^{(2)}, ..., z_i^{(p)}]$ as the Eq. (1) shows.

$$z_i^{(j)} = \begin{cases} S(x_i, u_j) & \text{if } u_j \text{ is a nearest neighbors in } x_i \\ 0 & \text{otherwise} \end{cases} \tag{1}$$

where $S(x_i, x_j) \geq 0$ is a given similarity function.

The proposed representation presents two attractive properties.

- **Better Construction:** Unlike those methods that all the data points are linearly combined their nearest neighbors in Euclidean space, local similarity representation utilizes the prior knowledge of a given similarity function. Such representation can be more accurate and sometimes be more sparse.
- **Computation Efficiency:** The existing landmark representation needs to solve a regression problem for every data point after using k-nn to find its nearest landmarks. When the number of data points increases, these methods can be non-scalable. The proposed representation only uses k-nn search to get nearest landmarks, then uses similarity function to get the encoded data without solving a regression problem. Obviously, such encoding method can largely speed up the landmark representation compared to the existing landmark presentations.

2.3 Spectral Embedding

Inspired by [12], the affinity matrix of landmark-based spectral clustering is designed as the following equation.

$$A = Z^T Z \tag{2}$$

where $Z = [z_1, ..., z_n], z_i \in \mathbb{R}^p$ and $p \ll n$. Z can be treated as the coordinates of the original data with landmarks basis. So the elements a_{ij} in A can be treated as the inner-product of x_i and x_j.

Now the original data is well sparsely represented by $Z \in \mathbb{R}^{p \times n}$. Let $\hat{Z}$ be $\hat{Z} = D^{1/2} Z$. The corresponding normalized Laplacian matrix can be rewritten as follow:

$$L = I - D^{-1/2} A D^{-1/2}$$

$$L = I - (D^{-1/2} Z^T)(Z D^{-1/2}) = I - \hat{Z}\hat{Z}^T$$

Considered the properties of Singular Vector Decomposition(SVD), the eigen-decompostion of a large matrix $\hat{Z}\hat{Z}^T$ can be efficiently computed by SVD on a tall and thin matrix Z.

2.4 Computation Complexity Analysis

Supposed there are n data points with dimensionality d and p landmarks are selected. The final step of all the mentioned methods is the same - to cluster the embedded data points into k cluster. We summarize the computation complexity of the proposed methods and other state-of-the-art methods as Table 1 shows.

To summarize the above solutions, Algorithm 1 shows the pseudo code of the proposed method.

Table 1. Comparisons between SC-LLC and comparative methods in terms of computation complexity

Method	Preprocessing	Construction	Embedding
SC	N/A	$O(n^2 \log n)$	$O(n^3)$
Nyström	N/A	$O(pnd)$	$O(p^3 + pn)$
FASP	$O(tpnd)$	$O(p^2 d)$	$O(p^3)$
LSC	$O(tpnd)$	$O(pnd)$	$O(p^3 + p^2 n)$
LSC-LSR	N/A	$O(pnd)$	$O(p^3 + p^2 n)$

Algorithm 1. Spectral Clustering with Local Similarity Representation

---

Require: Dataset $X \in \mathbb{R}^{n \times d}$,
  similarity function $S(x_i, x_j) \geq 0$,
  the number of landmarks p,
  the nearest neighbors r,
  cluster number k
Ensure: Clustering result $C = [c_1, ..., c_n]$
1: Select p landmarks $U = [u_1, ..., u_p]$ by random selection
2: For each data, compute their landmark representation $Z = [z_1, ..., z_n]$ using Eq. (1)
3: Compute the first largest k left-singular vectors Y of Z
4: Form $T \in \mathbb{R}^{n \times k}$ by from U normalizing its rows to norm 1 $t_{ij} = u_{ij} / \sqrt{\sum_k y_{ik}^2}$
5: Treat each row of T as a data, run k-means on these data and get clustering result $C = [c_1, ..., c_n]$

---

3   Experiments

In this section, several experiments are conducted to illustrate the effectiveness and the efficiency of the proposed method.

3.1   Data Sets

We conducted the experiments on four real-world data sets downloaded from UCI. Here is a brief introduction of all the four data sets.

Semeion: A handwritten digits database from around 80 persons. All the data is represented by its original pixels - 256 input attributes.

PenDigits: A handwritten digits database by collecting 250 samples from 44 writers. Each data contains 16 input attributes.

USPS: A handwritten digits database contains 11000 handwritten digits. All the data is represented by its original pixels - 256 input attributes.

MNIST: A famous handwritten digits database. All the data is represented by its original pixels - 784 input attributes.

The summary of all the four data sets is given as Table 2 shows.

Table 2. Summary of four experimental data sets

Data set	# of instances	# of attributes	# of classes
Semeion	1593	256	10
PenDigits	10992	16	10
USPS	11000	256	10
MNIST	60000	784	10

3.2   Comparative Methods

To illustrate the efficiency and effectiveness of our proposed methods, Four comparative methods are give as follow:

Nyström: Spectral clustering with Nyström method approximates the whole affinity matrix by sampling its columns. Spectral embedding with Nyström method can be computed by eigen decomposition on a small matrix and some matrix multiplication. For fair comparison, we implement it into Python 3 and sklearn.

FASP: Fast Approximate Spectral Clustering is a kind of k-means-based approximate spectral clustering. It runs k-means and gets some cluster centers as the sample to represent the whole data set. For fair comparison, we implement it into Python 3 and sklearn.

LSC: The first proposed landmark-based spectral clustering. It selects the landmarks by k-means and uses N-W estimator to get the landmark representation of the original data under the selected landmark basis. For fair comparison, we implement it into Python 3 and sklearn.

LSC-LSR: It is the abbreviate for our proposed method - Landmark-based Spectral Clustering with Local Similarity Representation.

3.3   Evaluation Metrics

We evaluate the spectral clustering methods with Normalized Mutual Information(NMI) and runtime. All the code is implemented in Python 3 and sklearn [13] under a Linux machine with Intel i7 and 12 GB memory.

Mutual information (MI) of two random variables is a measure of the mutual dependence between the two variables. Before introducing the mutual information, we firstly state the definition of the entropy.

The entropy of uncertainty for a partition set $H(X)$ is given by:

$$H(X) = \sum_{i=1}^{|X|} p(i) \log p(i)$$

where $p(i) = |X|/N$ is the probability that an object picked randomly from X falls into class X_i.

The mutual information between the grand-truth label(G) and cluster results(C) is given by:

$$\mathrm{MI} = \sum_{i=1}^{|G|} \sum_{j=1}^{|C|} P(i,j) \log \frac{P(i,j)}{P(i)P(j)}$$

where $P(i,j) = |G_i \cap C_i|/N$.

The normalized mutual information is defined as follow:

$$\mathrm{NMI}(G,C) = \frac{\mathrm{MI}(G,C)}{\sqrt{\mathrm{H}(G)\mathrm{H}(C)}}$$

Obviously, the value of NMI is nonnegative and not greater than 1. The higher value of NMI means the better cluster accuracy.

3.4 Results and Analysis

Each test are conducted for 20 time under 1000 landmarks with 5 neighbors. We compute the average NMI and runtime with its standard variance. The accuracy and runtime of four spectral clustering methods on all the data sets are reported in Tables 3 and 4. Several interesting points are found:

- Taking the accuracy evaluation into consideration, SC-LSR outperforms all the comparative methods on nearly all the data set. The main reason to achieve such performance might be the proposed landmark-based representation.

Table 3. NMI of SC-LSR and comparative methods

Method	Dataset			
	Semeion	PenDigits	USPS	MNIST
Nyström	0.49 ± 0.03	0.69 ± 0.01	0.26 ± 0.01	0.48 ± 0.00
FASP	0.58 ± 0.02	0.71 ± 0.03	0.61 ± 0.04	$\mathbf{0.66 \pm 0.04}$
LSC	0.57 ± 0.02	0.64 ± 0.02	0.58 ± 0.01	0.60 ± 0.02
LSC-LSR	$\mathbf{0.63 \pm 0.02}$	$\mathbf{0.80 \pm 0.02}$	$\mathbf{0.62 \pm 0.03}$	0.61 ± 0.02

Table 4. Runtime of SC-LSR and comparative methods

Method	Dataset			
	Semeion	PenDigits	USPS	MNIST
Nyström	2.03 ± 0.00	2.25 ± 0.10	$\mathbf{3.10 \pm 0.01}$	$\mathbf{10.31 \pm 0.59}$
FASP	1.04 ± 0.02	$\mathbf{1.56 \pm 0.17}$	9.00 ± 0.31	130.44 ± 5.62
LSC	1.46 ± 0.03	2.57 ± 0.19	14.85 ± 0.33	202.62 ± 4.67
LSC-LSR	$\mathbf{0.79 \pm 0.01}$	1.82 ± 0.15	4.99 ± 0.07	67.00 ± 0.59

– In some data sets, the k-means approximation methods - FASP and LSC usually spends more time than Nyström method and the proposed method. These methods select landmarks or sample points by k-means whose time complexity is $O(tpnd)$, where t is the number of iteration that k-means executes. There might be a various Euclidean geometry of the original data. So these methods must be time-consuming.

In order to further examine the behaviors of these methods, PENDIGITS data set is used to be conducted a thorough study.

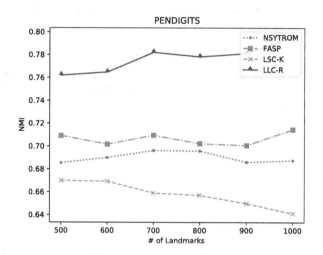

Fig. 1. NMI # of nearest landmarks on Semeion data set

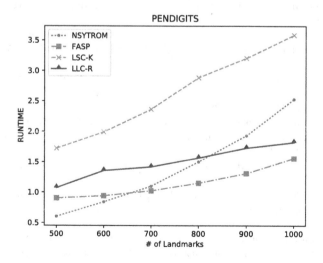

Fig. 2. Runtime # of nearest landmarks on Semeion data set

Consider all the methods must choose the number of landmarks or the number of sampling points p, plenty of tests on all of four methods are conducted for 20 times with a wide range of the number of landmarks as the results are shown in Figs. 1 and 2. It is clear that the clustering accuracy can increase slightly while the runtime can largely increase as the number of landmarks growing.

4   Conclusion

In this paper, we have proposed a landmark-based spectral clustering with local similarity representation. Similar to existing landmark-based spectral clustering methods, random selection is used to select the landmarks. By utilizing the prior information embedded in a given similarity function, local similarity representation is used to encode the original data ponits. By using the properties of singular vector decomposition, spectral embedding on the affinity matrix can be computed efficiently. The experimental results demonstrate the superior performance of the proposed method with existing spectral clustering methods.

Acknowledgment. The authors would like to thank the financial support of National Natural Science Foundation of China (Project NO. 61672528, 61403405, 61232016, 61170287).

References

1. Von Luxburg, U., Belkin, M., Bousquet, O.: Consistency of spectral clustering. Ann. Stat. **36**(2), 555–586 (2008)
2. Liu, X., Zhou, S., Wang, Y., Li, M., Dou, Y., Zhu, E., Yin, J.: Optimal neighborhood kernel clustering with multiple kernels. In: Proceedings of the 31st Conference on Artificial Intelligence, pp. 2266–2272 (2017)
3. Wu, Y., Zhang, B., Yi, X., Tang, Y.: Communication-motion planning for wireless relay-assisted multi-robot system. IEEE Wirel. Commun. Lett. **5**(6), 568–571 (2016)
4. Achanta, R., Shaji, A., Smith, K., Lucchi, A., Fua, P., Süsstrunk, S.: SLIC superpixels compared to state-of-the-art superpixel methods. IEEE Trans. Pattern Anal. Mach. Intell. **34**(11), 2274–2282 (2012)
5. Li, Z., Chen, J.: Superpixel segmentation using linear spectral clustering. In: Proceedings of the IEEE Conference on Computer Vision and Pattern Recognition, pp. 1356–1363 (2015)
6. Hartigan, J.A., Wong, M.A.: A k-means clustering algorithm. Appl. Stat. **28**(1), 100–108 (1979)
7. Fowlkes, C., Belongie, S., Chung, F., Malik, J.: Spectral grouping using the nystrom method. IEEE Trans. Pattern Anal. Mach. Intell. **26**(2), 214–225 (2004)
8. Yan, D., Huang, L., Jordan, M.I.: Fast approximate spectral clustering. In: International Conference on Knowledge Discovery and Data Mining, pp. 1–23 (2009)
9. Chen, X.: Large scale spectral clustering with landmark-based representation. In: Proceedings of the Twenty-Fifth AAAI Conference on Artificial Intelligence Large, number Chung 1997, pp. 313–318 (2011)

10. Wang, J., Yang, J., Yu, K., Lv, F., Huang, T.: Locality-constrained linear coding for image classification. In: Computer Vision and Pattern Recognition, pp. 27–30 (2014)
11. Wang, M., Fu, W., Hao, S., Tao, D., Wu, X.: Scalable semi-supervised learning by efficient anchor graph regularization. IEEE Trans. Knowl. Data Eng. **28**(7), 1864–1877 (2016)
12. Liu, W., He, J., Chang, S.-F.: Large graph construction for scalable semi-supervised learning. In: Proceedings of the 25th International Conference on Machine Learning, pp. 679–689 (2010)
13. Pedregosa, F., Varoquaux, G., Gramfort, A., Michel, V., Thirion, B., Grisel, O., Blondel, M., Prettenhofer, P., Weiss, R., Dubourg, V., Vanderplas, J., Passos, A., Cournapeau, D., Brucher, M., Perrot, M., Duchesnay, E.: Scikit-learn: machine learning in python. J. Mach. Learn. Res. **12**, 2825–2830 (2011)

Query Optimization Strategies in Probabilistic Relational Databases

Caicai Zhang[1(✉)], Zhongsheng Cao[2], and Hong Zhu[2(✉)]

[1] Zhejiang University of Water Resources and Electric Power, Hangzhou, China
caicaizhng@gmail.com
[2] School of Computer Science and Technology,
Huazhong University of Science and Technology, Wuhan, China
zhuhong@hust.edu.cn

Abstract. Most existing optimization strategies for relational algebra queries in probabilistic relational databases focus on accelerating probability computation of lineage expressions of answering tuples. However, none of them take into account simplifying lineage expression during query processing. To this aim, an optimization method that makes use of integrity constraints to generate simplified lineage expressions for query results is proposed. The simplified lineage expressions for two algebra operations are generated under functional dependency constraints and referential constraints separately. The effectiveness of the optimization strategies for relational algebra queries is demonstrated in the experiment.

Keywords: Probabilistic databases · Query optimization · Functional dependency constraints · Referential constraints

1 Introduction

Deterministic databases were invented to support applications that require precise data semantics, such as banking, payroll, and accounting. However, modern applications need to process uncertain data that are retrieved from diverse and autonomous sources [1], such as data cleaning [2,6], sensor networks [19,20], tracking moving objects [5,10], or healthcare information systems [11]. Informally, a probabilistic database is a probability distribution over a set of deterministic databases (namely, possible worlds) [18].

Query processing is an important task for probabilistic relational databases. Assumption query is also an important and special query over probabilistic relational databases. In this paper, we are going to study the optimization strategies for general relational queries and assumption query, respectively.

There are mainly two methods for probabilistic query processing. One is to integrate the probability computation into the query evaluation, the other is to first obtain the result tuples together with their lineage, and then compute the probability of the lineage as the probabilities of answering tuples. The former can only evaluate safe queries over independent probabilistic relational databases,

© Springer Nature Singapore Pte Ltd. 2017
D. Du et al. (Eds.): NCTCS 2017, CCIS 768, pp. 208–220, 2017.
https://doi.org/10.1007/978-981-10-6893-5_16

while the latter can be used for any relational queries over correlated probabilistic relational databases.

The computation of the lineage expressions for general relational algebras are listed as follows [7,8].

R → SELECT R.*, R.f FROM R

$\sigma_\phi(Q)$ → SELECT R.* FROM (Q) R WHERE ϕ

$\pi_A(Q)$ → SELECT R.A, **OR**(R.f) AS f FROM (Q) R GROUP BY R.A

$Q_1 \bowtie_\phi Q_2$ → SELECT R.*, S.*, **AND**(R.f, S.f) AS f FROM (Q_1) R, (Q_2) S WHERE ϕ

$Q_1 \cup Q_2$ → SELECT R.*, **OR**(R.f) AS f FROM (SELECT * FROM Q_1 UNION ALL SELECT * FROM Q_2) R GROUP BY R.*

$Q_1 - Q_2$→ SELECT R.*, **AND**(R.f, **NOT**(S.f)) AS f FROM (Q_1) R LEFT OUTER JOIN (Q_2) S ON $R.* = S.*$

While the procedure of obtaining the set of answering tuples and their lineage expressions over probabilistic relational databases are barely different from traditional relational databases, the probability computation of lineage expressions is to compute the probabilities of Boolean logical expressions. The time complexity of computing a Boolean expression is $O(2^n)$, where n is the number of variables appeared in the expression. There are many optimization strategies to accelerate the probability computation of a given Boolean expression.

The problem is that duplicate variables in the Boolean expressions still lead to huge cost of optimized probability computation. Therefore, we consider a different way of optimization strategy of query processing in probabilistic relational databases. The idea is to simplify the lineage expressions during their generation by taking integrity constraints into account.

The main contributions of this paper are as follows:

(1) We provide an optimization strategy to simplify lineage of projection operator under functional dependency constraints.
(2) We provide an optimization strategy to simplify lineage of join operator under referential constraints.
(3) We conduct an extensive experimental study to evaluate our query optimization strategies in different configurations, showing its efficiency and scalability.

The remainder of this article is organized as follows. Section 2 describes related works. Section 3 gives necessary background on probabilistic databases. Section 4 gives the optimization strategy for general query. Section 5 is our experimental study. Finally, Sect. 6 concludes the article with final remarks.

2   Related Work

In this section, we review related work in the areas of probabilistic databases and query evaluation.

There are significant amounts of work on representation formalism for uncertain data, e.g., [4,17,23]. In general, these studies can be divided into two categories, one is based on simple correlation model [4,23], which associates existence probabilities with individual tuples and assumes that the tuples are mutually independent or exclusive; the other is based on a richer representation formalism which can express complex correlations between tuples [17]. The latter data model which we adopted is more practical, because many application domains naturally produce correlated data and dependencies among tuples arises naturally during query evaluation even when one assumes that the base data tuples are independent [17].

There are also two categories of approach to query evaluation in probabilistic databases [21]. One approach is to integrate the probabilistic inference with the query computation step which could take advantage of standard data management techniques to speed up the probabilistic inference [13,14], but it can only compute correct probability for the set of queries restricting that has safe plans on simple correlation model. Queries that do not exist safe plans or queries on complex correlation model need to be processed by the other approach. The other approach is to separate the query evaluation and probability inference on the lineage expression [15].

Fink et al. [7,8] list the computation of the lineage expressions for general relational algebras. For example, the lineage expression for projection is the disjunction of formulae of each involved tuples; the lineage expression for join is the conjunction of formulae of each involved tuples. Probability inference on the lineage expression is to compute the probability of a formula composed of a set of Boolean variables being true. The time complexity of probability computation of an arbitrary formula is $O(2^n)$, where n is the number of variables in the formula. Given a formula, [8] incrementally decompose it to obtain sub-formulae in a tractable form called 1OF, where each variable occurs only once and for which probability computation can be done in linear time. This approach is based on incremental decomposition of a formula using three decomposition types.

3   Preliminary

Definition 1. *A probabilistic database in the extensional representation [3, 9, 16] is a discrete probability space $PDB = (W, P)$, where $W = \{w_1, \ldots, w_n\}$ is a set of traditional databases, called possible worlds, and $P : W \rightarrow [0, 1]$ is a function mapping from possible worlds to probability values, such that $\sum_{j=1}^n P(w_j) = 1$.*

The extensional representation of probabilistic databases can express any finite set of deterministic databases, however, it is not compact to enumerate all possible worlds and hence there is a need to have a concise representation formalism.

Definition 2. *A probabilistic database $\mathbb{D}$ in the intensional representation is a quadruple $\langle \mathfrak{R}, E, P, f \rangle$, where $\mathfrak{R}$ is a traditional relational database, E is a set of Boolean independent variables $\{e_1, \ldots, e_m\}$, P specifies the probability value* *of each variable being true. f associates each tuple t with a variable or a Boolean expression composing of variables, namely f(t), whose truth value determines the presence of t in the actual world and whose probability is defined by probabilities of composed variables* [9].

A possible world w_i is a traditional database instance such that the expression associated with the tuple in the possible world is true, the expression associated with the tuple not in the possible world is false. A joint value $V_j(E)(j \in [1, 2^m])$ of all variables in E determines a possible world w_i of the probabilistic database. $P(w_i) = \sum_{w_i \sim V_j(E)} P(V_j(E))$ and $\sum P(w_i) = 1$, where $w_i \sim V_j(E)$ represents the joint value $V_j(E)$ is a joint value leading to the possible world w_i.

4   General Query Optimization

4.1   Optimization Strategy for Projection Under Functional Dependency Constraints

Suppose that R is a probabilistic relation, and a set of attributes A in R functionally determine the other attributes in R, then the set of tuples with the same value of A and different values of other attributes are mutually exclusive. The lineage of answering tuples of projection is the disjunction of expressions of tuples with the same values on projection attributes. When the projection attributes functionally determine the other attributes in the query, the lineage of each answering tuple of projection is the disjunction of expressions of the set of tuples, which are mutually exclusive. The current methods for computing probability of lineage expressions extract duplicate variables in the expressions. The time complexity of probability computation mainly depends on the number of duplicate variables in the expressions. However, if a disjunction is composed of several mutually exclusive sub-expressions, then the probability of the disjunction is equal to the sum of probabilities of these sub-expressions. Furthermore, the time complexity of probability computation of each sub-expression depends on the number of duplicate variables in each sub-expression.

Theorem 1. *If a disjunction is composed of several mutually exclusive sub-expressions, then the probability of the disjunction is equal to the sum of probabilities of these sub-expressions.*

Theorem 2. *If a disjunction is composed of several mutually exclusive sub-expressions, the time complexity of probability computation of the disjunction is larger than the sum of time complexity of probability computation of these sub-expressions.*

Based on Theorems 1 and 2, a new computation sign ADD is introduced in the lineage expression. The sign ADD specifies the mutually exclusive correlation of sub-expressions in the disjunction expression. During probability computation of answering tuples, the sub-expressions are computed individually, then return the sum of their probabilities. Therefore, the computation of the lineage expressions for projection under functional dependency constraints is listed as follows.

$\pi_A(Q) \rightarrow$ select R.A, ADD(R.f) as f from (Q) R group by R.A

4.2 Optimization Strategy for Join Under Referential Constraints

Suppose that R and S are two probabilistic relations, and a set of attributes A in R reference a set of attributes A in S. Given a query $R \bowtie_A \pi_A(S)$, where there exist join operation between R and S, projection operation on $S.A$ and no other attributes of S involved, the lineage of answering tuples of the query is obtained as follows [7,8].

$R \bowtie_A \pi_A(S) \rightarrow$ select $R.*$, AND($R.f$, $S.f$) as f from R, (select A, OR(f) as f from S group by A) S' where R.A $= S'$.A.

The lineage of each answering tuple t is $f_{t_i \in R, t_i = t}(t_i) \wedge (\vee_{t_j \in S, t_j.A = t_i.A} f(t_j))$.

Since there exists referential constraint, for each tuple $t \in R$, $\neg f(t) \vee (\vee_{t_j \in S, t_j.A = t.A} f(t_j))$ is always true. Then, we have

$f_{t_i \in R, t = t_i}(t_i) \wedge \vee_{t_j \in S, t_j.A = t.A} f(t_j) = f(t_i)$.

Therefore, the lineage of answering tuples of the query can be obtained as follows.

$R \bowtie_A \pi_A(S) \rightarrow$ select $R.*$ from R

4.3 Algorithm

Based on the optimization strategies in Sects. 4.1 and 4.2, Algorithm 1 shows the approach of processing probabilistic relational queries.

Algorithm 1. CQuery($\mathbb{D} = \langle D, E, P, f \rangle$, Q)

Input: $\mathbb{D} = \langle D, E, P, f \rangle$, the probabilistic relational database
　　　　Q, the probabilistic relational query
Output: (RT_Q, P_Q)
 1: **if** Q satisfies the optimization strategy **then**
 2:　　$(RT_Q, L) \leftarrow$ Rewritten the query Q into a query involving lineage computation
　　　　according to the optimization strategy
 3: **else**
 4:　　$(RT_Q, L) \leftarrow$ Rewritten the query Q into a query involving lineage computation
 5: **end if**
 6: **for** $t \in RT_Q$ **do**
 7:　　Compute the existential probability $P(L(t))$ of tuple t.
 8:　　Insert $(t, P(L(t)))$ into (RT_Q, P_Q)
 9: **end for**
10: **return** (RT_Q, P_Q)

Example 1. Given a query $Q : \pi_A(R \bowtie S \bowtie T) = \pi_A(R \bowtie (\pi_B(S \bowtie T)))$, where R, S and T are three probabilistic relations listed in Table 1, and $R.A$ functionally determines $R.B$, according to the existing approach, the answering tuples and their lineage are shown as in Table 2(a). While the query satisfies the optimization strategy (1), according to the optimization approach introduced in this paper, the answering tuples and their lineage are shown as in Table 2(b).

Table 1. A probabilistic relational database $\mathbb{D}$

(a) Probabilistic relation R

RID	A	B	f
t_1	1	1	$f(t_1)$
t_2	1	2	$f(t_2)$
t_3	2	1	$f(t_3)$
t_4	2	2	$f(t_4)$

(b) Probabilistic relation S

RID	B	C	f
t_5	1	1	$f(t_5)$
t_6	1	2	$f(t_6)$
t_7	2	1	$f(t_7)$
t_8	2	2	$f(t_8)$

(c) Probabilistic relation T

RID	C	f
t_9	1	$f(t_9)$
t_{10}	2	$f(t_{10})$

Table 2. Lineage of query result

(a) Query result

A	f
1	$f(t_1) \wedge (f(t_5) \wedge f(t_9) \vee f(t_6) \wedge f(t_{10})) \vee f(t_2) \wedge (f(t_7) \wedge f(t_9) \vee f(t_8) \wedge f(t_{10}))$
2	$f(t_3) \wedge (f(t_5) \wedge f(t_9) \vee f(t_6) \wedge f(t_{10})) \vee f(t_4) \wedge (f(t_7) \wedge f(t_9) \vee f(t_8) \wedge f(t_{10}))$

(b) Query result with functional dependency constraints

A	f
1	$f(t_1) \wedge (f(t_5) \wedge f(t_9) \vee f(t_6) \wedge f(t_{10})) + f(t_2) \wedge (f(t_7) \wedge f(t_9) \vee f(t_8) \wedge f(t_{10}))$
2	$f(t_3) \wedge (f(t_5) \wedge f(t_9) \vee f(t_6) \wedge f(t_{10})) + f(t_4) \wedge (f(t_7) \wedge f(t_9) \vee f(t_8) \wedge f(t_{10}))$

(c) Query result with referential constraints

A	f
1	$f(t_1) \vee f(t_2)$
2	$f(t_3) \vee f(t_4)$

Based on the Shannon expansion [8], the probability of the lineage in Table 2(b) is computed by abstracting the common variables. Suppose there are no common variables in the expressions of tuples in the three tables, then the common variables in the lineage of answering tuple in Table 2(b) are the set of variables appeared in $f(t_9)$ and $f(t_{10})$. While the probability of lineage in Table 2(b) can be computed by adding the probabilities of two sub-expressions of ADD, and the probabilities of these sub-expressions can be computed individually.

$P(f(t_1) \wedge (f(t_5) \wedge f(t_9) \vee f(t_6) \wedge f(t_{10})) + f(t_2) \wedge (f(t_7) \wedge f(t_9) \vee f(t_8) \wedge f(t_{10})))$
$= P(f(t_1) \wedge (f(t_5) \wedge f(t_9) \vee f(t_6) \wedge f(t_{10}))) + P(f(t_2) \wedge (f(t_7) \wedge f(t_9) \vee f(t_8) \wedge f(t_{10})))$

If $R.B$ references $S.B$, and $S.C$ references $T.C$, then the query $Q : \pi_A(R \bowtie S \bowtie T) = \pi_A(R \bowtie (\pi_B(S \bowtie T)))$ can be simplified as $Q : \pi_A(R \bowtie_B \pi_B(S))$, which is equal to $Q : \pi_A(R)$. The query result is shown in Table 2(c).

5 Experiments

In this section, we describe an experimental study on the query optimization strategies. This section is organized as follows. Section 5.1 describes the experimental environment setup. Section 5.2 studies the performance of optimization strategies. Let Naive be the existing query processing approach, and CQuery be the query processing approach with the optimization strategies.

5.1 Experimental Environment Setup

A probabilistic relational database $\mathbb{D} = \langle D, E, P, f \rangle$ is actually stored as follows. D is stored as a traditional relational database (We use Oracle 10g), with an additional column f in each probabilistic relation; E and P are stored in another relation V_P. We implement three user-defined function: OR, AND, ADD. As described in query lineage, function OR generates an expression by linking each f with $\vee$, function AND generates an expression by linking each f with $\wedge$, and function ADD generates an expression by linking each f with $+$. For a query, the set of result tuples and the corresponding lineage expression are obtained by executing the query over the database management system, then the probabilities of answering tuples are obtained by computing the probabilities of lineage expression being true.

All of the algorithms are implemented in Java, and all of our experiments are conducted on a Pentium 2.5 GHz PC with 3 G memory, on Windows XP.

5.2 Comparison of Naive and CQuery

Synthetic Datasets. The synthetic datasets include three relations $R(A, B)$, $S(B, C)$ and $T(C)$. The f value of each tuple is an independent Boolean variable. The probability of each variable is assigned randomly and stored in table V_P. By the conditioning method, two set of datasets are generated by conditioning on functional dependency constraints and referential constraints separately.

Dataset1: 10 scales of datasets are generated as follows. First, insert 1 K tuples into R, S and T separately, in different scale of dataset, the B values with the same A value in $R(A, B)$ range from 10 to 20. In each data set, the expressions of tuples are updated by conditioning on the functional dependency constraint $R.A \rightarrow R.B$. We evaluate the query $Q : \pi_A(R \bowtie S \bowtie T) = \pi_A(R \bowtie (\pi_B(S \bowtie T)))$ on each scale of dataset.

The Naive approach rewrites the query into the following statement to obtain the set of answering tuples and their lineage, and then computes the probabilities of the lineage expressions.

select A, OR(f) as f from (select A, AND(R.f, ST.f) as f from R,

(select B, OR(f) as f from (select B, AND(S.f, T.f) as f from S, T where S.C = T.C) group by B) ST where R.B = ST.B) group by A

By taking account of functional dependency constraints, the CQuery approach rewrites the query into the following statement.

select A, ADD(f) as f from (select A, AND(R.f, ST.f) as f from R,
(select B, OR(f) as f from (select B, AND(S.f, T.f) as f from S, T where
S.C = T.C) group by B) ST where R.B = ST.B)

Dataset2: 10 scales of datasets are generated as follows. First, insert $1K$ tuples into R and S separately, in different scale of dataset, the C values with the same B value in $S(B, C)$ range from 10 to 20. In each data set, the expressions of tuples are updated by conditioning on the referential constraint $R.B$ references to $S.B$. We evaluate the query $Q : \pi_A(R \bowtie S)$ on each scale of dataset. We apply the linear complexity conditioning method for referential constraints introduced in [22] to update the expressions of tuples in R and S.

The Naive approach rewrites the query into the following statement to obtain the set of answering tuples and their lineage, and then computes the probabilities of the lineage expressions.

select A, OR(f) as f from (select A, AND(R.f, S'.f) as f from R,
(select B, OR(f) as f from S group by B) S' where R.B = S'.B) group by A

By taking account of referential constraints, the CQuery approach rewrites the query into the following statement.

select A, OR(f) as f from R group by A

Results and Analysis. Figure 1 shows the running time of the Naive method and the CQuery method over the synthetic datasets with functional dependency constraints (Dataset1). **(1) Results.** Figure 1 shows the running time of the CQuery is less than that of Naive. The running time of the CQuery is not affected by the distribution of B values in R, while the running time of Naive increases fast as the number of different B values with the same A value increases. **(2) Analysis.** After conditioning on the functional dependency constraint, the

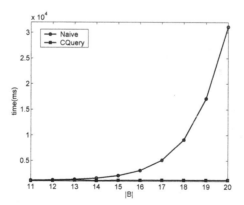

Fig. 1. Comparison: Naive vs CQuery. Evaluate $Q : \pi_A(R \bowtie S \bowtie T) = \pi_A(R \bowtie (\pi_B(S \bowtie T)))$ over $R(A, B)$, $S(B, C)$ and $T(C)$ with functional dependency constraints $R.A \rightarrow R.B$, while varying the number of different values of B corresponding to the same value of A in Table R.

tuples with the same A value in R are mutually exclusive, which means there are common variables in their expressions. The truth values of these common variables need to be enumerated to compute the probability of the lineage expressions of answering tuples. The number of the common variables ranges from 10 to 20, therefore, the running time of the Naive method increases fast as the number of different B values increases. In the CQuery method, the lineage expression of an answering tuple is the combination of the expressions of tuples with the same A value using ADD. The probability of the lineage expression of the answering tuple is the sum of the probabilities of expressions of tuples in the combination, and the probability of the expression of each tuple can be computed individually. After conditioning on functional dependency constraint, the expression of each tuple with the same A values corresponds to a possible world, and there are no duplicate variables inside the expressions of these tuples. Therefore, the computing time of probabilities of answering tuples for the CQuery method is considerably less than that for Naive method. Furthermore, the running time of the CQuery method is not affected by the distribution of B values in R.

Figure 2 shows the running time of the Naive method and the CQuery method over the synthetic datasets with referential constraints (Dataset2). **(1) Results.** Figure 2 shows the running time of the CQuery method is less than that of the Naive method. Furthermore, the running time of the CQuery method is not affected by the distribution of C values in S, while the running time of the Naive method increases fast as the different number of C values increases. **(2) Analysis.** Based on the conditioning method in [22], after conditioning on the referential constraint, there are common variables among the expressions of tuples in R and S with the same B value. Then there exist common variables in the lineage expressions of answering tuples in Naive method, and the number of common variables increases when increasing the number of different C values according to the same B value in S. The lineage expressions of answering tuples

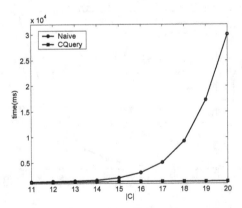

Fig. 2. Comparison: Naive vs CQuery. Evaluate $Q : \pi_A(R \bowtie S)$ over $R(A, B)$, $S(B, C)$ with referential constraints $R.B$ references to $S.B$, while varying the number of different values of C corresponding to the same value of B in Table S.

in the CQuery method is the combination of expressions of tuples in R with the same A value and different B values, and there are no common variables among these tuples. Therefore, the running time of the CQuery method is not affected by the distribution of C values in S.

Real Dataset. We use a real-world probabilistic dataset from the University of Stanford, the Trio project. *movies(movie-id, title, year, director)* stores the uncertainty about the movie information. ratings(movie-id, viewer-id, date, rating, confidence) stores the uncertainty about movie-viewer ratings. This dataset has been used in [12]. We normalize the data set by the data model introduced in Definition 2. Functional dependency constraints and referential constraints are inserted separately to set up the experiment.

(1) Data set generated by conditioning on the functional dependency constraint movie-id→(title, year, director)

The query evaluated in the experiment is as follows.

select movie-id from movies where $year > 1988$;

The Naive method rewrites the query into the following statement to obtain the set of answering tuples and their lineage, and then computes the probabilities of the lineage expressions.

select movie-id, OR(f) from movies where $year > 1988$ group by movie-id;

By taking account of functional dependency constraints, the CQuery method rewrites the query into the following statement.

select movie-id, ADD(f) from movies where $year > 1988$ group by movie-id;

Result on real dataset. Table 3(a) shows the running time of the Naive method and the CQuery method over the real dataset with functional dependency constraints. **(1) Results.** Table 3(a) shows that the running time of the CQuery method is less than that of the Naive method. **(2) Analysis.** In the Naive method, the lineage expression of answering tuples are computed by enumerating the values of duplicate variables. For the query evaluated in the experiment, the lineage expression of each answering tuple is the disjunction of expressions of tuples with the same movie-id value. And there are common variables among their expressions due to their mutually exclusive correlation. The number of the common variables ranges from 2 to 18. While in the CQuery method, the

Table 3. The time of the two query methods on real datasets

(a) Real dataset with functional dependency constraints

Naive	*CQuery*
29389ms	121ms

(b) Real dataset with referential constraints

Naive	*CQuery*
35389ms	116ms

lineage expression of each answering tuple is the combination of expressions of tuples with the same movie-id value with ADD operation. The probability of the expression of the answering tuple is the sum of the probabilities of every expression in the combination. The probability of the expression of each tuple in the combination can be computed individually. Since there are no common variables inside the expression of each tuple, the running time of the CQuery method merely varies.

(2) Data set generated by conditioning on ratings.movie-id references to movies.movie-id.

The query evaluated in the experiment is as follows.

select viewer-id from ratings, movies where ratings.movie-id=movies.movie-id and $ratings = 5$;

The Naive method rewrites the query into the following statement to obtain the set of answering tuples and their lineage, and then computes the probabilities of the lineage expressions.

select viewer-id, $OR(f)$ as f from

(select viewer-id, $AND(ratings.f, movies'.f)$ as f from ratings,

(select movie-id, $OR(f)$ as f from movies group by movie-id)

movies'

where ratings.movie-id=movies'.movie-id)

where $ratings = 5$ group by viewer.id

By taking account of referential constraints, the CQuery method rewrites the query into the following statement.

select viewer-id, $OR(f)$ as f from ratings where $ratings = 5$ group by viewer-id;

Results on real datasets. Table 3(b) show the running time of the Naive method and the CQuery method over the real dataset with referential constraints. **(1) Results.** Table 3(b) shows that the running time of the CQuery method is about 84% less than that of the Naive method. **(2) Analysis.** The number of tuples with the same *movie-id* value in *movies* ranges from 2 to 21. Thus, the number of duplicate variables in the lineage of answering tuples in the Naive method ranges from 3 to 22. While in the CQuery method, the query evaluated in the experiment is rewritten into the query over the *ratings* only, no duplicate variables exist in the lineage of answering tuples. Therefore, the running time of the CQuery method is less than that of the Naive method.

6   Conclusion

This paper proposed optimization strategies for processing several query algebras in probabilistic relational databases.

The lineage expressions of result tuples of several algebras can be simplified under integrity constraints. For project operator in probabilistic relational database, the lineage expression of result tuples is the disjunction of formulae of tuples with the same value on the project attribute. The time complexity of probability computation of lineage expressions depends on the number of duplicate variables in the disjunction expression. For functional dependency constraints, the lineage expression of specific projection which operates on sets of mutually exclusive tuples can replace disjunction with add. The probability of add of sub-expressions is the sum of probabilities of its sub-expressions. The time complexity of lineage expressions computation depends on the number of duplicate variables inside the formula of each mutually exclusive tuple. For referential constraints, join operator satisfying the specific condition can be transformed to be selection operator, the lineage expressions of result tuples are simplified at the same time. The simplified lineage expressions improve the efficiency of query processing in probabilistic relational databases.

References

1. Agreste, S., De Meo, P., Ferrara, E., Ursino, D.: Xml matchers: approaches and challenges. Knowl.-Based Syst. **66**, 190–209 (2014)
2. Ayat, N., Akbarinia, R., Afsarmanesh, H., Valduriez, P.: Entity resolution for probabilistic data. Inf. Sci. **277**, 492–511 (2014)
3. Cheng, R., Chen, J., Xie, X.: Cleaning uncertain data with quality guarantees. Proc. VLDB Endowment **1**(1), 722–735 (2008)
4. Cormode, G., Srivastava, D., Shen, E., Yu, T.: Aggregate query answering on possibilistic data with cardinality constraints. In: The 29th IEEE International Conference on Data Engineering (ICDE), pp. 258–269. IEEE Computer Society, Arlington (2012)
5. Dalvi, N., Ré, C., Suciu, D.: Probabilistic databases: diamonds in the dirt. Commun. ACM **52**(7), 86–94 (2009)
6. Feng, H., Wang, H., Li, J., Gao, H.: Entity resolution on uncertain relations. In: Wang, J., Xiong, H., Ishikawa, Y., Xu, J., Zhou, J. (eds.) WAIM 2013. LNCS, vol. 7923, pp. 77–86. Springer, Heidelberg (2013). doi:10.1007/978-3-642-38562-9_8
7. Fink, R., Olteanu, D.: Dichotomies for queries with negation in probabilistic databases. ACM Trans. Database Syst. **41**(1), 4–47 (2016)
8. Fink, R., Olteanu, D., Rath, S.: Providing support for full relational algebra in probabilistic databases. In: The 27th IEEE International Conference on Data Engineering (ICDE), pp. 315–326. IEEE Computer Society, Hannover (2011)
9. Fuhr, N., Rölleke, T.: A probabilistic relational algebra for the integration of information retrieval and database systems. ACM Trans. Inf. Syst. (TOIS) **15**(1), 32–66 (1997)
10. Lian, X., Chen, L.: Probabilistic top-k dominating queries in uncertain databases. Inf. Sci. **226**, 23–46 (2013)
11. Mahmood, N., Burney, S.A., Ahsan, K.: Generic temporal and fuzzy ontological framework (gtfof) for developing temporal-fuzzy database model for managing patient's data. J. UCS **18**(2), 177–193 (2012)
12. Mo, L., Cheng, R., Li, X., Cheung, D.W.l., Yang, X.S.: Cleaning uncertain data for top-k queries. In: The 29th IEEE International Conference on Data Engineering (ICDE), pp. 134–145. IEEE Computer Society, Brisbane (2013)
13. Qin, B.: Efficient queries evaluation on block independent disjoint probabilistic databases. In: Renz, M., Shahabi, C., Zhou, X., Cheema, M.A. (eds.) DASFAA 2015. LNCS, vol. 9050, pp. 74–88. Springer, Cham (2015). doi:10.1007/978-3-319-18123-3_5

14. Ré, C., Suciu, D.: Materialized views in probabilistic databases: for information exchange and query optimization. In: The 33rd International Conference on Very Large Data Bases, pp. 51–62. VLDB Endowment, University of Vienna, Austria (2007)
15. Roy, S., Perduca, V., Tannen, V.: Faster query answering in probabilistic databases using read-once functions. In: the 14th International Conference on Database Theory (ICDT), pp. 232–243. ACM, New York (2011)
16. Sarma, A.D., Benjelloun, O., Halevy, A., Widom, J.: Working models for uncertain data. In: The 22nd International Conference on Data Engineering (ICDE), pp. 2–7. IEEE Computer Society, Atlanta (2006)
17. Sen, P., Deshpande, A.: Representing and querying correlated tuples in probabilistic databases. In: The 23rd IEEE International Conference on Data Engineering (ICDE), pp. 596–605. IEEE Computer Society, Istanbul (2007)
18. Sen, P., Deshpande, A., Getoor, L.: PRDB: managing and exploiting rich correlations in probabilistic databases. VLDB J. **18**(5), 1065–1090 (2009)
19. Škrbić, S., Racković, M., Takači, A.: Prioritized fuzzy logic based information processing in relational databases. Knowl.-Based Syst. **38**, 62–73 (2013)
20. Song, W., Yu, J.X., Cheng, H., Liu, H., He, J., Du, X.: Bayesian network structure learning from attribute uncertain data. In: Gao, H., Lim, L., Wang, W., Li, C., Chen, L. (eds.) WAIM 2012. LNCS, vol. 7418, pp. 314–321. Springer, Heidelberg (2012). doi:10.1007/978-3-642-32281-5_31
21. Suciu, D., Olteanu, D., Ré, C., Koch, C.: Probabilistic databases. Synth. Lect. Data Manag. **3**(2), 1–180 (2011)
22. Tang, R., Shao, D., Ba, M.L., Wu, H.: Conditioning probabilistic relational data with referential constraints. In: Han, W.-S., Lee, M.L., Muliantara, A., Sanjaya, N.A., Thalheim, B., Zhou, S. (eds.) DASFAA 2014. LNCS, vol. 8505, pp. 413–427. Springer, Heidelberg (2014). doi:10.1007/978-3-662-43984-5_32
23. Widom, J.: Trio: a system for integrated management of data, accuracy, and lineage. In: CIDR, pp. 262–276. ACM, New York (2005)

Recommendation Method of Ore Blending Based on Thermodynamic Principle and Adaptive Step Size

Huan Wang[1], Bingyang Shen[2(✉)], Yuxing Gao[2], Yuning Cao[2], and Xiaojuan Ban[2]

[1] School of Civil and Resource Engineering,
University of Science and Technology Beijing, Beijing, China
wh@anmining.com
[2] School of Computer and Communication Engineering,
University of Science and Technology Beijing, Beijing, China
tinkleing@gmail.com, gaoyuxing1993@163.com, mail@caoyuning.com,
banxj@ustb.edu.cn

Abstract. In the modern metallurgical enterprises, it is necessary to design ore concentrates and production parameters according to the production, which is called ore blending. This paper presents a method of ore blending recommendation using thermodynamic principle and adaptive step size. The whole ore blending process is divided into three parts: blanking recommendation, parameter calculation and result correction. In the part of blanking recommendation, a case-based recommendation system is used to recommend the concentrate list. In the parameter calculation section, the SOMA is used to calculate the concentrate phase. And combined with the method of concentrate phase adjustment, an intelligent algorithm for rapid and accurate calculation of concentrate phase is proposed. Then the smelting parameters are calculated based on thermodynamic principle. In the result correction part, the high accuracy ore blending recommendation is achieved by combining adaptive step size with thermodynamic calculation software. Through the combination of three parts, a fast recommendation method for intelligent ore blending is proposed. The rationality and effectiveness of the method are verified by experiments.

Keywords: Ore blending recommendation · Concentrate phase calculation · Swarm intelligence algorithm · SOMA · Adaptive step size

1 Introduction

Ore blending is one of the most important parts in the metallurgical enterprise's production process. The technical department of the enterprise needs to design the concentrate list according to the existing stock. On the one hand, smelting products must meet the targets. On the other hand, it is necessary to maximize

© Springer Nature Singapore Pte Ltd. 2017
D. Du et al. (Eds.): NCTCS 2017, CCIS 768, pp. 221–232, 2017.
https://doi.org/10.1007/978-981-10-6893-5_17

the production efficiency of enterprises [1]. At present, new concentrate lists design cycle is too long, and it also consumes a lot of manpower and material resources.

In recent years, many enterprises and researchers have chosen to use expert system to improve enterprise efficiency. Kai-Lin et al. carried out the study of iron ore mixing optimal scheduling using ant colony optimization algorithm [2]. Zhang et al. designed a knowledge-based multi role decision support system for blast furnace ore mixing cost optimization [3]. Judging from the existing results, most of the current expert system adopt a single method, and can only predict the results of a certain stage. Its prediction results are also lack of authority and universality, and have no promotion value [4].

In this paper, the data mining method and artificial intelligence technology are adopted to simplify the ore blending process of the enterprise from concentrate lists in the actual production. Based on the principle of thermodynamics, a comprehensive study of multiple methods for ore blending has been carried out.

A case-based reasoning method is applied in ore blanking recommendation, which constructs the database by the data warehouse from the previous data acquisition system. And the case matching and recommendation are made according to the matching requirements proposed by the technical department.

In the parameter calculation process, SOMA is used to calculate concentrate phase. Combined with the knowledge of the metallurgical field, the calculation of phase calculation finally achieve the high precision by concentrate compounds relative atomic mass ratio on the SOMAs results. Subsequently, the thermodynamic parameter calculation software FactSage was adopted to recommend the process parameters and predict the melting results.

Then the combination of adaptive scheduling method and software is used in the result correction. By adjusting the input parameters of the software, the results of the calculations have been corrected [5,6].

Finally, at the end of the intelligent ore blending process, the output list is almost identical with the demand of the technical department. Figure 1 presents the framework for ore blending recommendation methods. From the experimental

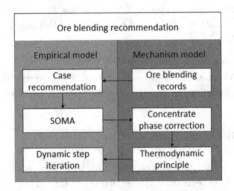

Fig. 1. Structure of ore blending recommendation

results, the ore blending system using has greatly shortened the time of ore blending process. And the recommendation result is highly accurate and authoritative, which has a strong production guidance significance.

2   Problem Analysis

2.1   Brief Description of Ore Blending

At present, the metallurgical process is mainly composed of two parts, ore blanking design and practical production. Blanking design is a design process of concentrate list. Concentrate list is designed by the technical department and copied to the production department, which guides the production department to carry out the actual smelting plan. Concentrate list mainly includes three parts: the total stock of concentrate, the type and amount of concentrates used and the control parameters of smelting process [7].

The total stock of concentrate shows the stock and monthly purchasing plan of the existing concentrates in the enterprise warehouse, and does not belong to the content of this study.

The type and amount of concentrates used illustrates what kinds of concentrates are needed for the ore blending and gives the elemental composition and concentrate dosage. According to the target of smelting, the technical department calculates the estimation value of the concentrate amount according to the different element composition of each kind of concentrate. The module inputs concentrate phase of x, and the content of the phase in the concentrates is $a_1, a_2, a_3, \ldots, a_n$. The amount of each concentrate is $d_1, d_2, \ldots, d_n$. Then the formula for x is

$$x = \frac{\sum_{k=1}^{n} a_k \cdot d_k}{\sum_{k=1}^{n} d_k} \tag{1}$$

Through the application of Formula (1), the technical department will get the composition of the material used in this process, and the thermodynamic theory will be carried out to analyze and predict the melting results.

The main parameter of the control is the 4 attributes, namely: matte grade, Fe_3O_4 content, SiO_2/Fe and SiO_2/CaO. These 4 attributes are the target value calculated by the technical department through the prediction of concentrate phase. In addition to these 4 attributes, the control parameter also include the use of oxygen ratio, air volume, silicon, calcium and other recommended production parameters.

Production process includes: the production department puts the concentrate specified in the concentrate list into the smelting furnace, and uses the recommended parameters for smelting production. At the end of production, the production department records the actual values of matte grade, Fe_3O_4 content, SiO_2/Fe and SiO_2/CaO. The target values of matte grade, Fe_3O_4 content, SiO_2/Fe and SiO_2/CaO are $T_1 T_2 T_3 T_4$, and the actual values as $M_1 M_2 M_3 M_4$. The production department calculates the absolute error and the mean absolute error of each item:

$$\Delta_k = |T_k - M_k| \quad k = 1, 2, 3, 4 \tag{2}$$

$$\delta_{MAE} = \frac{1}{N} \sum_{k=1}^{N} \Delta_k \quad N = 4 \tag{3}$$

Then the values of Δ_k the δ_{MAE} are copied to the technical department, which are analyzed by the technical department to summarize the experience for the next ore blanking.

To sum up, ore blanking recommendation process is the process of calculating the type, dosage and control parameters of the concentrates. The problem has been transformed into how to give high precise and authoritative concentrate dosage and control parameter according to the product index.

2.2   Ore Recommendation Analysis

Through the study of enterprise production process, the concentrate list using in the actual production has important reference value. The concentrates used in metallurgical enterprises will not change suddenly. Even if the variety of concentrates varies, the elemental composition of the concentrates is not very different [8]. In this way, the design of the new concentrate list can be guided by appropriate data mining techniques based on the history concentrate list.

We designed a data acquisition system to collect the concentrate list used in the production of the enterprise. When the data acquisition system has accumulated enough actual production parameters and concentrate lists, its data quantity has allowed for the research of intelligent ore recommendation technology.

Blanking recommendation is the first step of intelligent ore blending. When the technical department plans to design a new concentrate list, it needs to calculate the similarity between the demand and the previously lists, and use calculation results for blanking recommendation. In this paper, Euclidean distance is used as an evaluation criterion of similarity [9]. For n-dimensional space, there are two n-dimensional vectors $A(x_1, x_2, x_3, \ldots, x_n)$ and $B(y_1, y_2, y_3, \ldots, y_n)$. The Euclidean distance D is defined as

$$d = \sqrt{\sum_{k=1}^{n} (x_k - y_k)^2} \tag{4}$$

Since the concentrate used in each ore blending process will be different, the ingredients shall be filled out according to the materials used in this process. Then according to Formula (4) defines the calculation of d. Taking the minimum number of d concentrate list provides a reference for the design staff, which can reduce the workload of the technical department and enhance reliability of the new concentrate list.

The parameter recommendation is to calculate the thermodynamic reaction of the new concentrate list with FactSage. FactSage is an authoritative computational software in the field of thermodynamics. FactSage combines the principles of thermodynamics with the powerful numerical computation. Before calling the

FactSage software, the phase calculation should be carried out according to the composition of a certain concentrate element calculated by Formula (1). The i-type concentrates in the ore set have n elements, and the elements are calculated as $X_i(x_1, x_2, x_3, \ldots, x_n)$. The concentrate consists of m compounds, and the phase composition is defined as the m-dimensional vector $T_i(a_1, a_2, a_3, \ldots, a_m)$. Each component in the vector is the content of a compound of the concentrate. The calculation of the concentrate phase is the process of calculating T from the element composition X through the algorithm S:

$$X_i(x_1, x_2, x_3, \ldots, x_n) \to^S T_i(a_1, a_2, a_3, \ldots, a_m) \tag{5}$$

Then the material phase of the concentrate list is the sum of the phases of all concentrate:

$$T = \sum_{i=1}^{n} T_i \tag{6}$$

The software uses the phase composition to recommend the parameters and predict the melting results. The calculation result is an important reference for the final output of the ore blending recommendation system.

The result correction calculation is to adjust the result given by the parameters recommendation. The parameters recommendation is that the FactSage predicts the production of smelting results based on the current concentrate phase, which are often biased with the target value. In order to improve the practicality of the result, this paper recalculates the result of Factsage by dynamic iteration until the thermodynamic theoretical calculation and the target give the accuracy requirements. The theoretical calculation of the value of P, the technical sector requirements for the Q, the required accuracy of s, by Formula (2) to calculate Δ, if there is

$$\Delta < s \tag{7}$$

It can be concluded that the concentrate list given by the ore blending system is in full compliance with the technical requirements.

In summary, through the combination of blanking recommendation method, parameter recommendation method and result correction method, the result of intelligent ore blending recommendation will be greatly improved.

3   Ore Blanking Recommendation Using Case Recommendation Method

In this paper, the case-based reasoning method is used to realize the basic recommendation of concentrate list. Case-based reasoning is one of the methods of artificial intelligence, and its ability to solve problems depends on the number of cases in the case database [10].

The amount of blanking in the concentrate list is determined by the matte grade, Fe_3O_4 content, SiO_2/Fe and SiO_2/CaO of the smelting products. Therefore, it is possible to distinguish each blanking order from the 4 indicators.

Table 1. Copper materials and compositions

Copper material	Composition
NFCA	$CuFeS_2, CuS, Cu_5FeS_4, FeS_2, SiO_2, KAl_2(AlSi_3O_{10})(OH)_2$
FRONTIOR (ENRC)	$CuFeS_2, FeS_2, CuS, SiO_2, KAlSi_3O_8, CaO$
LUMWANA (LMC)	$CuFeS_2, Cu_5FeS_4, SiO_2, Mg_6Si_8O_{20}(OH)_4, KAlSi_3O_8$
LUBAMBE	$CuFeS_2, Cu_2S, SiO_2, KAlSi_3O_8, Cu_2(OH)_2CO_3$
CHIBULUMA (CHIB)	$Cu_5FeS_4, Cu_2S, SiO_2, Mg_6Si_8O_{20}(OH)_4, CaO$

The blanking database can be considered as a 4 dimensional Euclidean space, and each historical record is recorded as a vector in which the components are (a, b, c, d). When the technical department needs to design a new concentrate list, technical department fills in four indicators and the use of the type of copper material. And the main types of ore using in enterprise as shown in Table 1. The target input is represented by a vector as a four-dimensional vector $T(t_1, t_2, t_3, t_4)$. For the other blanking records $h_i(h_{i1}, h_{i2}, h_{i3}, h_{i4})$ in the database, calculate the European distance d_i:

$$d_i = \sqrt{\sum_{k=1}^{4}(t_k - h_{ik})^2} \tag{8}$$

At the end of the calculation sort d_i in ascending order, take the first five blanking records as a solution to the problem. The corresponding concentrate lists are displayed to the user for selection.

The technical department can obtain a historical concentrate list that is similar to the one expected by the blanking recommendation. But the demand for each blanking cannot be exactly the same. The technical department need to adjust the list of materials. In order to realize the intelligence of the distribution process, this paper uses the parameter recommendation and the result correction method after the recommended step.

4   Parameter Recommendation Calculation Based on Thermodynamic Principle

4.1   SOMA

The parameter recommendation is mainly based on the Equilib function of FactSage. Before the parameter is recommended, the phase calculation of the material should be carried out first, and FactSage requirements of the concentrate phase error of 0.01 or less.

In order to select the best optimization algorithm to calculate the phase, this paper uses the quasi-Newton method (BFGS), differential evolution method (DE), genetic algorithm (GA), Simulated Annealing (SA), Particle Swarm Optimization (PSO), and Self Organizational Migration Algorithm (SOMA) [11,12].

In the processor Intel E5-1603 v4 2.80 GHz, memory 16G workstation experiments on each algorithm for different concentrate fitting time required as shown in Fig. 2. It can be seen from the data that SOMA is the most suitable algorithm for the calculation of the concentrate.

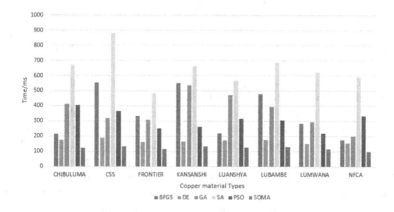

Fig. 2. Comparison of various algorithms for fitting concentrates

Self-organizing migration algorithm is a swarm intelligence algorithm. It treats particles in the solution space as individuals, and all individuals form a population. By imitating the competition and cooperation in the process of social animal foraging, we gradually converge until the optimal solution or the approximate optimal solution is obtained [13, 14].

According to the products studied in this paper, the most important elements are Cu, Fe and S. Therefore, the three kinds of elements in the concentrate are used as input, and the SOMA is used to fit the phase of the first kind of concentrate. The concentration of the three elements in the concentrate is vector $P(Cu, Fe, S)$, and the compounds in the concentrate has n species. The vector Q is calculated by the Formula (5) as the vector $Q(q_1, q_2, \ldots, q_n)$. In order to evaluate the fitting results of the algorithm, the element content of results was calculated by compound element composition as $P'(Cu', Fe', S')$

$$\Delta P(\Delta Cu, \Delta Fe, \Delta S) = (|Cu - Cu'|, |Fe - Fe'|, |S - S'|) \qquad (9)$$

$$\Delta d = \frac{\Delta Cu + \Delta Fe + \Delta S}{3} \qquad (10)$$

Through the reverse comparison of 30 sets of data, only using SOMA to fit the concentrate phase, Δd is about 0.4. Only using SOMA is unable to follow-up calculation. This paper studies the adjustment of SOMA by the exact method of material refinement.

4.2   Precise Adjustment Method

This paper sets Cu, Fe, S as the primary adjustment objectives of the adjustment method. We analyze all the ten kinds of concentrates used in the enterprise. Using the knowledge of the material domain, the relative atomic mass adjustment coefficient is given for the first kind of compound of each concentrate to correct the result of SOMA.

   We divides the mineral phase into two categories. The proportion of the first kind of compound phase is large, which has strong influence on the melting result and needs to be optimized by using the optimization algorithm. The proportion of the second phase is less, the prediction results are not directly affected and can be calculated by the atomic mass formula.

   Relative atomic mass adjustment mainly through two methods to improve the accuracy. According to the actual situation of the production, the content range of the compound which needs to be fitted is given, so that the SOMA can avoid the local optimal solution through the point of view of the earlier solution. Then the fitting result can be more accurate by changing the value of first kind of compound. For example, if the Cu content obtained by the fitting is high, the calculated value of the Cu-containing compound is reduced according to the relative atomic mass ratio of the compound. Define the Cu content obtained by the fitting is Cu, and the Cu content calculated by the reverse thrust is Cu'. Then calculate $diffCu$ first:

$$diffCu = |Cu - Cu'| \tag{11}$$

The quaternary compound containing Cu is defined as A, the relative atomic mass is a, the number of Cu atoms is i, and the adjusted content A' is

$$A' = A - diffCu \cdot \frac{a}{64 \cdot i} \tag{12}$$

Formula (12) is used as the concentrate phase of the first kind of compound. Other elements of the formula can be derived.

   For the second kind compounds of each concentrate, we found that these compounds will affect the accuracy of SOMA fitting. Therefore, the concentration of Cu, Fe, S elements in these compounds should be subtracted before they put into the SOMA. There are n kinds of constant compounds containing Cu, and their contents are defined as $Q(q_1, q_2, \ldots, q_n)$, and $a_1, a_2, \ldots, a_n$ is the relative atomic mass of the constant compound, the amount of Cu that needs to be subtracted before calculation dCu:

$$dCu = \sum_{k=1}^{n} q_k \cdot \frac{64}{a_k} \tag{13}$$

Similar to the Formula (13), the contents dFe and dS of Fe and S previously calculated can be obtained. Finally, when adjusting a phase, it will dynamically change the content of other corresponding elements. So adjust the order of compounds must be determined keeping the total amount of elements is the same as expected. Table 2 shows the results of the fitting calculations for the same concentrate use adjustment method. Method 1 uses the atomic mass adjustment and the SOMA. Method 2 subtracts the element constant on the basis of Method 1. And Method 3 used dynamic order adjustment on the basis of method 2.

Table 2. Different improvement program on the same group of minerals phase calculation results

Method	Cu	Cu'	Fe	Fe'	S	S'	Δd
SOMA	32.103	32.85886	22.486	22.80747	28.163	27.88065	0.45323
Method 1	32.103	32.12889	22.486	22.51774	28.163	28.19031	0.02831
Method 2	32.103	32.11301	22.486	22.49704	28.163	28.16730	0.00845
Method 3	32.103	32.10255	22.486	22.48625	28.163	28.16348	0.00039

Taking the NFCA for example, the adjustment process is briefly described as follows. Through the combination of three adjustment methods, the results of the SOMA fitting are adjusted, the accuracy of the phase calculation is of the order of 0.001.

Algorithm 1. Phase synthesis adjustment method

Require: The range of $CuFeS_2$, CuS, Cu_5FeS_4, FeS_2, element mass fraction, and elemental composition of concentrate
Ensure: Phase composition of NFCA
   Set the range of $CuFeS_2$, CuS, Cu_5FeS_4, FeS_2
   The phase is subtracted from dCu, dFe, dS in advance.
   Calculate $diffCu, diffFe, diffS$ between the fitted value and the actual phase.
   Calculates the phase that does not need to be adjusted by formula
   Call function AcomicMassAdjustment
   function ACOMICMASSADJUSTMENT($Phase of NFCA$)
      Applying the phase adjustment formula to adjust the Cu.
      Calculate diffFe and diffS between the fitted value and the actual phase.
      Applying the phase adjustment formula to adjust the S.
      Recalculate the diffFe.
      Applying the phase adjustment formula to adjust the Fe.
      return $result$
   end function

4.3   Parameter Recommended Calculation

The FactSage will calculate recommended parameters and the smelting results by using the concentrate phase. The recommended parameters include gun end pressure, oxygen ratio and other parameters. The results of the smelting include matte grade, Fe_3O_4 content, SiO_2/Fe, SiO_2/CaO, and the detailed composition of the gases and slag produced after melting.

However, the results of FactSage calculation may have some deviation from the target value which reduces the practical value of FactSage. In order to solve this problem, the result correction method is designed to correct the result of the FactSage.

5   Result Correction by Adaptive Step Size

5.1   Adaptive Step Size Correction

For the actual smelting process, the oxygen ratio and the amount of silicon added are easy to control, and also associated with the matte grade and SiO_2/Fe. In the result correction, by changing the oxygen ratio and the amount of silicon added recommended value, the new values will be the input of FactSage. Then call FactSage to make calculation, making matte grade and SiO_2/Fe of the calculation the same as target value. In each iteration, adjust the matte grade by adjusting the oxygen ratio, and adjust the SiO_2/Fe by adjusting the amount of silicon. The values of matte grade and SiO_2/Fe are Cu, $SiFe$, and the smelting results of this FactSage are Cu', $SiFe'$, and the inequality

$$dCu = |Cu - Cu'| < 0.2 \tag{14}$$

$$dSiFe = |SiFe - SiFe'| < 0.01 \tag{15}$$

When the Formula (14) and (15) are satisfied at the same time, it is considered that the ore distribution has fully met the requirements of the index.

This paper adopts the adaptive dynamic step size helps to reduce the number of iterations and shortens the computation time [15]. The size of the iteration step is determined by the difference between the target value and the FactSage prediction. After several experiments, we have determined a good dynamic iterative step size, part of the experimental results shown in Table 3.

Table 3. The number of FactSage calls of different step sizes schemes

Scheme	Oxygen ratio change	Silicon change	Iteration number
Fixed-step 1	1	1	198
Fixed-step 2	0.5	2	134
Adaptive step size 1	dCu	$dSiFe * 2$	57
Adaptive step size 2	$dCu * 2$	$dSiFe * 5$	32
Adaptive step size 3	$dCu * 4$	$dSiFe * 5$	65
Adaptive step size 4	$dCu * 2.5$	$dSiFe * 5$	16
Adaptive step size 5	$dCu * 2.5$	$dSiFe * 10$	5

Use Formula (14) and (15) to calculate the results for dCu, $dSiFe$. The next FactSage input oxygen ratio is M. The amount of silicon added is N

$$M = M' \pm dCu \cdot 2.5 \tag{16}$$

$$N = N' \pm dSiFe \cdot 10 \tag{17}$$

where the matte grade and SiO_2/Fe of the FactSage calculated value is lower than the target value to take a positive sign. According to Formula (16) and (17), the input data of FactSage is modified after the new oxygen ratio and the amount of added silicon are obtained. Then re-use FactSage for parameter recommendation and smelting results prediction until the simultaneous Formula (14) and (15).

The following gives a formal description of the best dynamic step size adjustment scheme:

Algorithm 2. Adaptive step size correction method

Require: The target values of matte grade and SiO_2 / Fe, concentrate phase
Ensure: Parameter recommendation results and prediction of melting results
1: **while** $dCu > 0.2 \&\& dSiFe > 0.01$ **do**
2:     Calculate dCu, dSi:Fe
3:     **if** $dCu > 0.2$ **then**
4:         $dO = dCu * 2.5$
5:     **end if**
6:     **if** $dSiFe > 0.01$ **then**
7:         $dSi = dSiFe * 10$
8:     **end if**
9:     Use the new arguments to call the FactSage calculation
10: **end while**

This iteration can produce the results that meet the requirements about five iteration. Make the intelligent ore blending recommended in full compliance with the needs of the user's single, without having to rely on the adjustment of expert experience.

6   Summary

In this paper, through the concentrate list recommendation, parameter recommendation and result correction method, the recommended concentrate list is fully in line with the demand, greatly reducing the time required for distribution process. According to the ore blending data in the enterprise, this method can be well applied to the recommendation of ore blending in metallurgical process. The present deficiency is that when the amount of data increases, case recommendation calculation takes too much time. The next step of this paper is to study the appropriate method for data recommendation in large data volume. Considering the combination of deep data mining methods and deep learning to improve the result of ore blending recommendation task.

Acknowledgements. This work was supported in part by The National Key Research and Development Program of China (Grant No. 2016YFB0700502, 2016YF- B1001404) and National Natural Science Foundation of China (No. 61572075).

References

1. Li, Z., Cui, Z.: Multi-objective optimization of ore blending based on genetic algorithm. J. Guangxi Univ. (National Science Edition) **05**, 1230–1238 (2013)
2. Kai-Lin, H.U., Ping, L.I.: The optimized scheduling for iron-making bulk ore blending process based on improved ant colony optimization. J. Shanghai Jiaotong Univ. **45**(8), 1105–1112 (2011)
3. Zhang, R., Lu, J., Zhang, G.: A knowledge-based multi-role decision support system for ore blending cost optimization of blast furnaces. Eur. J. Oper. Res. **215**(1), 194–203 (2011)
4. Ke, L., He, X., Ye, Y., He, H.: Current research situation and development trend of ore blending optimization technology. China Min. **26**(01), 77–82 (2017)
5. Huang, R., Lv, X.W., Bai, C.G., et al.: Solid state and smelting reduction of Panzhihua ilmenite concentrate with coke. Can. Metall. Q. **51**(4), 434–439 (2012)
6. Yu, W., Tang, Q., Chen, J., Sun, T.: Thermodynamic analysis of carbothermic reduction of a high-phosphorus oolitic iron ore by factsage. Int. J. Miner. Metall. Mater. **23**(10), 1126–1132 (2016)
7. Wu, S.L., Oliveira, D., Dai, Y.M., et al.: Ore-blending optimization model for sintering process based on characteristics of iron ores. J. Miner. Metall. Mater. **19**(3), 217–224 (2012)
8. Song, C.Y., Kai-Lin, H.U., Ping, L.I.: Modeling and scheduling optimization for bulk ore blending process. J. Iron Steel Res. (English Edition) **19**(9), 20–28 (2012)
9. Dokmanic, I., Parhizkar, R., Ranieri, J., et al.: Euclidean distance matrices: essential theory, algorithms, and applications. IEEE Signal Process. Mag. **32**(6), 12–30 (2015)
10. Ramon, L.D.M., Mcsherry, D., Bridge, D., Leake, D., Smyth, B.: Retrieval, reuse, revision and retention in case-based reasoning. Knowl. Eng. Rev. **20**(3), 215–240 (2005)
11. Chakraborty, A., Chakraborty, M.: Multi criteria genetic algorithm for optimal blending of coal. OPSEARCH **49**(4), 386–399 (2012)
12. Savic, M., Nikolic, D., Mihajlovic, I., et al.: Multi-criteria decision support system for optimal blending process in zinc production. Miner. Process. Extr. Metall. Rev. **36**(4), 267–280 (2015)
13. Deep, K., Dipti: A new hybrid Self Organizing Migrating Genetic Algorithm for function optimization. In: IEEE Congress on Evolutionary Computation, pp. 2796–2803 (2007)
14. Kadlec, P., Raida, Z.: Self-organizing migrating algorithm for optimization with general number of objectives. In: Radioelektronika, pp. 1–5. IEEE (2012)
15. Zanghirati, G., Zanni, L., Frassoldati, G.: New adaptive step size selections in gradient methods. J. Indus. Manag. Optim. **4**(2), 299–312 (2017)

A Survey of Personalised Image Retrieval and Recommendation

Zhenyan Ji[1(✉)], Weina Yao[1], Huaiyu Pi[1], Wei Lu[1], Jing He[2], and Haishuai Wang[3]

[1] Beijing Jiaotong University, Beijing 100044, China
{zhyji,15121693,16121731,luwei}@bjtu.edu.cn
[2] Victoria University, Melbourne, VIC 3011, Australia
lotusjing@gmail.com
[3] Washington University in St. Louis, St. Louis, MO 63130, USA
haishuai.wang@wustl.edu

Abstract. With the advent of web2.0 era, it has been becoming increasingly easy to create and share Internet content. Plenty of pictures are uploaded to the Internet every day. A primary challenge against traditional image retrieval technologies is how to help users quickly discover the images they need. Personalised image retrieval is a new trend in the field of image retrieval. It not only improves the accuracy of the existing retrieval systems, but also better meets the users' needs. Personalised image retrieval and recommendation (PIRR) can be grouped into two main categories, content-based PIRR and collaborative filtering (CF)-based PIRR. This paper first summarises the development of image retrieval and introduces different image retrieval solutions. Then the key technologies of content-based PIRR are analysed from three aspects, user interest acquisition, user interest representation and personalised implementation. Different techniques are compared and analysed. Regarding CF-based PIRR, the user-based, item-based and model-based CF-based PIRR are introduced and compared. At the end of the paper, we compare and summarise content-based PIRR and CF-based PIRR.

Keywords: Personalised image retrieval · Content-based · Collaborative filtering

1 Introduction

With the popularisation of digital photographic equipment (such as mobile phone, digital camera), mobile internet and social networking service, the amount of images on the Internet grows massively.

As a significant information carrier, images have many advantages over texts. Images could present more rich, visible and intuitive information, such as objects' shape, colour, texture and so on. The rapid growth of image data on the Internet makes image retrieval more difficult. How to discover the target images efficiently and accurately from massive image data? Many researchers have done a lot of work in this area.

© Springer Nature Singapore Pte Ltd. 2017
D. Du et al. (Eds.): NCTCS 2017, CCIS 768, pp. 233–247, 2017.
https://doi.org/10.1007/978-981-10-6893-5_18

In this paper, Sect. 2 introduces the categories of current image retrieval technologies. Section 3 elaborates content based and collaborative filtering (CF) based methods for personalised image retrieval and recommendation (PIRR).

2   Classification of Image Retrieval Technology

Image retrieval research has been carried out since the 1970s. After decades of study, the image retrieval technologies are mainly divided into five classes.

1. Text-based image retrieval (TBIR)

Traditional image retrieval systems usually use TBIR techniques. Images are annotated with keywords manually and then retrieved by keywords matching. TBIR essentially turns image retrieval into text retrieval. Since manual annotation is usually subjective and ambiguous, abundant visual contents of images cannot be expressed accurately and comprehensively by keywords [1]. How to obtain precise, standard and complete annotation in TBIR influences the retrieval accuracy directly. Meanwhile, manual tagging is time-consuming and brings high workload.

2. Content-based image retrieval (CBIR)

CBIR searches for images by their low-level features such as colour, shape, texture, etc. Searching processes are mainly divided into three steps, low-level feature extraction, feature fusion, and similarity measurement. CBIR returns images with similar characteristics.

Low-level features can be obtained automatically by image processing algorithms. It avoids the subjectivity of manual annotation and improves the retrieval efficiency significantly. The earliest successful application of CBIR is IBM QBIC system [2]. The other successful cases are UIUC's MARS [3], MIT's Photobook [4], Digital Library Project [5] of UC Berkeley, VisualSEEK system [6] of Columbia University, and so on.

3. Semantic-based image retrieval

Low-level features only represent images' visual characteristics, but people often search images by their semantic meanings. Different people may have the different semantic comprehension to the same image. Visually similar images may not be semantically equal [1]. The disparity between low-level features and high-level semantics is known as the "semantic gap", which causes the accuracy of CBIR declining dramatically. Semantic-based image retrieval trains a computer to learn human beings' logical reasoning ability and then analyses the visual features and perceives image contents from the human perspective. Instead of designing complex feature extraction algorithms to get more representative feature expression, semantic based method focuses on narrowing down the "semantic gap" to improve the search results. Many semantic based image retrieval systems have been developed, like Visengine [7], iFind [8], SemView [9], and so on.

4. Context-based image retrieval

Context based image retrieval is widely applied in web-based image retrieval. Images embedded in the web pages have plenty of context information, which can provide rich external information for image analysing and feature extraction. Web-based image retrieval searches images based on the structure of web pages and the contexts.

5. Personalised image retrieval and recommendation

To solve the problem of image overload and improve query efficiency, personalisation techniques are introduced to image retrieval systems. User preferences and image processing technologies are combined to enhance the retrieval accuracy.

Personalised image retrieval obtains images in a passive way. A user retrieves images via an image search engine. The system is driven by users' inputs and personalised information to get target images. A personalised image recommendation system actively recommends images, which a user may be interested in, to the user. The system mines a user's preference and pushes relevant images to the user. Both the image retrieval and the image recommendation need utilise a user's personalised information to search for target images and improve the efficiency and accuracy of the query. Personalised image retrieval and recommendation (PIRR) gains more and more attention and becomes a new generation of image retrieval [10].

PIRR technologies are analysed in the following parts.

3   PIRR

PIRR can be classified into two categories, content-based PIRR and CF-based PIRR.

3.1   Content-Based PIRR

The key components of the content-based PIRR are user interest acquisition, user interest representation and personalization implementation [10]. Figure 1 shows the general architecture of the system. The system collects image tags labelled by users and their past behaviours on images, such as browsing, clicking, saving and querying history. Then users' preferences are deduced via feature extraction, semantic correlation, etc. A user preference model is constructed with proper user interest representation method. The model is applied to the personalised image retrieval stage to acquire customised results. Meanwhile, user's feedback is gathered to optimise the result.

User Interest Acquisition. The main sources of user interests are the tags added by users, the past usage of users and users' feedback. There are different approaches to gather different kinds of user interest information.

1. Tag-based user interest acquisition

Recently social networking sites, such as Flickr, Instagram, Weibo, WeChat and so on, serve as effective information exchange platforms. A large number of users and images are accumulated. Besides images shared by users, the tags annotated by users

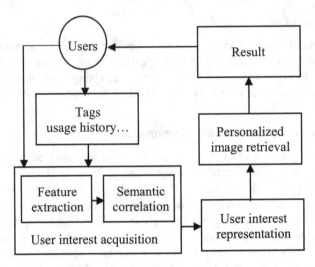

Fig. 1. General system architecture

often contain much more personalised information. Retrieval efficiency can be significantly improved by utilising the tags fully [11]. There are two main methods for mining tag information. One is using the tags directly as the personalised information to sort the images based on tag relevance [12, 13]. The other approach is collecting images posted by users and their tags to build a topic model for each user. In the model, images, which a user is interested in, are grouped into several topics. Each topic contains several keywords (tags). The query is mapped to the related topics to obtain results with users' preferences [14].

2. Past behaviour based user interest acquisition

Users' operations on images such as searching history, browsing, saving and so on, are recorded and saved in log files by the system. The usage information contains user's preference to images. For example, users' saving operations show that users are most likely to be interested in the saved images. A set of images that reflects the different interest level is obtained according to usage information. User interest description based on the content of the images is generated by mining the relevant information of the images. Qiu et al. [15] classified images by usage information to construct user interest model. Fan et al. [16] proposed an interactive personalised retrieval method. The method visualises the retrieval results and obtains users' interest image types based on users' clicking on the results. The search range is narrowed after several iterations. Yu et al. [17] designed a ranking algorithm that builds a ranking model with images' visual features and users' operations on the images.

Users' interests contained in browsing history and usage information cannot be used to build the users' profile directly because they are hidden in images' low-level features. Machine learning techniques, such as SVM [18], Bayesian classifier [19, 20], neural network [21], and k-means [22] are usually used to create an association between low-level features and high-level query concepts.

3. User feedback based interest acquisition

Traditional CBIR systems collect users' feedback on the results and adjust the outputs to reduce the deviation caused by the "semantic gap" [23, 24]. User's feedback is the explicit description of whether the object is interesting or not, such as providing positive or negative feedback, examining and modifying user interest specification and so on [25]. Relevance feedback is often adopted to improve the retrieval accuracy. In the personalization implementation phase, relevance feedback technology also plays an important role (see details in Sect. 3.3).

Besides the fore-mentioned user interest acquisition approaches, some demographic information (such as age, gender and occupation) can also be used as a reference to determine user preference. Identifying relevance between different users via social networks can also help to predict users' preferences [13, 26].

4. Comparison of user interest acquisition approaches.

Tag-based methods do not require the users' explicit participation during gathering interest. The processing is simple, fast and accurate. But the amount of labels added by users is limited and sometimes the labels are subjective and ambiguous. Even some spelling errors can seriously affect the accuracy of user interest description. Past behaviour based methods do not need user's explicit participation during gathering interest either. Users' preference information is implicitly expressed in users searching history, operation and other users' usage information. Searching accuracy decreases with the growing processing complexity and implicit preference. Additionally, users' historical behaviours cannot always reflect the users' latest preference. Users' feedback helps the system to update users' interest dynamically. However, users would rather have incorrect results than provide more detailed descriptions to the system in most cases, so relevance feedback also suffers from data sparsity problem.

Table 1 compares the three user interest acquisition approaches.

Table 1. Comparison of user interest acquisition approaches

User interest acquisition	Personalised information expression	User involved directly	Data size	Accuracy	Real-time analysis
Tag-based method	Explicit	No	Small	High	Yes
Past behaviour based method	Implicit	No	Large	Low	No
User feedback based method	Explicit	Yes	Small	High	Yes

User Interest Representation. The main user interest representation methods of content-based personalised image retrieval are the vector-based representation, topic model representation and ontology representation.

1. Vector-based representation

Vector-based representation refers to using vectors of a set of keywords or visual features to represent users' interests. The keywords can be input by users or obtained automatically by machine learning. Images contain rich information above-mentioned and different users have different concerns on the same image. The keywords or low-level features can only represent an image's general characteristic but cannot describe users' preferences accurately. To overcome the shortcoming of vector-based representation, Qiu et al. [15] adopted an improved vector-based method. The method builds the user interest model with an N-dimensional vector of features and related weights. High-frequency features have higher weights and low-frequency features have lower weights. The weights can be determined via a term weighting scheme such as TF, TF.IDF [27] or Okapi BM25 [28].

Vector-based representation is currently a popular interest representation method and can reflect the importance of each feature. However, it can't express the entire user interest precisely due to the limitation of its data structure. It is more suitable for short-term interest representation that represents content searched by a user in one retrieval process. Short-term interests can be represented by only one vector because they contain fewer features than long-term interests, which integrate preference information from several searching procedures [29].

2. Topic model representation

As the number of keywords describing users' interest increases, the dimension of feature vectors grows oversize and reduces the retrieval efficiency. Sometimes literally irrelevant words may be semantically associated, such as Apple, phone, Jobs, and so on. Under such circumstances, searching only by keyword similarity may lead to some deviation. Sang et al. [14] adopted a topic model to describe user interest and avoid the fore-mentioned problems. A topic model is used to describe the potential theme of a set of keywords. The same keyword may appear in different topics with a different probability. Computers analyse the corpus for each user via mathematical methods and calculate the probability of each tag belonging to each topic. The topic model can also solve the polysemy problem. For example, the system can figure out whether certain user regards the word "apple" as a fruit or a cell phone by analysing the user's topic model. Probabilistic Latent Semantic Analysis (PLSA) [14] and Latent Dirichlet Allocation (LDA) [30, 31] are often used for training user topic model.

The widely used bag-of-words model [32] in information retrieval systems can be regarded as a form of topic model representation. Bag-of-words model represents a document as an unordered collection of words with neglecting grammar and word order. Applying bag-of-words model to image processing brings the bag-of-visual-words model. An image is regarded as a collection of visual words, which are the low-level features such as SIFT features, of the image [33]. The bag-of-words model can express not only text features but also visual features of images, which makes the image retrieval system more scalable. However, bag-of-words model neglects the geometric information of the images entirely. It cannot represent the background of images, the relationship between objects, and other semantic information [34]. Yang et al. [35] divided an image into several regions to calculate the visual words of each part separately. Then they connected each part by the visual words to form a complete feature vector. This method integrates the spatial information, but it increases the computational complexity and has limited application. Liu et al. [36] proposed a context-based model for long queries. The query input can be a text in any length rather than just a few words or the image itself. The model can identify multiple topics from long queries and use visual words to return a set of images relevant to each topic.

3. Ontology representation

Ontology is a philosophical concept. Gruber from Stanford University defines ontology as an explicit specification of a conceptualised object [12]. The basic idea of ontology representation is to depict an interesting feature by an ontology concept vector. These ontologies usually take the form of hierarchical concept tree, and each node in the tree represents an interest class of the user. Fan et al. [16] developed the one-way IS-A hierarchical relationship between different themes based on concept ontology. Jia et al. [37] constructed structured indices for images' semantic features and utilised semantic feature vector to describe an image. Xing et al. [38] built user-ontology-based user model which combines concept, classification and non-classification information to provide more abundant and accurate user interest representation.

Table 2 compares the user interest representation methods.

Table 2. Comparison of user interest representation

User interest representation	Information capacity	Interest type	Feature type
Vector-base representation	Small	Short-term	Visual feature, semantic feature
Topic model representation	Large	Long-term	Semantic feature
Ontology representation	Large	Long-term	Semantic feature

In many image-related tasks, representative and distinguishable feature representations are very important, especially in the user-centered retrieval or recommendation tasks. The system should consider not only the image characteristics but also users' interests and intentions. So more efficient representation is required. It is a popular research area to utilise deep learning to obtain such feature representation [39–41] automatically.

Personalisation Implementation. Personalisation implementation is embodied in query optimisation or result optimisation, i.e., utilising personalised information to adjust input query information or optimising the results.

1. Similarity measurement

Personalised image retrieval measures image similarity from two aspects, distances between low-level features and semantic similarities. General distance measurements for the low-level features are Cosine Distance, Euclidean Distance, position-based measurements, Histogram intersection, etc. Burdescu et al. [42] measured semantic similarity by comparing the negative KL distance between a query image and the database images. Zhang et al. [18] obtained a distance matrix by optimising distances of nodes in the structured semantic network to minimise the distances of similar semantic nodes. Kurtz et al. [43] combined two strategies, automatic "soft" prediction of ontological terms and using dissimilarity measure to evaluate the similarity between images' annotations, and used the HSBD distance proposed by Kurtz [44] to evaluate the similarity.

2. Query optimization

Users usually cannot accurately describe their desired images. Low level features automatically extracted by computers only provide images' general descriptions without any personalised information. A user interest model can be used to optimise queries by adding or deleting partial query terms to or from the user's queries for a more accurate description [14]. Besides, queries can be optimised by adjusting the weights of query terms.

Relevance feedback is frequently used to get a personalised result. Rui et al. [45] proposed a weight adjusting method based on the feedbacks from users. Rocchio et al. [46] rectified initial query to make it approach to the best query based on the feedbacks. Porkaew et al. [47] grouped similar queries into the same cluster and then selected representative queries from the clusters to form a multipoint query. Su et al. [25] proposed NPRF (Navigation-Pattern-based-Relevance-Feedback) that combines the above three methods to overcome the redundant browsing problem related to traditional relevance feedback.

3. Result optimization

Result optimisation consists of result re-ranking and result filtering.

Result re-ranking extracts the semantic information of the retrieval results and compares it with the user interest model. Then the retrieval results are sorted based on their relevance to the user interests.

Result filtering discards some images according to user interests. Result filtering can be regarded as a supplement to result in re-ranking and often used after result re-ranking.

Result Re-ranking and result filtering are often combined to achieve more accurate retrieval results. Obviously, result optimisation's kernel is training user interest model. Traditional machine learning algorithms, such as decision tree, supervised vector machine, Naive Bayes and so on, are widely used for result optimisation [19, 48–50].

3.2 CF-Based PIRR

Besides content sharing, social networking can also establish the association between users. In a social network, users usually join some virtual communities interested to establish relationships with other users who share their interests. We can infer users' interested images by mining the relevance among users or images. This method is called collaborative filtering (CF). The similarities of users or images are measured by users' rating matrix for images. To achieve a personalised searching result, heuristic method or probability statistical methods are utilised to infer the unknown ratings based on existing ratings. CF-based PIRR can be divided into user-based CF, item-based CF and model-based CF.

User-Based CF. User-based CF is based on the assumption that a user may like the items that are liked by users with similar interests. The measurement of users' similarities here are not demographic information but their rating data for images, i.e., users with similar ratings have the similar preference.

Considering each row of a user-item-rating matrix as a user, similarities of the user vector to all other user row vectors are calculated. The similarity is usually calculated by Euclidean distance, Pearson correlation coefficient, cosine similarity, and so on. Then prediction and recommendation are made according to the top K most similar users' rating [51].

Another popular user-based recommendation method is association recommendation. Association recommendation mines association rules by using the purchasing or rating records of the first K users, and makes recommendations according to the rules and user history records [52].

User-based CF need not describe users' preferences with image content features, which can avoid "semantic gap" problems. Different users have different nearest neighbours so that recommendation lists are personalised. With sufficient data, user-based CF can achieve a high accuracy and is widely used.

However, some problems are revealed with the constantly growing of users and images. The first is "cold start" problem [53]. When a new user joins, it is difficult to find users with similar interest because there is a lack of the user's ratings for the images. The second is "data sparsity" problem. In fact, images rated by users make up a small percentage of total images on the internet, so that the nearest neighbour algorithm is unable to make recommendations to some users and the algorithm accuracy declines.

Item-Based CF. Item-based CF is based on the assumption that a user may like the images similar to those he/she likes before. Image similarities are measured by users' ratings for the images instead of image visual features. Each column of a user-item-rating matrix is regarded as an item/image, and then similarities of the image to the other images are calculated for prediction and recommendation [54].

Item-based CF is more acceptable than user-based CF because images preferred before are more reliable than users with similar tastes to a user. Adjustments can be made quickly when users' interests change.

Item-based CF also suffers "cold start" problem. When new images are added to the system, they cannot be recommended to any user due to lacking of user history data [55, 56]. Compared with user-based CF, item-based CF does not take into account the characteristics of different users so that it has limited performance on personalization. Additionally, data sparsity problem also affects the accuracy of retrieval and recommendation. Tiraweerakhajohn et al. [57] combined item attribute similarity and item rating similarity. This method alleviates the "cold start" and data sparsity problems by introducing content information to the item-based CF. Lei et al. [58] and Ye [59] also took advantage of association rules mining for item rating prediction to solve the above mentioned problems.

Both user-based and item-based CF use nearest neighbour algorithms for the recommendation with different similarity measurements based on user or item. They both have the problem, computation complexity increasing as the number of images or users grows. When images rarely change, and the number of users is much larger than the number of images, the item-based recommendation is more efficient. However, when there is many images and images are frequently updated, user-based CF performs better.

User-based CF and item-based CF complement each other and are usually combined to use.

Model-Based CF. Both user-based CF and item-based CF rely on users' ratings for items. As the amount of images grows, it's difficult for both to process data in real time. Model-based CF utilises historical data to train a model, and then the model is used for prediction and recommendation. The approach can use SVD (Singular Value Decomposition), NMF (Non-negative matrix factorization), MDPs (Markov decision processes) model [60], classification, clustering, decision tree and so on to train a model.

Model-based CF can solve the cold start problem, adapt to sparse data, and process data in real time [61]. However, it is insensitive to users' new preferences, and model training processes are complex and time-consuming.

3.3 Comparison of PIRR Methods

Table 3 compares content-based PIRR and CF-based PIRR. Content-based PIRR is affected by semantic gap problem. Compared with the content-based approach, CF-based PIRR requires only users' historical rating data instead of image contents. CF-based PIRR can avoid manual intervention such as manual annotation, and is suitable for any image type. In fact, CF has been broadly applied to the personalized recommendation for different kinds of data such as movies, music, news and so on. CF-based PIRR can take full advantage of association information among users in social networks. However, some problems exist, such as cold start problem [62, 63], rating data sparsity, historical rating data failing to capture user interest changes, and so on [64]. To solve the problems, a hybrid method [63, 65, 66] that combines content-based filtering and PIRR is used. Widisinghe et al. [67] took into account users' changing preferences in different contexts and proposed a hybrid approach based on context and PIRR for image recommendation. Liu et al. [68] combined image content processing and user preferences into a hybrid Sparse Topic Model (STM), and used the probability matrix decomposition technique to solve data sparsity problem.

Table 3. Comparison of two PIRRs

Methods	Solution	Advantages	Disadvantages
CF-based PIRR	Predicting the rating of user u for image i by the ratings for i from similar users to u	• content independent • cross-genre	• no profile information for new user • no rating data for new items • hard to find new interest • rely on user rating scores • scalability • data sparsity
Content-based PIRR	Recommending images similar to the images the user used to like	• timely update • interpretability • user rating independent	• no profile information for new user • over-specialization

4   Conclusions

Image retrieval technologies can be grouped into text-based image retrieval, content-based image retrieval, semantic-based image retrieval, context-based image retrieval, PIRR. PIRR technologies are categorised into content-based PIRR, CF-based PIRR. In a content-based PIRR system, image contents are usually represented by low-level features and user preferences are usually textual descriptions of image contents, such as text tags. Therefore, content-based PIRR can be regarded as an approach combining content-based and text-based image retrieval technology. Inevitably it has some problems existed, such as the inaccuracy of tags, "semantic gap" between the low-level features and the high-level semantics, etc. CF-based PIRR effectively overcomes these shortcomings. Users with similar preferences are identified by users' ratings for images, and the similarity can be used to infer the images that the target user may be interested in. PIRR only needs users' rating data and does not require any knowledge of images. Therefore, it can adapt to any image type. However, CF-based PIRR is confronted with some problems such as cold start, data sparsity, etc. It can only retrieve the known interest content and cannot discover users' interest change. Hybrid methods combine content-based method and PIRR method to solve the fore-mentioned problems. How to embed content features of images into CF-based PIRR more efficiently still remains an open problem. Besides, there are some new challenges, such as user privacy protection and capturing user interest dynamic change, to be met.

Acknowledgements. This project was supported by NSFC (61272353).

References

1. Datta, R., Joshi, D., Li, J., Wang, J.Z.: Image retrieval: ideas, influences, and trends of the new age. ACM Comput. Surv. (Csur) **40**(2), 5 (2008)
2. Flickner, M., Sawhney, H., Niblack, W., Ashley, J., Huang, Q., Dom, B., Gorkani, M., Hafner, J., Lee, D., Petkovic, D.: Query by image and video content: the QBIC system. Computer **28**(9), 23–32 (1995)
3. Mehrotra, S., Rui, Y., Chakrabarti, K., Ortega, M., Huang, T.S.: Multimedia analysis and retrieval system. In: Proceedings of the 3rd International Workshop on Information Retrieval Systems (1997)
4. Pentland, A., Picard, R.W., Sclaroff, S.: Photobook: content-based manipulation of image databases. Int. J. Comput. Vision **18**(3), 233–254 (1996)
5. Wilensky, R.: UC Berkeley's digital library project. Commun. ACM **38**(4), 60 (1995)
6. Smith, J.R., Chang, S.-F.: VisualSEEK: a fully automated content-based image query system. In: Proceedings of the Fourth ACM International Conference on Multimedia, pp. 87–98. ACM (1997)
7. Xu, X., Peng, B., Sun, Z.: A semantic-based image retrieval system: VisEngine. Comput. Eng. **4**, 021 (2004)
8. Zhang, H., Wenyin, L., Hu, C.: IFIND—A system for semantics and feature based image retrieval over Internet. In: Proceedings of the Eighth ACM International Conference on Multimedia, pp. 477–478. ACM (2000)

9. Wang, W., Wu, Y., Zhang, A.: SemView: a semantic-sensitive distributed image retrieval system. In: Proceedings of the 2003 Annual National Conference on Digital Government Research, pp. 1–4. Digital Government Society of North America (2003)

10. Ghorab, M.R., Zhou, D., O'Connor, A., Wade, V.: Personalised information retrieval: survey and classification. User Model. User-Adap. Inter. **23**(4), 381–443 (2013)

11. Skowron, M., Tkalčič, M., Ferwerda, B., Schedl, M.: Fusing social media cues: personality prediction from twitter and instagram. In: Proceedings of the 25th International Conference Companion on World Wide Web, pp. 107–108. International World Wide Web Conferences Steering Committee (2016)

12. Liu, D., Hua, X.-S., Wang, M., Zhang, H.: Boost search relevance for tag-based social image retrieval. In: IEEE International Conference on Multimedia and Expo, ICME 2009, pp. 1636–1639. IEEE (2009)

13. Cheung, M., She, J.: Bag-of-features tagging approach for a better recommendation with social big data. In: Proceedings of the 4th International Conference on Advances in Information Mining and Management (IMMM 2014), pp. 83–88 (2014)

14. Sang, J., Xu, C., Lu, D.: Learn to personalized image search from the photo sharing websites. IEEE Trans. Multimedia **14**(4), 963–974 (2012)

15. Qiu, Z.W., Zhang, T.W.: Individuation image retrieval based on user multimedia data management model. Acta Electron. Sin. **36**(9), 1746–1749 (2008)

16. Fan, J., Keim, D.A., Gao, Y., Luo, H., Li, Z.: JustClick: personalized image recommendation via exploratory search from large-scale Flickr images. IEEE Trans. Circuits Syst. Video Technol. **19**(2), 273–288 (2009)

17. Yu, J., Tao, D., Wang, M., Rui, Y.: Learning to rank using user clicks and visual features for image retrieval. IEEE Trans. Cybern. **45**(4), 767–779 (2015)

18. Zhang, H., Zha, Z.-J., Yang, Y., Yan, S., Gao, Y., Chua, T.-S.: Attribute-augmented semantic hierarchy: towards bridging semantic gap and intention gap in image retrieval. In: Proceedings of the 21st ACM International Conference on Multimedia, pp. 33–42. ACM (2013)

19. Jayech, K., Mahjoub, M.A.: New approach using Bayesian Network to improve content based image classification systems. IJCSI Int. J. Comput. Sci. Issues **7**(6), 53–62 (2010)

20. Hu, T., Yu, J.: Max-margin based Bayesian classifier. Front. Inf. Technol. Electron. Eng. **17**(10), 973–981 (2016)

21. Krizhevsky, A., Sutskever, I., Hinton, G.E.: Imagenet classification with deep convolutional neural networks. In: Advances in Neural Information Processing Systems, pp. 1097–1105 (2012)

22. Lin, C.-H., Chen, C.-C., Lee, H.-L., Liao, J.-R.: Fast K-means algorithm based on a level histogram for image retrieval. Expert Syst. Appl. **41**(7), 3276–3283 (2014)

23. Liu, Y., Zhang, D., Lu, G., Ma, W.-Y.: A survey of content-based image retrieval with high-level semantics. Pattern Recogn. **40**(1), 262–282 (2007)

24. Wu, J., Xiao, Z.-B., Wang, H.-S., Shen, H.: Learning with both unlabeled data and query logs for image search. Comput. Electr. Eng. **40**(3), 964–973 (2014)

25. Su, J.-H., Huang, W.-J., Philip, S.Y., Tseng, V.S.: Efficient relevance feedback for content-based image retrieval by mining user navigation patterns. IEEE Trans. Knowl. Data Eng. **23**(3), 360–372 (2011)

26. Adomavicius, G., Tuzhilin, A.: Toward the next generation of recommender systems: a survey of the state-of-the-art and possible extensions. IEEE Trans. Knowl. Data Eng. **17**(6), 734–749 (2005)

27. Paik, J.H.: A novel TF-IDF weighting scheme for effective ranking. In: Proceedings of the 36th International ACM SIGIR Conference on Research and Development in Information Retrieval, pp. 343–352. ACM (2013)

28. Whissell, J.S., Clarke, C.L.: Improving document clustering using Okapi BM25 feature weighting. Inf. Retrieval **14**(5), 466–487 (2011)
29. Zhang, J., Zhuo, L., Shen, L., He, L.: A personalized image retrieval based on user interest model. Int. J. Pattern Recogn. Artif. Intell. **24**(03), 401–419 (2010)
30. Nie, W., Li, X., Liu, A., Su, Y.: 3D object retrieval based on Spatial+LDA model. Multimedia Tools Appl. **76**(3), 4091–4104 (2017)
31. Li, X., Ouyang, J., Lu, Y.: Topic modeling for large-scale text data. Front. Inf. Technol. Electron. Eng. **16**(6), 457–465 (2015)
32. Zhang, Y., Jin, R., Zhou, Z.H.: Understanding bag-of-words model: a statistical framework. Int. J. Mach. Learn. Cybern. **1**(1), 43–52 (2010)
33. Tu, N.A., Dinh, D.-L., Rasel, M.K., Lee, Y.-K.: Topic modeling and improvement of image representation for large-scale image retrieval. Inf. Sci. **366**, 99–120 (2016)
34. Shekhar, R., Jawahar, C.: Word image retrieval using bag of visual words. In: 2012 10th IAPR International Workshop on Document Analysis Systems (DAS), pp. 297–301. IEEE (2012)
35. Yang, J., Jiang, Y.-G., Hauptmann, A.G., Ngo, C.-W.: Evaluating bag-of-visual-words representations in scene classification. In: Proceedings of the International Workshop on Multimedia Information Retrieval, pp. 197–206. ACM (2007)
36. Liu, L.: Contextual topic model based image recommendation system. In: 2015 IEEE/WIC/ACM International Conference on Web Intelligence and Intelligent Agent Technology (WI-IAT), pp. 239–240. IEEE (2015)
37. Jia, D., Berg, A.C., Li, F.F.: Hierarchical semantic indexing for large scale image retrieval. In: IEEE Conference on Computer Vision and Pattern Recognition, pp. 785–792 (2011)
38. Jiang, X., Tan, A.-H.: Learning and inferencing in user ontology for personalized Semantic Web search. Inf. Sci. **179**(16), 2794–2808 (2009)
39. Geng, X., Zhang, H., Bian, J., Chua, T.-S.: Learning image and user features for recommendation in social networks. In: Proceedings of the IEEE International Conference on Computer Vision, pp. 4274–4282 (2015)
40. Lei, C., Liu, D., Li, W., Zha, Z.J., Li, H.: Comparative deep learning of hybrid representations for image recommendations. In: IEEE Conference on Computer Vision and Pattern Recognition, pp. 2545–2553 (2016)
41. Song, G., Jin, X., Chen, G., Nie, Y.: Two-level hierarchical feature learning for image classification. Front. Inf. Technol. Electron. Eng. **17**(9), 897–906 (2016)
42. Burdescu, D.D., Mihai, C.G., Stanescu, L., Brezovan, M.: Automatic image annotation and semantic based image retrieval for medical domain. Neurocomputing **109**, 33–48 (2013)
43. Kurtz, C., Depeursinge, A., Napel, S., Beaulieu, C.F., Rubin, D.L.: On combining image-based and ontological semantic dissimilarities for medical image retrieval applications. Med. Image Anal. **18**(7), 1082–1100 (2014)
44. Kurtz, C., Beaulieu, C.F., Napel, S., Rubin, D.L.: A hierarchical knowledge-based approach for retrieving similar medical images described with semantic annotations. J. Biomed. Inform. **49**, 227–244 (2014)
45. Rui, Y., Huang, T.S.: A novel relevance feedback technique in image retrieval. In: Proceedings of the Seventh ACM International Conference on Multimedia (Part 2), pp. 67–70. ACM (1999)
46. Rocchio, J.J.: Relevance feedback in information retrieval. In: Salton, G. (ed.) The Smart Retrieval System: Experiments in Automatic Document Processing, pp. 313–323. Prentice Hall Inc., Englewood Cliffs (1971)
47. Porkaew, K., Chakrabarti, K.: Query refinement for multimedia similarity retrieval in MARS. In: Proceedings of the Seventh ACM International Conference on Multimedia (Part 1), pp. 235–238. ACM (1999)

48. Tao, D., Tang, X., Li, X., Wu, X.: Asymmetric bagging and random subspace for support vector machines-based relevance feedback in image retrieval. IEEE Trans. Pattern Anal. Mach. Intell. **28**(7), 1088–1099 (2006)

49. Johnson, M., Shotton, J., Cipolla, R.: Semantic texton forests for image categorization and segmentation. In: Criminisi, A., Shotton, J. (eds.) Decision Forests for Computer Vision and Medical Image Analysis. Advances in Computer Vision and Pattern Recognition, pp. 211–227. Springer, London (2013)

50. Tong, S., Chang, E.: Support vector machine active learning for image retrieval. In: Proceedings of the Ninth ACM International Conference on Multimedia, pp. 107–118. ACM (2001)

51. Zhao, S., Du, N., Nauerz, A., Zhang, X., Yuan, Q., Fu, R.: Improved recommendation based on collaborative tagging behaviors. In: Proceedings of the 13th International Conference on Intelligent User Interfaces, pp. 413–416. ACM (2008)

52. Gong, S.J.: Personalized recommendation system based on association rules mining and collaborative filtering. In: Wang, Y. (ed.) Applied Mechanics and Materials, pp. 540–544. Trans Tech Publ, Zürich (2011)

53. Ju, B., Qian, Y., Ye, M.: Preference transfer model in collaborative filtering for implicit data. Front. Inf. Technol. Electron. Eng. **17**(6), 489–500 (2016)

54. Sarwar, B., Karypis, G., Konstan, J., Riedl, J.: Item-based collaborative filtering recommendation algorithms. In: Proceedings of the 10th International Conference on World Wide Web, pp. 285–295. ACM (2001)

55. Zhou, K., Yang, S.-H., Zha, H.: Functional matrix factorizations for cold-start recommendation. In: Proceedings of the 34th International ACM SIGIR Conference on Research and Development in Information Retrieval, pp. 315–324. ACM (2011)

56. Yuan, Z., Huang, C., Sun, X., Li, X., Xu, D.: A microblog recommendation algorithm based on social tagging and a temporal interest evolution model. Front. Inf. Technol. Electron. Eng. **16**(7), 532–540 (2015)

57. Tiraweerakhajohn, C., Pinngern, O.: A combination of content-based filtering and item-based collaborative filtering using association rules. In: The 1st International Conference on Electrical Engineering/Electronics, Computer, Telecommunications and Information Technology. ECTI, Thailand (2004)

58. Lei, W., Qing, F., Zhou, J.: Improved personalized recommendation based on causal association rule and collaborative filtering. Int. J. Distance Educ. Technol. (IJDET) **14**(3), 21–33 (2016)

59. Ye, H.: A personalized collaborative filtering recommendation using association rules mining and self-organizing map. JSW **6**(4), 732–739 (2011)

60. Thorat, P.B., Goudar, R., Barve, S.: Survey on collaborative filtering, content-based filtering and hybrid recommendation system. Int. J. Comput. Appl. **110**(4), 31–36 (2015)

61. Ma, Z., Leijon, A.: A model-based collaborative filtering method for bounded support data. In: 2012 3rd IEEE International Conference on Network Infrastructure and Digital Content (IC-NIDC), pp. 545–548. IEEE (2012)

62. Fernández-Tobías, I., Braunhofer, M., Elahi, M., Ricci, F., Cantador, I.: Alleviating the new user problem in collaborative filtering by exploiting personality information. User Model. User-Adap. Inter. **26**(2–3), 221–255 (2016)

63. Yang, C., Zhou, Y., Chen, L., Zhang, X., Chiu, D.M.: Social-group-based ranking algorithms for cold-start video recommendation. Int. J. Data Sci. Anal. **1**(3–4), 165–175 (2016)

64. Candillier, L., Meyer, F., Boullé, M.: Comparing state-of-the-art collaborative filtering systems. In: Perner, P. (ed.) MLDM 2007. LNCS, vol. 4571, pp. 548–562. Springer, Heidelberg (2007). doi:10.1007/978-3-540-73499-4_41

65. Sanchez, F., Barrilero, M., Uribe, S., Alvarez, F., Tena, A., Menendez, J.M.: Social and content hybrid image recommender system for mobile social networks. Mob. Netw. Appl. **17**(6), 782–795 (2012)
66. Lekakos, G., Caravelas, P.: A hybrid approach for movie recommendation. Multimedia Tools Appl. **36**(1), 55–70 (2008)
67. Widisinghe, A., Ranasinghe, D., Kulathilaka, K., Kaluarachchi, R., Wimalawarne, K.A.D.N. K.: picSEEK: collaborative filtering for context-based image recommendation. In: International Conference on Information and Automation for Sustainability, pp. 225–232 (2010)
68. Liu, X., Tsai, M.H., Huang, T.: Analyzing user preference for social image recommendation. arXiv:1604.07044 [cs.IR] (2016)

A Fast Interactive Item-Based Collaborative Filtering Algorithm

Zhenyan Ji[1(✉)], Zhi Zhang[1], Canzhen Zhou[1], and Haishuai Wang[2]

[1] Beijing Jiaotong University, Haidian 100044, China
zhyji@bjtu.edu.cn
[2] Washington University in St. Louis, St. Louis, MO 63130, USA
haishuai.wang@wustl.edu

Abstract. A recommender system becomes more and more popular in e-commerce. Usually prediction results cannot satisfy users' requirements fully, and sometimes it even contains totally irrelevant items. To reflect users' newest preference and increase the quality of recommendation, a fast interactive item-based collaborative filtering algorithm is proposed. Firstly, we propose an item-based collaborative filtering algorithm with less time and space complexity. Then we introduce interactive iterations to reflect users' up-to-date preference and increase users' satisfaction. The experiments show that our fast interactive item-based CF algorithm has better recall and precision than traditional item-based CF algorithm.

Keywords: Recommender system · Item-based collaborative filtering · Interactive recommendation · Iteration

1 Introduction

With the rapid development of e-commerce and social networks, internet information grows explosively. How to find useful information efficiently from mass information? A recommender system can predict users' potential desire based on their historical preference and mine meaningful information for them. Usually a computer completes the recommendation processing without manual intervention. However, a recommender system usually cannot provide users with the most satisfying prediction, sometimes it even irritates users by recommending totally irrelevant items. Imagine this, if you are able to provide feedback to the recommender, is there an improvement of the quality in the following recommendation?

Recommending algorithm can be divided into four categories, collaborative filtering recommending algorithm, content-based filtering recommending algorithm, hybrid recommending algorithm (combining collaborative filtering and content-based filtering), and personality-based recommending algorithm [1]. Here we focus on collaborative filtering algorithm whose data source has no content. There are two main collaborative filtering algorithms (CF), user-based CF algorithm and item-based CF algorithm. In this paper, we discuss primarily the improvement on item-based CF algorithm.

D. Du et al. (Eds.): NCTCS 2017, CCIS 768, pp. 248–257, 2017.
https://doi.org/10.1007/978-981-10-6893-5_19

Collaborative filtering suffers from the problems such as cold start, scalability, scarcity, and etc. It cannot give accurate result. How to reflect user's up-to-date preferences and produce more accurate result to users? Much effort has been put into improving the model of data training process. But we improve the item-based CF algorithm by introducing manual intervention in the evaluation process, i.e., the recommend process.

This paper has research contributions:

1. Propose an interactive item-based CF algorithm with less time and space complexity but higher precision and recall rate.
2. Implement the interactive item-based CF algorithm and compare it with the general item-based CF algorithm.
3. Experimentally proves that by interactive iteration, performance of item-based CF algorithm can be improved by introducing interactive iterations

The remainder of the paper is organized as the following. Section 2 provides the basic background knowledge of item-based CF algorithm's recommending process and Sect. 3 describes the defects of it. In Sect. 4, we present the improved item-based CF with interactive iteration in detail including how it can solve the existing flaws. Section 5 describes our experimental evaluations between general item-based CF and the improved one. Finally, Sect. 6 includes concluding remarks and future work's direction.

2 Related Work

Item-based CF [2, 3] is a kind of CF algorithms, which calculated similarity of items based on memorized ratings and generated a recommendation for target users, [4] presented a ranking algorithm called FolkRank improved with item-based CF. Additionally, some efforts have been made to improve item-based CF algorithm. [5] improved item-based CF algorithm by incorporating external aggregate ratings information. [6] combined item-based CF with genetic algorithms using rating behaviors. [7] adopted BP neural networks to fill the vacant ratings to decrease source data sparsity. [8] reduced the number of item pair comparison through simple clustering to accelerate algorithm's speed. [9] focused on improving the recommending performance when dataset is sparse. [10] implemented the pipeline recommendation algorithm based on MapReduce. [11] implemented the item-based CF on the distributed cluster platform Hadoop. [12] introduced user relevance score into the similarity calculations to improve CF. [17] propose an improved collaborative filtering recommendation algorithm based on dynamic item clustering method. [18] propose an Item-based Fuzzy Clustering Collaborative Filtering in order to ensure the benefits of a model-based technique improving the quality of suggestions. [19] uses tag-based method to calculate the similarity between users and in the process of calculating item similarity, which makes use of TAG to calculate interest points, thereby it enhances the credibility of item similarity and guarantees the quality of recommendation quality as well. [20] introduces three kinds of Stability Degree into similarity computation and improves the accuracy of item-based CF algorithm.

Improvements are usually made in similarity calculation step. Rare improvements are made in the recommending process to improve the item-based algorithm. To reflect users' current preferences, we propose an interactive item-based CF algorithm.

3   Item-Based Collaborative Filtering (CF)

The basic idea of item-based CF algorithms [2, 3] is to calculate the similarity between items and the relevance between users and items, and then recommend the items with highest similarity to target users. The whole process can be roughly divided into three steps, calculating similarity between items, predicting users' preferences on items, and recommending top related items to a certain user. We describe the three steps in detail as the below.

3.1   Item Similarity Computation

For each items, we compute its similarity with every other items in the dataset. The first step is to identify the users who have rated both given items. Then the similarities between items are calculated based on the ratings given to the items by users who have rated both of them. There are multiple similarity algorithms such as cosine-based similarity, correlation-based similarity and adjust-cosine similarity [2, 3]. We adopt cosine-based similarity, which indicates that items and their ratings are viewed as vectors and the cosine of the angle between two vectors are regarded as their similarity. To be precise, the similarity between item i and j is given by

$$\text{sim}(i,j) = \cos(\vec{i},\vec{j}) = \frac{\vec{i} \cdot \vec{j}}{\|\vec{i}\|_2 * \|\vec{j}\|_2} \tag{1}$$

where "•" denotes that the dot product of vector i and j.

3.2   Prediction Computation

After computing similarities between items, the next step is to measure the possibility for a certain user to purchase a certain item. There are several algorithms to calculate predictions, such as regression, weighted-sum and etc. Here we introduce weighted-sum method. As the name literally tells us, to get a prediction for a user u on an item i, the algorithm takes all the items (item N) similar to the target item i. From the similar items, user's rating for each of the items (item N) is weighted by the similarity between it (item N) and the target item i. Finally, the predicted rating is calculated by scaling the prediction by the sum of similarities sim(i,j) [2, 3, 13]. The algorithm is as the below.

$$P(u,i) = \frac{\sum_{all\ rated\ items,N}(sim(i,N) * rate(u,N))}{\sum_{all\ rated\ items,N}(|sim(i,N)|)} \tag{2}$$

3.3   Item Recommendation

The last step is recommendation, which is easier to understand than the former two steps. From the prediction or recommendation list, top k items are popped up and recommended to active users. For example, if we want to recommend 10 items to a user u, we choose the top 10 items in the recommendation list, i.e. the 10 items with highest $P(u, i)$.

4   Defect of Traditional Item-Based Collaborative Filtering (CF)

Traditional item-based CF algorithm cannot be dynamically updated due to the computation complexity. So they cannot be applied into the interactive environment.

Association rule mining is one of the rationales of collaborative filtering algorithms [14, 15], which is to find out all implications that satisfy certain support level and confidence level from all datasets. Suppose set $I = \{i_1, i_2, \cdots, i_m\}$, i_k (k = 1, 2, ..., m) is item. If $X \in I$, then X is an item set. And if $|x| = k$, then X is a k-itemset. Transaction binary group T = (tid, X), tid is the transaction number and transaction's only identifier. The data set $D = \{t_1, t_2, \cdots, t_n\}$. And the implications that association rule mining is going to find out is the one that satisfy the condition where A → B, $A \in I, B \in I$ and $A \cap B = \varnothing$. Support level s of X is X's transactions' percentage of all transactions, denoted by

$$s(X) = p(X) = (\sup(X))/(|D|) \tag{3}$$

confidence level c of X is $X \cup Y$'s transactions' percentage of transactions include X, denoted by

$$c(X) = p(X|Y) = (\sup(X \cup Y))/(\sup(X)) \tag{4}$$

Since the time complexity and space complexity of association rule mining are very high, the algorithm using it as a theoretical basis cannot be applied to online environment, especially for interactive online environment. So traditional item-based CF algorithm based on association rule mining can't be implemented to online environment unless being edited to a less time-and-space-consuming version.

5   Interactive Item-Based Collaborative Filtering (CF)

The interactive item-based CF algorithm focuses on the third step of the item-based CF process, the recommend process. On one hand, it improves precision and recall rate by splitting up the recommendation process into several smaller iterations. For example, if we decide that we recommend 20 items to each user, then the interactive item-based CF algorithm randomly makes the recommendation size at least 2 times fewer than the original size. Here we set the size to be 5 for each iteration, and the algorithm iterates the recommending process 4 times in total. At the end of each iteration, it compares the results with the test data. If the prediction results agree with test data, we assume that the user 'likes' this recommendation, that is, this recommendation fits the user's inclination, otherwise it supposes the prediction doesn't fit. In this way we simulate the real world's conditions where we can get users' interactive feedbacks. After receiving the feedbacks, the interactive item-based CF algorithm immediately updates the prediction model mentioned in 2.2 with rating information from the user. That simply means, for user u and item i rated by user u, it updates P(u, j) by adding sim(i, j)*rate(u, i) on the denominator, and adding sim(i, j) on the numerator. The update of prediction can be denoted as

$$P(u,j) = \frac{\sum_N (sim(i,N) * r(u,N)) + sim(i,j) * r(u,j)}{\sum_N (|sim(i,N)|) + sim(i,j)} \tag{5}$$

r(u,i) indicates user u's rating on item i, and N indicates all the items that has been rated by user u.

On the other hand, in order to reduce the complexity of this algorithm so that it adapts to the interactive recommendation, we only consider conditions when A and B are all I-itemset when we consider implications like $A- > B$. In this way we can get correlation matrix M between items, and is on behalf of $i- > j$'s confidence level. We can also consider the interactive algorithm as an algorithm to conduct linear transformation. It takes a vector that shows history matching relation between users and items as an input, and a vector that shows expected matching relation between users and items as an output, as shown in Fig. 1.

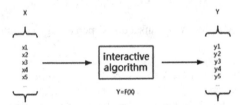

Fig. 1. Interactive algorithm conducts linear transformation, taking a vector showing history matching relation between users and items as an input, and a vector showing expected matching relation between users and items as an output

When recommending to user u, let the system's input vector be

$$X = \{x_1, x_2, x_3, \ldots, x_k\},$$

and the result be

$$Y = \{y_1, y_2, y_3, \ldots, y_k\}.$$

The mapping relation is: $Y = MX$, where $y_i = \sum_{i=1}^{k} x_i * M_{ij}$. Considering the user has submitted the feedback data for certain recommendation, when the system input is changed to X', output is Y', let $D = X' - X$, then $Y' = Y + MD$. In this way, system's calculation pressure can be considerably alleviated, as most elements of vector D are 0, and the actual complexity of calculation is reduced to $O(n)$.

The new recommendation algorithm's time complexity is $O(nm)$, space complexity of system is $O(m^2)$ n is the number of items user i has purchased, m is the number of items in system, if the system stores every user's recommendation result, then time complexity is $O(m)$. Buffered length is much less than m considering the influence of confidence level, which means time complexity less than $O(m)$. This update process is much more effective to fit the interactive iteration purpose comparing with the traditional item-based CF algorithm.

6 Experimental Evaluation

To evaluate the quality of a recommendation algorithm, we usually use recall and precision rate. Recall rate refers to the fraction of relevant instances retrieved, while precision rate is the fraction of retrieved instances that are relevant. Enhancing recall and precision rate has always been the top goal for recommendation systems. All our experiments ran on a PC with 2 GHz CPU and 8 GB RAM.

6.1 Data Set

We use MovieLens [16] 1 M Dataset as our dataset. The dataset contains more than 1,000,000 ratings from 6040 users over 3952 movies. We divide the dataset into two parts, the train set and the test set. We decided to use 70% of the total dataset as train set and the remaining 30% as test set.

6.2 Evaluation Metrics

We use precision and recall to evaluate the experiment results. We have customized the definitions of precision and recall for recommendation systems based on the corresponding definitions in the field of information retrieval

In recommendation system, precision is the proportion of correctly recommended items (i.e., the recommended items that are accepted by users) to all the recommended items.

$$precision = \frac{|\{relevant\ items\} \cap \{recommended\ items\}|}{recommended\ items} \tag{6}$$

In recommendation system, recall is the proportion of correctly recommended items to all the items that are accepted by users whatever they are recommended or not.

$$recall = \frac{|\{relevant\,items\} \cap \{recommended\,items\}|}{relevant\,items} \qquad (7)$$

From the above formulas, we can conclude that precision value and recall value are in the range [0, 1]. A perfect precision value 1.0 means that all items recommended are accepted by users although it says nothing about if all the accepted items are recommended by the recommendation system. A perfect recall value 1.0 means that all items accepted by users are recommended, but it says nothing about how many incorrectly recommended items are in the recommendation list.

6.3 Experiments

All our experiments ran on a PC with 2 GHz CPU and 8 GB RAM.

In the experiments, we compare our interactive item-based CF with the traditional item-based CF in order to see the improved performance. We set recommendation size 10 items for each iteration, that is, a group of ten more items are recommended at the end of each iteration. First iteration comprises 10 items while second comprises 20, third 30 and fourth 40 and so on. To simulate users' feedback, recommendation results are compared with the test dataset. If the results are in the test dataset, it means that the user gives a positive feedback and they 'like' the item. Otherwise it means that the user gives a negative feedback and they 'dislike' the item. The experiment results are shown in Figs. 2 and 3, where x-axis denotes the size of recommendation set and y-axis denotes the recall or precision rate.

Figure 2 shows recall comparison of interactive item-based CF and traditional item-based CF. Figure 3 shows precision comparison of two item-based CF. When interactive item-based CF makes the first recommendation, its recall and precision rate are slightly higher than the traditional item-based CF due to lacking of users' feedback. After the first iteration, its recall rate rises up and becomes much higher than the traditional item-based CF's recall rate because of the accumulated improvements in each iteration. With the recommendation size increasing, so does the gap between the interactive algorithm and the traditional one.

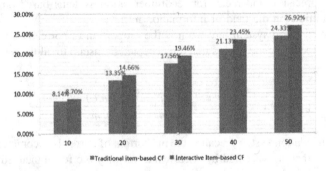

Fig. 2. Recall of interactive item-based CF become higher than traditional item-based CF after first iteration, and as the recommendation size increases, so does the gap between the two algorithms

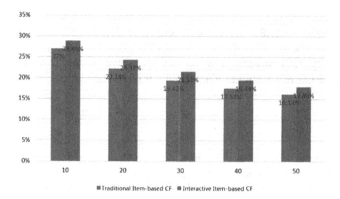

Fig. 3. Precision of interactive item-based CF is originally higher than traditional item-based CF and after first iteration, and as the recommendation size increases, so does the gap between those two algorithms

Meanwhile we have recorded the time taken by different algorithms in recommendation in the course of experiments. Interaction brings certain calculation burden to the system, yet within acceptable range. In this experiment we made 30,000 recommendations and each recommendation comprises 10 items. Figure 4 presents the recorded time taken by them (in milliseconds).

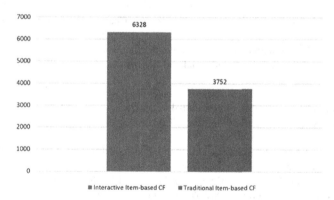

Fig. 4. Interaction mode brings certain calculation burden to the system, yet within acceptable range

7 Conclusions

In this paper we have explained that getting users' feedbacks would help enhance item-based CF algorithm's performance. We propose an approach of improving the item-based CF algorithm by interactive iteration. We divide the whole recommendation into multiple recommendation iterations. After each recommendation iteration is over, we gain feedback from users and update the recommendation model to improve the results. With the feedbacks, the results can reflect users' up-to-date preferences. Furthermore, in order to make the current item-based algorithm fit for an interactive environment, we also improve the item-based CF algorithm so that it has less time and space complexity. Experiments show that the interactive method indeed improves the recall and precision of traditional item-based CF recommendations.

References

1. Park, D.H., Kim, H.K., Choi, I.Y., Kim, J.K.: A literature review and classification of recommender systems research. Expert Syst. Appl. **39**(11), 10059–10072 (2012)
2. Sarwar, B., Karypis, G., Konstan, J., Riedl, J.: Item-based collaborative filtering recommendation algorithms. In: Proceedings of the 10th International Conference on World Wide Web, pp. 285–295. ACM (2001)
3. Deshpande, M., Karypis, G.: Item-based top-n recommendation algorithms. ACM Trans. Inf. Syst. (TOIS) **22**(1), 143–177 (2004)
4. Gemmell, J., Schimoler, T., Ramezani, M., Christiansen, L., Mobasher, B.: Improving folkrank with item-based collaborative filtering. In: Recommender Systems & the Social Web (2009)
5. Umyarov, A., Tuzhilin, A.: Improving collaborative filtering recommendations using external data. In: Eighth IEEE International Conference on Data Mining, ICDM 2008, pp. 618–627. IEEE (2008)
6. Xiao, J., Luo, M., Chen, J.-M., Li, J.-J.: An item based collaborative filtering system combined with genetic algorithms using rating behavior. In: Huang, D.-S., Han, K. (eds.) ICIC 2015. LNCS, vol. 9227, pp. 453–460. Springer, Cham (2015). doi:10.1007/978-3-319-22053-6_48
7. Gong, S., Ye, H.: An item based collaborative filtering using bp neural networks prediction. In: International Conference on Industrial and Information Systems, IIS 2009, pp. 146–148. IEEE (2009)
8. Ben Shimon, D., Rokach, L., Shapira, B., Shani, G.: Fast item-based collaborative filtering. In: Proceedings of the International Conference on Agents and Artificial Intelligence-Volume 2, pp. 457–463. SCITEPRESS-Science and Technology Publications, Lda (2015)
9. Pirasteh, P., Jung, J.J., Hwang, D.: Item-based collaborative filtering with attribute correlation: a case study on movie recommendation. In: Nguyen, N.T., Attachoo, B., Trawiński, B., Somboonviwat, K. (eds.) ACIIDS 2014. LNCS, vol. 8398, pp. 245–252. Springer, Cham (2014). doi:10.1007/978-3-319-05458-2_26
10. Zhao, Z.-L., Wang, C.-D., Wan, Y.-Y., Huang, Z.-W., Lai, J.-H.: Pipeline item-based collaborative filtering based on MapReduce. In: 2015 IEEE Fifth International Conference on Big Data and Cloud Computing (BDCloud), pp. 9–14. IEEE (2015)
11. Lu, F., Hong, L., Changfeng, L.: The improvement and implementation of distributed item-based collaborative filtering algorithm on Hadoop. In: 2015 34th Chinese Control Conference (CCC), pp. 9078–9083. IEEE (2015)
12. Latha, R., Nadarajan, R.: User relevance for item-based collaborative filtering. In: Saeed, K., Chaki, R., Cortesi, A., Wierzchoń, S. (eds.) CISIM 2013. LNCS, vol. 8104, pp. 337–347. Springer, Heidelberg (2013). doi:10.1007/978-3-642-40925-7_31

13. Cadegnani, S., Guerra, F., Ilarri, S., del Carmen Rodríguez-Hernández, M., Trillo-Lado, R., Velegrakis, Y.: Recommending web pages using item-based collaborative filtering approaches. In: Cardoso, J., Guerra, F., Houben, G.J., Pinto, A., Velegrakis, Y. (eds.) KEYSTONE 2015. LNCS, vol. 9398, pp. 17–29. Springer, Cham (2015). doi:10.1007/978-3-319-27932-9_2

14. Agrawal, R., Imieliński, T., Swami, A.: Mining association rules between sets of items in large databases. Paper presented at the Proceedings of the 1993 ACM SIGMOD international conference on Management of data, Washington, D.C., USA (1993)

15. Agrawal, R., Srikant, R.: Algorithms for mining association rules in large databases. In: Proceedings of the 20th VLDB Conference Santiago, Chile, pp. 141–182 (1994)

16. Harper, F.M., Konstan, J.A.: The movielens datasets: History and context. ACM Trans. Interact. Intell. Syst. (TiiS) 5(4), 19 (2016)

17. Wen, J., Zhou, W.: An improved item-based collaborative filtering algorithm based on clustering method. J. Comput. Inf. Syst. 8(2), 571–578 (2012)

18. Birtolo, C., Ronca, D., Armenise, R.: Improving accuracy of recommendation system by means of Item-based Fuzzy Clustering Collaborative Filtering. In: 2011 11th International Conference on Intelligent Systems Design and Applications (ISDA), pp. 100–106. IEEE (2011)

19. Hui, S., Pengyu, L., Kai, Z.: Improving item-based collaborative filtering recommendation system with tag. In: 2011 2nd International Conference on Artificial Intelligence, Management Science and Electronic Commerce (AIMSEC), pp. 2142–2145. IEEE (2011)

20. Mu, X., Chen, Y., Zhang, L.: An improved similarity algorithm based on stability degree for item-based collaborative filtering. In: 2010 International Conference on Computer Design and Applications (ICCDA), pp. V3-494–V493-498. IEEE (2010)

Parallel and Distributed Computing

The Impact of the Mesh Partitioning Factors on CFD Simulation

Chen Cui[1], Juan Chen[1(✉)], Feihao Wu[1], Miao Wang[1], Yuyang Sun[2], and Xinhai Xu[1]

[1] State Key Laboratory of High Performance Computing, College of Computer, National University of Defense Technology, Changsha, China
juanchen@nudt.edu.cn
[2] College of Computer, National University of Defense Technology, Changsha, China

Abstract. Mesh partitioning plays an important role in Computational Fluid Dynamics (CFD) simulation. However, it is difficult to produce a good mesh partitioning to achieve a high performance simulation because it is a NP-complete problem to solve this problem. A good mesh partitioning may be determined by many factors. Nowadays, there is a lack of systematic guidelines and comprehensive analyses for how to produce a high quality mesh partitioning. Considering that it is difficult to break through in theory, we prefer to explore how the factors related to mesh partitioning influence CFD simulation based on a large amount of experimental analyses. In this paper, we evaluate the impact of changing the mesh partitioning factors on mesh partitioning quality and simulation performance according to the following five factors: the number of processor faces, subdomain aspect ratio, load, partitioning direction and mapping. We design a series of rules to make various and numerous mesh partitioning changes based on four commonly used methods (Simple, Metis, Scotch and Manual) in OpenFOAM. Furthermore, we conduct the parallel simulation for two representative cases (cavity case and damBreak case) in OpenFOAM framework. The experimental results certify that changing mesh partitioning factors really influences the simulation performance. Then we provide some analyses and advices, which will definitely be helpful to guide mesh partitioning in the future.

Keywords: Mesh partitioning · CFD simulation · Mesh partitioning quality · Simulation performance

1 Introduction

In parallel Computational Fluid Dynamics (CFD), how to obtain a high quality mesh partitioning is a key problem that determines the simulation performance. In CFD simulation, computation is performed iteratively on mesh elements such as nodes, finite elements or finite control volumes (also called cells). Then the

© Springer Nature Singapore Pte Ltd. 2017
D. Du et al. (Eds.): NCTCS 2017, CCIS 768, pp. 261–276, 2017.
https://doi.org/10.1007/978-981-10-6893-5_20

information is exchanged between elements that are adjacent. Mesh partitioning is needed for the efficient execution when the simulation is performed on parallel machines, that is, mapping the mesh onto processors so that the number of mesh elements each processor gets is evenly balanced and the amount of inter-processor communication required by the information exchange between elements that are adjacent is minimized [1]. It is well known that this problem is NP-complete [2]. Because that mesh partitioning can be affected by the model of physical problem, the mesh geometry, the number of mesh elements, the mesh density, the number of subdomains and so on, it is almost impossible to obtain the theoretically optimal mesh partitioning. There are some commonly used mesh partitioning techniques at present, but none of them can deal with all CFD problems. In addition, the current researches on mesh partitioning usually focus on the mesh partitioning optimization for solving specific problems. There is a lack of systematic and comprehensive analysis of mesh partitioning so far. Considering that it is difficult to break through in theory, our idea is the experimental analysis by changing several key factors that may affect mesh partitioning and observing the subsequent mesh partitioning quality and simulation performance. Our purpose is to obtain mesh partitioning changes by designing relatively more changes of these factors and then to evaluate the impact of these factors on mesh partitioning quality and simulation performance.

Many factors will have an impact on mesh partitioning, which in turn will affect CFD simulation. Generally speaking, most research interests related to mesh partitioning are focused on the balanced load on each processor (each processor gets roughly an equal number of mesh elements) and the minimum inter-processor communication overhead (the number of cut edges is minimized). There are a variety of mesh partitioning techniques over the last few decades that focus on these two criteria, and they can be roughly classified as geometry-based approaches such as the recursive coordinate bisection (RCB) [3] and the space filling curve (SFC) [4], and graph-based approaches such as the recursive spectral bisection (RSB) [5] and the multilevel graph partitioning [6]. However, there are some other cases where the load balance and the number of cut edges may no longer be the only factors that determine the mesh partitioning quality and simulation performance [7]. For example, if the decomposition is used to construct pre-conditioners, the shape of subdomains, which can be measured by the aspect ratio (AR) of subdomains, will heavily influence the quality of preconditioning and, thus, the overall execution time [8]. Furthermore, even if the above factors are kept consistent, there exist some other factors affecting the CFD simulation, such as the partitioning direction [9,10]. Finally, as with many other task mappings [11,12], we find that different mappings of the subdomains onto processors will also have an impact on CFD simulation.

Nowadays, there is a lack of systematic guidelines for mesh partitioning. Sometimes, improper mesh partitionings will prevent from achieving a satisfying simulation performance and even will lead to an unsuccessful simulation. Because of the complexity of this problem and the fact that the mesh partitioning effectiveness is affected by many factors, mesh partitioning has become one of the most critical factors that can affect the simulation performance. In order to obtain beneficial guidelines for good mesh partitioning, we can start with the study on the impact of changing the factors related to mesh partitioning on CFD simulation. In order to enumerate as many mesh partitioning results as possible, we make some rules to produce relatively more changes for each of five factors related to mesh partitioning. We find that the simulation performance, such as the number of iterations and the simulation speed, is really affected with the changes of these five factors. More important, a large amount of experiments and analyses could tell us which kind of mesh partitioning will benefit CFD simulation. The lack of systematic and effective methods for this field also highlights the significance of our research.

In this paper, we systematically evaluate the impact of changing the five factors in mesh partitioning process on mesh partitioning quality and CFD simulation: the number of processor faces (boundary faces of a processor shared with other processors), subdomain aspect ratio, load, partitioning direction and mapping. Note that we choose the number of processor faces rather than the number of cut edges. This is because in Finite Volume Method (FVM), the number of processor faces and the number of cut edges are equivalent for the measurement of communication overhead. For each cut edge, there are two processor faces that belong to different processors. The problems this experiment has mainly focused on and solved are as follows:

- We take the idea of enumeration to design various and numerous mesh partitioning changes, hoping to make the evaluation more adequate. The difficulties here mainly lie in the design of enumeration rules and how to fit them with current commonly used mesh partitioning methods.
- We evaluate the impact of the above mesh partitioning factor changes on mesh partitioning quality and simulation performance. What we need to consider is how to select appropriate metrics for evaluating the partitioning quality and simulation performance. In this paper, we take the load imbalance and the maximum number of processor faces as the metrics to evaluate the mesh partitioning quality, and take the number of iterations and the execution time as the metrics to evaluate the simulation performance.
- We plot a series of variable trends under different factor changes and analyze the relationship between mesh partitioning and simulation performance, followed by some advices for improving the simulation performance, which will be helpful to guide the future mesh partitioning.

The rest of the paper is organized as follows. Section 2 reviews the related work. Section 3 introduces the basic idea for designing our experiments. In Sect. 4, we show the experimental results and the detailed evaluations. Section 5 concludes the paper.

2   Related Work

There are various mesh partitioning techniques over the last few decades [3–6]. And there are many representative mesh partitioning software packages based on these techniques, such as Metis [13], Scotch [14], Jostle [15] and Zoltan [16]. Among which, Metis is based on a multi-level graph partitioning while Scotch is based on a divide and conquer approach.

Some works deal with the evaluation of mesh partitioning quality and subsequent simulation performance from some perspectives based on certain partitioning methods. In [17] the author compares the performance including CPU time, speedup and load imbalance of different partitioning methods based on an application case. In [18], the authors test Metis and Scotch algorithms and they compare the quality of them in terms of the number of subdomain elements and the number of processor faces. The research in [19] shows a study on the performance analysis of some partitioning algorithms. The work in [10] presents a study on the impact of partitioning directions on CFD parallel performance. There are some works related to the evaluation of subdomain aspect ratio [20,21]. Moreover, some recent experiments have shown that task mapping can significantly influence the performance of parallel applications [11,12].

All experiments in this paper are conducted on Open Source Field Operation And Manipulation (OpenFOAM) [22], a widely used open source platform based on the FVM [23–25]. Both Metis and Scotch are implemented in OpenFOAM based on third-party packages. Moreover, there are two other mesh partitioning methods in OpenFOAM. One is Simple, a method refers to simple geometric decomposition, and the other is Manual, by which the user directly specifies the allocation of each cell to a particular processor. In our experiments, we will refer to the aforementioned four methods.

3   Methodology

In this section, in order to evaluate the impact of changing the five factors on simulation performance, we design various and numerous mesh partitioning changes based on following five perspectives: the number of processor faces, subdomain aspect ratio, load, partitioning direction and mapping.

3.1   Changing the Number of Processor Faces

First, based on Simple method and the cavity case (a case involving isothermal, incompressible flow in a two-dimensional square domain) [22] in OpenFOAM, we focus on the impact of changing the number of processor faces on the CFD simulation while the load remains unchanged. We produce a 2×2 mesh partitioning by a horizontal line and a vertical line, as Fig. 1(a) shows. The P_ID in Fig. 1 means No. of subdomains. We call this mesh partitioning the initial partitioning. In order to obtain more mesh partitioning results with different numbers of processor faces, we rotate the two lines by some certain counterclockwise angles as Fig. 1(b), (c) and (d) show, during which the load balance remains unchanged. We call this rule the Simple-RotateTwoLines. We achieve eleven representative mesh partitioning results in all. These eleven rotation angles are $7.5°$, $15°$, $22.5°$, $30°$, $37.5°$, $45°$, $52.5°$, $60°$, $67.5°$, $75°$, $82.5°$, respectively. Figure 1(b), (c) and

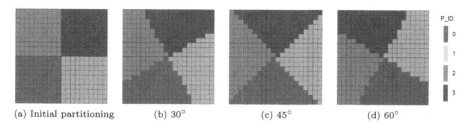

(a) Initial partitioning   (b) 30°   (c) 45°   (d) 60°

Fig. 1. Mesh partitioning results (partial) of original cavity case with Simple-RotateTwoLines

(d) only show three of them. In the later section, we will compare the simulation performance of these eleven mesh partitionings.

3.2   Changing Subdomain Aspect Ratio

Not only the number of processor faces, but also the shape of mesh partitioning will also affect the simulation performance. The shape of mesh partitioning is usually measured by the aspect ratio of subdomains [20,21]. There is a certain class of solution techniques where the shape of subdomains will heavily influence the quality of preconditioning and thus the overall execution time [8]. For example, the time needed by parallel Domain Decomposition Preconditioned Conjugate Gradient (DD-PCG) [26,27] solver, where the decomposition is used to construct preconditioners, is determined by two factors: the maximum time that is needed by any of the subdomain solutions and the number of iterations of the global conjugate gradient. Both factors are at least partially determined by the shape of the subdomains, and the later factor is heavily influenced by the aspect ratio of the subdomains [7].

In OpenFOAM, there are a range of preconditioners for preconditioning of matrices in the PCG solvers [22]. Among which, Diagonal Incomplete-Cholesky (DIC) is frequently used in many cases. In this section, we study the impact of the aspect ratio on the DIC-PCG solver of OpenFOAM platform based on the cavity case. The pressure is solved by DIC-PCG solver in the cavity case.

Firstly, we need to measure the aspect ratio of subdomains. We adopt the definition in [20,21], where the aspect ratio of a two dimensional (2D) subdomain with area ΩS and perimeter ∂S is evaluated by expression $AR = \partial S/4\sqrt{\Omega S}$. This expression suggests that the ideal shape is assumed as square for 2D problem. Note that all geometries are generated in three dimensions in OpenFOAM, but the cavity case we used is specified a empty boundary condition for front and back planes, which means we can treat it as 2D problem.

Next, on the premise of load balancing, we obtain subdomains with different aspect ratios by changing the numbers of partitionings in both x and y directions. In order to get more partitioning results where the mesh is equally divided in two directions, we modify the geometry of the original cavity case as Fig. 2(b) shows, and generate a mesh with $48 \times 48 \times 1$ cells, which is called the modified cavity

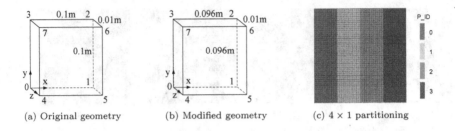

(a) Original geometry   (b) Modified geometry   (c) 4 × 1 partitioning

Fig. 2. The geometry of cavity case and one partitioning result with Simple-$X \times Y$ Partitioning

case. Several $X \times Y$ mesh partitionings are constructed based on the modified cavity case, among which the value of X or Y can be 1, 2, 4, 8, 16. We call this rule the Simple-$X \times Y$ Partitioning. Figure 2 shows the geometry of cavity case and one of partitioning results under this rule.

3.3 Changing Load

It is hard to guarantee a perfect load balance for each mesh partitioning, so it is necessary to study the impact of changing the load on simulation performance. In this section, we consider three methods to change the load: rotation method, translation method and method that sets varying processor weights.

Firstly, we use rotation method and translation method to change the load of mesh partitioning. The idea of rotation is similar to that of Simple-RotateTwoLines, but the difference is that only the vertical line is rotated counterclockwise in the same way as Simple-RotateTwoLines while the horizontal line is fixed. The difference of the numbers of cells between subdomains will increase with increasing rotation angles, thereby the load change will be realized. We call this rule the Simple-RotateOneLine. Figure 3 shows partial rotation results under this rule.

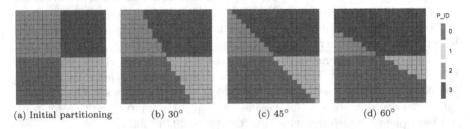

(a) Initial partitioning   (b) 30°   (c) 45°   (d) 60°

Fig. 3. Mesh partitioning results (partial) of original cavity case with Simple-RotateOneLine

The basic idea of translation method is to move the vertical line of the mesh partitioning in horizontal direction or move the horizontal one in vertical direction, so as to change the size of subdomains and thereby make the load unbalanced. We call this rule the Simple-Translation. Figure 4 gives partial results of damBreak case (the feature of this case is a transient flow of two fluids separated by a sharp interface, or free surface) [22] with this rule. Note that in order to improve the resolution of interface of damBreak, we refine the mesh according to the OpenFOAM user guide.

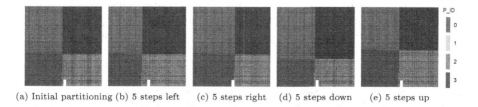

(a) Initial partitioning (b) 5 steps left   (c) 5 steps right   (d) 5 steps down   (e) 5 steps up

Fig. 4. Mesh partitioning results (partial) of damBreak case with Simple-Translation

When we use Metis or Scotch methods, the weights of processors can be set by the optional keyword processorWeights and then the mesh will be decomposed according to the processorWeights. So secondly, we set different values for processorWeights to change the load of mesh partitioning based on Metis and Scotch. We assume there are eight parts of equal weights, which are allocated among four processors. We can get five different allocation results as shown in Figs. 5 and 6. The ratio of each mesh partitioning represents the proportion of

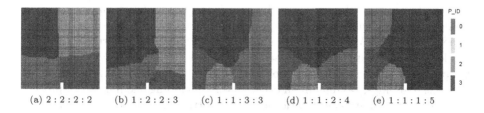

(a) 2 : 2 : 2 : 2   (b) 1 : 2 : 2 : 3   (c) 1 : 1 : 3 : 3   (d) 1 : 1 : 2 : 4   (e) 1 : 1 : 1 : 5

Fig. 5. Mesh partitioning results of damBreak case with Metis-ProcessorWeights

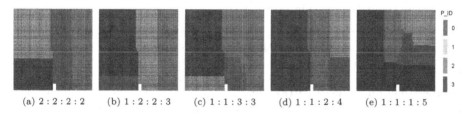

(a) 2 : 2 : 2 : 2   (b) 1 : 2 : 2 : 3   (c) 1 : 1 : 3 : 3   (d) 1 : 1 : 2 : 4   (e) 1 : 1 : 1 : 5

Fig. 6. Mesh partitioning results of damBreak case with Scotch-ProcessorWeights

weights processor 0 to processor 3 own in these eight parts. We call these two rules the Metis-ProcessorWeights and the Scotch-ProcessorWeights respectively.

3.4   Changing Partitioning Direction

Partitioning direction will also affect the simulation performance even though other factors are identical in two mesh partitionings [10]. In this section, we produce two rectangular partitionings and two triangular partitionings. For each two of them, there is a horizontal partitioning and a vertical partitioning. Figure 7 shows the partitioning results, the last two of which are obtained by the Manual method in OpenFOAM. We call this rule the Manual-PartitioningDirection. The only difference is the partitioning direction between Fig. 7(b) and (c), as well as Fig. 7(d) and (e).

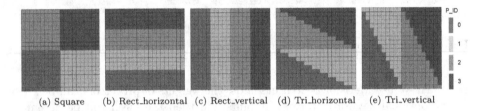

(a) Square   (b) Rect_horizontal   (c) Rect_vertical   (d) Tri_horizontal   (e) Tri_vertical

Fig. 7. Mesh partitioning results of original cavity case with Manual-Partitioning Direction

3.5   Changing Mapping

In order to compare the impact of different mappings on CFD simulation when subdomains are mapped onto processors after partitioning, we have designed various mappings. We first produce a 2 × 2 mesh partitioning formed with four subdomains by Simple method based on modified cavity case, and then modify the processor number of each subdomain. In order to emphasize on the impact of different mappings, we remain all other factors, including the number of processor faces, subdomain aspect ratio, load and partitioning direction, unchanged. There are 24 (24 = 4! = 4×3×2×1) different mappings to map four subdomains onto four processors totally. We call this rule the Simple-TraversalMapping. We will test all these mappings in next section.

3.6   Metrics for Evaluating Mesh Partitioning Quality
and Simulation Performance

In order to evaluate mesh partitioning quality and simulation performance, we choose four metrics: the load imbalance, the maximum number of processor faces, the CFD execution time and the number of iterations.

A mesh partitioning with good quality should satisfy the following two conditions: the numbers of cells for each processor are equal as much as possible and the maximum communication overhead between processors is minimum. In [17], the author takes the load imbalance to measure the first criteria. The load imbalance is defined like this: the number of processors multiplies the maximum number of cells among processors, and then the multiplied result is divided by the whole mesh cells. In [18], the authors take processor faces as the metric for communication overhead and they think that less processor faces will lead to less inter-processor communication.

A CFD simulation with high performance should perform a fast simulation speed and a high iterative convergence rate. In OpenFOAM, the execution time (elapsed CPU time) in the solving process reflects the simulation speed, and the number of iterations reflects the iterative convergence rate.

4 Experimental Results and Analyses

In this section, we carry out our experiments using the methods in Sect. 3. We show the load imbalance, the maximum number of processor faces, the execution time and the number of iterations of different mesh partitionings. Then the results are analyzed to evaluate the impact of changing the five factors on mesh partitioning quality and simulation performance. All experiments are carried out for five times and the average of experiment data is adopted here, aiming at reducing the accidental errors that may occur in a single experiment. Instead of the number of iterations for all variables, here we only consider the number of iterations for p (pressure). This is because p is solved by DIC-PCG solver in both cavity and damBreak cases and the number of iterations of p is far greater than that of other variables by about one order of magnitude in cavity case and by about two order of magnitude in damBreak case.

4.1 Changing the Number of Processor Faces

In Fig. 8, the results of initial partitioning, which is represented by the rotation angle of 0, are given to facilitate the contrast analysis. As we can see from Fig. 8(a), with the increase of rotation angle, the load imbalance keeps unchanged. In the case of balanced load, the rotation of the two lines can lead to changes of the maximum number of processor faces. Different numbers of processor faces mean different communication overhead, so that the execution time will also be different as shown in Fig. 8(b). Moreover, from Fig. 8(a) and (b) we can conclude that the trend of the number of iterations is also roughly the same as that of the maximum number of processor faces.

4.2 Changing Subdomain Aspect Ratio

As Table 1 shows, when the number of subdomains is constant, the number of iterations and the execution time will change with the aspect ratio, and a

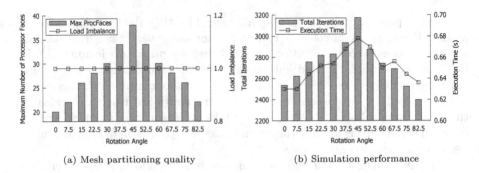

(a) Mesh partitioning quality   (b) Simulation performance

Fig. 8. Experimental results of original cavity case with Simple-RotateTwoLines

Table 1. Experimental results of modified cavity case with Simple-$X \times Y$ Partitioning. For each mesh partitioning, the subdomain aspect ratio, the number of iterations (second line) and the execution time (third line, and the unit is s) are reported.

X	Y				
	1	2	4	8	16
1	AR(1,1) = 1	AR(1,2) = 1.06066	AR(1,4) = 1.25	AR(1,8) = 1.59099	AR(1,16) = 2.125
	12095	14179	15182	16382	18753
	10.368	6.288	4.152	3.09	2.796
2	AR(2,1) = 1.06066	AR(2,2) = 1	AR(2,4) = 1.06066	AR(2,8) = 1.25	AR(2,16) = 1.59099
	14387	14354	15580	17110	20084
	6.318	3.978	2.94	2.63	2.674
4	AR(4,1) = 1.25	AR(4,2) = 1.06066	AR(4,4) = 1	AR(4,8) = 1.06066	AR(4,16) = 1.25
	15182	15782	16022	17727	20420
	4.144	2.974	2.602	2.56	2.788
8	AR(8,1) = 1.59099	AR(8,2) = 1.25	AR(8,4) = 1.06066	AR(8,8) = 1	AR(8,16) = 1.06066
	16554	17119	17424	18791	21867
	3.084	2.674	2.582	2.7	3.262
16	AR(16,1) = 2.125	AR(16,2) = 1.59099	AR(16,4) = 1.25	AR(16,8) = 1.06066	AR(16,16) = 1
	18733	19909	20299	21445	24072
	2.832	2.742	2.828	3.548	4.426

smaller aspect ratio will result in a smaller number of iterations and a shorter execution time. For example, when we fix the number of subdomains as 16, there are five items on back diagonal line. Among these items, the middle item with $AR(4, 4) = 1$ has the smallest number of iterations and the shortest execution time. This indicates that an ideal subdomain shape, such as a square shape, will benefit the simulation performance. Moreover, there are some differences of simulation performance even though $AR(X, Y) = AR(Y, X)$.

4.3 Changing Load

Figures 9, 10 and 11 show the experimental results of changing load.

As shown in Fig. 9(a) and (b), though the maximum numbers of processor faces are still symmetrical with respect to 45°, the execution time curve is very

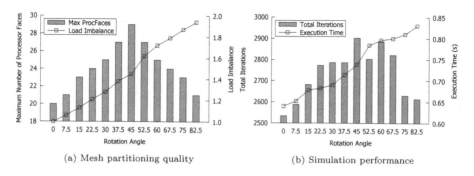

(a) Mesh partitioning quality   (b) Simulation performance

Fig. 9. Experimental results of original cavity case with Simple-RotateOneLine

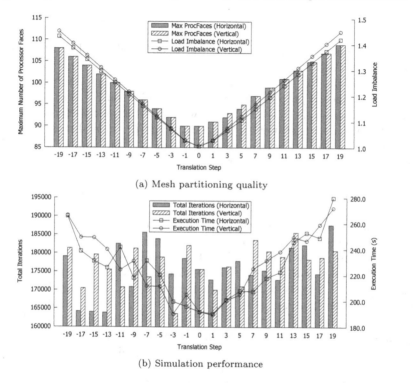

(a) Mesh partitioning quality

(b) Simulation performance

Fig. 10. Experimental results of damBreak case with Simple-Translation

similar to the load imbalance curve, which means that the load imbalance has a greater impact on the execution time in this case. Execution time of applications mainly includes computation time and communication time. Load imbalance will increase the computation time. Meanwhile the increase of the number of processor faces will affect the communication time. It seems that the latter influence is much less than the former one in this case. Similar relationships between the

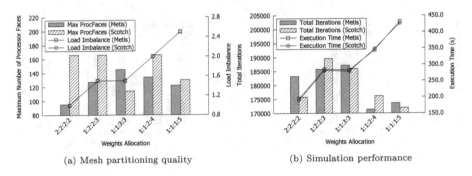

(a) Mesh partitioning quality   (b) Simulation performance

Fig. 11. Experimental results of damBreak case with Metis-ProcessorWeights and Scotch-ProcessorWeights

load imbalance and the execution time can be observed from Fig. 10(a) and (b), as well as Fig. 11(a) and (b).

In Fig. 9(a) and (b), the relationship between the number of iterations and the maximum number of processor faces is similar to that in Fig. 8(a) and (b). But for damBreak case, the relationship between them is quite different as shown in Fig. 10(a) and (b), as well as Fig. 11(a) and (b). In addition, there is no positive correlation between the execution time and the number of iterations. More iterations do not mean longer execution time, as can be seen in Figs. 9(b), 10(b) and 11(b).

Figure 11(a) and (b) indicate that although the mesh partitioning shapes are different for Metis and Scotch under the current rules, the two methods are basically consistent in terms of the load imbalance and the execution time. However, from the perspective of the number of processor faces, Metis generally has less processor faces than Scotch as Fig. 11(a) shows, where there is only an exception for allocation 1 : 1 : 3 : 3. The load imbalance of weights allocations 1 : 2 : 2 : 3 and 1 : 1 : 3 : 3 is approximately equal because that the maximum weights are same here and this leads to the roughly equal numbers of cells. Furthermore, as we can see from Fig. 11(a) and (b), the speed of parallel CFD applications depends on the simulation speed of the largest subdomain. More specifically, the execution time of parallel CFD applications is changing with the size of the largest subdomain. If the size of the largest subdomain of two different mesh partitionings is similar, so is the execution time.

4.4   Changing Partitioning Direction

As shown in Fig. 12, when partitioning the mesh along the vertical direction, we can get a little more iterations comparing with partitioning the mesh along the horizontal direction. Combined with the result of [10], where the number of iterations of the vertical partitioning, on the contrary, are less than that of the horizontal partitioning for a 2D tube flow case, it is indicated that the impact of partitioning direction on CFD problems is the case dependent.

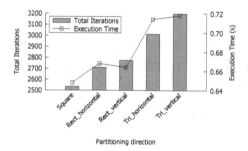

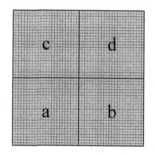

Fig. 12. Simulation performance of original cavity case with Manual-PartitioningDirection

Fig. 13. An illustration of processor number vector (a, b, c, d) of Simple-TraversalMapping

4.5 Changing Mapping

As shown in Fig. 14, there are 24 different mappings which are represented by a series of processor number vectors. The relationship between the processor number vector and the practical mapping is illustrated in Fig. 13. As we can see from Fig. 14, the number of iterations and the execution time will change with the mapping. The original mapping of Simple method (represented by vector $(0, 1, 2, 3)$) has more iterations and longer execution time compared with some other mappings. This indicates that maybe we can improve the simulation performance by changing the mapping of a mesh partitioning. In addition, there is another interesting phenomenon that the position of processor 0 in the vector (that is, which sobdomain the processor 0 possesses) determines the simulation performance of different mappings.

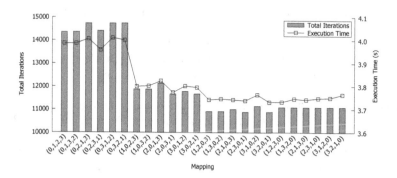

Fig. 14. Simulation performance of modified cavity case with Simple-TraversalMapping

4.6   Analyses

From the above analyses of the experimental results we find that:

- Load balancing is the most important factor that affects mesh partitioning quality and simulation performance. The execution time of parallel CFD applications is usually changing with the size of the largest subdomain. If the size of the largest subdomain of two different mesh partitionings is similar, so is the execution time.
- When the load is balanced, other factors such as the number of processor faces, subdomain aspect ratio, partitioning direction and mapping will also have an impact on simulation performance.
- The smaller the number of processor faces or the smaller the subdomain aspect ratio, then the less the iterations and the shorter the execution time.
- Under the premise that load, the number of processor faces and subdomain aspect ratio are constant, we can possibly improve simulation performance by changing the partitioning direction or the mapping of a mesh partitioning.
- There is no positive correlation between the execution time and the number of iterations, and more iterations do not mean a longer execution time.

We need to pay attention to above factors in mesh partitioning to improve partitioning quality and simulation performance.

5   Conclusion

In this paper, we systematically evaluate the impact of changing the five factors in mesh partitioning process on mesh partitioning quality and CFD simulation performance: the number of processor faces, subdomain aspect ratio, load, partitioning direction and mapping. In order to obtain as many mesh partitioning changes as possible, we adopt some rules to design various and numerous mesh partitioning changes based on four commonly used mesh partitioning methods (Simple, Metis, Scotch and Manual) in OpenFOAM. Through the experiments with the cavity case and the damBreak case, we have obtained some analytical results that can contribute to the future mesh partitioning.

Acknowledgements. The authors would like to thank to the funding from the National Natural Science Foundation of China under grant No.61221491, No.61303071, No.61303068, No.61303063, No.61303061 and No.61120106005, and Open Fund (No. 201402-01, No.201503-01 and No.201503-02) from State Key Laboratory of High Performance Computing.

References

1. Schloegel, K., Karypis, G., Kumar, V.: Graph partitioning for high performance scientific simulations. Army High Performance Computing Research Center (2000)
2. Walshaw, C., Cross, M.: Mesh partitioning: a multilevel balancing and refinement algorithm. SIAM J. Sci. Comput. **22**(1), 63–80 (2000)

3. Berger, M.J., Bokhari, S.H.: A partitioning strategy for nonuniform problems on multiprocessors. IEEE Trans. Comput. **36**(5), 570–580 (1987)
4. Aftosmis, M., Berger, M., Murman, S.: Applications of space-filling-curves to cartesian methods for CFD. In: 42nd AIAA Aerospace Sciences Meeting and Exhibit, p. 1232 (2004)
5. Simon, H.D.: Partitioning of unstructured problems for parallel processing. Comput. Syst. Eng. **2**(2–3), 135–148 (1991)
6. Karypis, G., Kumar, V.: A fast and high quality multilevel scheme for partitioning irregular graphs. SIAM J. Sci. Comput. **20**(1), 359–392 (1998)
7. Diekmann, R., Preis, R., Schlimbach, F., Walshaw, C.: Shape-optimized mesh partitioning and load balancing for parallel adaptive FEM. Parallel Comput. **26**(12), 1555–1581 (2000)
8. Vanderstraeten, D., Keunings, R.: Beyond conventional mesh partitioning algorithms and the minimum edge cut criterion: Impact on realistic applications. Technical report. Society for Industrial and Applied Mathematics, Philadelphia, PA (United States) (1995)
9. Farhat, C., Maman, N., Brown, G.W.: Mesh partitioning for implicit computations via iterative domain decomposition: impact and optimization of the subdomain aspect ratio. Int. J. Numer. Methods Eng. **38**(6), 989–1000 (1995)
10. Li, H., Xu, X., Tang, Y., et al.: A multi-user performance analysis framework for CFD simulations. Prog. Comput. Fluid Dyn. Int. J. **17**(4), 199–211 (2017)
11. Bhatelé, A., Kalé, L.V., Kumar, S.: Dynamic topology aware load balancing algorithms for molecular dynamics applications. In: Proceedings of the 23rd International Conference on Supercomputing, pp. 110–116. ACM (2009)
12. Aktulga, H.M., Yang, C., Ng, E.G., Maris, P., Vary, J.P.: Topology-aware mappings for large-scale eigenvalue problems. In: Kaklamanis, C., Papatheodorou, T., Spirakis, P.G. (eds.) Euro-Par 2012. LNCS, vol. 7484, pp. 830–842. Springer, Heidelberg (2012). doi:10.1007/978-3-642-32820-6_82
13. Karypis, G., Kumar, V.: A software package for partitioning unstructured graphs, partitioning meshes, and computing fill-reducing orderings of sparse matrices. Department of Computer Science and Engineering, Army HPC Research Center, University of Minnesota, Minneapolis, MN (1998)
14. Pellegrini, F., Roman, J.: Scotch: a software package for static mapping by dual recursive bipartitioning of process and architecture graphs. In: Liddell, H., Colbrook, A., Hertzberger, B., Sloot, P. (eds.) HPCN-Europe 1996. LNCS, vol. 1067, pp. 493–498. Springer, Heidelberg (1996). doi:10.1007/3-540-61142-8_588
15. Walshaw, C., Cross, M.: JOSTLE: parallel multilevel graph-partitioning software – an overview. In: Magoules, F. (ed.) Mesh Partitioning Techniques and Domain Decomposition Techniques, pp. 27–58. Civil-Comp Ltd. (2007)
16. Devine, K., Boman, E., Heaphy, R., Hendrickson, B., Vaughan, C.: Zoltan data management service for parallel dynamic applications. Comput. Sci. Eng. **4**(2), 90–97 (2002)
17. Shang, Z.: Large-scale CFD parallel computing dealing with massive mesh. J. Eng. **2013**, 6 (2013). Article ID 850148
18. Šidlof, P., Horáček, J., Řidký, V.: Parallel CFD simulation of flow in a 3D model of vibrating human vocal folds. Comput. Fluids **80**, 290–300 (2013)
19. Wang, M., Tang, Y., Guo, X., Ren, X.: Performance analysis of the graph-partitioning algorithms used in OpenFOAM. In: 2012 IEEE Fifth International Conference on Advanced Computational Intelligence (ICACI), pp. 99–104. IEEE (2012)

20. Walshaw, C., Cross, M., Diekmann, R., Schlimbach, F.: Multilevel mesh partitioning for optimising aspect ratio. In: Hernández, V., Palma, J.M.L.M., Dongarra, J.J. (eds.) VECPAR 1998. LNCS, vol. 1573, pp. 285–300. Springer, Heidelberg (1999). doi:10.1007/10703040_23
21. Rao, A.R.M.: Parallel mesh-partitioning algorithms for generating shape optimised partitions using evolutionary computing. Adv. Eng. Softw. **40**(2), 141–157 (2009)
22. OpenFOAM User Guide: Version 2.3.0, 5 February 2014
23. Guo, X.W., Zou, S., Yang, X., Yuan, X.F., Wang, M.: Interface instabilities and chaotic rheological responses in binary polymer mixtures under shear flow. RSC Adv. **4**(105), 61167–61177 (2014)
24. Zhang, T.T., Yang, W.J., Lin, Y.F., Cao, Y., Wang, M., Wang, Q., Wei, Y.X.: Numerical study on flow rate limitation of open capillary channel flow through a wedge. Adv. Mech. Eng. **8**(4), 1–11 (2016). doi:10.1177/1687814016645487
25. Li, C., Yang, W., Xu, X., Wang, J., Wang, M., Xu, L.: Numerical investigation of fish exploiting vortices based on the kármán gaiting model. Ocean Eng. **140**, 7–18 (2017)
26. Bramble, J.H., Pasciak, J.E., Schatz, A.H.: The construction of preconditioners for elliptic problems by substructuring. I. Math. Comput. **47**(175), 103–134 (1986)
27. Bramble, J.H., Pasciak, J.E., Schatz, A.H.: The construction of preconditioners for elliptic problems by substructuring. II. Math. Comput. **49**(179), 1–16 (1987)

Bat Algorithm Based Low Power Mapping Methods for 3D Network-on-Chips

Jiazheng Li[1,2], Guozhi Song[1(✉)], Yue Ma[1], Cheng Wang[3],
Baohui Zhu[1], Yan Chai[1], and Jieqi Rong[1]

[1] School of Computer Science and Software Engineering,
Tianjin Polytechnic University, Tianjin 300387, China
guozhi.song@gmail.com
[2] School of Information Sciences, University of Illinois at Urbana-Champaign,
Champaign, IL 61820, USA
[3] School of Information Science, Yunnan University, Kunming 650500,
Yunnan, China

Abstract. Mapping a task graph as a distribution of Intellectual Property (IP) cores onto a Network-on-Chip (NoC) is a NP-hard problem that significantly affects the performance metrics of the whole system including power, delay, load balance and heat. Intelligence optimization algorithms are widely used to solve mapping problems. Bat Algorithm (BA), a novel metaheuristic algorithm mimicking hunting behaviors of bats, which has never been applied in NoCs, is used in low power mapping methods for 3D NoCs in this paper for the first time. The BA based mapping algorithm shows better performance than other mainstream mapping algorithms in terms of the optimization efficiency and power consumption. However, the concept of the basic BA has obvious disadvantages. To improve the basic BA, we propose a Group-Searching Bat Algorithm (GSBA) that can better utilize individual bats. This improved mapping algorithm performs much better than the traditional BA, especially when the scale of the application graph is large.

Keywords: Network-on-Chip · Mapping algorithm · Low power · Bat Algorithm · Parallel computing

1 Introduction

Along with the rapid development of VLSI technology, processing elements (PE) integrated on a single chip are becoming more. Network-on-Chip is a novel architecture of System-on-Chip proposed to adapt this tendency [1]. Key problems of NoCs are categorized into three parts, i.e. NoC infrastructure, communication paradigm, and application mapping [2]. From 2D to 3D NoCs, how to map applications onto NoCs is always a crucial issue attracting scholars all over the world. A good mapping algorithm can be helpful in reducing power consumption and execution time, balancing the load, and decreasing communication delay, thus improving the whole efficiency and performance of a system [3]. Mapping for NoCs is a NP-hard problem, so intelligence algorithms are excellent methods to solve it [4].

© Springer Nature Singapore Pte Ltd. 2017
D. Du et al. (Eds.): NCTCS 2017, CCIS 768, pp. 277–295, 2017.
https://doi.org/10.1007/978-981-10-6893-5_21

Bats, one of the most fascinating species, have the amazing ability of using acoustic wave to locate their preys and avoid obstacles. This behavior is called echolocation. Inspired by echolocation of bats, Xin-She Yang proposed a novel metaheuristic algorithm-Bat Algorithm [5]. BA and BA-based methods has been widely used in numerical optimization, engineering optimization and other optimization areas.

However, the concept of BA has never been applied to solve NoC mapping problems. In this paper, we introduce the BA concept to 3D NoC mapping for the first time. The BA-based mapping algorithm shows better performance than other two mainstream heuristic mapping algorithms, i.e. Genetic Algorithm (GA) and Particle Swarm Algorithm (PSO). After careful analysis, we find that the basic BA has certain shortcomings. To increase the efficiency of BA, we propose an improved BA called GSBA. The experimental results show that GSBA is far superior to BA in terms of convergence and power consumption.

The rest of this paper is organized as followings. Section 2 introduces basic concepts and necessary formulation of 3D NoC mapping problem and process. The standard BA for numerical optimization is elaborated in Sect. 3. Based on the givens of previous sections, Sect. 4 applies the standard BA in 3D NoC mapping and compares it with GA and PSO. Summarizing and analyzing some flaws of basic BA, Sect. 5 proposes a parallel computing approach called GSBA to improve it, and does experiments and simulations to verify the efficiency of the improved algorithm. Finally, Sect. 6 gives the conclusion of this paper and expectation of future works.

2   Problem Formulation for 3D NoC Mapping

In this paper, each mapping process is based on the condition that the Application Characteristic Graph (ACG) to be mapped and the Topology Architecture Graph (TAG) of a NoC are given. We also assume that a node of the ACG represents an IP core operating certain tasks. Here an IP core could be any functional modules such as a microprocessor. The aim of mapping is to distribute the IP cores on the ACG onto the resource nodes on the TAG of the NoC in one-to-one correspondence properly, trying to find one arrangement that consumes the power as low as possible.

2.1   Definitions and Constraint Conditions

To clearly demonstrate the mapping problem, here we give three necessary definitions and according examples.

Definition 1. Given an ACG $G(V, E)$ where a node $v_i \in V$ represents an IP core identified by an integer, a directed edge $e_{i,j} \in E$ represents the communication path between cores v_i and v_j and the weight of this edge represents the communication traffic between the two cores. Figure 1 shows a classical ACG called Picture-In-Picture (PIP).

Definition 2. Given a TCG $T(R, P)$ where a node $r_i \in T$ represents a resource node (namely, a PE), a directed edge $p_{i,j} \in P$ represents the communication path between nodes r_i and r_j and $h_{i,j}$ represents the Manhattan distance between the two nodes.

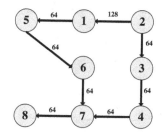

Fig. 1. Classical ACG PIP

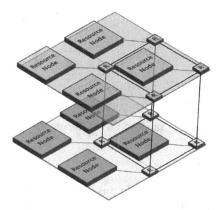

Fig. 2. A $2 \times 2 \times 2$ mesh structure NoC

Figure 2 gives an example of a $2 \times 2 \times 2$ Mesh structure NoC and Fig. 3 shows its according TAG.

Definition 3. Knowing an ACG with m cores and a TCG with n nodes (n ≥ m), one mapping assignment is represented by $(x_1, x_2, x_3, \ldots x_m)$ where x_i means putting the ith core of the ACG on the x_i th node on the TCG. Here we give an example of this real-number coding method: the mapping result of PIP ACG onto the $2 \times 2 \times 2$ NoC TAG shown in Fig. 3 is represented by (4, 1, 2, 3, 7, 6, 8, 5) (Fig. 4).

Based on the definitions above, the mapping process can be described as: given G and T, we try to find the mapping function $map()$ that would optimize the objective function. The mapping process must meet some specific constraint conditions as followings meanwhile.

$$\forall v_i \in V \Rightarrow map(v_i) \in R \qquad (1)$$

$$\forall v_i \neq v_j \Leftrightarrow map(v_i) \neq map(v_j) \qquad (2)$$

$$size(G) \leq size(T) \qquad (3)$$

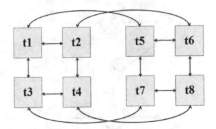

Fig. 3. The TAG of the NoC in Fig. 2

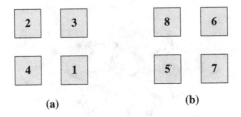

Fig. 4. One mapping result of PIP ACG onto the TAG in Fig. 3

2.2 Power Model for Mapping

The aim of optimized mapping methods in this paper is trying to reduce the total power consumption as much as possible. So power models for 3D NoCs are closely connected with the design of the objective function (i.e. the fitness function in the intelligence optimization process).

We use the power model given in [6]. The average energy consumed of transmitting one bit data form nodes r_i to r_j is calculated by

$$E_{bit}^{i,j} = \mu E_{Rbit} + \mu_H E_{LHbit} + \mu_V E_{LVbit} \tag{4}$$

where μ represents the number of routers from r_i to r_j, μ_H and μ_V represent numbers of horizontal and vertical links in the communication path respectively, and E_{LHbit} and E_{LVbit} represent consumed power of transmitting one bit data through one horizontal and one vertical link respectively.

The total power consumption thus would be represented as

$$E_{total} = \sum_{i=1}^{m} \sum_{j=1}^{m} (E_{bit}^{i,j} \times weight_{i,j}) \tag{5}$$

where $weight_{i,j}$ represents the communication traffic from r_i to r_j. This paper aims to minimize E_{total}.

3   Basic Concepts of Standard Bat Algorithm

Bats, the only mammal species with wings in the world, have amazing capability of echolocation. The frequencies of acoustic waves emitted by bats vary from different kinds of bats. Typical frequencies range from 25 to 150 kHz. Each ultrasonic burst typically lasts 5 to 20 ms. And a bat typically emits 10 to 20 bursts per second. When hunting and getting closer to their preys, the pulse emission rate can be sped up to about 200 pulses per second. The loudness of the pulses would normally decrease when flying to the preys. Modeling the echolocation behaviors of bat, BA was proposed [5]. Applied in various test problems, BA has shown its excellent efficiency in global engineering optimization [7]. BA performs nicely in terms of both local search and global search.

3.1   Global Search

In BA, we regard an individual bat as one solution of the optimization problem. The principle of BA global search is that other bats move towards the current best individual at some certain paces in one iteration. The bats change their positions according to the following rules.

$$V_i^{t+1} = V_i^t + \left(X_i^t - X_*\right)f_i \tag{6}$$

$$X_i^{t+1} = X_i^t + V_i^{t+1} \tag{7}$$

where V_i^t is the velocity of the ith individual bat at time t and X_i^t is its according position, X_* is the current global best position, and f_i is the frequency of this bat that controls how long one pace is calculated by

$$f_i = f_{min} + (f_{max} - f_{min})\beta \tag{8}$$

where $[f_{min}, f_{max}]$ is the range of frequencies corresponding to the wavelength range $[\lambda_{min}, \lambda_{max}]$, and $\beta \in [0, 1]$ is a random number. The selection of f_i is related to the problem to be solved.

3.2   Local Search

The concept of BA local search is that one individual bat moves a small step around its neighborhood to look for a better solution. The movement of this individual bat can be mathematized as

$$X_{new} = X_{old} + \varepsilon \overline{A^t} \tag{9}$$

where $\varepsilon \in [-1, 1]$ is a random number and $\overline{A^t}$ is the average loudness of all bats at time t.

As in nature, the loudness A_i and the pulse emission rate R_i need to be updated during the optimization. As the iterations proceed, A_i decreases while R_i increases as

$$A_i^{t+1} = \alpha A_i^t \tag{10}$$

$$R_i^{t+1} = R_i^0[1 - \exp(-\gamma t)] \tag{11}$$

where α and γ are constants, and R_i^0 is the maximum pulse emission rate. Here α actually resembles the cooling factor in simulated annealing algorithm (SA). For any $0 < \alpha < 1$ and $\gamma > 0$, there is

$$ast \rightarrow \infty, A_i^t \rightarrow 0, R_i^t \rightarrow R_i^0 \tag{12}$$

3.3 Specific Steps

The specific steps of standard BA can be elaborated as followings.

Step (1) Confirm the objective function $f(X)$, the population scale and the number of iteration times.

Step (2) Randomly initialize the population and velocities V_i^0 of individuals.

Step (3) Use formula (8) to give each individual bat a constant frequency f_i.

Step (4) Initialize A_i^0 and R_i^0 for each individual bat.

Step (5) Find the current global best position X_* according to the fitness function.

Step (6) Update velocities and positions of individuals by formulas (6) and (7).

Step (7) For each individual bat, generate a random number $rand1_i$; if $rand1_i > R_i^t$, use formula (9) to accomplish the local search.

Step (8) Calculate the new fitness value of each individual.

Step (9) For each individual bat, generate a random number $rand2_i$; if $rand2_i < A_i^t$ and $f(X_{new}) < f(X_{old})$, accept the new solution.

Step (10) Increase R_i and decrease A_i using (10) and (11).

Step (11) Find the new global best individual.

Step (12) If the number of iteration times is met, output the best solution X_*; otherwise, jump to Step (6) and proceed the iteration.

4 Standard BA Based Mapping Method for 3D NoC

BA has been successfully applied in many domains, especially NP-hard problems, and shown its great efficiency. Wang et al. used BA in path planning for uninhabited combat air vehicle (UCAV) [8]. Bahman and Rasoul proposed an improved BA to develop strategies for Battery Energy Storage (BES) management [9]. Osaba et al. presented the first Discrete Bat Algorithm to solve Traveling Salesman Problem (TSP) and Asymmetric Traveling Salesman Problem (ATSP) [10]. Tangherloni et al. adopted BA in biochemical kinetic values parameter estimation [11].

However, such an efficient algorithm has never been used in the research on NoC design. Targeting at reducing power consumption of mapping applications onto 3D NoCs, we firstly try BA in the field of NoC.

However, we could not directly apply the standard BA, which is for continuous optimization problems, in 3D NoC mapping, a NP-hard combinatorial optimization problem with very strict constraint conditions. What we could do is to introduce the principle and the basic thought of BA to 3D NoC mapping, and properly modify them due to the particularity of our target problem.

4.1 Basic Idea

Heuristic algorithms have been the main methods in 3D NoC mapping [4]. The basic principle of all heuristic algorithms is generating a population group in which the individuals change following some special rules with various algorithms. We have mentioned in Sect. 2 that one mapping assignment is represented by $(x_1, x_2, x_3, \ldots x_m)$ where m is the number of IP cores to be mapped, and constrained that IP cores of an ACG and PEs on a TAG are in one-to-one correspondence. So one population of individuals used in our optimization is a set of mapping results.

In the iteration process, we use the searching principles of BA. To achieve global search, other non-best individuals are moving towards the current global best at a settled pace in each iteration. The "pace" here is different from one pace in numerical optimization. We define one pace movement of a non-best individual bat is changing one or two IP cores' positions, making the layout of this individual more alike with that of the current global best individual X_*. For a non-best individual X_i, this procedure is shown in Fig. 5 where we define $X_{i(k)}$ as the position of the kth IP core in the solution X_i.

And we also have the local search method. The procedure could be described as: randomly select an IP core and put it on another position of the NoC; if there is already an IP core on this position, swap the positions of the two IP cores. We call this shaking a mapping assignment.

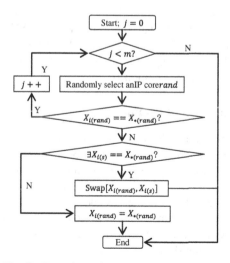

Fig. 5. Procedure of one pace movement of X_i

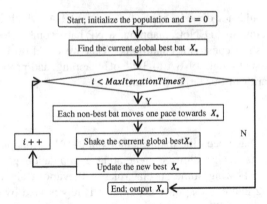

Fig. 6. BA based 3D NoC mapping algorithm

Combining the global search method and the local search method, we have the BA based optimization mapping algorithm for 3D NoC, as shown in Fig. 6.

4.2 Fitness Function Design

Actually, in the optimization process, only when the fitness value of one individual bat gets better, we accept the change. Fitness function is the criterion to evaluate a solution.

We extract our fitness function from the power model mention in formula (4) and (5). And we use XYZ routing algorithm [12] in our simulations. So the fitness function used in our optimization could designed as

$$Fitness = \sum_{i=1}^{m} \sum_{j=1}^{m} [(X_{i,j} + Y_{i,j})weight_{i,j} + Z_{i,j}] \tag{13}$$

where $X_{i,j}$, $Y_{i,j}$ and $Z_{i,j}$ are the numbers of links from core i to core j on x-axis, y-axis and z-axis respectively. Because of Through Silicon Vias (TSV) technology [13], the energy consumed vertically would be far less than the energy consumed horizontally. So $Z_{i,j}$ does not multiply by $weight_{i,j}$. From formula (13) we could see that the smaller the fitness value is, the better the solution is.

4.3 Comparison with GA and PSO on Convergence

After designing the algorithm and the fitness function. To verify the efficiency and superiority of BA based mapping algorithm, we conduct experiments comparing BA with GA [14] and PSO [15] under the same conditions. In this section, we use three classical ACGs: Multi-Window Displayer (MWD), Video Object Plane Decoder (VOPD) and Double Video Object Plane Decoder (DVOPD), as shown in Fig. 7.

To compare the three algorithms in terms of convergence, we run each algorithm for 10 times for each ACG, and we draw the average curve of 10 times experiments for clear description and avoiding deviation.

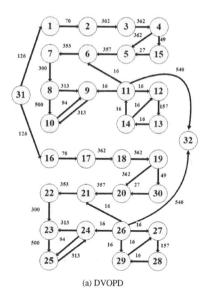

(a) DVOPD

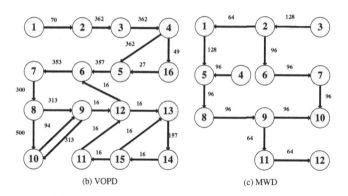

(b) VOPD   (c) MWD

Fig. 7. Three classical ACGs

MWD has 12 cores and 14 edges. We map it onto a 2 × 2 × 3 mesh structure 3D NoC. And here the population of 3 algorithms is 50 and the number of max iteration times is 100. The average curves of 3 algorithms for mapping MWD are shown in Fig. 8.

VOPD has 16 cores and 21 edges. We map it onto a 3 × 3 × 3 mesh structure 3D NoC. And here the population of 3 algorithms is 100 and the number of maximum iteration times is 200. The average curves of 3 algorithms for mapping VOPD are shown in Fig. 9.

DVOPD has 32 cores and 44 edges. We map it onto a 4 × 4 × 3 mesh structure 3D NoC. And here the population of 3 algorithms is 200 and the number of max iteration times is 300. The average curves of 3 algorithms for mapping VOPD are shown in Fig. 10.

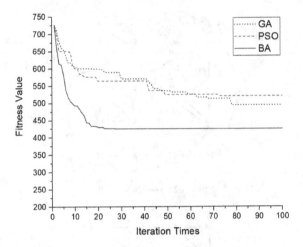

Fig. 8. Curves of 3 algorithms for mapping MWD

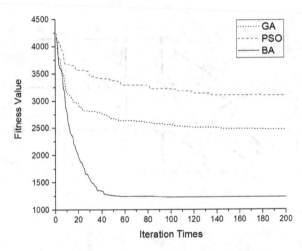

Fig. 9. Curves of 3 algorithms for mapping VOPD

From the mapping curves of 3 algorithms for 3 classical ACGs, we could see that for all the ACGs, BA could find better solutions with smaller fitness values. And for ACGs with larger scales, BA performs much better than other two algorithms.

4.4 Comparison with GA and PSO on Power Consumption

After getting the mapping results, to compare the power consumption situations, we generate communication files of the mapping results, and do simulations according the communication files on Access Noxim 0.2 platform [16]. Main simulation parameters are given in Table 1.

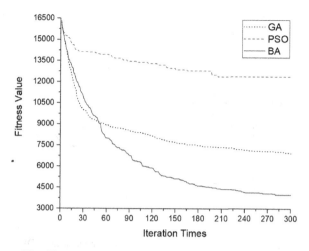

Fig. 10. Curves of 3 Algorithms for Mapping DVOPD

Table 1. Simulation parameters

Simulation parameter	Default value
Packet injection rate	0.02
Packet injection mode	Memory-less poisson distribution
Sizes of packets	2 to 10 flits
Channel buffer	8 flits

Setting the parameters, we do simulations using the final mapping results we obtained in the last part. For each ACG, the power consumption for every 10 mapping assignments of 3 algorithms are simulated and drawn in boxplots in the following Figs. 11, 12 and 13. Each calculated power consumed is for the whole system running an ACG.

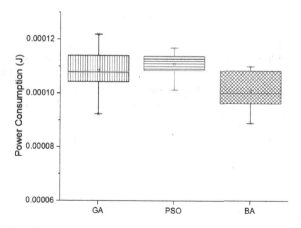

Fig. 11. Power consumption comparison for mapping MWD

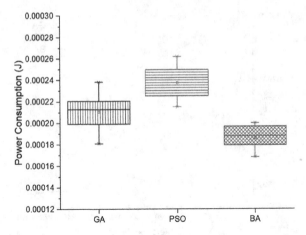

Fig. 12. Power consumption comparison for mapping VOPD

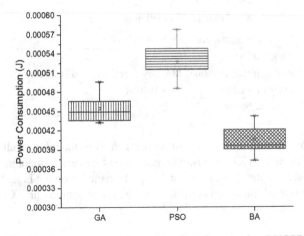

Fig. 13. Power consumption comparison for mapping DVOPD

We can observe that BA shows lower power consumption than GA and PSO. And the larger the scale of the ACG is, the more obviously BA excels other two algorithms. For MWD, the average power consumption of 10 times simulations of BA is 6.82% lower than that of GA and 8.91% lower than that of PSO. For VOPD, this figure of BA is 11.37% and 21.43% lower than those of GA and PSO respectively. For DVOPD, this figure of BA is 10.77% and 29.81% lower than those of GA and PSO respectively.

5   GSBA Based Mapping Method for 3D NoC

We successfully used standard BA in 3D NoC mapping in the last section. It has shown its great efficiency and searching ability. However, standard BA has certain defect like lack of diversity and instability of optimization accuracy. To improve the traditional BA, many approaches have been proposed. Fister et al. hybridized BA using Differential Evolution (DE) strategies [17]. Zhao and He presented a binary BA with chaos and Doppler effect [18]. Xue has done very deep research on BA and proposed several improvements [19]. And in this paper, aiming at increase the utilization of individuals and improve the diversity of populations, we propose a Group-Searching Bat Algorithm (GSBA).

5.1   GSBA Principles and Steps

Figure 14 is an example of showing one shortcoming of standard BA. For DVOPD, we use different population scale of BA for 10 times and draw the average curve.

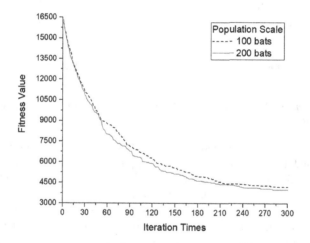

Fig. 14. 100-bat and 200-bat population scale for mapping DVOPD

It is obvious that the 200-bat population does not excel 100-bat population very much. This means that as the scale of population increase, standard BA cannot efficiently utilize each individual bat as we hope. The method that, all other bats move towards the current global best, lacks of diversity. To improve this, we introduce a group-searching method based on parallel computing into BA.

The basic principle of GSBA is that instead of only choosing the global best, we divide the population into several groups, and find the group best bats. In the iterations, each non-best individual in a group moves towards its group best. In this way, the bats in different groups fly to their own group best bat independently and simultaneously, thus the utilization of individual bats and diversity of the population are improved.

Except from this, to connect different groups and maintain the overall globality of the algorithm, after the group movements, we let each other group best individual move towards the global best. We also reinforce the local search to increase the searching accuracy. The specific steps of GSBA based mapping algorithm for 3D NoC are given in Fig. 15.

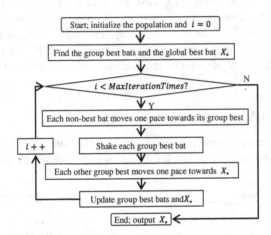

Fig. 15. GSBA based 3D NoC mapping algorithm

5.2 Experimental Results of Three Classical ACGs Comparing BA and GSBA

In this part, we do experiments and simulations to compare BA and GSBA in terms of convergence and power consumption by mapping three classical ACGs. Here the iteration times and population scales, and the NoCs structures are the same as Sect. 4.

To map MWD, the 50-bat population is divided into 5 groups. The convergence and power comparison between BA and GSBA are shown in Figs. 16 and 17.

To map VOPD, the 100-bat population is divided into 10 groups. The convergence and power comparison between BA and GSBA are shown in Figs. 18 and 19.

To map DVOPD, the 200-bat population is divided into 10 groups. The convergence and power comparison between BA and GSBA are shown in Figs. 20 and 21.

From these Figs, we could see that for MWD with the smallest scale, the optimization efficiency and power consumption of the two algorithms are almost the same. However, for VOPD and DVOPD with larger scales, the superiority of GSBA is obvious. In mapping VOPD, the average total power consumption of GSBA is 5.34% lower than that of standard BA. In mapping DVOPD, the average total power consumption of GSBA is 10.11% lower than its counterpart.

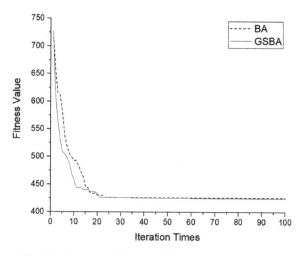

Fig. 16. Curves of BA and GSBA for mapping MWD

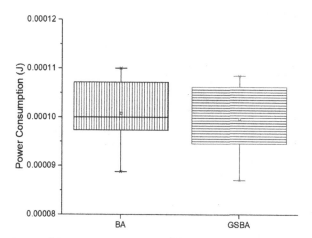

Fig. 17. Power consumption comparison for mapping MWD

5.3 Experimental Results of Five Random ACGs Comparing BA and GSBA

In this part, we do experiments and simulations to compare BA and GSBA in terms of convergence and power consumption by mapping five randomly generated ACGs. We use the random ACG generator TGFF [20] to make random ACGs in different scales. We generate 5 ACGs with 13 cores and 12 edges, 21 cores and 24 edges, 41 cores and 48 edges, 81 cores and 99 edges, and 101 cores and 129 edges respectively.

To map a random ACG with 13 cores and 12 edges, we use the 3 × 3 × 3 Mesh structure heterogeneous NoC. The number of iteration times is 100 and the population scale is 50. We divide the 50-bat population into 5 groups.

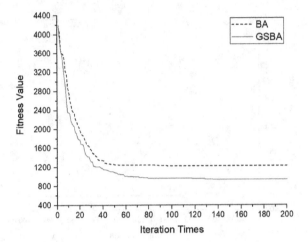

Fig. 18. Curves of BA and GSBA for mapping VOPD

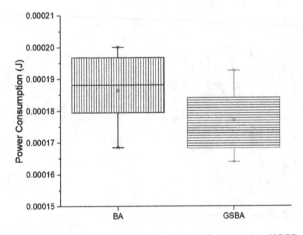

Fig. 19. Power consumption comparison for mapping VOPD

To map a random ACG with 21 cores and 24 edges, we use the $3 \times 3 \times 3$ Mesh structure heterogeneous NoC. The number of iteration times is 200 and the population scale is 10. We divide the 100-bat population into 10 groups.

To map a random ACG with 41 cores and 48 edges, we use the $4 \times 4 \times 3$ Mesh structure heterogeneous NoC. The number of iteration times is 200 and the population scale is 300. We divide the 200-bat population into 10 groups.

To map a random ACG with 81 cores and 99 edges, we use the $5 \times 5 \times 4$ Mesh structure heterogeneous NoC. The number of iteration times is 300 and the population scale is 200. We divide the 200-bat population into 10 groups.

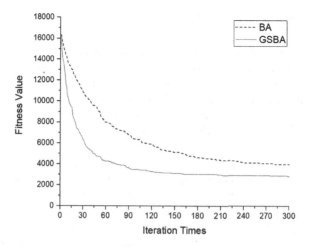

Fig. 20. Curves of BA and GSBA for mapping DVOPD

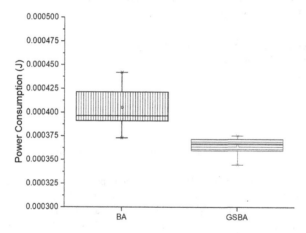

Fig. 21. Power consumption comparison for mapping DVOPD

To map a random ACG with 101 cores and 129 edges, we use the 5 × 5 × 5 Mesh structure heterogeneous NoC. The number of iteration times is 300 and the population scale is 200. We divide the 200-bat population into 10 groups.

For the random ACG in 13/12 scale, the average total power consumption of GSBA is 14.75% lower than that of standard BA. For the random ACG in 21/24 scale, that of GSBA is 10.32% lower than that of standard BA. For the random ACG in 41/48 scale, that of GSBA is 21.59% lower than that of standard BA. For the random ACG in 81/99 scale, that of GSBA is 30.16% lower than that of standard BA. For the random ACG in 101/129 scale, that of GSBA is 24.64% lower than that of its counterpart. Given the experimental data for five random ACGs in different scales, it is undoubted that GSBA has better efficiency and low power consumption than its counterpart, especially when the scale of the ACG is larger.

6   Conclusion and Future Work

In this paper, we successfully apply a novel heuristic algorithm called bat algorithm in low power mapping design methods for 3D NoC. This new algorithm performs better than other two mainstream mapping algorithms in terms of convergence and power consumption. However, we find that standard BA has certain weakness, thus proposing GSBA to increase the individual utilization and diversity of BA. Experimental results show that the improved BA with group-searching strategy is much superior to standard BA.

The limitation of this paper is that we optimize only one metric for 3D NoC. In our future work, we will focus on designing multi-objective optimization methods [21, 22], based on BA and its improvements, to optimize more than one performance metrics of power, heat, delay and load balance simultaneously.

And for the proposed GSBA, it is apparent that GSBA with different numbers of groups would perform very differently. In the future, we will explore the relationship between the efficiency and performance of GSBA and how to divide the population into groups by both experimental verification and theoretical support, trying to find the optimal group division method.

Acknowledgement. The authors were support by National Training Program of Innovation and Entrepreneurship for Undergraduates No. 201710058042 and 201710058009. We thank the anonymous reviewers for commenting on this paper.

References

1. Benini, L., De Micheli, G.: Networks on chips: a new SoC paradigm. Computer **35**(1), 70–78 (2002)
2. Ogras, U.Y., Hu, J., Marculescu, R.: Key research problems in NoC design: a holistic perspective. In: Proceedings of CODES+ISSS, Jersey City, NJ, pp. 69–74, September 2005
3. Hu, J., Marculescu, R.: Energy- and performance-aware mapping for regular NoC architectures. IEEE Trans. Comput. Aided Des. Integr. Circ. Syst. **24**(4), 551–562 (2005)
4. Huang, C., Zhang, D.K., Song, G.Z.: Survey on mapping algorithm of three-dimensional network on chip. J. Chin. Comput. Syst. **37**(2), 193–201 (2016)
5. Yang, X.S.: A new metaheuristic bat-inspired algorithm. In: González, J.R., et al. (eds.) Nature Inspired Cooperative Strategies for Optimization (NISCO 2010). SCI, vol. 284, pp. 65–74. Springer, Heidelberg (2010)
6. Wang, X.H., Liu, P., Yang, M., Palesi, M., Jiang, Y.T., Huang, M.C.: Energy efficient run-time incremental mapping for 3-D networks-on-chip. J. Comput. Sci. Technol. **28**(1), 54–71 (2013)
7. Yang, X.S., Gandomi, A.H.: Bat algorithm: a novel approach for global engineering optimization. Eng. Comput. **29**(5), 464–483 (2012)
8. Wang, G.G., Guo, L.H., Duan, H., Liu, L., Wang, H.Q.: A bat algorithm with mutation for UCAV path planning. Sci. World J. (2012). Article ID 418946
9. Bahman, B.F., Rasoul, A.A.: Optimal sizing of battery energy storage for micro-grid operation management using a new improved bat algorithm. Int. J. Electr. Power Energy Syst. **56**(3), 42–54 (2014)

10. Osaba, E., et al.: An improved discrete bat algorithm for symmetric and asymmetric traveling salesman problems. Eng. Appl. Artif. Intell. **48**(C), 59–71 (2016)
11. Tangherloni, A., Nobile, M.S., Cazzaniga, P.: GPU-powered bat algorithm for the parameter estimation of biochemical kinetic values. In: IEEE International Conference on Computational Intelligence in Bioinformatics and Computational Biology (CIBCB 2016), Chiang Mai, Thailand, October 2016
12. Zhang, D.K., Huang, C., Song, G.Z.: Survey on three-dimensional network-on-chip. J. Softw. **27**(1), 155–187 (2016)
13. Black, B., Annavaram, M., Brekelbaum, N., DeVale, J., Jiang, L., Loh, G.H. et al.: Die stacking (3D) microarchitecture. In: IEEE/ACM International Symposium on Microarchitecture, pp. 469–479. IEEE Xplore (2006)
14. Addo-Quaye, C.: Thermal-aware mapping and placement for 3-D NoC designs. In: Proceedings of IEEE International SOC Conference, pp. 25–28. IEEE Xplore (2005)
15. Yang, W., Zhang, Z., Liu, Y.J.: Improved particle swarm optimization algorithm based mapping algorithm for 3D-Mesh CMP. Appl. Res. Comput. **30**(5), 1345–1348 (2013)
16. Jheng, K.Y., Chao, C.H., Wang, H.Y., Wu, A.Y.: Traffic-thermal mutual-coupling co-simulation platform for three-dimensional network-on-chip. In: International Symposium on VLSI Design Automation and Test, vol. 54, pp. 135–138. IEEE Explore (2010)
17. Fister, Jr., I., Fong, S., Brest, J., Fister, I.: A novel hybrid self-adaptive bat algorithm. Sci. World J. (2014). Article ID 709738
18. Zhao, D.S., He, Y.Z.: A novel binary bat algorithm with chaos and doppler effect in echoes for analog fault diagnosis. Analog Integr. Circ. Sig. Process **87**(3), 437–450 (2016)
19. Xue, F.: Research and application of heuristic intelligence optimization based on bat algorithm. Doctoral Dissertation, Beijing University of Technology (2016)
20. Dick, R.P., Rhodes, D.L., Wolf, W.: TGFF: task graphs for free. In: Proceedings of the Sixth IEEE International Workshop on Hardware/Software Codesign (CODES/CASHE 1998), pp. 97–101 (1998)
21. Tornero, R., Sterrantino, V., Palesi, M., Orduna, J.M.: A multi-objective strategy for concurrent mapping and routing in networks on chip. In: IEEE International Symposium on Parallel and Distributed Processing (IPDPS), Rome, Italy, May. 2009
22. Yang, X.S.: Bat algorithm for multi-objective optimisation. Int. J. Bio Inspir. Comput. **3**(5), 267–274 (2012)

A Hybrid Adaptive Dissemination Solution Based on Geographic Distance for Vehicular Ad Hoc Networks

Qi Fu[1]([⊠]), Anhua Chen[1], Yunxia Jiang[1], Zhigang Chen[2], and Yankai Song[1]

[1] School of Computer Science and Engineering,
Hunan University of Science and Technology, Xiangtan, China
jackiefq@163.com, {ahchen,yunxia}@hnust.edu.cn,
2997487948@qq.com
[2] College of Information Science and Engineering,
Central South University, Changsha, China
czg@csu.edu.cn

Abstract. Increasing amount of vehicles are being equipped with embedded sensors, processing and wireless communication capabilities. This has opened a myriad of possibilities for varying applications on safety, public collaboration and participation. Message dissemination is one of the many fundamental services in Vehicular Ad hoc Networks (VANETs). For this purpose, in this paper we describe HADD, a hybrid adaptive dissemination protocol based on geographic distance. Contrary to other existing approaches that focus exclusively on always-connected networks, it is designed to operate under any kind of road traffic condition. We propose a new geographic-based broadcast suppression strategy to broadcast the message waiting in the local buffer queue to other vehicles. Finally, HADD employs a rate control scheme that sets the pace at which messages must be transmitted according to the perceived network data traffic, thus avoiding channel overloading. Hence, HADD adapts not only to the varying road traffic condition, but also to the perceived wireless channel quality. When compared to two related and well-accepted protocols under Manhattan grid scenarios, we show that, overall, HADD is more reliable and efficient in terms of message delivery.

Keywords: VANETs · Message dissemination · Broadcast suppression · Rate control · OMNet++

1 Introduction

Recently Vehicular Ad Hoc Networks (VANETs) has emerged as an exciting research and application area including safety, infotainment, traffic efficiency and driver assistance, etc. Although, considered as a class of Mobile Ad Hoc Network, the unique characteristics of VANETs, such as unpredictable mobility and vehicle density, geographically constrained topology, etc., bring new challenges to physical communication, end-to-end data transport, distributed routing, congestion control, etc [1]. In fact, the major design goal of VANETs is to decrease traffic accidents and enhance driving safety. So the essential components of information management techniques employed for various application services mainly include four respects like data gathering, aggregation, validation and dissemination [2]. This paper focus on a certain mechanism about message (like beacon or safety message, etc.) dissemination based on current research works.

The existing data dissemination mechanisms and protocols proposed for VANETs are usually based on the following techniques: flooding, broadcasting, neighbour knowledge based exchange and cluster based approach [3]. These strategies operate on vehicles in an ad hoc manner and also with roadside base stations using the DSRC (Dedicated Short Range Communications) links. A robust and efficient designing of dissemination strategy for VANETs is a challenging task because of: (1) Data generated by vehicles must be kept alive. (2) Data dissemination mechanism must work efficiently for both sparse and dense VANETs. (3) Data dissemination strategy should be robust against the variations in the transmitted signal power level of vehicles. (4) Data dissemination process must be intelligent to identify the target dissemination area. The aim of data dissemination is to transport information to the intended recipients while meeting some design requirements.

This work is organized as follows. Section 2 presents more related works about dissemination solutions for VANETs. Section 3 presents the proposed dissemination solution for VANETs. Section 4 discusses simulation and performance analysis. Finally, Sect. 5 concludes this work and presents some future directions.

2   Related Work

Data dissemination in VANETs is a well-studied topic. However, despite the fact that VANETs are intermittently connected by nature [4], most solutions focus exclusively on always-connected scenarios. Moreover, the solutions that do focus on both connected and intermittently connected scenarios either employ some kind of infrastructure. These proposed mechanisms generally can be divided into four categories: forwarding based, broadcasting based, push based and routing protocols based dissemination mechanisms [2].

2.1   Forwarding Based Mechanism

Data forwarding is an essential responsibility of a VANET's communication device. However, the network topology of VANETs is continuously changing due to the dynamic variation in the vehicle's mobility, so the forwarded data must be repeated since some vehicles are most likely to be out of wireless radio range. Moreover, the data load on the wireless channel should be not to exceed the wireless bandwidth threshold and be controlled. Hence, devising of dissemination protocols with different QoS requirements (e.g., minimum communication delay) for varying dynamic topology is a challenging task.

For instance, Greene et al. [5] proposed application-specific utility descriptions to managing VANETs resources for diverse data traffics dissemination. Each application in VANETs is assigned a specific micro-utility function, specifying its desired spatial and temporal data delivery characteristics, when multiple competing applications share constrained communication resources. These micro-utilities travel with the data to guide critical in-transit resource decisions such as dropping data and storing data for later data forwarding.

Sommer et al. [6] proposed a distributed forwarding scheme-Adaptive Traffic Beacon (ATB), which considers message utility, observations of past channel conditions, measurements of current conditions, and tentative estimations of future conditions, such a mechanism can efficiently adapt to highly dynamic environments both proactively and reactively, but to maintain a congestion-free wireless channel.

Hiroki et al. [7] proposed a novel Delay Tolerant Network (DTN) approach which is a combination of street segment based route detection by using the road map information, the route selection based on transmission delay estimation along each street segment and at each intersection and the dynamic next-hop selection among the neighbour vehicular wireless nodes only by the local location information of all the neighbour ones.

Huang et al. [8] used mathematical analysis and simulation results to demonstrate that, when the vehicle density is large, the farthest forwarder may experience large number of collisions, which bring about the high contention delay. They proposed an vehicle density based forwarding (VDF) protocol for safety message dissemination in IEEE 802.11-based multihop VANETs. The protocol adaptably chooses the forwarder according to the vehicle density to obtain the good trade-off between contention delay and forwarding hops.

2.2 Broadcasting Based Mechanism

The kind of dissemination mechanism can either broadcast data to vehicles in each direction, or perform a directed broadcast to other vehicles around it. To improve the reliability of broadcasting strategy for VANETs, the communication could be relayed using only vehicles traveling in the same direction, opposite direction and both directions. Moreover, the delay requirements for diverse applications should be satisfied. At the same time, the dissemination approach should be capable to eliminate the message redundancy.

For instance, Harry et al. [9] proposed an original methodology to study the performance of 802.11p VANETs with an empirically verified stochastic traffic model. Based on the information of car density at from the traffic model, the 802.11p broadcasting model is developed under a new metric-Broadcasting Performance Index (BPI) used to characterize the broadcasting performance and packet collision probability in VANETs.

Maia et al. [10] proposed a video dissemination protocol which is designed to operate under extremely dynamic road traffic condition. It is a geographic-based broadcast suppression strategy that gives a higher priority to rebroadcast to specific vehicles. Moreover, vehicles store and carry received data in a local buffer in order to forward them to vehicles that were not covered by the first dissemination process, probably as a result of collisions or intermittent disconnections. Finally, it adopts a rate control mechanism to set the pace at which messages must be transmitted according to the perceived network data traffic, thus avoiding channel overloading.

Bakhouya et al. [11] proposed a distributed statistically-based broadcast suppression protocol, that is the Adaptive Information Dissemination (AID). Based on the inter-arrival time between message receptions, a vehicle decides whether to rebroadcast the message by assuming it was already transmitted by other neighbouring vehicles. However, this scheme operates only on connected networks.

He et al. [12] investigated the data collection problem in VANETs under rapid evolving traffic conditions and proposed an adaptive approach to carry or forward the data packet based on current traffic information. The objective is to minimize the network communication overhead while satisfying the data collection time constraint. They formulated the data collection problem as a scheduling optimization problem and prove it is NP-complete. An optimal dynamic programming solution and a genetic algorithm based heuristic solution were developed to solve the problem under different application scenarios.

2.3   Push Based Mechanism

In push based strategy, the distribution of some state data will be managed by data center and be repeated for defined time duration while vehicles are inside a specific geographical event area. The specific algorithm to optimize this repetition process also should be developed. Moreover, when the transmission range of vehicles is too strong, it creates interference and reduces the network throughput. On the contrary, the vehicle may not communicate with other vehicles. Hence, push-based mechanism with smart dissemination algorithms that adjusts according to the transmitted signal power level is needed.

For instance, Zhao et al. [13] proposed a data pouring (DP) and buffering paradigm to address the data dissemination problem. In DP, data are periodically broadcast to vehicles on the road. In DP with intersection buffering (DP-IB), data poured from the source are buffered and rebroadcast at the intersections. This approach also provided analytical models to explore the dissemination capacity (DC) of the proposed scheme, which provide guidelines on choosing the system parameters to maximize the DC under different delivery ratio requirements in VANETs.

Baiocchi et al. [14] defined an architectural model for the integration of VANETs and cellular networks, according to a push mode paradigm where VANETs are used primarily to disseminate service announcements and general interest messages. In the provision of location and context aware services, VANETs role can be twofold: On one side the VANET can be used to disseminate advertisement data to a multiplicity of users; on the other side the service can be accessed both via the VANETs itself and a 3G/4G network. This heterogeneous access may depend on coverage time, user position/activity/profile and network conditions.

Pandey et al. [15] assumed a hybrid VANETs consisting of stationary info-stations and moving vehicles. These info-stations are installed at every major intersection of the city to form a Distributed Hash Table (DHT) based broker overlay among themselves and act as rendezvous points for related publications and subscriptions. The vehicles can take the role of publisher, subscriber or broker depending upon the context.

This publish/subscribe communication paradigm provides decoupling in time, space, and synchronization between communicating entities, and presents itself as an elegant solution for data dissemination in VANETs.

Bian et al. [16] proposed a new geo-based Named Data Networking (NDN) forwarding strategy to achieve efficient and reliable packet delivery in urban VANET scenarios. They investigated the caching redundancy problem with the default full-path caching scheme in VANETs and presented some heuristic strategies to reduce the unnecessary cached copies.

GPCR [17] prefers vehicles located in the middle of intersections to avoid the obstacle effect on wireless communication, while CLWPR [18] takes multiple factors into consideration including distance, sending queue length, frame error rate, etc.

2.4   Routing Protocols Based Mechanism

For one way and two ways in the context of VANETs traffics, vehicles moving in both directions could yield the best performance, but vehicles in the opposite direction needed better routing protocols to increase the data dissemination performance. Hence, multi-hopping mechanism should be used while maintaining a path from the source to the destination. However, multi-hop techniques consume lot of wireless resources due to redundant retransmissions and increase the communication delay, so the designing of efficient and reliable safety data dissemination algorithms will be complicated and scalable. Moreover, some specific data dissemination models used for multi-hop path is needed as well due to the VANETs characteristics such as high-speed movement, short connection lifetime etc. The proposed models could also be capable to provide some QoS parameters for routing protocols implementation like latency, reachability, etc.

For instance, Lee et al. [19] proposed a proactive urban monitoring middleware, named MobEyes that exploits node mobility to opportunistically diffuse sensed data summaries among neighbour vehicles and to create a low-cost index to query monitoring data. This strategy is evaluated in terms of indexing completeness, harvesting time, and overhead.

Bhoi et al. [20] proposed a routing protocol that uses the urban road network information such as multi-lane and flyover to send the data to the destination with a minimum packet forwarding delay. The next path for data forwarding is selected based on a path value calculated by the Road Side Unit (RSU) for each path connected to a junction.

Sotirios et al. [21] proposed a new position-based routing algorithm called Junction-Based Routing. This approach makes use of selective greedy forwarding up to the node that is located at a junction and is closer to the destination. If a local optimum is reached, a recovery strategy is applied with minimum angle method.

Nawaz Ali et al. [22] investigated that considering the remaining delay tolerance of submitted requests and the knowledge of fixed road layout, the performance of the cooperative load balancing system could be further improved significantly. Then they proposed an Enhanced Cooperative Load Balancing (ECLB) approach. The ECLB approach could balance the overload of junction-RSUs and edge-RSUs more freely and could maximize the overall system performance also. The ECLB approach reduced the number of deadline conflict requests which helps positively to improve the overall system performance. The ECLB approach even could operate efficiently if a vehicle deviates from the initial selected route in the middle of the routing.

Liu et al. [23] analyzed the dynamic traffic characteristics in standalone RSU-based VANETs and proposed to use different channels to disseminate different types of data and apply push and pull data dissemination techniques based on the volume of requests at the RSU server.

Shi et al. [24] proposed a social-based routing scheme to enable the efficient and effective message routing among passengers. In this scheme, passengers are divided into different communities based on the improved K-Clique community detection algorithm (IKC). For determining the forwarding and dropping order of message, a Social-based Message Buffering scheme (SMB) at vehicles was devised with their closeness and contribution considered. A Bilateral Forwarder Determination method (BFD) was also proposed to make the optimal message forwarding.

3   Proposed Solution

In VANETs, data dissemination becomes even harder due to the wireless medium and high dynamicity. To perform data dissemination in a reliable and efficient way without incurring a high load into the network, we proposed a Hybrid Adaptive Dissemination based on geographic Distance (HADD). HADD selects a minimum set of vehicles to reinforce the data broadcasting or to suppress it at different pace and time. HADD tries to reduce the load sent to the wireless link layer by decreasing the amount of redundant

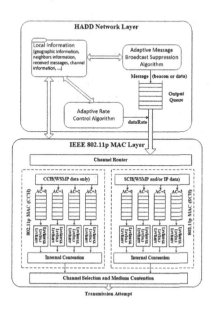

Fig. 1. General architecture of HADD

retransmissions. Figure 1 shows the general architecture of HADD. As can be observed, HADD operates above the IEEE 802.11p MAC layer [25] and consists of the adaptive message broadcast suppression algorithm and adaptive rate control algorithm.

In HADD, the independently of the neighbour vehicle density and received messages will be kept in a local information buffer to be later forwarded to a set of vehicles. When a vehicle receives a new message, it executes the broadcast suppression algorithm, based on its neighbour vehicle information and the adaptive contention confliction result of the MAC layer, to calculate a waiting delay to rebroadcast the message. When the related delay timer expires, the vehicle places such message into an output queue controlled by the rate control part. On the other side, the rate control mechanism based on MAC layer information (like the channel load, confliction, etc.) will decide when the message in output queue is sent down to the MAC layer to be disseminated. Thus, we assume each vehicle is equipped with a GPS and periodically broadcasts its geographic information in beacons to perform the cooperative data dissemination.

3.1   Message Broadcast Suppression Algorithm

The goal of broadcast suppression strategy is to avoid the broadcast storm problem caused by redundant and uncoordinated retransmissions, which is characterized by severe packet losses, high delay etc. To solve these issues, we propose a new distance-based broadcast suppression mechanism (Algorithm 1). At first, when a vehicle v receives a broadcast with a new message m (Line 9), it distinguishes the type (beacon or data) of message. For the beacon message, it will update the vehicle's neighbour set N with the ID embedded in message m (Line 12). Then we calculate the each distance from n ($n \in N$) to current vehicle and get the average distance (*avgDist*) from n to current vehicle (Line 13-14). After that, we get the distance ratio (*distRatio*) of *avgDist* to R (Line 15). If the *distRatio* is close to 1, it means that some neighbour vehicle may gradually leave the current vehicle, so we should reduce the time to send beacon message to maintain the stable of its neighbour set for data dissemination. Otherwise, we should appropriately increase this time to reduce the beacon broadcast conflicting (Line 16–20). Meanwhile, for the data message broadcast, if the received m is a new data message, we buffer it first. Then we verify whether there is any neighbour with a distance to the sender (v) of the message (m) greater than the communication radius R (Lines 25–26). If there is any such neighbour, we calculate the distance from current vehicle to v and calculate the distance ratio (Line 25–29) used to decide the broadcast delay (Line 30–34). If the message is received data message and is rebroadcast beyond the maximum times, it will discarded and we need to recalculate the contention windows value of each access category (AC) based on conflicting number in lower MAC layer and readjust them (Line 35–38). Otherwise, we rebroadcast the message with the initial value (Line 39). After that, when the timer expires, the data message will be inserted into the output queue (Line 40–41).

Algorithm 1: The message broadcast suppression algorithm

1 Initialize

2 $N \leftarrow$ set of one-hop neighbours;

3 $R \leftarrow$ communication radius;

4 **avgDist** $\leftarrow$ average distance from vehicle to its neighbour $n \in N$

5 $D_{max} \leftarrow$ max distance threshold from message source to destination

6 $C_{sch}^{collision} \leftarrow$ number of ACs confliction in SCH;

7 $N_{collision}^{max} \leftarrow$ the max collision number in MAC layer

8 $T_0 \leftarrow$ origin delay;

9 **Event** receive message m from neighbour v

10 //beacon broadcast suppression

11 if(isNewBeacon(m){

12   update vehicle's neighbours set N with m;

13   foreach $n \in N$ do {

14   count the average distance (**avgDist**) to current vehicle; }

15   distRatio = **avgDist**/R ;

16   if distRatio > P$_{threshold}$ //Probability threshold value

17     $T_{delay} = T_0 \times (1\text{-distRatio})$;

18   **else**

19     $T_{delay} = T_0 \times (1\text{+distRatio})$;

20   scheduleBeaconBroadcastAt(currentTime+T_{delay});

21 }

22 //data message broadcast suppression

23 if(isNewDataMsg(m) {

24   insert m to ReceivedMsg(m) queue;

25   isNeighbour $\leftarrow$ true;

26   foreach $n \in N$ do { if (n.distance(v) > R) isNeighbour $\leftarrow$ false }

27   if(!isNeighbour){

28       $Dist \leftarrow$ distance to v;

29   distRatio $\leftarrow |\ Dist$ -$D_{max}|/\ R$;

30   if v is inside forwarding set of this vehicle then

31         $T_{delay} \leftarrow T_0 \times (1 - distRatio)$;

32   else

33         $T_{delay} \leftarrow T_0 \times (2 - distRatio)$;

34   scheduleMsgReBroadcastAt(currentTime + T_{delay}); }

35   }else if(isMaxRetransNum (m)) {

36   discard m;

37       $CW_{Csch} \leftarrow \left| \dfrac{CW_{max}^{ACi} - CW_{min}^{ACi}}{(N_{collision}^{max} -1)^2} \times C_{sch}^{collision\,2} + CW_{min}^{ACi} \right|$;

38   adjustAC_CW(CW_{Csch});

39   }else{ scheduleMsgReBroadcastAt(currentTime + T_0); }

40 **Event** message broadcast timer for m is expired

41   Insert m into the output queue

The above dissemination idea is to make vehicles have a greater chance of not interfering in the transmissions of one another with different intervals. Therefore, HADD combines dynamic contention window with a distance-based to suppress relative message broadcast. In this strategy, vehicles are given a waiting delay to broadcast or rebroadcast based on the distance to the sender of the message. The higher the distance to the sender, the lower the waiting delay to transmit. It is worth noticing that when the timer to broadcast or rebroadcast expires, the vehicle does not broadcast or rebroadcast message immediately. Instead, it places the message into an output queue used by the rate control mechanism.

3.2 Adaptive Rate Control Algorithm

By employing both beacon and data message broadcast suppression mechanism, HADD is able to deliver messages under different road and vehicle traffic conditions. However, as the vehicle traffic density increases, so does the number of vehicle competing to access the channel, independently of the effectiveness of the employed broadcast suppression mechanism. Therefore, to make the proposed solution adaptable to the available bandwidth, a rate control (RC) mechanism (see Algorithm 2) is also proposed in HADD to determine how fast messages in the output queue are sent down to the lower MAC layer when a vehicle notices that the communication channel starts to deteriorate. Hence, as the broadcast suppression timer for beacon or message finally expires, such message will be inserted into an output buffer queue controlled by the RC mechanism for proper dissemination. This mechanism removes messages from the output queue at the same operational rate. Meanwhile, when messages are lost, RC reduces the rate accordingly by using the average number of lost message retrieved from the MAC layer by now.

Algorithm 2: The adaptive rate control algorithm

---

1 **Initialize**
2 R_{data} ← current data sending rate from MAC Layer;
3 *avgMsgLost* ← average lost message number at the
    channel by now;
4 T_{send_delay} ← message sending delay;
5 T_{lost} ← timer for counting the average number of the
    message lost at channel
6 **Event** message sending timer expires
7   remove *m* from the output queue
8   send *m* down to MAC layer;
9   if the timer for *avgMsgLost* expires{
10   update *avgMsgLost* at channel in MAC Layer
11   scheduleLostMsgTimer(*currentTime*+T_{lost});   }
12   *newDataRate* ← R_{data} / (1+ *avgMsgLost*);
13   T_{send_delay} ← *m*.length() / *newDataRate*;
14   sendDownMsgAt(*currentTime* + $T_{send\ delay}$);

In summary, as the timer used by the RC component expires (Line 6), a message *m* is removed from the front of the output queue (Line 7) and immediately sent down to the MAC layer (Line 8). At present, the RC mechanism must decide when the next message will be forwarded down to the MAC. Therefore, we first update the average number of the message lost if the relative timer expires and reschedule the timer if necessary (Line 9–11), then we calculate the new operational data rate with a new average number of the message lost by now due to collisions (Line 12). Then we can calculate the approximate transmission delay (Line 13) which is used to set up a timer for the next transmission (Line 14) to decrease the load on the communication channel. We argue that by using this simple strategy, HADD is able to adapt to both varying road traffic conditions and to the amount of data traffic on the wireless channel.

4   Performance Analysis

To evaluate the performance of the HADD, we conducted several simulations using the well-established OMNet++4.6 network simulator [26] and a road traffic simulator SUMO [27]. We also compared HADD to Flooding and AID protocols. Flooding is a simple dissemination scheme in which all vehicles immediately rebroadcast received messages exactly once. Meanwhile, AID relies on a distributed statistically-based broadcast suppression approach to determine whether a vehicle should rebroadcast under connected networks condition.

4.1   Simulation Setup

To show that HADD is a proper solution for message dissemination under different road traffic conditions, we evaluated all protocols under different vehicle traffic densities in a grid scenario (see Fig. 2). The scenario is a Manhattan grid with two road side units (RSUs) located on the top left (sink RSU) and bottom right corner (source RSU) of the scenario. One of these units is the source RSU which regularly broadcasts data message. This data message is received by vehicles driving within the scenario and forwarded such that it reaches the sink RSU. We use the SUMO mobility simulator to build the street layouts and to generate realistic vehicle movements. To assess different road traffic conditions, we vary the density in the Manhattan grid from 40 vehicles/km^2 to 400 vehicles/km^2.

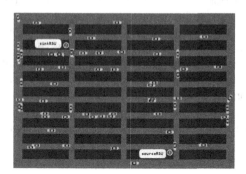

Fig. 2. Manhattan grid scenario with two RSUs

We also use the Veins 4.4 framework [28], since it implements both an obstacle model and the IEEE 802.11p standard for vehicle communications. As parameters to our simulations, we set the bit rate at the MAC layer to 18 Mbps and the transmission power to 0.98 mW. This results in a transmission range (R) of about 200 m under the two-ray ground propagation model. Moreover, the source messages are inserted into the network at two different data rates, 1 Mbps and 2 Mbps. These messages are transmitted only on the Service Channel. Table 1 shows a summary of the main parameters used in our performance analysis.

Table 1. Simulation parameters

Parameter	Value
Transmission range (R)	200 m
Transmission power	0.98 mw
Rate in MAC layer	18 Mbps
Base delay (T_0)	200 ms
Beacon frequency	1 Hz
Number of data message per run	400
Vehicle density (vehicles/km^2)	40–400

The metrics used to evaluate the reliability, scalability and efficiency of HADD includes:

- **Delivery ratio**, it is the percentage of data messages generated by the source vehicle that is actually delivered to intended recipients. It is expected that dissemination protocols must achieve a delivery ratio of 100%.
- **Collisions**, it is the average number of collisions per vehicle to disseminate all data messages. A high number of collisions indicate that a given protocol is not able to avoid the broadcast storm problem.

4.2 Simulation Results

Figure 3 shows the performance of the delivery ratio under different vehicle traffic densities and different transmission rates in our simulation scenario. In particular, looking at the results for the transmission rate of 1 and 2 Mbps, when the vehicle density is low, none of the protocols guarantee 100% delivery under such lower densities. However, we can see that HADD is the more reliable solution than the other two protocols. As the traffic density increases, HADD reaches a delivery ratio of nearly 100%. It is worth noticing that, the delivery ratio performance of HADD is not much affected by the transmission rate. The explanation is that, despite the rate control mechanism employed by HADD, HADD uses a suppression-store–forward

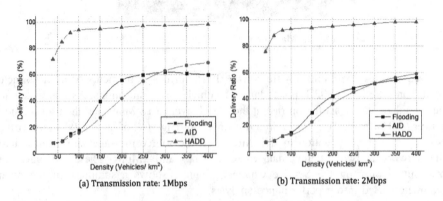

(a) Transmission rate: 1Mbps   (b) Transmission rate: 2Mbps

Fig. 3. Delivery ratio vs. density

communication model. Therefore, it works as a recovery mechanism for messages losses caused by collisions. On the other hand, the low delivery results of Flooding and AID can be attributed to the fact that these solutions don't rely on any suppression-store–forward mechanism. As another consequence, their performance deteriorates with the increase of the transmission rate. For instance, for a traffic density of 400 vehicles/km^2, when the transmission rate increases from 1 Mbps to 2 Mbps, Flooding's and AID's delivery performance decrease about 30% to 40%. This happens due to channel overloading, message collisions and, consequently, message losses. Finally, this result clearly shows that our proposed solution meets the strict delivery ratio requirement for message dissemination.

Figure 4 shows the performance of the collisions under different traffic densities and different transmission rates within the Manhattan grid scenario. At higher traffic densities, it becomes clear that HADD generates a much lower number of collisions when compared to the other protocols. For instance, at a transmission rate of 1 Mbps and a traffic density of 400 vehicles/km^2, the number of collisions for HADD is about 84% less when compared to AID and 86% less than Flooding. Moreover, the number of collisions for HADD is not much affected by the increase of the transmission rate.

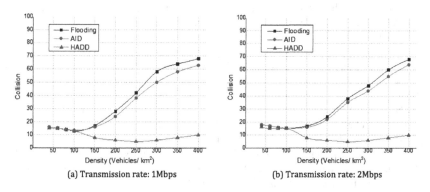

(a) Transmission rate: 1Mbps   (b) Transmission rate: 2Mbps

Fig. 4. Number of collisions vs. density

5 Conclusion

In this paper, we proposed HADD, a hybrid adaptive dissemination protocol for VANETs with diverse traffic conditions. HADD selects a minimum set of vehicles to reinforce the data broadcasting or to suppress it at different pace and time. In HADD, vehicles store received messages in a local information buffer and forward them whenever the timer for certain message expires. Our results showed that this increases the delivery capabilities for HADD under both low and high traffic density scenarios. A rate control mechanism is also proposed in order to set the pace at which vehicles should transmit messages into the communication channel. The performance analysis shows that HADD is adaptable not only to the varying vehicle traffic density, but also to the available bandwidth. As future work, we plan to work on a more effective store–carry–forward mechanism based on traffic prediction in order to increase the delivery results and to decrease the overhead.

Acknowledgments. This work was partially supported by the National Science Foundation, under grant No. 61379057 and No. 61672540.

References

1. Cunha, F., et al.: Data communication in VANETs: protocols, applications and challenges. Ad Hoc Netw. **44**, 90–103 (2016)
2. Kakkasageri, M.S., et al.: Information management in vehicular ad hoc networks: A review. J. Netw. Comput. Appl. **39**, 334–350 (2014)
3. Kakkasageri, M.S., et al.: A survey on information dissemination in VANETs". In: Daher, R., Vinel, A. (eds.) Roadside Networks For Vehicular Communications: Architectures. Applications And Test Fields. IGI Global Publishers, USA (2012)
4. Uppoor, S., Fiore, M.: Large-scale urban vehicular mobility for networking research. In: IEEE Vehicular Networking Conference, VNC 2011, pp. 62–69 (2011)
5. Greene, D., et al.: Utility-driven information dissemination in VANETS. In: 14th World Congress On Intelligent Transportation Systems, Beijing, China, 9–13 October 2007
6. Sommer, C., et al.: Traffic information systems: efficient message dissemination via adaptive beaconing. IEEE Commun. Mag. **49**(5), 173–179 (2011)
7. Hanawa, H., Higaki, H.: DTN data message transmission by inter-vehicle communication with help of road map and statistical traffic information in VANET. UIC-ATC-Scalcom. **42**, 814–820 (2014)
8. Huang, J., et al.: Vehicle density based forwarding protocol for safety message broadcast in VANET. Sci. World J. (2014). doi:http://dx.doi.org/10.1155/2014/584164
9. Harry, J.F., et al.: A stochastic traffic modeling approach for 802.11p VANET broadcasting performance evaluation. In: 2012 IEEE 23rd International Symposium on Personal, Indoor and Mobile Radio Communications - (PIMRC), Sydney, NSW, pp. 1077–1083 (2012)
10. Maia, G., et al.: A rate control video dissemination solution for extremely dynamic vehicular ad hoc networks. Perform. Eval. **87**, 3–18 (2015)
11. Bakhouya, M., et al.: An adaptive approach for information dissemination in vehicular ad hoc networks. J. Netw. Comput. Appl. **34**(6), 1971–1978 (2011)
12. He, Z.J., Zhang, D.Q.: Cost-efficient traffic-aware data collection protocol in VANET. Ad Hoc Netw. **55**, 28–39 (2017)
13. Zhao, J., et al.: Data pouring and buffering on the road: a new data dissemination paradigm for vehicular ad hoc networks. IEEE Trans. Veh. Technol. **56**(6), 3266–3276 (2007)
14. Baiocchi, A., et al.: Infotainment services based on push-mode dissemination in an integrated VANET and 3G architecture. J. Commun. Netw. **15**(2), 179–190 (2013)
15. Pandey, T., et al.: Publish/subscribe based information dissemination over VANET utilizing DHT. Front. Comput. Sci. **6**(6), 713–724 (2012)
16. Bian, C., Zhao, T., Li, X.M., et al.: Boosting named data networking for data dissemination in urban VANET scenarios. Veh. Commun. **2**, 195–207 (2015)
17. Lochert, C., Mauve, M., Füßler, H., Hartenstein, H.: Geographic routing in city scenarios. Mob. Comput. Commun. Rev. **9**(1), 69–72 (2005)
18. Katsaros, K., Dianati, M., Tafazolli, R., Kernchen, R.: CLWPR: a novel cross-layer optimized position based routing protocol for VANETs. In: Vehicular Networking Conference, pp. 139–146. IEEE (2011)

19. Lee, U., et al.: Dissemination and harvesting of urban data using vehicular sensing platforms. IEEE Trans. Veh. Technol. **58**(2), 882–901 (2009)
20. Bhoi, S.K., et al.: A path selection based routing protocol for urban vehicular ad hoc network (UVAN) environment. Wirel. Netw. **23**(2), 311–322 (2017)
21. Tsiachris, S., et al.: Junction-based geographic routing algorithm for vehicular ad hoc networks. Wirel. Pers. Commun. **71**(2), 955–973 (2013)
22. Md. Nawaz Ali, G.G., et al.: Efficient data dissemination in cooperative multi-RSU Vehicular Ad Hoc Networks (VANETs). J. Syst. Soft. **117**, 508–527 (2016)
23. Liu, K., Lee, V.: Adaptive data dissemination for time-constrained messages in dynamic vehicular networks. Transp. Res. Part C: Emerg. Technol. **21**(1), 214–229 (2012)
24. Shi, J.L., et al.: Social-based routing scheme for fixed-line VANET. Comput. Netw. **113**, 230–243 (2016). doi:10.1016/j.comnet.2016.12.016
25. IEEE, Wireless LAN Medium Access Control (MAC) and Physical Layer (PHY) specifications amendment 6: wireless access in vehicular environments. IEEE standards (2010)
26. Varga, A., Hornig, R.: An overview of the OMNeT++ simulation environment. In: International Conference on Simulation Tools and Techniques for Communications, Networks and Systems & Workshops, Simutools 2008, pp. 1–10 (2008)
27. Krajzewicz, D., et al.: Recent development and applications of SUMO-simulation of urban mobility. Int. J. Adv. Syst. Measur. **5**(3&4), 128–138 (2012)
28. Sommer, C., et al.: Bidirectionally coupled network and road traffic simulation for improved IVC analysis. IEEE Trans. Mob. Comput. **10**(1), 3–15 (2011)

Computational Model

Near Optimal Online Resource Allocation Scheme for Energy Harvesting Cloud Radio Access Network with Battery Imperfections

Sijing Duan, Zhigang Chen$^{(\boxtimes)}$, and Deyu Zhang

School of Software, Central South University, Changsha 410083, China
czg@csu.edu.cn

Abstract. In energy harvesting wireless networks, the energy storage devices are usually imperfect. In this paper, we investigate dynamic online resource allocation scheme for Energy Harvesting Cloud Radio Access Network (EH-CRAN) by jointly considering the EH process, data admission, and a practical battery model with finite battery capacity, energy charging and discharging loss. We use Lyapunov optimization technique and design data queue and energy queue to formulate a stochastic optimization problem, and decompose the formulated problem into three subproblems, including data scheduling, power allocation and routing scheduling. Based on the solutions of these subproblems, an online resource allocation algorithm is proposed to maximize the user utility while ensuring the sustainability of RRHs. Furthermore, this algorithm does not require any prior statistical information of the system, e.g., channel state, data arrival and EH process. Both performance analysis and simulation results demonstrate the proposed algorithm can achieve close-to-optimal utility.

Keywords: Cloud Radio Access Networks (C-RANs) · Resource allocation optimization · Energy harvesting (EH) · Battery imperfections

1 Introduction

With the evolution of wireless communication networks and the widespread use of smart devices, mobile data traffic is growing rapidly in recent years. To meet such huge data demand, operators need to deploy many base stations (BSs) to increase network coverage, which will lead to the growth of operating expenditure and energy consumption. In this case, the academia and industry proposed a promising solution, the Cloud Radio Access Network (C-RAN), which can achieve great capacity improvement at a relative low cost while offering high spectral efficiency (SE). As show in Fig. 1, the typical C-RAN architecture splits the traditional cellular network into two parts, the distributed remote radio heads (RRHs) and baseband units (BBUs) [1]. The data processing and control function are centralized into a visualized BBU pool, while the RRHs are closely

© Springer Nature Singapore Pte Ltd. 2017
D. Du et al. (Eds.): NCTCS 2017, CCIS 768, pp. 313–327, 2017.
https://doi.org/10.1007/978-981-10-6893-5_23

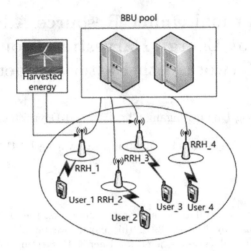

Fig. 1. The architecture of EH-CRAN

deployed to mobile user side across the network [2] and transmit data to users to provide service.

Due to increasing threats of global warming and climate change concerns, green wireless communications have recently drawn intense attention [3]. Therefore, from the perspective of energy efficiency, the densely deployment of RRHs will increase energy consumption and contribute a considerable portion of carbon footprint, it is desirable to adopt energy harvesting (EH) technology to improve energy efficiency in C-RAN, one solution is equipping RRHs with EH devices, these devices can recharge their batteries with renewable environmental energy sources, e.g., sunlight and wind. Intuitively, EH is a powerful technique to extend C-RAN operational lifetime. However, in reality, the EH devices are affected by various battery imperfection, e.g., battery degradation [4] (the batteries have limited number of charge/discharging cycles), energy leakage [5], imperfect knowledge of state of charge [6], storage losses [7,8] or circuity cost [9]. In order to take full advantage of EH technology, it is necessary to consider battery imperfections.

Resource management for EH-CRAN with battery imperfections faces some new challenges which have not been investigated. Firstly, the process of EH is random and changing with time, which is usually affected by weather factors, it provides C-RAN with more difficulties than powered by electricity grid, and makes more challenging for energy management. Secondly, considering the finite battery capacity, the harvested energy in the RRHs batteries cannot exceed the capacity bound and should be fully exploited to serve radio communication, and the energy depletion for data transmission should be controlled within available battery bound. Furthermore, owing to the aging battery equipments and circuit board leakage, there will be energy loss during the process of battery charging and discharging, so how to make RRHs provide high-quality radio communication services to mobile users with the non-ideal battery imperfection and dynamic EH process is important, and the EH-CRAN requires a low-complexity and online resource allocation algorithm to efficiently utilize the energy harvested by RRHs.

Many existing literature have focused on energy efficiency in C-RAN [10–13] without adopting EH technology, so their approaches are based on static model and cannot be applied into EH-CRAN which requires joint management of data buffers and energy buffers to optimize the network performance. In addition, several works [14,15] take dynamic EH process into consideration in C-RAN, whereas they assume energy storage devices are ideal, however, there exists battery constraints and storage inefficiencies in real network operation, the energy queue dynamics would not coincide with ideal queue updating. As a result, the algorithm and schemes designed in these works cannot be applied in stochastic network online resource allocation management for the EH-CRAN with battery imperfections. Moreover, some literature [4,16–18] consider the battery imperfection in general wireless sensor network, but cannot match the EH-CRAN scenarios.

In this paper, we investigate the resource management scheme for EH-CRAN with finite battery capacity, energy charging/discharging loss over time, by jointly considering the data buffers and energy buffers management of RRHs. Our objective is to maximize the time-average user utility and to provide users with high quality service, while ensuring the stability of network and persistent energy supplement under imperfect battery conditions. To this end, we formulate an user utility maximization problem. To handle this issue, we develop an online resource allocation algorithm to achieve close-to-optimal user utility, while jointly considering data admission, power allocation and routing scheduling by using Lyapunov stochastic network optimization technique [19]. In addition, we analyze the performance of proposed algorithm in the presence of practical battery imperfections, without considering any prior statistical information of channel changing state, random data arrival, and EH process. Simulation results demonstrate the proposed algorithm can achieve close-to-optimal utility.

The paper is organized as follows. Section 3 presents the network system model. Section 4 gives the dynamic resource allocation scheme and proposes an online resource allocation algorithm for EH-CRAN. Section 5 shows the performance analysis of the proposed algorithm, followed by simulations in Sect. 6. Section 7 concludes this paper.

2   Related Work

There have been many previous works on C-RAN which studied energy efficient resource allocation [11–14]. Reference [10] proposed a joint optimization solution for resource block assignment and power allocation to maximize EE performance in heterogeneous C-RANs . Wang et al. [11] adopted two cloud-based techniques to enhance both performance and EE by jointly studying energy minimization and resource allocation in C-RAN. The author in [12] proposed an energy-efficient resource allocation algorithm, which can improve the quality of service (Qos) performance for D2D communications underlaying C-RAN. In [13], the author designed a resource allocation algorithm to maximize user EE in the uplink OFDMA based C-RAN. However, the above literature only focus on how to improve efficient energy performance, not to consider the random EH process, so they cannot be applied in EH-CRAN. Accordingly, there are several literature paying attention to the application of EH technology in EH-CRAN. Zeng et al. [14] proposed a new structure which can enable RRHs to harvest energy from radio signals transmitted by neighbor RRHs and user terminals. Qiao et al. [15] introduced a hierarchical framework for the designing and analysis of heterogeneous C-RAN with energy harvesting. However, they ignored the battery imperfections in practical systems, in general, an optimum resource allocation algorithm without considering these aspects is imperfect. This paper is different from the previous works, our model includes the realistic scenario of battery degradation over time. To this end, we take the practical imperfect battery status into consideration, and propose an online resource allocation policy without considering any statistical knowledge of the environment.

3   System Model

We consider an EH-CRAN consisting of N RRHs and M users, denoted by $\mathcal{N} = \{1, \cdots n, \cdots, N\}$ and $\mathcal{M} = \{1, \cdots m, \cdots, M\}$ respectively. RRHs deliver data to users for downlink transmission through channels $\mathcal{K}$ denote as $\mathcal{K} = \{1, \cdots k, \cdots, K\}$. Each RRH is equipped with an EH devices, e.g.,solar panel or wind turbine. In order to describe the dynamics of network, we define data queue and energy queue in this paper, the data queue stores the random data arrival, while the energy queue saves energy that harvested from the ambient source. The network system operated in slotted time indexed by $t \in \{1, \cdots, T\}$.

3.1   Transmission Model

Let $\boldsymbol{C}(t)$ denote the channel state in each time slot, $\boldsymbol{P}(t)$ as the power vector and $\boldsymbol{P}(t) = [P_{n,m}(t), \forall[n, m] \in \mathcal{K}]$, where $P_{n,m}(t)$ denotes the power allocated to channel k at time slot t. We assume each RRH has a peak power constraint such that:

$$0 \leq \sum_{m \in \mathcal{M}} P_{n,m}(t) \leq P_{\max} \tag{1}$$

Given the channel state $\boldsymbol{C}(t)$, the network allocates a power value $\boldsymbol{P}(t)$ for data transmission, we define a transmission rate-power function over the link $[n, m]$ as follows:

$$\theta_{n,m}(t) = \theta_{n,m}(\boldsymbol{C}(t), \boldsymbol{P}(t)). \tag{2}$$

Because the allocated power is upper bounded, there is a finite constant θ_{max} such that: $\theta_{n,m}(t) \leq \theta_{max}$. Now let $\theta_{n,m}^k(t)$ denote the transmission data allocated to channel k in time slot t. It is clear that we have:

$$\sum_{k \in \mathcal{K}} \theta_{n,m}^k(t) \leq \theta_{n,m}(t) \tag{3}$$

In the EH-CRAN, denote $Q_{n,m}(t)$ the data queue backlog maintained by RRH n, and let $A_{n,m}(t)$ denote the amount of data admitted by RRH n in time slot t. The total data of user m in BBU pool is denoted as A_{max}, and the request data cannot exceed A_{max}, so we have:

$$\sum_{n \in \mathcal{N}} A_{n,m}(t) \leq A_{max}, \forall n \in \mathcal{N}, m \in \mathcal{M} \tag{4}$$

For the given data admission and rate-power allocation, the queue length $Q_{n,m}(t)$ evolves across time as follows:

$$Q_{n,m}(t+1) = Q_{n,m}(t) - \sum_{k \in \mathcal{K}} \theta_{n,m}^k(t) + A_{n,m}(t) \tag{5}$$

The data queue backlog is empty at time slot 0 with $Q_{n,m}(0) = 0$. We define the network stable if it satisfies the following:

$$\overline{Q}(t) = \lim_{T \to \infty} \frac{1}{T} \sum_{t=0}^{T-1} \sum_{n \in \mathcal{N}} \sum_{m \in \mathcal{M}} \mathbb{E}[Q_{n,m}(t)] \leq \infty \tag{6}$$

3.2 Imperfect Battery Model

Each RRH is equipped with a finite energy storage device (i.e., battery) to store energy. The batteries have some loss and energy degradation during charging and discharging. Define $\lambda \in (0,1]$ as the charging and discharging efficiency, and $\eta \in (0,1]$ as the storage efficiency. (e.g., $\lambda = 0.6$ means that 60% of charged and discharged energy is useful, $\eta = 0.6$ means 40% of the stored energy will be lost).

Let $B_n(t)$ represent the energy queue backlog in time slot t, it indicates the remaining energy in the battery, denote the battery capacity as B_{max}, and the power allocation value $P_{n,m}(t)$ should satisfy the following constraint:

$$\sum_{m \in \mathcal{M}} P_{n,m}(t) \leq \lambda \eta B_n(t) \tag{7}$$

where the $\lambda \eta$ indicates the discharging loss and energy degeneration. The amount of energy from ambient sources by RRH n in each time slot t is denoted by $b_n(t)$, which is upper bounded by b_{max}, i.e.,

$$0 \leq b_n(t) \leq b_{max} \tag{8}$$

and the energy queue updates as the following equation:

$$B_n(t+1) = \eta B_n(t) - \frac{\sum_{m \in \mathcal{M}} P_{n,m}(t)}{\lambda} + \lambda b_n(t) \tag{9}$$

and the energy queue is upper bounded:

$$\lambda b_{max} \leq (1 - \eta) B_{max} + \frac{P_{max}}{\lambda} \tag{10}$$

Constraint (10) is necessary to maintain the stability of the energy queue $B_n(t)$. If $\lambda b_{max} \geq (1 - \eta) B_{max} + \frac{P_{max}}{\lambda}$, the maximum energy arrival is greater than the largest energy departure. In this case, there will be one channel of energy queue $B_n(t)$ that grows unbounded.

We assume the battery capacity is large enough to accommodate the largest possible charging/discharging range, thus we have:

$$B_{max} \geq \frac{P_{max}}{\lambda} + \lambda b_{max} \tag{11}$$

3.3 Network Utility Maximization

The network utility relys on total users' utility which can be expressed by:

$$G(t) = \sum_{m \in \mathcal{M}} U(\sum_{n \in \mathcal{N}} A_{n,m}(t)) \tag{12}$$

where $U(\cdot)$ denote the utility function. The maximum first derivative of $U(\cdot)$ is γ_{max}, which is assumed to be increasing, and strictly concave, continuously differentiable w.r.t. $\sum_{n \in \mathcal{N}} A_{n,m}(t)$, we adopt the utility function to be a logarithm function $log(1 + A_{n,m}(t))$.

In this stochastic system, the EH process and channel state are changing over time, and we aim to design an effective online resource allocation algorithm to schedule admission data $\boldsymbol{A}(t) = [A_{n,m}(t), \forall[n,m] \in \mathcal{K}]$, allocate admission power $\boldsymbol{P}(t)$, and control the routing scheduling decisions $\boldsymbol{\theta}(t) = [\theta_{n,m}(t)], \forall[n,m] \in \mathcal{K}]$ in each time slot, so as to maximize the time-average utility. Define the network state as $\Phi(t) = \{\boldsymbol{A}(t), \boldsymbol{P}(t), \boldsymbol{\theta}(t)\}$, the time-average user utility maximization problem can be formulated as:

$$U^* = \max_{\Phi} \lim_{T \to \infty} \frac{1}{T} \sum_{n \in \mathcal{N}} \mathbb{E}[G(t)]$$

$$s.t. (1)-(9) \tag{13}$$

the above expectation is taken over variable system parameters which are included in network state.

4 Dynamic Resource Allocation Scheme

In this section, we will propose a dynamic resource allocation scheme based on the system model in the above section, the problem (13) is a stochastic optimization problem which jointly considering the data transmission and energy harvesting. It is usually hard to solve and require prior information about the network. To this end, we use Lyapunov technique in [20] to develop a low-complexity online algorithm without requiring other statistical knowledge of stochastic EH and channel information.

4.1 Problem Transformation

To start, we first choose a queue perturbation parameter Υ_n. Here, we define Lyapunov function as follows:

$$L(t) = \frac{1}{2} \sum_{n \in \mathcal{N}} \sum_{m \in \mathcal{M}} (Q_{n,m}(t))^2 + \frac{1}{2} \sum_{n \in \mathcal{N}} (B_n(t) - \Upsilon_n)^2 \qquad (14)$$

The intuition behind the using of the Υ_n is to keep the Lyapunov function small, we intend to push the energy queue to Υ_n. In this case, if we choose proper value of Υ_n, the energy queues always have enough energy for data transmission. Based on the Lyapunov function $L(t)$, the 1-slot conditional Lyapunov drift is defined as:

$$\Delta(t) = \mathbb{E}[L(t+1) - L(t)|\Phi(t)] \qquad (15)$$

it measures the increase of $L(t)$ in each slot. Our objective is to make the data queue tend to zero, nevertheless the energy queue push towards full to ensure sufficient energy supply, in this way, we can minimize $\Delta(t)$. We further incorporate the user utility into Lyapunov drift $\Delta_V(t)$ to derive the drift-minus-utility in function $\Delta_V(t)$:

$$\Delta_V(t) = \mathbb{E}[(\Delta(t) - VG(t))|\Phi(t)] \qquad (16)$$

where V is a parameter to achieve tradeoff between user utility and queue backlog, we can guarantee stability of system and maximize the user utility by minimizing the $\Delta_V(t)$. To simplify the optimization problem, we first develop the upper bound of $\Delta_V(t)$ in Theorem 1, then transform the problem into minimizing the upper bound to achieve the close-to-optimal solution. To start, we define a constant $\Pi = A_{\max} + \theta_{\max}$, the meaning will be shown later.

Theorem 1. *The value of $\Delta_V(t)$ is bounded by*

$$\Delta_V(t) = \Delta(t) - VG(t)) + \Pi \sum_{n \in \mathcal{N}} \sum_{m \in \mathcal{M}} \sum_{k \in \mathcal{K}} \theta_{n,m}^k(t)$$

$$\leq B + \mathbb{E}[\Theta(t)|\Phi(t)] \tag{17}$$

where B is constant and independent with V, which can be expressed by:

$$B = \frac{1}{2}(\theta_{\max}^2 + A_{\max}^2)$$
$$+ \frac{1}{2} \max\{[\frac{P_{\max}}{\lambda} + (1 - \eta)\Upsilon_n]^2, [-\lambda b_{\max} + (1 - \eta)\Upsilon_n]^2\} \tag{18}$$

and $\Theta(t)$ is given as follows:

$$\Theta(t) = \sum_{n \in \mathcal{N}} \sum_{m \in \mathcal{M}} [Q_{n,m}(t)A_{n,m}(t) - VG(t))]$$
$$- \sum_{n \in \mathcal{N}} \sum_{m \in \mathcal{M}} \sum_{k \in \mathcal{K}} \theta_{n,m}^k(t)[Q_{n,m}(t) - \Pi]$$
$$- \frac{\eta}{\lambda}(B_n(t) - \Upsilon_n) \sum_{n \in \mathcal{N}} \sum_{m \in \mathcal{M}} P_{n,m}(t) + \sum_{n \in \mathcal{N}} \eta(B_n(t) - \Upsilon_n)[\lambda b_n(t) - (1 - \eta)\Upsilon_n] \tag{19}$$

The proof of Theorem 1 is provided in the Appendix. As we can see in Eq. (19), we can get the value of B by using the system parameters in the system model, so we only need to minimize the $\Theta(t)$ by optimizing the data admission $\boldsymbol{A}(t)$, power allocation $\boldsymbol{P}(t)$, routing scheduling decision $\boldsymbol{\theta}(t)$.

4.2   Characters of Rate-Power Function

In these paper, we consider the data transmission through Orthogonal channel that the wireless channel does not interference with each other, so we derive the rate function for simplicity, let $d_{n,m}$ denote the channel coefficient, ρ^2 represent the noise variance, we have:

$$\theta_{n,m}(t) = log\left(1 + \frac{d_{n,m}^2(t)P_{n,m}(t)}{\rho^2}\right)$$

We readily have

$$\mu = \max \frac{d_{n,m}^2(t)}{\rho^2}.$$

here, μ is finite if all channel gains $d_{n,m}^2(t)$ are bounded.

4.3 The Proposed Algorithm

Now, we propose the algorithm:

In every slot t, observing states $\{b(t), \theta(t)\}$, and the queues $\{Q(t), B(t)\}$, we determine data scheduling $A_{n,m}^*(t)$, power allocation $P_{n,m}^*(t)$, and routing scheduling $\theta_{n,m}^{k^*}(t)$ as follows:

- (Data Admission). From the Eq. (19), we can compose the first term to optimize the admitted data $A_{n,m}(t)$:

$$\textbf{(DA)} \min_{A(t)} \sum_{n \in \mathcal{N}} \sum_{m \in \mathcal{M}} [Q_{n,m}(t) A_{n,m}(t) - \dot{V} G(t))]$$

$$\text{s.t. (4).}$$

In the above equation, the first term is linear, the second term utility function is a twice-differentiable and concave function. So the objective function **DA** is a convex function, and **DA** problem is a convex optimization problem which can be efficiently solved by using convex programming [21].
- (Power Allocation). Define the weight as the "perturbed" queue-backpressure:

$$O_{n,m}^k(t) = [Q_{n,m}(t) - \Pi_n]^+; \tag{20}$$

In the Eq. (20), the perturbation weight $\Pi_n = A_{\max} + \theta_{\max}$ is to ensure a deterministic upper bound on data queue size [20]. Based on such bound, we can choose the proper value of V and Υ_n for the proposed algorithm and yield a feasible online control policy for (13). Then, define the channel weight $O_{n,m}(t) = \max O_{n,m}^k(t)$. Let $P^*(t)$ be the optimal solution of the following problem:

$$\textbf{(PA)} \min_{P(t)} \sum_{n \in \mathcal{N}} \sum_{m \in \mathcal{M}} [\sum (\frac{\eta}{\lambda}(B_n(t) - \Upsilon_n) \sum_{m \in \mathcal{M}} P_{n,m}(t) - O_{n,m}(t)\theta_{n,m}(t))]$$

$$\text{s.t. (1), (7).}$$

The perturbed energy backlog $(B_n(t) - \Upsilon_n)$ is weighted by $\frac{\eta}{\lambda}$ in the **PA** problem to determine the optimal power allocation, the weights are responsible for the battery degeneration and discharging loss. We consider the simple case without channel interference, so the power allocation can be solved in a distribute manner.

The optimal power allocation $P^*(t)$ is the variable of rate-power function $\theta_{n,m}(t)$, we can achieve the optimal $\theta_{n,m}^*(t) = \theta_{n,m}(S(t), P^*(t))$.
- (Routing and Scheduling). For each RRH n, we choose the $k^* \in \arg \max_k O_{n,m}^k(t)$. If $O_{n,m}^{k^*}(t) \geq 0$, set

$$\textbf{(RS)} \max_{\theta(t)} \theta_{n,m}^{k^*}(t) = \theta_{n,m}^*(t)$$

$$\text{s.t. (2), (3).}$$

It is the max-weight matching problem, which can be solved by Hungarian algorithm. We allocate the full rate over the channel k to achieve the maximum positive weight over this channel.

- **(Queue Updation).** Update $Q_{n,m}(t)$ and $B_n(t)$ according to (5) and (9) respectively.

5   Performance Analysis

We now present the performance analysis of the proposed algorithm. Below, the parameter γ_{max} is the largest first derivative of the utility function.

- **Upper bounds of data queues and energy queues**

The following Theorem 2 indicates the finite upper bounds of data queue length and energy queue . If the data queue is finite, it indicates the system stable.

Theorem 2. *The data queues and energy queues satisfy the following inequalities with any channel state $S(t)$ and harvested energy $b(t)$:*

$$0 \leq Q_{n,m}(t) \leq \gamma_{\max}V + A_{\max}, \forall n, m \tag{21}$$

$$0 \leq B_n(t) \leq \gamma_{\max}V + P_{\max} + b_{\max}, \forall n \tag{22}$$

We can see from Theorem 2 that the energy queue size is deterministically upper-bounded by a constant of size V. It provides an explicit characterization of the size of the energy storage device to achieve the desired utility performance. Such explicit bounds are particularly useful for practical EH-CRAN system deployments. Moreover, when RRH n allocates nonzero power to any of its channel, $B_n(t) \geq P_{\max}$.

The proof of Theorem 2 is provided in Appendix.

- **Optimality of the proposed algorithm**

Theorem 3. *Suppose that the optimal network utility that can be achieved by an optimal algorithm is Y^* and the network utility $\overline{U}$ achieved by our algorithm, the gap between them is bounded by:*

$$\overline{U} \geq Y^* - \frac{B}{V}. \tag{23}$$

The Theorem 3 shows that the achieved user utility increases with larger V. The weight V represents how much we emphasize on utility maximization. The proof of Theorem 3 can be proved on the basis of Lyapunov optimization theory. The proof is omitted due to space limit, the details of proof method can be found in [22] according to the Theorem 4.5.

6 Simulation Result

In this section, simulation results are provided to evaluate the proposed algorithm. In the simulation, we consider the EH-CRAN consisting of 10 RRHs and 20 users in the circular area with a radius of 300 m. We assume imperfect batteries at RRHs, with storage efficiency $\eta < 1$, and charge/discharge efficiency $\lambda \leq 1$. The amount of maximum newly arrival data $A_{max} = 3$ Mb. The peak power $P_{max} = 2$ W. The transmission rate $\theta = 2$ Mb. The battery capacity $B_{max} = 160$ W. We also assume that the harvested energy $b_n(t)$ is i.i.d for each RRH. Furthermore, we have $\gamma_{max} = 1$, $\mu = 2$, $b_{max} = 5$ W. We run simulation experiment with different value of V, and the total operating time is $T = 1500$ s.

As shown in Fig. 2, the energy buffers increase linearly at beginning and fluctuate slightly around average value. It indicates that RRHs harvest energy

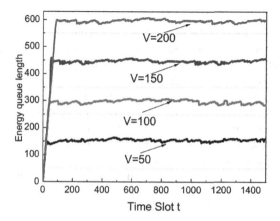

Fig. 2. Energy queue dynamics

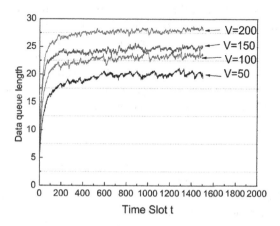

Fig. 3. Data queue dynamics

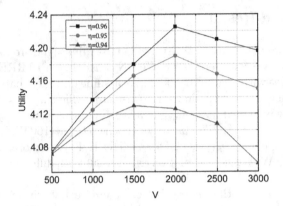

Fig. 4. Utility versus value of V

to charge batteries from ambient source. When the batteries are charged to certain value, RRHs starts to transmit data which is a discharging process. Both charging and discharging will push energy queue to appear balance. Furthermore, the higher the value of V, the higher the peak of energy queue backlog. So it is necessary to equip larger capacity battery with higher value of V.

Figure 3 shows the dynamics of data queue under different value of V. At the startup phase, there is not enough energy for data transmission, the backlog of data queues grow linearly from 0 as the value of V increases, finally they converge and fluctuate around a time-average value. Actually, RRHs prefer to maximize network gain by requesting as much data as possible, once the energy harvesting device batteries store sufficient energy, RRHs begin to deliver data to users. So it appears fluctuation, which indicates the balance between data requesting and transmission.

Figure 4 shows the network utility of the proposed algorithm under different value of V. When we set the value of $\lambda = 1$, $\eta = 0.96, 0.95, 0.94$, the network utility increases at start phase and decreases after reaching the maximum value. Besides, a large V implies that high energy is required to render $P_{n,m}(t) > 0$ for transmission. However, it is difficult to maintain high energy in the presence of energy degeneration. As a result, when the utility decreases with the increasing of V. The optimality gap with the proposed algorithm does not monotonically decrease with V any more in the presence of battery imperfections.

7   Conclusion

In this paper, a dynamic resource allocation scheme was proposed for a general EH-CRAN system. Taking imperfect finite-capacity energy storage devices into consideration, we formulated a stochastic optimization problem to maximize the user utility which subjects to energy availability constraints. Based on Lyapunov optimization technique, an online control algorithm was proposed to make data admission, power allocation and routing decisions, without requiring any statistical knowledge of channel, newly data arrival, and EH processes. Both performance analysis and simulation results show that the proposed algorithm can efficiently utilize the harvested energy to provide a feasible and near-optimal control solution for EH-CRAN. In the future work, we will focus on the EH-CRAN powered by hybrid energy source with battery imperfections.

Acknowledgement. This work is supported by the National Natural Science Foundation of China (Grant No.71633006, Grant No. 61672540, Grant No. 61379057). This work is supported by The Fund of Postgraduate Student Independent Innovation Project of Central South University (2017zzzts625).

Appendix

Proof of Theorem 1

Squaring both sides of the queueing equation in (5), and using the fact that $([Q-b]^+ + a)^2 \le a^2 + b^2 + 2Q(a-b)$, we can have:

$$\frac{1}{2}\left([Q_{n,m}(t+1)]^2 - [Q_{n,m}(t)]^2\right)$$

$$\le \frac{1}{2}(\theta_{\max}^2 + A_{\max}^2) - Q_{n,m}(t)[\sum_{n \in \mathcal{N}}\sum_{m \in \mathcal{M}}\theta_{n,m}(t) - A_{n,m}(t)] \qquad (24)$$

similarly, we can also derive

$$\frac{1}{2}([B_n(t+1) - \Upsilon_n]^2 - [B_n(t) - \Upsilon_n]^2)$$

$$\le -\frac{1}{2}(1-\eta^2)[B_n(t) - \Upsilon_n]^2 + \frac{1}{2}\left[\frac{\sum_{m \in \mathcal{M}}P_{n,m}(t)}{\lambda} - \lambda b_n(t) + (1-\eta)\Upsilon_n\right]$$

$$\le \frac{1}{2}\max\left\{[\frac{P_{\max}}{\lambda} + (1-\eta)\Upsilon]^2, [-\lambda b_{\max} + (1-\eta)\Upsilon_n]^2\right\}$$

$$- \frac{\eta}{\lambda}(B_n(t) - \Upsilon_n)[\lambda b_n(t) - (1-\eta)\Upsilon_n] \qquad (25)$$

Proof of Theorem 2

We prove Eq. (21) by inductions. Since Eq. (21) holds at $t = 0$, we show that if Eq. (21) holds at slot t, i.e., $Q_{n,m}(t) \le \gamma_{\max}V + A_{\max}$, then it also holds at slot $t+1$. If $Q_{n,m}(t) \le \gamma_{\max}V + A_{\max}$, then it is easy to see that $Q_{n,m}(t+1) \le V\gamma_{\max} + A_{\max}$ according to the data availability constraint (3). Suppose $Q_{n,m}(t) \ge V\gamma_{\max}$, we prove Eq. (21) by showing that the objective function of **DA** problem monotonically increases with $A_{n,m}(t)$. Therefore, the $A_{n,m}^*(t) = 0$ is the optimal solution for the **DA** problem. Taking derivative of the objective function in the **DA** problem w.r.t. $A_{n,m}(t)$ yields $Q_{n,m}(t) - VU'(\sum_{n \in \mathcal{N}}A_{n,m}(t))$. Recalling the $\gamma_{\max}$ denotes the upper bound of the first derivative of the user utility, it can be found that the derivative of the objective function is larger than 0. Therefore, minimizing the objective function yields $A^*_{n,m}(t) = 0$, which proves Eq. (21).

The proof of Eq. (22) is similar.

References

1. Demestichas, P., Georgakopoulos, A., Karvounas, D., Tsagkaris, K.: 5G on the horizon: key challenges for the radio-access network. IEEE Veh. Technol. Mag. **8**(3), 47–53 (2013)
2. Checko, A., Christiansen, H.L., Yan, Y., Scolari, L.: Cloud ran for mobile networksa technology overview. IEEE Commun. Surv. Tutor. **17**(1), 405–426 (2015)
3. Wang, X., Zhang, Y., Chen, T., Giannakis, G.B.: Dynamic energy management for smart-grid-powered coordinated multipoint systems. IEEE J. Sel. Areas Commun. **34**(5), 1348–1359 (2016)
4. Michelusi, N., Badia, L., Carli, R., Corradini, L.: Energy management policies for harvesting-based wireless sensor devices with battery degradation. IEEE Trans. Commun. **61**(12), 4934–4947 (2013)
5. Devillers, B., Gunduz, D.: A general framework for the optimization of energy harvesting communication systems with battery imperfections. J. Commun. Netw. **14**(2), 130–139 (2012)
6. Michelusi, N., Badia, L., Zorzi, M.: Optimal transmission policies for energy harvesting devices with limited state-of-charge knowledge. IEEE Trans. Commun. **62**(11), 3969–3982 (2014)
7. Tutuncuoglu, K., Yener, A., Ulukus, S.: Optimum policies for an energy harvesting transmitter under energy storage losses. IEEE J. Sel. Areas Commun. **33**(3), 467–481 (2015)
8. Biason, A., Zorzi, M.: Energy harvesting communication system with SOC-dependent energy storage losses (2016)
9. Ni, W., Dong, X.: Energy harvesting wireless communications with energy cooperation between transmitter and receiver. IEEE Trans. Commun. **63**(4), 1457–1469 (2015)
10. Peng, M., Zhang, K., Jiang, J., Wang, J.: Energy-efficient resource assignment and power allocation in heterogeneous cloud radio access networks. IEEE Trans. Veh. Technol. **64**(11), 5275–5287 (2014)
11. Wang, K., Yang, K., Magurawalage, C.S.: Joint energy minimization and resource allocation in C-RAN with mobile cloud. IEEE Trans. Cloud Comput. **99**(1) (2015)
12. Zhou, Z., Dong, M., Ota, K., Wang, G.: Energy-efficient resource allocation for D2D communications underlaying cloud-RAN-based LTE-A networks. IEEE Internet Things J. **3**(3), 428–438 (2016)
13. Sun, Y., Li, C., Huang, Y., Yang, L.: Energy-efficient resource allocation in C-RAN with fronthaul rate constraints. In: International Conference on Wireless Communications and Signal Processing, pp. 1–6 (2016)
14. Zeng, T., Zhen, M.A., Wang, G., Zhong, Z.: Green circuit design for battery-free sensors in cloud radio access network. China Commun. **12**(11), 1–11 (2015)
15. Qiao, G., Leng, S., Zhang, Y., Zeng, M., Xu, L.: Multiple time-scale energy scheduling with energy harvesting aided heterogeneous cloud radio access networks. In: IEEE/CIC International Conference on Communications in China, pp. 1–6 (2016)

16. Biason, A., Zorzi, M.: On the effects of battery imperfections in an energy harvesting device, pp. 1–7 (2016)
17. Chalasani, S., Conrad, J.M.: A survey of energy harvesting sources for embedded systems. In: Southeastcon, pp. 442–447 (2008)
18. Mao, Z., Koksal, C.E., Shroff, N.B.: Near optimal power and rate control of multi-hop sensor networks with energy replenishment: basic limitations with finite energy and data storage. IEEE Trans. Autom. Control **57**(4), 815–829 (2012)
19. Neely, M.J.: Energy optimal control for time-varying wireless networks. IEEE Trans. Inf. Theor. **52**(7), 2915–2934 (2006)
20. Huang, L., Neely, M.J.: Utility optimal scheduling in energy-harvesting networks. IEEE/ACM Trans. Netw. **21**(4), 1117–1130 (2013)
21. Boyd, S., Vandenberghe, L., Faybusovich, L.: Convex optimization. IEEE Trans. Autom. Control **51**(11), 1859–1859 (2006)
22. Neely, M.: Stochastic network optimization with application to communication and queueing systems. Syn. Lect. Commun. Netw. **3**(1), 211 (2010)

Singular Point Probability Improve LSTM Network Performance for Long-term Traffic Flow Prediction

Boyi Liu[1,4], Jieren Cheng[1,2(✉)], Kuanqi Cai[3], Pengchao Shi[3], and Xiangyan Tang[1]

[1] College of Information Science and Technology,
Hainan University, Haikou 570228, China
cjr22@163.com
[2] State Key Laboratory of Marine Resource Utilization in South China Sea,
Haikou 570228, China
[3] Mechanical and Electrical Engineering College,
Hainan University, Haikou 570228, China
[4] University of Chinese Academy of Sciences, Beijing 100000, China

Abstract. Traffic flow forecasting is the key in intelligent transportation system, but the current traffic flow forecasting method has low accuracy and poor stability in the long-term period. For this reason, an improved LSTM Network is proposed. Firstly, the concept and calculation method of time singularity ratio of traffic data stream is proposed to predict long-term traffic flow. The singular point probability LSTM (SPP-LSTM) is presented. Namely, the algorithm discard the LSTM network unit form the network temporarily according to the singular point probability during the training process of the depth learning network, so as to get SPP-LSTM model. Finally, the paper amends the SPP-LSTM by ARIMA to realize the accurate prediction of 24-hour traffic flow data. Theoretical analysis and experimental results show that the SPP-LSTM has a high accuracy rate, stability and wide application prospect in the long-time traffic flow forecast with hourly period.

Keywords: LSTM · Singular point · Depth learning · Traffic flow forecasting

1 Introduction

With the development of social economy and transportation, traffic problems appear more frequently. ITS (Intelligent Transportation System) has been developed rapidly [1, 2]. Accurate traffic flow forecasting is the prerequisite and the key step to realize ITS, it is conducive to improving the efficiency of transport operations and the quality of people's travel. The current researches are mainly to solve the short-term traffic flow forecasting problem. Accuracy of the long-term traffic flow forecasting is low. The paper made a research on this problem, and proposed a new traffic flow prediction algorithm with higher accuracy and longer prediction time.

One of the representative traffic flow prediction algorithms is Davis and Nihan's Nonparametric Regressive Model [3] applied to traffic flow prediction in 1991. Without

© Springer Nature Singapore Pte Ltd. 2017
D. Du et al. (Eds.): NCTCS 2017, CCIS 768, pp. 328–340, 2017.
https://doi.org/10.1007/978-981-10-6893-5_24

prior knowledge, it can perform more accurate than parametric modeling only with sufficient historical data, but its complexity is also high. Dougherty proposed neural network [4] for traffic flow prediction in 1995, which is suitable for complex and non-linear conditions, and it can be effective to predict when the data is incomplete and inaccurate with good adaptability and fault-tolerance, but it requires a lot of learning data and the training process is complex; The classification regression tree method [5] for the traffic flow forecast proposed by Yanyan et al. in 2013 has a better prediction effect and interpretability, but requires a lot of training data and certain skills for parameter adjustment. In addition, plenty of traffic flow forecasting methods based on the above methods, deep belief network model [6], support vector machine [7], wavelet neural network model [8], hybrid neural network model [9] have been proposed in recent years.

The traffic flow forecasting model proposed above has certain improvement in accuracy, but its prediction time of high precision is limited to 5 min–15 min while its prediction accuracy is not high during 30 min–60 min, and its stability is poor. Aiming at this problem, this paper proposed an unequal interval combining model based on improved LSTM [10] and ARIMA [11], which can guarantee the higher accuracy rate on the basis of increasing the prediction time and the length of the time period.

2 Improvement of LSTM Neural Network

2.1 LSTM Neural Network

The LSTM neural network [12] is a special type of RNN (recurrent neural networks) [13]. RNN is an efficient and accurate depth neural network, which has outstanding effect in long-term dependence on data learning [14] and has been applied well in the field of machine translation [15], pattern recognition [16] and so on. However, it has a problem called "gradient disappearance" [17]. And LSTM was raised to solve the problem of RNN, which is characterized by the ability to learn long-term dependency information. LSTM was proposed by Hochreiter and Schmidhuber in 1997 [18]. In recent years, LSTM has derived many variants, of which the relatively popular variant with the added "peephole connection" is proposed by Gers and Schmidhuber in 2000 [19]. In addition, Yao proposed a variant using the Depth gate [20], it is different from LSTM that it also decides what to forget and what new information to add. Another novel modified variant is the Gated Recurrent Unit (GRU) proposed by Cho et al. in 2014 [21], which combined the forget gate and input gate to a single update gate.

LSTM neural network is a special RNN, it can learn from the information of a long-term to solve the problem of gradient disappearance by increasing the memory unit. Therefore, this paper applied it to the hourly traffic flow forecast of the middle and long-term period for the first time.

2.2 LSTM Neural Network Based on Self-adaptive Probabilities

The LSTM neural network has the function of preventing the gradient disappearance and long-term memory, but it also has the problem of over-fitting [22]. The so-called over-fitting phenomenon is that the trained model has a good performance on the training data set, but its performance on the test set is poor [24]. The causes of this phenomenon include excessive noise interference, high model complexity and so on. In this paper, the situation that the LSTM neural network is applied to the traffic flow prediction, making the noise interference an important incentive for the over-fitting phenomenon.

To solve the over-fitting problem, Hinton proposed a solution that uses Dropout in 2014 [22]. Although Hinton, et al. proposed Dropout to reduce the probability of over-fitting, but they do not go into the calculation method seriously of the key parameter involved in Dropout - the probability of selective discarding neurons, while they use the empirical value of 0.5. The reason is that the network structure generated randomly is the most in this case. In recent years, the empirical value is also used in the related applications based on LSTM. In order to solve this problem, this paper made a study and proposed the method of calculating the probability value of selective discarding neurons in Dropout to improve the self-adaptive over-fitting of LSTM neural network.

In the improved scheme proposed in this paper, the probability value of selective discarding neurons is replaced by the traffic data time singularity ratio. The reason is that the over-fitting phenomenon has a certain relationship with the amount of the noise. Too much noise will lead to the situation that the training result performs well on the training noise while it performs badly on the real data, which will lead to the poor performance on the test set; and it is really easy to fall into the local feature optimal solution when the noise is too small. Therefore, the proportion of singular points has an important impact on the training results. And the probability value of selectively discarding neurons in Dropout also expresses the proportion of the screening of data to a certain extent. Therefore, there is a large degree of critical link between the two. At the same time, it was found in this paper that if we use the time singularity ratio as the probability value of selectively discarding neurons in Dropout, we can guarantee that the singular points are not discarded totally and they exist to a certain degree. It can presented by the follow formulas:

$$\frac{N_d}{N_j} = \frac{N_q}{N} \tag{1}$$

$$N_j = N_d + N_u \tag{2}$$

It can be deduced formula (1), (2) that:

$$\frac{N_{qd}}{N_j} \leq \frac{N_d}{N_j} \tag{3}$$

In the formula above, N_d represents the number of discarded nodes, N_j represents the number of nodes of each layer, N_q represents the number of singular points, N represents the number of all nodes in the single-layer network, N_u represents the number of nodes that is not discarded in the single-layer network, N_{qd} represents the number of nodes in the single-layer network that are both discarded and belong to noise. It can be seen that the improved method proposed in this paper can make the probability of selecting the node needed to delete randomly in Dropout more reasonable, and its effect to prevent over-fitting problem is more prominent.

We call the improved neural network adaptive to prevent over-fitting LSTM neural network: Singular Point Probability LSTM (SPP-LSTM). The SPP-LSTM are shown as follows:

Formula expressions are as shown below, the unimproved formulas are as follows:

$$z_i^{(l+1)} = w_i^{(l+1)} y^l + b_i^{(l+1)},$$ (4)

$$y_i^{(l+1)} = f(z_i^{(l+1)}).$$ (5)

The formulas of Adaptive to prevent over-fitting LSTM neural network are as follows:

$$p = \frac{N_q}{N},$$ (6)

$$r_j^{(l)} \sim Bernoulli(p),$$ (7)

$$\tilde{y}_i^{(l)} = r_j^{(l)} \times y^{(l)},$$ (8)

$$z_i^{(l+1)} = w_i^{(l+1)} \tilde{y}_i^{(l)} + b_i^{(l+1)},$$ (9)

$$y_i^{(l+1)} = f(z_i^{(l+1)}).$$ (10)

In the formulas (9) and (10) above, $z_i^{(l+1)}$ represents the value of the i-th neuron of the $l + 1$-th layer, $w_i^{(l+1)}$ represents the weight of the i-th connection of the $l + 1$-th layer, $b_i^{(l+1)}$ represents the bias of the i-th neuron of the $l + 1$-th layer, $y_i^{(l+1)}$ represents the output of the i-th neuron of the $l + 1$-th layer, f represents the activation function, p represents the expectation of probability, $r_j^{(l)}$ reflects the case whether the j-th neuron of the l-th layer is discarded or not, $\tilde{y}_i^{(l)}$ represents the output of the No. i neuron of the No. l layer after Dropout.

2.3   Traffic Data Flow Time Singularity Ratio Definition and Algorithm

To obtain the value of the time singularity ratio of the traffic flow proposed in this paper, it is necessary to obtain the number of singular points and the number of all the sample points, where the latter is known. Therefore, we only need to calculate the number of singular points. And for the detection methods of singular point, domestic and foreign scholars have been studied [25], but in this paper, we need to carry out the detection of singular point in traffic flow. In view of the high temporality of traffic flow, a method of self-adaptive singular point detection using time series is proposed (Fig. 1).

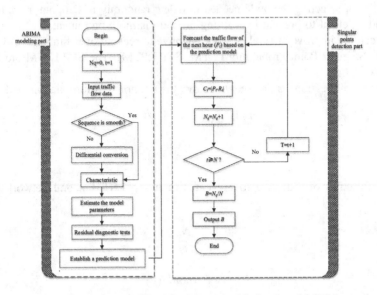

Fig. 1. Flowchart of singular ratio determination method in improved LSTM neural network

3   Combination Forecasting Model Based on SPP-LSTM and ARIMA

3.1   Traffic Flow Predicting Method Based on SPP-LSTM

After putting forward SD-LSTM, this paper applied it into the traffic flow prediction according to its features of great learning capacity on long term dependence of data and anti-overfitting. Then we made experiments, the traffic flow prediction result is obtained by using the improved LSTM model. we found that the result of using improved LSTM model to predict the traffic flow is better, and the most measurement figures of MAPE are under 20. Meanwhile, most of the MAPE figures are under 10 in the time of heavy traffic flow. At the same time, this paper analyzed the time slot of high MAPE figures and found that low traffic flow base would cause high MAPE figures. However, the traffic flow base of 6 o'clock was not low while the MAPE figure of it was high. Aiming at this, SPP-LSTM-ARIMA model is raised in this paper to predict the traffic flow.

3.2   SPP-LSTM-ARIMA Combination Predicting Method

This paper found that the main reason led to high MAPE in 6 o'clock is that the traffic flow changed severely during this period. The complicated features and high real time meant that LSTM cannot learn the whole features of this time slot. Thus, the prediction using deep learning method is not suit for this time slot. Meanwhile, ARIMA algorithm does not demand too much on data volume, and it has high real time and low algorithm complexity [26]. In result, this paper aimed at solving the non-ideal result of 6 o'clock predication by bringing in traffic flow prediction method based on ARIMA. ARIMA doesn't have the training process of data learning, so it is much suit for shorter period prediction. And the result is not ideal in the medium and long-term prediction. Aiming at this problem, this paper solved it by combining LSTM and ARIMA with non-equal interval, that is the non-equal interval traffic flow prediction method based on SPP-LSTM neural network and ARIMA (a.k.a. SPP-LSTM-ARIMA).

Non-equal interval, that is, in the prediction period of LSTM, regarding 1 h as unit time; in prediction period of ARIMA, regarding 15 min as unit time. Under this circumstance, the traffic flow prediction in different periods for one day forms the condition of the combination of non-equal intervals, as shown in Fig. 2. Below.

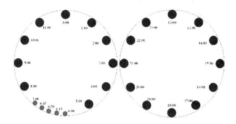

Fig. 2. SPP-LSTM-ARIMA non-equal interval combination diagram (Color figure online)

In the figure above, the prediction in 6 o'clock used 15 min as a circle (red dot), the prediction of other time slots regarded 1 h as a circle (black dot). Then, by the mode of non-equal interval combination, we combined the advantages of LSTM and ARIMA models together to improve the real time and accuracy of the traffic flow prediction.

The above theoretical analysis proves that SPP-LSTM-ARIMA can reach higher accuracy in the traffic flow prediction. At last, this paper proved it through experiment.

4   Experiment

4.1   Data and Environment of the Experiment

The experimental data in this paper comes from the traffic flow data set published publicly in the official website of British Columbia of Canada [27], and the experiment is based on the data from Vancouver Richmond region. The road condition at the monitoring point are shown in Fig. 3. And the specific location is shown in Fig. 4. During the process of the experiment, a total of 43824 h of data (from January 1, 1999

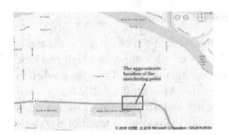

Fig. 3. Monitoring point and its surrounding roads

Fig. 4. The location of the monitoring point

to December 31, 2003) of the monitoring point are used, with data of May 21, 2003 and after as test data and data before that date as training data. The total test data has 5400 h and the total training data has 38424 h.

Firstly, this paper took a week as a cycle and number of weeks as label, and extracted traffic flow in the data by day. As shown in Figs. 5, 6, 7, 8, 9, 10 and 11. The abscissa is time and the ordinate is traffic flow. It can be seen from the figures that the number of different days in a week has a relatively fixed trend, which further proves the feasibility of using the model obtained by LSTM training.

Thus, this model can be used to model the different days of a week based on the trend. Through a large number of data training, we added the characteristics of a week to the model, so that the training model can adapt to the changing trend each week

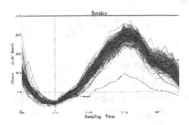

Fig. 5. Traffic flow data of Sunday

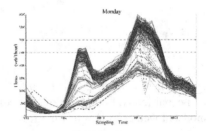

Fig. 6. Traffic flow data of Monday

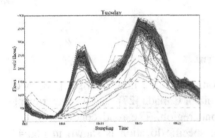

Fig. 7. Traffic flow data of Tuesday

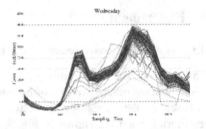

Fig. 8. Traffic flow data of Wednesday

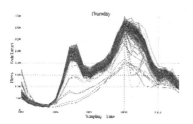

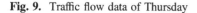

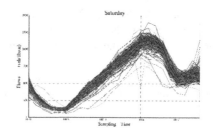

Fig. 9. Traffic flow data of Thursday

Fig. 10. Traffic flow data of Friday

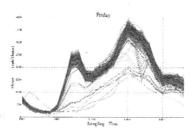

Fig. 11. Traffic flow data of Saturday

during the four years, and the law of the four years also has enough universality. The forecasting model obtained by four years' traffic flow data training is more consistent with long historical trends, and a lower error rate is guaranteed in this dimension. In the training process, we increased the training input vector to 24 h, and regarded the output of the forecast data as the traffic flow for the next hour. By using the method of deep learning, the characteristics of traffic flow information are excavated, and 24 h' traffic flow is entered in real time. This paper took the factors of real-time traffic flow and historical traffic flow into account, ensured real-time and improved accuracy at the same time.

The experiment of this paper is implemented by python 3.5.2 language in the 2-core 4-thread, 2.5 GHz, 8G memory computer with Linux system (Ubuntu 16.04 64-bit), where the traffic flow is collected every 1 h.

4.2   Result and Analysis of SPP-LSTM-ARIMA Traffic Flow Prediction

The formula below shows the method of calculating the MAPE value of the data deviation. As shown in Fig. 10. The MAPE value [28] is changing during the training process of LSTM by the data training set. It can be seen from the figure that the MAPE value decreases with the increase of epoch [29], and the MAPE value tends to be stable after the epoch value reaches 40. It shows that the number of the training done to sample set in this paper is enough sufficient.

Finally, the SPP-LSTM-ARIMA model obtained from the training of the data set is tested in the test data set in this paper. Subsequently, this article selected some of the results and made them visualized. Figure 12 shows the forecast value and the actual value of one month of the results; as can be seen from the graph, in the LATM-AR experimental test results, the predicted traffic flow data is basically consistent with the actual data and the method has high accuracy.

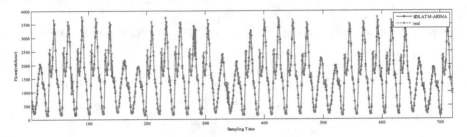

Fig. 12. The predicted values obtained by SPP-LSTM-AR method compared with the real values in a month

4.3 Comparison of the Results of Different Kinds of Traffic Flow Forecast Method

Using the training data set and the test data set, this paper compared the commonly used ARIMA prediction method and the latest proposed AR-RBLTFa method in reference [17] with the SPP-LSTM-ARIMA method proposed in this paper. Figure 13 shows the comparison of the data of working days, Fig. 14 shows the comparison of the data of Non-working days. As can be seen from the figure, compared with the commonly used ARIMA prediction method, AR-RBLTFa method and SPP-LSTM-ARIMA have higher accuracy.

After obtaining the traffic flow data of the three methods, in order to measure the error of the three methods much better, the MAPE value and the absolute error of the three methods are calculated and compared in this paper. Figure 15 shows the

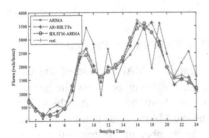

Fig. 13. Comparison of experimental results of different methods of working days

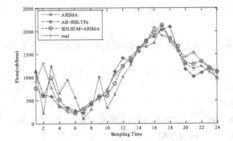

Fig. 14. Comparison of experimental results of different methods of non-working days

comparison of MAPE values of working days of the three methods; Fig. 16 below shows the comparison of MAPE values of non-working days of the three methods; Fig. 17 shows the comparison of the absolute error of working days of the three methods; Fig. 19 below shows the comparison of the absolute error of non-working days of the three methods; Fig. 18 below shows the comparison of RMSE values of working days of the three methods; Fig. 20 below shows the comparison of RMSE values of non-working days of the three methods; And RMSE calculation method is as shown in the Formula (12) below:

As can be seen in Figs. 15, 16, 17, 18, 19 and 20, ARIMA has the greatest error among the three kinds of error criteria, and the error of the AR-RBLTFa method is slightly larger than that of the SPP-LSTM-ARIMA. However, the AR-RBLTF method is not stable enough. Which is easy to produce serious potential hazard in the practical application. Then, the practical error of the three methods is quantitatively compared, as shown in Table 1. As can be seen from the table, the accuracy rate is: SPP-LSTM-ARIMA > AR-RBLTFa > ARIMA, while the error stability is: SPP-LSTM-ARIMA > AR-RBLTFa > ARIMA. Therefore, the SPP-LSTM-ARIMA proposed in this paper has higher accuracy and stability.

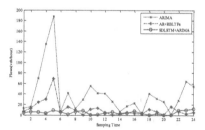

Fig. 15. Comparison of MAPE values of workday of three methods

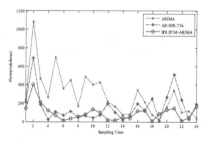

Fig. 16. Comparison of MAPE values of non-workday of three methods

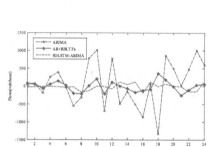

Fig. 17. Comparison of absolute errors of workday of three methods

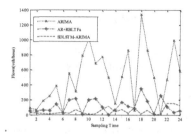

Fig. 18. Comparison of RMSE of workday of three methods

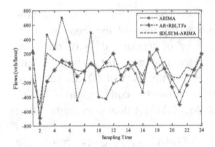

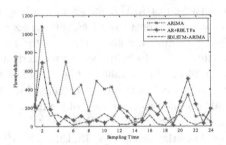

Fig. 19. Comparison of absolute errors of non-workday of three methods

Fig. 20. Comparison of RMSE of non-workday of three methods

Table 1. Quantitative comparison of three methods

Evaluating indicator	ARIMA	AR-RBLTFa	SPP-LSTM-ARIMA
MPAE	40.43	14.46	10.26
RMSE	611.4	184.49	176.90
Absolute error	498.59	156.41	138.25
Error entropy (normalized)	1	0.24	0.09

At last, this paper summarized the advantages and disadvantages of the three methods, as shown in Table 2 below:

Table 2. Comparison of three prediction methods

Algorithm	Accuracy	Dependence on historical data	Stability of forecast data	Real-time of the prediction
ARIMA	General	Slight low	Low	Predict on time
AR-RBLTFa	High	High	General	Predict on time
SPP-LSTM-ARIMA	Slight high	Slight high	High	Delay in variable scale adjustment

5   Conclusion

Aiming at the problem of traffic flow prediction algorithm cannot reach ideal result in medium and long-term slot, the SPP-LSTM method is put forward. This article defined the calculation method of time singularity ratio of the traffic flow firstly, improved LSTM neural network and put forward the probability values of selectively discarding neurons of the Dropout model by using time singularity ratio as self-adaptive data environment to deal with the problem of over-fitting in LSTM neural network and achieve adaptively of the traffic flow data set. Then, this article applied SPP-LSTM neural network in the traffic flow prediction. Aiming at the 6 o'clock error, the ARIMA model is introduced to predict traffic flow of 6 o'clock accurately by using the combination of non-equal intervals, which raised up the accuracy of the whole method. At last, this article verified the method by experiment and compared it with other methods. The result shows that SPP-LSTM-ARIMA proposed in this article has higher accuracy and stability. This method converts the traffic big data to practical value by using big data technology and machine learning. And it has broad application prospects. Especially in recent years, the rapid development of cloud computing and large data technology, making the proposed traffic flow prediction algorithm has a greater application prospects.

Acknowledgments. This work was supported by the National Natural Science Foundation of China (Project no. 61762033, 61363071), The National Natural Science Foundation of Hainan (Project no. 617048), Hainan University Doctor Start Fund Project (Project no. kyqd1328). Hainan University Youth Fund Project (Project no. qnjj1444). State Key Laboratory of Marine Resource Utilization in the South China Sea, Hainan University. College of Information Science and Technology, Hainan University. Nanjing University of Information Science and Technology (NUIST), A Project Funded by the Priority Academic Program Development of Jiangsu Higher Education Institutions, Jiangsu Collaborative Innovation Center on Atmospheric Environment and Equipment Technology.

References

1. Alam, M., Ferreira, J., Fonseca, J.: Introduction to intelligent transportation systems. In: Intelligent Transportation Systems, pp. 1–17. Springer, Heidelberg (2016)
2. Moral-Muñoz, J.A., Cobo, M.J., Chiclana, F., et al.: Analyzing highly cited papers in Intelligent transportation systems. IEEE Trans. Intell. Transp. Syst. **17**(4), 993–1001 (2016)
3. Davis, G.A., Nihan, N.L.: Nonparametric regression and short-term freeway traffic forecasting. J. Transp. Eng. **117**(2), 178–188 (1991)
4. Dougherty, M.: A review of neural networks applied to transport. Transp. Res. Part C Emerg. Technol. **3**(4), 247–260 (1995)
5. Yanyan, X., Zhaixi, K.X., et al.: Short-term prediction method of freeway traffic flow. J. Traffic Transp. Eng. **2**, 114–119 (2013)
6. Liu, F., Liu, B., Sun, C., et al.: Deep belief network-based approaches for link prediction in signed social networks. Entropy **17**(4), 2140–2169 (2015)
7. Bai, C., Peng, Z.R., Lu, Q.C., et al.: Dynamic bus travel time prediction models on road with multiple bus routes. Comput. Intell. Neurosci. **2015**, 63 (2015)
8. Yanchong, C., Darong, H., Ling, Z.: A short-term traffic flow prediction method based on wavelet analysis and neural network. In: 2016 Chinese Control and Decision Conference (CCDC), pp. 7030–1034. IEEE (2016)
9. Moretti, F., Pizzuti, S., Panzieri, S., et al.: Urban traffic flow forecasting through statistical and neural network bagging ensemble hybrid modeling. Neurocomputing **167**, 3–7 (2015)
10. Tian, Y., Pan, L.: Predicting short-term traffic flow by long short-term memory recurrent neural network. In: 2015 IEEE International Conference on Smart City/SocialCom/SustainCom (SmartCity), pp. 153–158. IEEE (2015)
11. Butt, M.: Selection of forecast model for consumption (four sectors) and transmission (two Pipelines) of natural gas in Punjab (Pakistan) based on ARIMA model. Int. J. Adv. Stat. Probab. **3**(1), 115–125 (2015)

12. Zhu, X., Sobhani, P., Guo, H.: Long short-term memory over recursive structures. In: Proceedings of the 32nd International Conference on Machine Learning, pp. 1604–1612 (2015)
13. Rakkiyappan, R., Chandrasekar, A., Cao, J.: Passivity and passification of memristor-based recurrent neural networks with additive time-varying delays. IEEE Trans. Neural Netw. Learn. Syst. 26(9), 2043–2057 (2015)
14. LukošEvičlus, M., Jaeger, H.: Reservoir computing approaches to recurrent neural network training. Comput. Sci. Rev. 3(3), 127–149 (2009)
15. Bahdanau, D., Cho, K., Bengio, Y.: Neural machine translation by jointly learning to align and translate. arXiv preprint arXiv:1409.0473 (2014)
16. Liang, M., Hu, X.: Recurrent convolutional neural network for object recognition. In: Proceedings of the IEEE Conference on Computer Vision and Pattern Recognition, pp. 3367–3375 (2015)
17. Pascanu, R., Mikolov, T., Bengio, Y.: On the difficulty of training recurrent neural networks. In: ICML (3), vol. 28, pp. 1310–1318 (2013)
18. Hochreiter, S., Schmidhuber, J.: Long short-term memory. Neural Comput. 9(8), 1735–1780 (1997)
19. Gers, F.A., Schmidhuber, J., Cummins, F.: Learning to forget: continual prediction with LSTM. Neural Comput. 12(10), 2451–2471 (2000)
20. Yao, K., Cohn, T., Vylomova, K., et al.: Depth-gated recurrent neural networks (2015)
21. Chung, J., Gulcehre, C., Cho, K.H., et al.: Empirical evaluation of gated recurrent neural networks on sequence modeling. arXiv preprint arXiv:1412.3555 (2014)
22. Srivastava, N., Hinton, G.E., Krizhevsky, A., et al.: Dropout: a simple way to prevent neural networks from overfitting. J. Mach. Learn. Res. 15(1), 1929–1958 (2014)
23. Zaremba, W., Sutskever, I., Vinyals, O.: Recurrent neural network regularization. arXiv preprint arXiv:1409.2329 (2014)
24. Bailey, D.H., Borwein, J.M., de Prado, M.L., et al.: Pseudomathematics and financial charlatanism: the effects of backtest over fitting on out-of-sample performance. Not. AMS 61(5), 458–471 (2014)
25. Awad, A.I., Baba, K.: Singular point detection for efficient fingerprint classification. Int. J. New Comput. Architectures Appl. (IJNCAA) 2(1), 1–7 (2012)
26. Pati, J., Shukla, K.K.: A comparison of ARIMA, neural network and a hybrid technique for Debian bug number prediction. In: 2014 International Conference on Computer and Communication Technology (ICCCT), pp. 47–53. IEEE (2014)
27. Traffic data program of British Columbia. Public Traffic Data [EB/OL]. http://www.th.gov. bc.ca/trafficData/legacy/TDP-97-03.html
28. Chen, J., Wang, Y., Gu, C., et al.: Enhancement of the mechanical properties of basalt fiber-wood-plastic composites via maleic anhydride grafted high-density polyethylene (MAPE) addition. Materials 6(6), 2483–2496 (2013)
29. Dunleavy, K., Pittaluga, S., Maeda, L.S., et al.: Dose-adjusted EPOCH-rituximab therapy in primary mediastinal B-cell lymphoma. N. Engl. J. Med. 368(15), 1408–1416 (2013)

A Bi-directional Evolution Algorithm for Financial Recommendation Model

Jingming Xue[1,2(✉)], Lu Huang[3], Qiang Liu[1], and Jianping Yin[1]

[1] College of Computer, National University of Defense Technology,
Changsha 410076, China
13787170450@163.com
[2] Bank of Changsha Co., Ltd., Changsha 410076, China
[3] Department of Computer, ChangSha Electric Power Technical College,
Changsha 410131, China

Abstract. By the challenge of rich data and poor information, recommender systems technology emerged as the time require and vigorous developed to more and more powerful vitality. However, in some real-world applications such as financial domain, the recommender systems of financial products usually require a long-term significant financial commitment as their utility, because it is not realized immediately depending on several external factors like market returns or governmental regularizations. In this paper, we propose a **bi-direction evolution recommendation system** (BDE_RS) to address this problem, which tries to balance the precision and the gains of the recommendation system. Portfolios are recommended based on the distance of investor and portfolio models which are composition of finite number financial assets with various weights. Based on investor transaction and investor profile, we design and construct recommendation using ARM technique for portfolio management. Extensive experiments conducted on benchmark and real-world data sets demonstrate that our proposed approach outperforms other state-of-the-art methods.

Keywords: Recommendation system · BDE_RS · Protfolio management

1 Introduction

In recent years, as people rapidly improve their ability to utilize the information technology production and collect data, thousands of databases are used in business manager, government's official business, scientific research and project development etc. How to acquire useful information from the high-dimensional data is an important problem. To deal with this information overload problem, researchers have proposed recommender systems that automatically analyze users' usage data to recommend good information resources. Typically, a recommender system analyzes data about items' or about interactions between users and items to find associations among items and users [1–4].

© Springer Nature Singapore Pte Ltd. 2017
D. Du et al. (Eds.): NCTCS 2017, CCIS 768, pp. 341–354, 2017.
https://doi.org/10.1007/978-981-10-6893-5_25

Recommender systems are information filtering and decision supporting systems that present items in which the user is likely to be interested in a specific context [5]. Naturally, research on the problem of context-based recommendation has gained a lot of attention: given a set of users, a set of items and some context, find the underlying items that users may be interested in. These methods are expected to alleviate the sparsity issue, thus to improve the quality of recommendations because the factors behind prediction are assumed coming from two parts, rating and context. When rating is not available, the prediction can be still inferred from context. However, some existing recommendation systems based on context information only give minor improvements above the rating-based methods. [4] found the prediction quality drops when the context is sparser than rating data and explored the potential of integrating visual features to improve context-based Matrix Factorization methods for movie recommendations. [6] address a friend recommendation system that suggests new links between user nodes within the network. They present a different clustering indexes and a novel user calibration procedure using Genetic Algorithm (GA).

Knowledge-based recommender systems perform a needed function in a world of ever-expanding information resources. Unlike other recommender systems, they do not depend on large bodies of statistical data about particular rated items or particular users. [7] has shown that the knowledge component of these systems need not be prohibitively large, since they need only enough knowledge to judge items as similar to each other. The goal of a trust-based recommendation system is to generate personalized recommendations from known opinions and trust relationships. To get the recommended information, the user must join the trust network as soon as possible, and the majority of new users in the social network are often isolated nodes. So it is difficult for the user to provide recommended information, trust-based recommendation system is not very good to be able to solve the problem of new user.

Compared to the subjects of conventional recommender systems, financial products usually require a long-term significant financial commitment as their utility is not realized immediately but depending on several external factors like market returns or governmental regularizations. A novel row-sparsity inducing regularization term, $\ell_{2,1}$-norm, is integrated into the objective function of ELM, which has an effect of eliminating the potential noisy and auto-correlated neurons [8]. Zhu et al. [9] proposed a distance based multiple kernel extreme learning machine (DBMK-ELM), which provides a two-stage multiple kernel learning approach with high efficiency. In order to reduce the risk of such a choice, users tend to formulate stricter expectations to these products rather than to conventional e-commerce ones, thus applying a recommender system in financial domains is a challenging task. From a business perspective, a common challenge that several financial institutions are facing is the lack of an intelligent decision support system [10]. As sales activities of financial products require expert knowledge, recommender systems offer great benefits for financial services by both improving the efficiency of sales representatives and automatizing decision making process for the clients. Therefore, a significant demand is observed for these decision support systems.

To meet the demand of personalized financial decision support, we propose a **bi-direction evolution recommendation system** (BDE_RS) using a novel incremental learning model. The financial ecosystem is a structured community of individuals or organization, which compose of nodes that are connected through one or more particular kind of interdependence, like values, ideas, interests and trading. In this paper, we consider users as the active entities that perform interactions (e.g. viewing, purchasing, rating, etc.) in the system. We call items the objects (e.g. products, movies, songs, etc.) with which the user can interact. The parameter setting that characterizes the environment (e.g. time, device, location) is defined as context; furthermore, we consider the actual preferences (e.g. filters, rules, item types) as constraints of the recommendations. Both users and items can be described by metadata (e.g. age, gender for users; genre, price for items). Recommender systems apply several data mining algorithms such as popularity-based methods, collaborative and content-based filtering, hybrid techniques, knowledge-based methods or case-based reasoning depending on the characteristics of the domain, the quality of available data and the business goals.

In addition, the new recommendation model can analyze and filter the financial products with less returns in the future and improve the investment gains of investors. The experimental results show that the recommended products have better gains during the several days after the recommended product day and the proposed model can provide reliable investment guidance for the target investors and let them get more investment returns.

The rest of this paper is organized as follows. Section 2 briefly reviews the definitions and theories of *association rule mining* (ARM) and the framework of the collaborative filtering algorithm based on user association rule mining. Section 3 demonstrates the motivation and the framework of the proposed model. Section 4 presents the simulation experiment and empirical analyses of the proposed model. Finally, Sect. 5 gives some conclusion remarks and discussion regarding future works.

2   Related Work

2.1   Collaborative Filtering Algorithm

Collaborative filtering or recommender systems use a database about user preferences to predict additional topics or products that a new user might like. [11] proposed two general classes of collaborative filtering algorithms. Memory-based algorithms operate over the entire user database to make predictions. In Model-based collaborative filtering, in contrast, uses the user database to estimate or learn a model, which is then used for predictions. In the past, many researchers have explored collaborative filtering (CF) from different aspects ranging from improving the performance of algorithms to incorporating more resources from heterogeneous data sources [12]. We firstly review some state-of-the-art CF methods. The k-nearest neighborhood algorithm is an early CF method [13], which has been applied in some real-world RSs. However, this method does not work well when the data is very sparse because it may fail to find similar users or items. Recently, latent factor models have become the most prevalent approach in CF. Therein, matrix factorization (MF) methods have become dominant in recent years. Recent developments have demonstrated the power of RBMS [3]. [4] found that some existing recommendation systems based on context information only give minor improvements above the rating-based methods. The prediction quality drops when the context is sparser than rating data.

However, individual-based CF approaches cannot be directly used for long-term time serial. Because in some real-world applications such as financial domain and e-commerce platforms, financial products usually require a long-term significant financial commitment as their utility is not realized immediately but depending on several external factors like market returns or governmental regularizations. Motivated by this, we propose a bi-direction evolution recommendation system using incremental learning to address this problem, which tries to balance the precision and the gains of the recommendation system.

2.2   Association Rule Mining Analysis

The framework of association rule mining was introduced into the data mining community at large by Agrawal et al. [14]. Their work was motivated by the desire to mine associations over sales transactions for market basket analysis and stressed the algorithmic aspects of the mining process [15]. ARM is used in stock market for predicting trading-based relationships between stocks [27]. In this section, we will briefly review the definitions and theories of association rule mining (ARM) and collaborative filtering (CF).

ARM is a well studied methodology to discover interesting relations between attributes in a large-scale dataset. The intention of association rule mining is to discover the strong rule using different measurements. Based on the concept of strong rules, we can identify recommended products [16].

Definitions. We now introduce the basic confidence of the ruleterminology of association rules. A *transaction* is a set of items, where the items of a transaction represent items that were purchased concurrently by a user. An *association rule* is a rule with the form X → Y, where X and Y are sets of items. X and Y are called as the body and the head of the rule, respectively. The intended meaning of this rule is that the presence of X in a transaction implies the presence of Y in the same transaction with a probability.

Each association rule X → Y has two measures relative to a given set of transactions: its *confidence* and its *support*. The confidence of the rule is the percentage of transactions that contain Y among transactions that contains X; The support of the rule is the percentage of transactions that contain both X and Y among all transactions in the input data set. As an example, assume that

Table 1. Sample transactions

Transaction ID	Purchased items
1	$\{A, B, C\}$
2	$\{A, D\}$
3	$\{A, B, C, E\}$
4	$\{B, E, F\}$

we have a database of transaction as listed in Table 1, for association rule "$\{A\}$ $\to \{B, C\}$", the confidence of the rule is 66%, and the support of the rule is 50%.

Use of Association Rule Mining in Financial Recommendation System

- **Data structure**
  The data structure that we use for recommendation system is as follows.
  financial_product_detail
  $P = \{product\_id, product\_detail\}$.
  Investor_detail
  $C = \{investor\_id, name, birth\_date, gender,$
  $location, initial\_cash, currency\}$
  Transaction_detail
  $T = \{transaction\_id, investor\_id,$
  $purchased\_product\_id\_1, ...\}$
- **Recommendation based on investors profile**
  Whenever an investor logins to the site, a recommendation system would give recommendation based on the investor's profile. At the time of login, the system finds the investor's age group, gender, location and risk tolerance. From this data, the system can find all list of investors that are belongs to the same group with signed investor. To find the group of the investors, the association rule mining algorithm is used [18].

2.3   Bi-directional Principal Component Analysis

In this section, we will briefly review the methods of the Bidirectional principal component analysis. Given K training samples $\{A_1, A_2, ..., A_k\}$ with mean matrix $\overline{A}$, for arbitrary data $A_k \in \mathbb{R}_{m*n}$, we can represent it as m row vectors.

$$A_k = \begin{pmatrix} A_{1k} \\ A_{2k} \\ ... \\ A_{mk} \end{pmatrix} \tag{1}$$

Assume $\overline{A}^j$ denote the j-th row vector of $\overline{A}$, we define the row scatter matrix

$$S^{row} = \frac{1}{K_m} \sum_{k=1}^{K} \sum_{i=1}^{m} (A_k^i - \overline{A}^i)^T (A_k^i - \overline{A}^i)$$

$$= \frac{1}{K_m} \sum_{k=1}^{K} (A_k - \overline{A})^T (A_k - \overline{A}) \tag{2}$$

The eigenvectors of the first q largest eigenvalues of S^{row} construct the row projection matrix $W = (w_1, w_2, ..., w_q)$.

Similarly, by treating an matrix A_k as n column vectors $A_k = \{A_{k1}, A_{k2}, ..., A_{kn}\}$, the corresponding column scatter matrix can be defined as

$$S^{col} = \frac{1}{K_n} \sum_{k=1}^{K} \sum_{i=1}^{n} (A_k^i - \overline{A}^i)(A_k^i - \overline{A}^i)^T$$

$$= \frac{1}{K_n} \sum_{k=1}^{K} (A_k - \overline{A})(A_k - \overline{A})^T \tag{3}$$

Eigenvectors of the first p largest eigenvalues of S^{col} construct the column projection matrix $H = (h_1, h_2, ..., h_p)$. In the BDPCA procedure, the transformation $Y_k = H^T A_k W \in \mathbb{R}^p * q$ is used to extract the feature matrix from data A_k and then to recommendation via nearest neighbor (NN) classifier.

3   Methodology

In this section, we first briefly discuss our motivation. Then, we introduce our BDE-RS framework using incremental learning.

3.1   Motivation

The process of recommendation is divided in two steps: a filtering procedure followed by an ordering. Filtering is an important step, because it separates the nodes with higher possibilities to be a recommendation, consequently reducing the total number of nodes to be processed in the network. The ordering step considers some process to put the most relevant nodes in the top of the resulting list. As expected, the result depends on the user the recommendation is generated for. Therefore, [19,20] present two general-purpose knowledge-based recommender systems with intelligent user interface, which can be flexibly applied on various financial products.

Due to the increasing complexity of product assortments and high cost pressure, one of the major challenges of today's retail banking is to improve the efficiency and effectiveness of sales processes. Financial service advisory is a knowledge-intensive task which in many cases overwhelms sales representatives thus leading to low quality results for the customer [19].

Recently, a new technique called association rule mining is proposed to solve the above problems [14,17,21]. The main idea behind ARM is to discover the strong rule using different measurement. Based on the concept of strong rules we can identify recommended product.

Usually, in ARM method, recommender system has to read all the transaction T and generate the subset of the transaction D. For real time application this procedure consumes high time and it also requires high computation. To overcome these limitations, an incremental learning method is a straightforward alternative. In fact, there are two major reasons for building incremental algorithms. The first reason is that in some cases, when the number of training dataset is very large, the batch algorithm cannot process the entire training set due to large computational or space requirements of the batch approach. The second reason is when the learning algorithm is supposed to operate in a dynamical settings, where all the training data is not given in advance, and new training samples may arrive at any time, and they have to be processed in an online manner. As far as we know, incremental learning has been studied for many years in machine learning community. Many incremental learning methods have also been developed for various applications. Unfortunately, only a few number of papers propose machine learning methods for personalized recommendation in financial domain.

3.2   The Framework of the Proposed Model

As mentioned in Sect. 2.3, directly incremental learning on the two scatter matrices S^{col} and S^{row} seems very difficult even impossible, since they are formulated as two cumulate summations. According to the work of [22], we can obtain a useful proposition through matricization of a tensor, they arrange the training samples in a tensor form, then rearrange the entries of the tensor to form several fat matrices, which refer to k-mode unfolding or matricization. The incremental ARM algorithm is shown in Algorithm 1.

4   Experiments and Results

In this section, we study and compare the performance of the proposed model with other method. In general, during the savings deposit interest rate rises (Fig. 1), the accuracy of the recommendation algorithm is higher, but during the deposit interest rate fall, the accuracy of recommendation algorithm is very low or even completely incorrect. Thus, in the course of falling, the experimental results can test a recommendation algorithm. In order to make the experiment results more objective and realistic, we use portfolios return to test whether the recommended asset has a good return from 30 to 360 days after that. For target investor, the higher the yields the investor gets, the better the effect of the recommendation model.

Algorithm 1. The incremental ARM algorithm

Input:
  The initial tensor λ consisting of K training datasets, the newly added sample set, dimensions k_{col} and k_{row}.

Output:
  The updated left singular subspaces of augmented matrices.
  1: Initialization;
  2: Select the principal components corresponding to the first k_{col} and k_{row} largest eigenvalues of S^{col} and S^{row}, respectively, i.e.
  3: Mean updating,
  4: QR decomposition, and
  5: small SVD;
  6: Record the updated singular subspaces $[U_{k_{col}}, Q_U]\ddot{U}$ of $\hat{A}^{(1)}$, and $[U_{k_{row}}, Q_V]\ddot{V}$ of $\hat{A}^{(2)}$
  7: Repeat steps 2–6 until the whole incremental learning process terminates, then output the final updated singular systems.

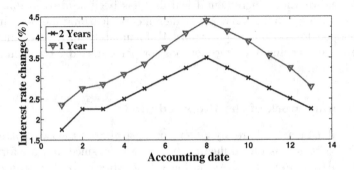

Fig. 1. Deposit interest rate change chart (2008–2015)

4.1   Evaluation Metrics

In this paper, we use the metrics Mean Average Precision (MAP) and Area Uder the ROC Curve (AUC) to evaluation models.

 – **MAP** computes the mean of the average precision scores over all portfolios P.

$$MAP = \frac{1}{|P|}\sum_{p \in P}\frac{1}{|P_h|}\sum_{p=1}^{P_h}\frac{p}{\hat{r}(P_{h,p})} \qquad (4)$$

where P_h denotes the relevant assets w.r.t portfolio p and $\hat{r}(P_{h,p})$ denotes the rank of the P_{th} relevant assets.
 – **AUC** measures the probability that the rank of relevant assets A^+ is higher than irrelevant assets A^-

$$AUC = \frac{\sum_{i \in A^+} + \sum_{k \in A^-}\delta[rank(i) < rank(k)]}{|A^+| \cdot |A^-|} \qquad (5)$$

where $\delta(.)$ returns 1 if $rank(i) < rank(k)$ and 0 otherwise.

4.2   Experimental Results and Analysis

This work aim to demonstrate the applicability of the BDE_RS Using Association Rule Mining. As a case study, benchmark and real-world datasets have been chosen for applying the proposed method.

A Case Study on MovieLens. The MovieLens datasets are widely used in education, research, and industry. They are downloaded hundreds of thousands of times each year, reflecting their use in popular press programming books, traditional and online courses, and software. These datasets are a product of member activity in the MovieLens movie recommendation system, an active research platform that has hosted many experiments since its launch in 1997 [23].

This dataset (ml-20m) describes 5-star rating and free-text tagging activity from MovieLens, a movie recommendation service. It contains 20000263 ratings and 465564 tag applications across 27278 movies. These data were created by 138493 users between January 09, 1995 and March 31, 2015. This dataset was generated on October 17, 2016. Users were selected at random for inclusion. All selected users had rated at least 20 movies. No demographic information is included. Each user is represented by an id, and no other information is provided.

To compare our approach with state-of-the-art methods, we evaluate the following methods in experiments:

- **kNN.** This is a baseline method to recommend movies watched by the top-k most similar groups
- **OCMF.** This method performs one-class MF on the binary group ratings where the weights are set according to a specified strategy [24].
- **DLGR.** This is a deep learning approach, where the variance parameters of the DW-RBM are set according to a specified strategy [25].
- **BDE_RS.** This is our proposed method.

Table 2. MAP and mean AUC of all comparative models

Model	MAP	AUC
kNN ($k = 5$)	0.1595	0.9347
OCMF	0.2811	0.9811
DLGR	0.3236	0.9880
BDE_RS	0.3492	0.9895

The results of MAP and mean AUC are reported in Table 2. The baseline method kNN does not achieve a good performance because it is hard to find a set of groups with identical taste over a sparse dataset. For the similar reason, OCMF and DLGR also do not perform very well.

A Case Study on BCSs. In order to examine whether the proposed model has made improvement in prediction accuracy, we select data at many different periods of the BCS's (Bank of Changsha Co., Ltd.)[1] real trading market in China as the experiment data. According to [26], we randomly select 512,000 users from the investor user database to fuzzy clustering and divide those users into several categories according to the threshold of clustering. By the nature of the clustering, the value of the threshold can control the number of the user categories. The value of the threshold and the number of the user categories are inversely related. The threshold can be in the range from 0 to 1. If the threshold is set too high, we will get very few user categories. Contrarily, if the threshold is set too small, we will get much more user categories. For example, if the threshold is set to 1, we will get 512,000 user categories. Clearly, if the threshold is set to 0, we will get one user categories. The complexity of clustering increases exponentially with the number of the user categories.

According to their own and family risk endurance and investment preference, investors can choose different investment instrument. Under normal circumstances, according to investment preferences, investors are divided into the following four categories: cautious, defensive, speculative and enterprising. After making several experiments, we set the clustering threshold $\lambda = 0.7129$ in this paper and then divide 512,000 users into four categories in Table 3.

Table 3. The users clustering results

Category name	Users numbers	Percentage (%)
Cautious	134,656	26.3
Defensive	223,232	43.6
Speculative	89,088	17.4
Enterprising	65,024	12.7
Totals	512,000	100

After the users clustering, we use Algorithm 1 based on the cosine similarity to calculate the similarity between the target user and the other users. We can find out the nearest neighbor users of the target user according to the similarity value.

With the complement classified for the target user, we can get the k clustered users and get the asset allocation from those users. Due to limited paper space, we selected bank financial products as the research portfolio in Fig. 2.

Figure 3 shows that different portfolio recommendation models will bring different asset returns. We compute the mean return rate of 12 trading weeks for 20 portfolios in two different assets which were recommended by the proposed method and the traditional method in the above periods. Assuming that the

---
[1] BCS was established in May 1997, is the first regional joint-stock commercial banks in Hunan province of China.

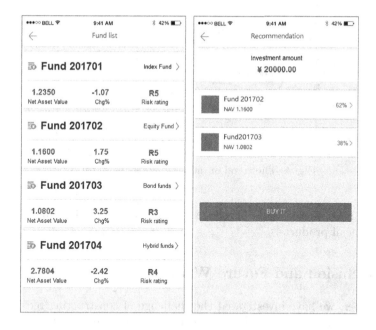

Fig. 2. The list of financial products and the result of e propsed model

target user bought the frontal assets in the recommend assets set, we find that the target user with appropriate operating will get far better asset return rate as the top line indicated in Fig. 3.

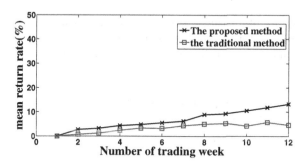

Fig. 3. Mean return rate comparing of two methods

To further study on this topic, we apply the algorithm to the online financial sale system, Fig. 4 shows that different methods will influence the ratio of online financial sales. From 1 to 3 stages, the traditional algorithms [3, 27] are introduced into the recommendation system, After 3 stages, we start our proposed method into the DBE_RS. As we can be seen from the Figure 4, there is

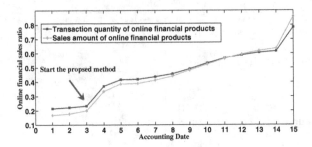

Fig. 4. The trend of online financial sales ratio

a rapid increase in the radio of sales amount and transaction quantity of the online financial products.

5   Conclusion and Future Work

In this paper, we have investigated the challenge of constructing recommender system in financial domain. To overcome this challenge, we have proposed a Bi-directional evolution learning model for recommender system, which incorporates coupling relations between and within users and items. Meanwhile, we propose an incremental learning approach to overcome the deficiencies of current ARM. Essentially, our model aims to learn high-level comprehensive features to represent investor preference so as to avoid the vulnerabilities in a shallow representation. The empirical evaluation on a real-world dataset demonstrates that the proposed approach can achieve much better performance than other state-of-the-art models.

In the future, an interesting work is how to further improve the accuracy of the proposed recommendation model by adopting several intelligent processing techniques, e.g., machine learning, time series analysis, the latest fuzzy clustering, etc.

Acknowledgments. This work was supported by the National Natural Science Foundation of China (Project no. 61303189, 61232016).

References

1. Huang, Z., Chung, W., Chen, H.: A graph model for e-commerce recommender systems. J. Am. Soc. Inform. Sci. Technol. **55**(3), 259–274 (2014)
2. Sayyed, F.R., Argiddi, R.V., Apte, S.S.: Generating recommendations for stock market using collaborative filtering. Int. J. Comput. Eng. Sci. **3**, 46–49 (2013)
3. Georgiev, K., Nakov, P.: A non-IID framework for collaborative filtering with restricted Boltzmann machines. In: International Conference on Machine Learning, pp. 1148–1156 (2013). JMLR.org

4. Zhao, L., Lu, Z., Pan, S.J., Yang, Q.: Matrix factorization+ for movie recommendation. In: Proceedings of the Twenty-Fifth International Joint Conference on Artificial Intelligence, pp. 3945–3951 (2016)

5. Zibriczky, D.: Recommender systems meet finance: a literature review. In: International Workshop on Personalization and Recommender Systems in Financial Services (2016)

6. Silva N.B., Tsang, I.R., Cavalcanti, G.D.C., et al.: A graph-based friend recommendation system using Genetic Algorithm. In: Evolutionary Computation, pp. 1–7. IEEE (2010)

7. Burke, R.: Knowledge-based recommender systems (2000)

8. Zhou, S., Liu, X., Liu, Q., et al.: Random Fourier extreme learning machine with $l_{2,1}$ - norm regularization. Neurocomputing **174**(PA), 143–153 (2014)

9. Zhu, C., Liu, X., Liu, Q., Ming, Y., Yin, J.: Distance based multiple kernel ELM: a fast multiple kernel learning approach. Math. Probl. Eng. **2015**, 1–9 (2015)

10. Cheng, H., Lu, Y.C., Sheu, C.: An ontology-based business intelligence application in a financial knowledge management system. Exp. Syst. Appl. **36**(2), 3614–3622 (2009)

11. Breese, J.S., Heckerman, D., Kadie, C.: Empirical analysis of predictive algorithms for collaborative filtering. In: Fourteenth Conference on Uncertainty in Artificial Intelligence, pp. 43–52. Morgan Kaufmann Publishers Inc. (1998)

12. Adomavicius, G., Tuzhilin, A.: Toward the next generation of recommender systems: a survey of the state-of-the-art and possible extensions. In: Multimedia Services in Intelligent Environments, pp. 734–749. Springer, Heidelberg (2013)

13. Su, X., Khoshgoftaar, T.M.: A survey of collaborative filtering techniques. Adv. Artif. Intell. **2009**(12), 4 (2009)

14. Agrawal, R., Imielinski, T., Swami, A.N.: Mining association rules between sets of items in large databases. In: Proceedings of the 1993 ACM SIGMOD International Conference on Management of Data, SIGMOD Conference, pp. 207–216 (1993)

15. Lin, W., Alvarez, S.A., Ruiz, C.: Efficient adaptive-support association rule mining for recommender system. Data Min. Knowl. Disc. **6**(1), 83–105 (2002)

16. Parikh, V., Shah, P.: E-commerce recommendation system using association rule mining and clustering. Int. J. Innov. Adv. Comput. Sci. **91**, 944–952 (2015)

17. Paranjape-Voditel, P., Deshpande, U.: An association rule mining based stock market recommender system. In: International Conference on Emerging Applications of Information Technology, pp. 21–24. IEEE (2011)

18. Fan, Y., Mai, J., Ren, X.: A rough set-based clustering collaborative filtering algorithm in e-commerce recommendation system. In: International Conference on Information Management, Innovation Management and Industrial Engineering, pp. 401–404 (2009)

19. Kiener, A., Kiener, A.: Knowledge-based interactive selling of financial services with FSAdvisor. In: Conference on Innovative Applications of Artificial Intelligence, pp. 1475–1482. AAAI Press (2005)

20. Felfernig, A., Jeran, M., Stettinger, M., et al.: Human computation based acquisition of financial service advisory practices. In: International Workshop on Personalization and Recommender Systems in Financial Services (2015)

21. Sobhanam, H., Mariappan, A.K.: Addressing cold start problem in recommender systems using association rules and clustering technique. In: International Conference on Computer Communication and Informatics, pp. 1–5. IEEE (2013)

22. Ren, C.X., Dai, D.Q.: Incremental learning of bidirectional principal components for face recognition. Pattern Recogn. **43**(1), 318–330 (2010)

23. Harper, F.M., Konstan, J.A.: The movieLens datasets: history and context. ACM (2016)
24. Hu, Y., Koren, Y., Volinsky, C.: Collaborative filtering for implicit feedback datasets. In: IEEE International Conference on Data Mining, pp. 263–272 (2008)
25. Hu, L., Cao, J., Xu, G., et al.: Deep modeling of group preferences for group-based recommendation. In: Twenty-Eighth AAAI Conference on Artificial Intelligence, pp. 1861–1867. AAAI Press (2014)
26. Yang, Y., Li, J., Yang, Y.: An efficient stock recommendation model based on big order net inflow. Math. Probl. Eng. **2016**(9), 1–15 (2016)
27. Paranjape-Voditel, P., Deshpande, U.: An association rule mining based stock market recommender system. In: Second International Conference on Emerging Applications of Information Technology, pp. 21–24 (2011)

Author Index

Printed in the United States
By Bookmasters